Management in
the Fire Service

Prepared by

Didactic Systems, Inc.

 **National Fire Protection
Association**
NFPA®

Batterymarch Park, Quincy, MA 02269

About the Author

This textbook was prepared by Didactic Systems, Inc., of Cranford, New Jersey, specialists in the preparation of management development materials. Didactic Systems serves as consultant on management development and training matters for many governmental agencies as well as for some of the country's largest corporations. Didactic Systems has prepared, for the National Fire Protection Association, a series of Fire Service Management Exercises, including: FSME-1, *Handling Personnel Problems at Company Level;* FSME-2, *Prefire Planning;* FSME-3, *Fire Fighting Tactics;* and FSME-4, *Strategic Command Decisions.*

The comprehensive modern management concept presented in this text and widely known as the linking elements concept was originally conceived by Erwin Rausch, President of Didactic Systems, Inc. Since its conception, the linking elements concept, which serves as a teaching strand throughout this text, has been expanded and refined to become an essentially universal guide for modern managerial action at all supervisory levels.

Seventh Printing
October 1988

NFPA No. TXT-3
ISBN: 0-87765-097-7
Library of Congress No.: 77-76527
Printed in U.S.A.

Contents

CHAPTER 4   **Modern Management Concepts**   64

CHAPTER 5   **Managing by Objectives**   102

CHAPTER 6   **Management Functions in the Fire Service**   146

Acknowledgments

Didactic Systems acknowledges with gratitude the many persons and organizations who cooperated in the preparation and development of this textbook. Special thanks go to the following:

> Captain Arthur Kiamie of the Cranford, NJ Fire Department, who served as consultant and whose advice was invaluable throughout the development of this project.

> Dr. Robert G. Kahmann, Jr., of Somerset County College, who helped with the original planning and reviewed as many chapters as his heavy schedule permitted.

The cooperation of the many publishers and representatives of the fire service who gave permission to use excerpts from their publications and management training materials is deeply appreciated. Didactic Systems, Inc., is also indebted to the many people and organizations who contributed helpful ideas, suggestions, and materials, including:

> Acton, MA Fire Dept., Malcolm S. McGregor, Chief
> American Insurance Association, John J. Jablonsky, Assistant
>   Vice President, Engineering and Safety Service
> Bloomfield, NJ Fire Dept., Earl J. McCormick, Chief
>   Captain Robert Mellilo, Training Officer
> Edison, NJ Fire Dept., Chief H. Ray Vliet
> Elizabeth, NJ Fire Dept., Deputy Chief Charles Swody
> Irvington, NJ Fire Dept., N. Bellarosa, Chief
>   William S. Holleran, Chief Engineer
> Linden, NJ Fire Dept., Frank Miklos, Chief
> Merck and Company, Roger A. McGary, Fire Chief (Also Assistant Chief,
>   East Franklin Township Volunteer Fire Company)
> Montclair, NJ Fire Dept., Captain Louis Luibl
> New Rochelle, NY Fire Dept., Chief Bell
> New York City Fire Dept., John J. Hart, Director, Management Planning
>   Deputy Chief Matthew Farrell
>   Battalion Chief William Manny
>   Battalion Chief James McKenna
>   Captain James Hallinan
> Plainfield, NJ Fire Dept., Chief Maurice Reilley
>   Captain Robert Horner
> Westfield NJ Fire Dept., Paul A. Battiloro, Deputy Chief, Bureau of
>   Fire Prevention

Finally, the following writers and editors on the staffs of Didactic Systems, Inc., and the National Fire Protection Association, as well as those writers, editors, and artists who contributed independently, deserve well-earned recognition for their efforts:

Chester Babcock	Joel Haness	Adrianna Ortisi
James Bartlett	Joseph Lahey	Craig Pearson
Ann Coughlin	Harvey Lieberman	Erwin Rausch
Amy Dean	Frank Lucas	Mary Strother
Ruth Gastel	Dennis Oppenheim	Keith Tower

Introduction to
Management in the Fire Service

Management in the Fire Service explores the skills and techniques used by competent management in business, government, and voluntary organizations, with particular emphasis on their application to the fire service. Although management in the fire service might appear to be a single topic, it is actually two separate entities: (1) management, and (2) management as it applies to the fire service. For this reason, this text can be divided into two segments.

The first segment of *Management in the Fire Service* (Chapters One through Five) primarily concerns itself with the essentially universal fundamental concepts and principles of modern management theory, presenting them as much as possible within the framework of a fire service environment. The second segment of the text (Chapters Six through Twelve) emphasizes fire service situations. It attempts to indicate how the aforementioned principles apply to specific fire service functions. The second segment is, therefore, far more detailed in its discussion and explanation of the functions for which fire service officers have managerial responsibility.

Chapter One, "Introduction to Modern Management," explains the purposes of the text and discusses a few fundamental management issues. It includes an overview of the fire service officer's need for self-development in the face of the increasingly complex functions and challenges the fire officer faces. The chapter emphasizes that, although management concerns in the fire service are somewhat unique, the same basic principles apply to fire service that provide guidance for any management activity.

Decision making, the one management skill that overlaps all other managerial skills, is introduced as a basis for further in-depth treatment later in the text. Two helpful techniques in decision making — decision trees and decision matrices — are explained and illustrated in the chapter.

Also included in the first chapter is discussion of two other areas that apply to all aspects of management: (1) communications, and (2) motivation. The importance of effective communications skills and the creation of a work environment that inspires personnel to extend their best efforts are summarized in this chapter, and a review of some of the basics involved in good communications is presented as a reminder of the skills that every manager should strive to improve.

The second chapter of the text, "Management Theory — Its Roots and Growth," shows how modern management theory grew out of the search for technical improvements in the way work is done. In addition to the early thoughts on management science, the chapter discusses the way management thinking and theory broadened to include an analysis of the activities of the manager, as well as how the manager's work could be made more efficient and, at the same time, effective.*

The early evolution of large organizations is briefly surveyed in Chapter Two, with examples of management practices represented in several historic settings. Management as a science and an art is then traced from its formal beginnings to the twentieth century. Frederick Taylor's approach to management, with its primary emphasis on working efficiency and economic reward, is examined in depth, as is the work of other advocates of scientific management, including Henry L. Gantt and Frank and Lillian Gilbreth.

The chapter outlines the classical principles of organizational management as formulated by Henri Fayol. These include the management cycle, which consists of the functions of planning, organizing people and materials, commanding, coordinating, and controlling, and such ideas as unified authority and responsibility, chain of command, specialization, and unified direction or objectives. The preparation of plans of action based on these principles is investigated and illustrated with examples.

Also introduced in Chapter Two is the most important outgrowth of the management cycle — management by objectives (or management with goals). With the introduction of management by objectives (one of the major management concepts for helping managers to become more effective), the chapter lays the foundation for later in-depth treatment of this subject.

The beginnings of behavioral theories of management, which soon paralleled management science and often disputed it, are surveyed in Chapter Three, "The Impact of Behavioral Science on Modern Management." The importance of the content of this chapter as an integral part of any study of modern management is reflected by the fact that more major research and work has probably been done in the area of the behavioral sciences than in any other branch of management theory.

Included in the chapter is some further analysis of the work of Frederick Taylor (the father of management science). Beginning with the work of Elton Mayo, extensive treatment is given to some of the major psychological and sociological studies that suggested important relationships between productivity and the worker's feelings, sense of belonging to a group, and sense of self-esteem.

Discussions of the growing role of behavioral scientists in proposing human relations models of organization are included in Chapter Three, as are the conclusions of behavioral science research as possible foundations for more effec-

---

*Efficient signifies optimal output from a given amount of input, such as more pieces produced per hour of production. Another example of efficiency is better results per manager in specific terms, such as higher profit, lower costs, larger quantity shipments, pieces of material per unit output, or, specifically, better service. Effective, in contrast, is a much broader term. Effectiveness includes not only the immediate results, but also concerns itself with the impact of today's actions on the future. For example, an effective manager is one who makes efficient use of personal time, who follows policies and procedures that will bring efficiency in the use of materials and in the use of time of subordinates, but who, however, does not sacrifice actions or expenditures that build for the future, in order to have better results today.

tive managerial leadership styles. Summaries are offered of Douglas McGregor's "Theory X" and "Theory Y" models, Blake and Mouton's *Managerial Grid*, Frederick Herzberg's "Motivation/Hygiene Theory," A. H. Maslow's "Hierarchy of Needs," the work of Chris Argyris, David McClelland's achievement motivation theories, Clare Graves' "Levels of Psychological Existence," and Raymond Miles' human resources approach. Norman R. Maier's work on the technical and acceptance quality requirements involved in decisions is presented as still further background for more extensive treatment of decision making later in the text.

"Modern Management Concepts," the fourth chapter of the text, introduces modern management concepts primarily based on awareness of the constantly varying interaction between the leader, the followers, and the situation. Organizational development as a new discipline is discussed, as well as techniques for better alignment of organizational needs with the characteristics and aspirations of the people who serve in it.

To achieve such alignment of the coordination requirements of the organization with the willingness of people to cooperate, emphasis is placed on the need to develop and blend clusters of skills that fire service officers must sharpen in order to do the best possible job. This includes the skills needed for helping to form a dynamic unit that is capable of responding to a changing environment while, at the same time, maintaining a healthy balance of morale and control.

The chapter also includes a detailed discussion of the comprehensive modern management concept known as the linking elements concept. The linking elements concept is introduced as a practical format for guiding managers in the achievement of their goals, and as a basis for a teaching strand woven throughout the remaining chapters of the text.

Chapter Five, "Managing by Objectives," continues the discussion of managing by objectives introduced earlier in the text by presenting further, more in-depth treatment of this important modern management concept. The chapter attempts to synthesize, or blend, the often-conflicting philosophies behind high emphasis on employee satisfaction and concentration on task accomplishment.

Objectives at various fire service organizational levels are illustrated with examples. Their use as a foundation for objective-type performance reviews and appraisals is compared with the earlier, more subjective type of employee evaluation procedures that were essentially based on personality characteristics.

In an attempt to establish the major background information upon which later conclusions are founded, an explanation of the process of managing by objectives is presented based on the following concerns: (1) What goals should be set? (2) How should goals be determined? (3) Who should be involved in the goal-setting process, and at what stage? (4) What new goals could emerge from goals' review sessions? (5) How and when should performance be reviewed?

The influence of objectives on organizational procedures, methods, and performance standards is analyzed through illustrations and examples. Successes and failures in the implementation of management by objectives techniques are also analyzed. The fundamental teaching thrust of this chapter is that managing by objectives, when properly applied in conjunction with one of the linking elements, can be used in the fire service by any manager, platoon commander, company officer, or chief as a basic framework for developing an improved organizational unit and for achieving the highest possible level of performance. Although managing by objectives might at first appear to be a simple concept, it has, in practice, many complicated aspects. For example, it is far more difficult to create an environment in which people strive to achieve objectives than it is to state the goals or think about them. However, managing by objectives is generally accepted as a very fundamental and practical approach to managing which, when applied correctly, can point the way to improvement in all other management areas.

Chapters One through Five complete the foundation and general principles of the modern management concepts and theories which, in the remaining chapters of the text, are applied, as relevant, to specific requirements and functions of organizational units in the fire service. Thus, Chapter Six, "Management Functions in the Fire Service," serves, in part, as an overview of the remaining chapters, which recommend a general approach that an officer can use to gradually improve the overall performance of a particular fire department unit.

The chapter also serves as an introduction to the remainder of the text by examining the interrelationships of the various functions of management in the fire service and discussing the application of modern management concepts to these functions. Because these functions are managed by and through people, the roles of departmental officers as managers are examined. For purposes of this text, the major part of the work of the fire service officer is considered to consist of managerial responsibilities in the following areas: (1) fire prevention activities, (2) fireground command activities, (3) management of physical resources, consisting of facilities (real estate and buildings), apparatus, equipment, and supplies, (4) management of the organizational units' personnel functions, and (5) training.

Fire prevention encompasses all of the means used by the fire service to decrease the incidence of uncontrolled fire. Because of the importance attached to fire prevention activities, the content of both Chapters Seven and Eight of *Management in the Fire Service* is devoted to fire service management functions related to fire prevention.

Chapter Seven summarizes the objectives of fire prevention by presenting an in-depth treatment of this important area, including: background information on early fire laws; national standards and codes; operational tasks and concerns; organization for fire prevention; personnel assignment and fire prevention priorities; the roles of fire service officers in fire prevention; and the importance of inspections — including detailed information on the inspection process itself.

Chapter Eight's presentation of prefire planning emphasizes: the importance of prefire planning, including information gathering, analysis, and dissemination; the drafting, use, and application of prefire plans; and the relationship between prefire planning and inspections. The loss prevention related functions discussed in the chapter are: public education, fire ignition sequence investigation, water supplies and systems as a management concern, loss prevention records and reports, and the legal aspects involved in loss prevention activities.

Modern management principles concerned with effective utilization of personnel and equipment under emergency conditions are explored in Chapter Nine, "Fireground Command Management Functions." Common tactical and strategic situations are used as illustrative examples.

Management of the physical resources available to a fire department, and the uses of budgets as a management tool are examined in Chapter Ten, "Management of Physical Resources," in light of the total management concept. Administrative procedures for control and performance improvement as they concern utilization of facilities, equipment, and supplies are covered.

The presentation of fire service personnel management functions contained in Chapter Eleven, "Personnel Management," concerns the development and implementation of forward-looking, positive personnel practices. Interpersonal relations between company officers and fire fighters and clerical personnel are discussed. Work assignment, participative decision making and goal setting, performance evaluations, recognition practices, discipline, and relations with labor organizations are covered.

Chapter Twelve, "Training as a Management Function," explores management techniques for improving technical efficiency and motivation through appropriate continuing training of fire fighters. Because training activities provide the opportunity to develop the skills and knowledge necessary to implement tactical operations, these techniques include: (1) diagnosis of training needs for each individual and for the group, and (2) development of plans to eliminate individual and group deficiencies.

All chapters in *Management in the Fire Service* culminate with applicable bibliographies, some of which attempt to detail specific original historical publications for portraying the evolution of management theories. End-of-chapter activities are intended to elicit from the student explanations concerning the practical application of the content of the chapters to future fire service responsibilities as they apply to management theories and functions.

Chapter One

Introduction to

Modern Management

THE SCOPE OF MANAGEMENT PRINCIPLES

This book is intended as a basic management text for present and potential members of the fire service, and for students and members of other fire science related professions. To those familiar with the fire service, it might seem that management is totally different there than it is elsewhere. There is some truth to this: the fire service has many unique management problems. For example, the personnel in few other organizations need to be constantly ready for instant changes from tranquil, routine duties to the sudden intensity of fire fighting emergencies.

The uniqueness of fire service management problems is largely the result of the distinctly individualized nature of the fire service, as described in the following excerpt from the National Fire Protection Association (NFPA) *Fire Protection Handbook:*[1]

> The fire service has many unique management problems. It requires a distinct team spirit; it has a need for a strong disciplinary influence due to the need for concerted and instant reaction on the fireground; it requires a high quality of leadership from its officers; it has a continuing training demand; it requires an extremely wide range of technical competence; it has a labor-employer relationship not comparable to that in other occupations; it requires an ability to deal with the public under both minor and major crisis situations. The fire service is not profit oriented, and has an obscure productivity pattern. It is a major consumer of tax dollars, uses costly equipment, is heavily dependent on manpower, and at present has no satisfactory means of measuring effectiveness in relation to cost. Despite these problems, the fire service has generally performed well for many years.

Yet, despite its very unique characteristics, the same basic principles that provide guidance for any management activity — from managing one's personal

1

life to managing a grocery store, bank, manufacturing concern, or other profit-oriented business — apply to management in the fire service. Thus, the problems that confront the fire service officer are similar in many ways to those that need to be resolved by the line managers in government, manufacturing, service industries, and retailing situations. To help illustrate this similarity, this book provides examples that are drawn both from the fire service and from other areas of management activity.

Similarity with Other Organizations

Management concepts and principles are essentially universal. For example, every manager is aware of the fundamental principle that management is concerned with the accomplishment of predetermined goals through the efforts of people. This principle, like other basic management principles, is applicable to all organizations that have managerial functions — including industry, government, volunteer organizations, and service institutions.

Managers, particularly at higher levels, have always been aware of the great similarities in managing different organizations because they know that the required technical knowledge exists among the people in the organizations, and that they can draw on that expertise. At lower levels of management, on the other hand, managers usually must possess some of that technical expertise themselves. Direct supervision of work requires that the manager understands the intricacies of the work at least sufficiently to recognize what is right and what is wrong. Managers who achieve higher levels must supervise more and more different types of functions and, naturally, can no longer be personally present to individually supervise each one of them. This is why the higher levels of government draw their managers from all walks of life: industry, labor, and other governmental agencies and institutions. A manager who gains experience in an industrial environment can usually do well in a position as a high-level government official. This frequent interchange of managers between different professions and occupations is evidence that, because fundamental management principles exist, it is usually possible for managers to adapt quickly to new environments.

Acceptance of Management Principles

In the fire service it is commonly believed that the application of good management principles must start from the top. This belief is prevalent because line officers frequently feel that, at their levels, it is virtually impossible to practice leadership styles that are not in keeping with those of their superiors. However, this is not always so, as can be seen from the fact that some fire officers are more competent than others. Clearly, the more competent officers are either better leaders or better managers, or both. Either intuitively, or because they have acquired greater knowledge about good management techniques and approaches, they achieve better performance from their units.

A similar common belief that some fire fighters have about management, is t the upper levels of management are not receptive to their ideas and suggestions. Here, too, there is some truth to the belief that little can be achieved except if, or when, the officers are in a receptive mood. However, if that were all that is involved, how might it be explained that some people exert a greater influence than others upon those to whom they report?

Many people believe that good management is merely common sense, steadily applied. Yet nothing could be further from the truth. Decisions that seem obvious and simple from the fire fighter's point of view often are far more difficult, and carry more risks and potential problems for the future, when seen from the wider perspective of the line officer or the chief. For these reasons, the study of management theory can be of great value to the more experienced members of the fire service who have never had extensive formal education in management, as well as to those members who are either new in such positions or who aspire to them.

GENERAL APPLICATION OF MANAGEMENT PRINCIPLES

When one embarks on a steady program to learn a new subject or to learn more about a subject with which one is not thoroughly acquainted, there are often topic areas that might seem to lack direct relevance or that are of little interest. It is easy to dismiss them by assuming that one does not really need the information because there is no immediate application. To do so, however, is to omit some segment that may, later, be of considerable interest and value.

Sometimes high-level managers and fire service officers think back to how they felt about their initial training in management. Many recall that often they considered such training as being too generalized and of too little direct value to themselves. Some recall that they felt their training should have been more specifically related to problems with which they were familiar. However, as they progressed to higher-level positions (from first-line supervisor or even from fire fighter to higher-level manager), they often found that many of the topics that had originally seemed to be general and impractical later proved to be highly pertinent and quite meaningful.

What might appear as generalities to the inexperienced eye take on deeper layers of meaning as one becomes more familiar with a given subject. These deeper layers of meaning are always present, and the student who faces a topic or subject area for the first time must exert considerable effort to dig them out. The results of such effort can be highly rewarding in the future, even if during the present the learner does not have the opportunity to quickly apply the newly gained knowledge.

There are areas, however, where newly acquired management principles can almost always be applied. For example, few people realize how significantly their personal lives can be affected by the application of good management techniques. Careful planning and well thought-out decisions can lead to better use of limited family resources. A higher standard of living and fewer frustrations are the inevitable rewards of wider perspective, greater insight, and enhanced skills with which to manage the same amount of income. The general application of management principles to one's personal life can help to bring about more meaningful relationships with others, and can also help in situations such as parents guiding their children more effectively.

Common Sense and Intuitive Decisions

As previously stated, many people believe that common sense is an adequate guide for the general application of management principles. Intuitively, people tend to believe that they will do the "right thing" when the need arises. While intuitive reactions can seem right because they come about naturally, they can very often be deceptive and thus lead to poor results. Examples of erroneous, intuitive, natural reactions are easy to find. For example, we need only to step suddenly on the brake when driving a car and watch the reactions of the passengers. Inevitably, they will brace themselves by stiffening their arms against the dashboard or the seat in front of them and, with both feet, will push hard on an imaginary brake as though an accident were about to happen. This is an intuitive natural reaction, yet a wrong reaction: nothing is potentially more dangerous than a futile attempt to prevent the impact of a high-speed collision with arms and legs that are too weak to resist. If an accident were to occur, such stiffening of the limbs would only lead to more severe injuries. Once the arms and legs (too weak to withstand the impact) give way, the body is thrown into the windshield with additional force. Very often in the process, an arm, a leg, or even a skull can be broken. The correct stance to take is exactly the opposite; to lean forward loosely and to brace one's head and body against the next closest car segment, such as the dashboard or the back of the seat in front.

Similar intuitive (yet wrong) decisions are made by salespersons who charge ahead when a prospect or customer voices an easily refutable objection. Rather than attempting to find the concern that prompted the objection in the first place, such salespersons address the words that may be only a weak reflection of the customer's actual feelings. The same is true of a supervisor who, when faced with pressure from higher levels of management, immediately passes that pressure along. The supervisor also acts intuitively — and sometimes wrongly, as does the business manager who cuts advertising when business slows down, or the teacher who chides students for asking "silly" questions. The examples are legion, yet the conclusion is obvious: intuitive reactions are often not the best. A few moments of thought between impulse and action can often bring about better actions — and better results.

For good management decisions, managers need a conceptual framework that provides logical consistency while making it possible to act quickly. That framework is usually based on a theory. To paraphrase the famous English economist John Maynard Keynes:

> Practical men who believe themselves to be exempt from theoretical influences are usually the slaves of some defunct theorist.

This is not surprising, for although some people scorn strict adherence to theory as being impractical, it is commonly realized that without sound theory there would be no basis for most of our endeavors. Thus, it would seem that there is nothing more practical than good theory.

The Uses of Theory

There are many requirements that a useful management theory must satisfy if it is to be practical, including the following:

1. First, a theory must fit real situations. It must be evident, to those affected, that the theory correctly depicts the real world and does not contain significant variations from that reality.

2. A management theory, if it is to be of real value, must give equal consideration to both sides.

   a. The organizational unit's need for performance in all the dimensions — productivity, quality, the ability to adapt quickly to changing situations, etc.

   b. The individual employee's or volunteer's need to gain maximum satisfaction from work.

3. There are three influences on the effectiveness of a manager that a practical theory must take into consideration.

   a. The manager's personality and leadership style.

   b. The capabilities, maturity, and personalities of the subordinates.

   c. The situation in which both are involved.

4. A useful theory must be applicable at all organizational levels. In the fire service a theory must be as useful to a chief as it is to a platoon leader.

5. A management theory must provide a workable guide for an accurate analysis of performance problems that exist so that the specific causes of such problems can be identified and overcome.

MANAGEMENT AND SUPERVISION

Frequently the words *management* and *supervision* are used synonymously, and supervisors are sometimes referred to as managers while managers are referred to as supervisors. There is, however, a significant distinction: it is possible to *manage* an activity without *supervising* anyone. Supervision refers to directing the activities of other people, which management does not necessarily require. On the other hand, anyone who supervises the work of other people automatically *is* a manager because supervision of others requires specific planning, setting of goals, and the organization, direction, and evaluations that are so essential to the management task.

Generally, the title "manager" is reserved for higher-level management, while the title "supervisor" is used to refer to those managers who directly supervise the line personnel doing the work. It would appear to be more appropriate to speak of first-line supervision, middle-level supervision, and top-level supervision.

THE TRANSITION FROM FIRE FIGHTER TO OFFICER

A difficult period in the life of a new officer is when it becomes necessary to take charge of a group of former co-workers. To become fully established as a competent manager is not a simple task. Part of the task includes gaining the respect of the members of the company and, at the same time, exerting strong leadership qualities. Also, a new officer must be careful not to add to any hard feelings that may exist because others weren't chosen for promotion. Sensitivity to the feelings of others is necessary, and a new officer will become more quickly established if the following suggestions are kept in mind:

• Do not try to make many changes too fast. Team members often resent changes in the procedures or policies they have been accustomed to. A slow approach is sometimes the most effective approach and can often help prevent additional resistance.

• Remember that the team might attempt to test a new officer's commitment and attitudes. Here, too, rash responses are likely to be costly. Moving with deliberation in response to such trials (except, of course, on the fire-ground) is usually the best approach. If in doubt as to what course of action to take, consultation with another officer, the direct superior, or the personnel officer will usually help a new officer avoid the types of mistakes that might later be regretted.

• Become well-aware of the distinction between "process" and "content." Although this is a simple distinction, it is a distinction that is sometimes difficult to always keep in mind. For example, if an instructor is teaching about pump operation, then the topic — pump operation — is the "content" of the activity. At the same time, there is a "process" going on: the acquisition of information by the learners — the learning process. The inadequate or inexperienced instructor may concentrate solely on explaining the topic ("content"). Such an instructor is likely to lecture and possibly not be aware that some of the learners have fallen asleep, though their eyes may still be open. The competent instructor, in contrast, would, while being occupied with discussing "content," watch the "process" of information transmittal or acquisition of information by the learners. Such an instructor would constantly be asking what else could be done to help students learn more effectively, how could students apply the information so it would be more meaningful to them, and how could students search for the portions of the topic that they still did not understand in order to gain a broader comprehension of the subject. This subject is discussed in further detail in Chapter Twelve, "Training as a Management Function."

On the fireground, the "content" of the activity concerns the fire and how it is to be contained and extinguished. The "process" that the truly competent officer remembers, though, concerns the effectiveness with which a team is coordinated, how it responds, what major problems occur that need to be rectified for the future, etc. A new officer must be self-disciplined enough to realize the importance of keeping "process" in mind while performing routine daily activities. A constant awareness of "process" helps provide the foundation for planning for the future, because it is in "process" that long-run effectiveness is developed — an effectiveness that constantly improves a team's ability to cope with its environment.

• Consider careful planning as an important key to success. For example, a fire service officer must always think of tomorrow and beyond. While the bulk of the work still deals with current matters, there is much that is important in preparations for work to be accomplished at some later date. For instance, the chief's most important work concerns long-range planning so that the department will be able to fulfill its needs for many years in the future. This is necessary because new stations and equipment take years to obtain. The battalion chief must think in intermediate terms, must devote time to scheduling personnel, and must plan how to develop personnel and techniques that will help make each of the districts more effective. The company officer, concerned only with one team, also must think about the development of personnel skills and capabilities in order to help improve overall performance.

Thus, while urgent matters that need to be accomplished during the daily routine are still primarily planned on a day-to-day basis, a task of importance for the company officer is the on-going, long-range planning necessary for matters that will take place in weeks and possibly in months or years.

• Realize that another major key to success is self-development. An officer's success ultimately depends on the ability to expand knowledge and learn new skills that will help improve the service and the communication the unit provides to the community.

Need for an Open-communications Environment

New supervisors have a tendency to see their roles and functions in a somewhat different perspective than that which leads to maximal performance. A new supervisor, or one who has never received appropriate training, is likely to have developed a mental picture of the job that does not match the way that same position is seen by the supervisor's managers. If the higher managers themselves are not adequately prepared to clearly communicate the responsibilities that they believe the lower-level managers should assume, or if they have insufficient contact with the actual problems and situations in the units they oversee, then there will frequently be a large and disturbing gap between the work that lower-level supervisors perform and that which would be most suited for their responsibilities. Too often the result is that unreasonable demands are being placed on lower-level managers; they are expected to do things for which inadequate time is allotted, or that appear to be impossible to handle without additional support. Higher-level managers in such a situation feel that their subordinates are not capable of performing their responsibilities in the expected professional manner. These problems are especially prevalent wherever higher-level managers fail to establish a working environment in which open communications can exist. How to resolve and overcome some of these problems is discussed in greater detail in the later chapters of this text.

INTRODUCTION TO DECISION MAKING
AS A MANAGEMENT SKILL

One skill that directly affects and overlaps all other managerial skills is decision making. Many management training programs attempt to help their participants learn decision making in a general form. To do so is an almost self-defeating process because decision making is so complex that it takes on an infinite variety of forms. Improvement in decision making must partially come from the application of general principles but, to a greater extent, from the specific ways in which these principles can be applied to the decisions in particular circumstances. How to make better decisions is discussed in various sections of this book: particularly in Chapter Five, "Managing by Objectives," where various facets of the participation of other people are discussed; in Chapter Nine, "Fireground Command Management Functions," where the application of decision to fireground strategy is explored; and in Chapter Ten, "Management of Physical Resources," where important decisions are involved in budgetary considerations and the purchase of apparatus.

Inexperienced decision makers often err by regarding decisions as primarily one choice or the other. Some decisions, of course, are that way. For example, one either stays in bed or gets out of bed. In most situations, however, particularly those relating to management decisions, there are usually a fairly large number of possible choices from which the decision maker may select. A little thought may often bring many of these to light.

Decisions on granting a privilege, for instance, seem at first to be simple "yes" or "no" choices. Upon closer examination, it turns out that there are many ways to say "yes" and many ways to say "no." A fire fighter requesting a new uniform or a change in vacation may be told "yes" in such a way that future requests are encouraged. On the other hand, "no" may be said in such a way that the person turned down thoroughly understands the reasons and does not feel bitter about the outcome. Unskilled managers often say "no" in such a way that difficulties and hard feelings result.

Recognizing the many possibilities that do exist is much easier when one follows the formal decision-making process. It is, therefore, appropriate to discuss decision making in the abstract — as a process that helps to select those courses of action that are likely to be most successful.

First, it is necessary to recognize that a decision is not a single act. It usually is a process, because making a single decision is not the important thing. It is in the chains of decisions that have to be made, and how they are linked to each other, that good skills in decision making are manifested.

Decision making consists of chains of decisions for different situations, such as for: solving problems, performing routine duties, completing a specific project or task, or seeking opportunities for improvement. In each case, the chain of decision consists of: definition decisions, analysis decisions, execution decisions, and follow-up decisions for correcting courses of action.

Each of these, by itself, is also a chain. With respect to problem solving, for instance, the definition "decision" consists of a series that answer questions such as: What is the problem? Has the problem occurred in the past? What is the difference from the previous problem? How does this problem affect the goals?

Analysis decisions involve questions such as: What data is necessary to make this decision? Where can such data be obtained? Is enough data now available? What alternatives should be considered? What additional data is needed to evaluate these alternatives? How can the data be applied to evaluate the alternatives? Which of the alternatives is best now? Which alternative steps are best after the first one (second one, third one, etc.) has been taken? When should other people be involved?

Execution decisions involve questions such as: What resources will be needed for this task? In what sequence should the tasks be performed? What people should be involved? Who should do what? In what way should each of these people be involved in making further decisions?

Follow-up decisions involve answers to questions such as: Where are there deviations from the plan? What should be done about these deviations from the planned or expected results? This last question, then, leads directly back into the initial chain. If there is a deviation from the plan, then this, in effect, becomes a problem, and the problem-solving chain starts from the beginning. For other types of decision chains, such as for seeking out opportunities, similar questions can be asked.

The second segment of the basic decision-making concept concerns the process for making each of the little decisions in each chain. For this, it must be recognized that decisions come in all sizes. To lift one's finger involves, in effect, a decision. It is one that is made almost totally subconsciously, and no effort is required. On the other hand, the decision to get out of bed in the morning is one that requires considerably more effort. Usually, it is a rather routine decision where very little analysis is necessary. There are many decisions that a manager makes that are equally routine; however, decisions of increasing complexity comprise the majority of a manager's responsibilities.

The more complex decisions correspondingly require more thought. The most complex decisions, of course, are no longer single decisions but, rather, chains of decisions. As a matter of fact, most decisions that are of any consequence do involve a series, and it is the entire series that is analyzed at one time.

When formal analysis of a decision is needed, it contains the following steps:

1. What data is required?
2. Simultaneously, what alternatives should be considered?
3. When the initial alternatives have been determined, what additional data is required to evaluate these alternatives?
4. What additional alternatives are suggested by the collection of the data?
5. How can the data be applied to evaluate the best alternative?
6. To what extent does this evaluation produce still additional alternatives?
7. What further data may be required in order to evaluate each of these

additional alternatives?

8. When has sufficient data been gathered to support the selection of the best alternative or when is it more important to make a good decision now, rather than a better decision at a later date?

9. Which alternative is indeed the best one?

Keeping these steps in mind whenever the need for a decision arises can be quite helpful, frequently to ensure that all alternatives that deserve consideration have indeed been considered. Two helpful techniques in decision making are briefly explained in the following paragraphs. These two techniques are: (1) decision trees, and (2) decision matrices. In addition to these, other techniques that are helpful in decision making are discussed in later chapters of this text.

Decision Trees

Decision trees are devices that help to define and evaluate alternatives. A decision tree depicts the questions that should be asked at every step in a decision chain: what alternatives are available at this point, and what consequences should be expected from each? A decision tree starts by asking what alternatives exist at the moment. For example, a very simple decision tree could be built for a short trip from one town to the next. Thus, assuming that three routes are available, that the trip must be made during the rush hour, and that it is important to get to the next town by a specific time, the possible alternatives might be: (1) a limited-access highway, and (2) two major truck routes, each of which has some stretches containing traffic lights. These alternatives are depicted in Figure 1.1.

Once these first branches of the tree have been drawn, the following consequences for each end point of this first set of branches need to be considered. These consequences are depicted in Figure 1.2.

1. For the limited access highway: (a) the possibility of heavy, slow moving traffic — about 40 minutes, (b) the possibility of complete blockage due to an accident — maximum probable time two hours, (c) no obstruction, free traffic flow — 15 minutes.

2. For truck route I: (a) heavy traffic, slow moving — about 60 minutes, (b) total obstruction, good connection to limited access highway at four points

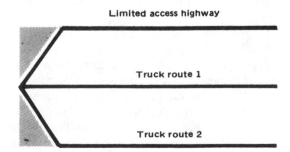

Fig. 1.1.   Diagram of the alternatives for use as a basis for the example of the simple decision tree described above.

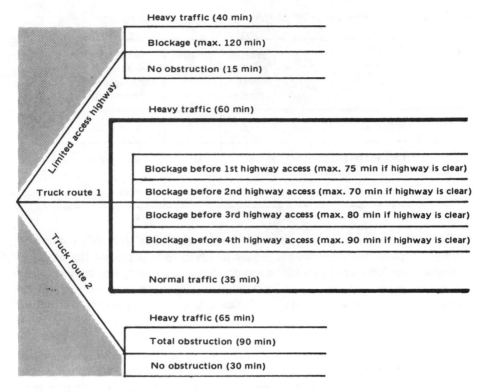

Fig. 1.2.   Diagram illustrating the consequences for each end point of the first set of branches for the simple decision tree shown in Figure 1.1.

— 1¼ to 1½ hours, (c) normal traffic — 35 minutes.

3. For truck route II: (a) heavy traffic, slow moving — about 65 minutes, (b) total obstruction — good access to side streets that would require 95 minutes, (c) normal traffic — ½ hour.

In order to select the best course, some experts say that probability should be estimated to each branch of the tree. Still other experts say that probabilities are not that practical, and that decisions should be made based on the decision maker's judgment about the value of the various alternatives, without mathematical analysis.

For those who would like more help with evaluating the various alternatives, decision matrices (described in the following subparagraphed section) can be useful. It is important to note that simple decision trees are usually quite obvious and therefore not needed. Nevertheless, for more difficult decisions, drawing of decision trees (even if the alternatives seem to be evident) can often bring awareness of additional alternatives that are not immediately apparent.

Anyone who makes use of this particular technique for complex decisions finds that it brings a certain discipline to the analysis that is absent without the diagram.

Table 1.1. Matrix for a Decision Tree

	Shortest possible time (Minutes)	Longest probable time (Minutes)	Reliability (Assurance that estimate is accurate)
Limited access highway	15	120	Low
Truck route 1	35	90	Medium
Truck route 2	30	95	High

One other advantage of decision trees lies in their ability to clearly communicate alternatives when several people are involved in seeking out the best approach. Decision trees have one major disadvantage — they are cumbersome. Therefore, decision trees should be used with discretion, and only on those decisions where they can provide significant advantage to justify the effort.

Decision Matrices

Any decision that has at least two dimensions can be organized as a matrix. Some insights into the relative disadvantages of the various alternatives can be gained from such an arrangement. Tables 1.1 and 1.2 illustrate two very simple matrices that lead to some interesting insights. Both are very simple matrices because they are tables containing only four boxes. A more complex type of table can be used for most decisions to evaluate alternatives. It lists all those alternatives that are worth serious consideration on separate lines, and each column designates a criterion against which it should be evaluated. For example, Table 1.1, "Matrix for a Decision Tree," partially evaluates the decision tree alternatives, and Table 1.2, "Matrix for Evaluation of Engines Being Considered for Purchase," compares the desirability of several pieces of fire department apparatus.

As previously stated, for those who would like more help with evaluating the various alternatives, decision matrices can be useful. In many decision matrices there are usually some tangible considerations, such as money or time factors that can be quantified in numbers, and intangible considerations, such as people's feelings about aspects of the decision.

The matrix shown in Table 1.2 is, of course, neither as complete nor as specific as a matrix that could actually be constructed to compare all of the advantages and disadvantages of actual pieces of apparatus. However, it is sufficiently complete to demonstrate the use of the technique. The column headings such as "Cost," "Maximum Pump Capacity," etc., would be different for every decision, and would have to be selected to suit the particular needs of the situation.

Table 1.2. Matrix for Evaluation of Engines Being Considered for Purchase

	Cost	Maximum pump capacity	Operating costs per hour	Special advantages	Special disadvantages	Fire fighters' preferences
Engine (Manufacturer A)	X dollars	R gpm	O dollars	Best piping arrangement, good crew cover	Highest expected maintenance	High
Engine (Manufacturer B)	Y dollars	S gpm	P dollars	Best controls and air pack mounts	Difficult to connect to more preconnects	Medium
Engine (Manufacturer C)	Z dollars	T gpm	Q dollars	Best hose bed size and turning radius	Smallest water tank	Medium

While matrices such as the one shown in Table 1.2 do not provide a definitive answer as to which pieces of equipment are the most desirable, they do ensure that all the relevant data has been considered and that a detailed evaluation has been made. Such detailed evaluations help ensure that better decisions will be made more often. While strict adherence to the decision-making process and the use of these techniques does not necessarily guarantee that only good decisions will be made, such adherence does guarantee, however, that poor decisions will be made less frequently.

It should be noted that each of the preceding techniques ties together to provide considerable support when a manager faces a difficult decision:

1. The steps in the decision-making process ensure an orderly and organized approach to the decision sequence.

2. The decision tree provides a framework for reviewing the possible causes of action and helps stimulate creative thinking in the search for more desirable alternatives than those that are immediately apparent.

3. Decision matrices are useful in evaluating which alternative represents the best choice.

All the steps in the process, and the techniques, serve three purposes: (1) in difficult decisions they provide a path and tools to help arrive at the best possible source of action; (2) when thoroughly understood they form an automatic thought process that serves as a guide in all decisions, thereby helping to bring about what is commonly referred to as "good judgment"; and (3) they provide a shorthand record of the thinking that led to the decision without the need of lengthy documentation.

COMMUNICATIONS AND MOTIVATION

Two other areas that apply to all aspects of management are: (1) communications, and (2) motivation. It is generally accepted that better communications skills can substantially improve operations by helping to avoid errors and ensuring better cooperation and relationships between people. Thus, many attempts have been made to help managers improve their ability to communicate. In this text, communications skills are discussed in several chapters, including those skills necessary for good counseling and those considered as most essential for giving instructions and commands.

A manager's ability to create a work environment that helps create a motivated team, and the ability to inspire personnel to extend their best efforts through motivation are also emphasized throughout the text.

Communications

To thoroughly treat all aspects of communications would require many extensive volumes. Such complete treatment would not be in keeping with the purpose of this text. Therefore, the following outline of some of the basics involved in good communications is included here as a reminder of the skills that every manager should work to improve in order to obtain better results and thus become a more proficient manager. They include:

1. The ability to put thoughts into words as clearly and concisely as possible. While some people consider this an innate talent at which some people are better than others, it has been shown that this is a skill that can be improved with practice — especially with study and experience in expressing oneself in writing.[2, 3]

2. Closely related to putting thoughts into words is the ability to choose words and word configurations that are appropriate to specific occasions.[4] Especially important is the ability to select those thoughts, or points, that shape the total presentations so that they can influence and persuade. The ability to influence and persuade is of great value to any person, but especially to those in managerial positions.[5]

3. Another highly important skill for communicators is the art of listening. Much has been written, and many attempts are being made, to help people listen more attentively. There are many types of listening, however, all of which need to be sharpened to improve communications skills. Of prime importance is the type of listening that is needed to understand a message that is being transmitted. People who have good comprehension of a topic often understand rather quickly, while others must listen more attentively and hear more words before they achieve adequate understanding. This is important to both the sender and the receiver. The sender must gear the speed of communication to the receiver's ability to accept, and the receiver must pay attention in proportion to the speed of transmission in order to understand the topic.

There are also levels of comprehension that must be considered. In some messages, such as listening to the morning news on the radio, the comprehension that is needed may be minimal — possibly not much more than that used in listening to soothing music.

However, when listening to instructions, attention to detail is much more important; for thorough learning, in a classroom or alone, the attention to detail and listening must be very high.

Another dimension to listening concerns those things that are not actually said but that are implied. Deeper meanings can be obtained by listening to the emotional overtones of another person as expressed by voice inflection. In many social and professional interactions people often mean something other than what they say; thus, the listener doesn't always understand the intent of the words, and understands only a portion of that part of the message that was in the actual words themselves.[6]

4. Nonverbal communications. Some keys to the secondary messages — those that are not verbally expressed — lie in the symbols and the nonverbal communications that accompany them. Everything influences the messages — the facial expression, the visual, gestural, and aural signs and symbols, the stance, the clothing, the relationship between the people involved, and the environment in which the communication takes place. Some people say that less than half of the significance of the message is transmitted with words. This statement is proven by the preference of most people for personal contact (rather than impersonal contact by telephone) on all complex or lengthy matters. Most people generally feel that the types of subjects that can be discussed in depth over the telephone are limited, and that important subjects should be handled on a face-to-face basis.

5. The emotional impact of words. Words carry emotional impact. This impact can be seen much more clearly when, rather than relying on the tone of the voice alone, the other person's reaction is visible. The ability to understand the emotional reactions of others to certain words and phrases is another aspect of communications that is of great value to people in managerial positions.[7]

6. The use of properly worded questions and the ability to apply the results of feedback, or the answers to questions, to gradually achieve understanding and agreement is another important aspect of communications. (See Chapter Twelve, "Training as a Management Function," for more in-depth treatment of this subject.)

7. The successful utilization of appropriate visual aids. A means of communications that is of major significance to persons in managerial situations is the use of visual aids that can help to achieve greater speed and clarity in the transmission of messages.

Motivation

How to create a work environment that can help produce a motivated team is a major topic throughout this text. Although many managers speak of motivating and training people, all too often these words have little meaning. In reality, no human being can be *motivated* and no one human being can be trained by someone else. People, however, can *find motivation* for their work in a favorable environment. They can also find the desire to learn, and the enhanced ability to learn, in an environment that encourages self-development.

It is the manager's job to see that an environment is gradually developed, if it does not already exist, that allows people to find higher levels of motivation. This requires the continuing development of the manager's skills in the technical sense, as well as in managerial and leadership areas.

· ACTIVITIES

1. Explain why fire service line officers often feel that it is futile, at their levels, to practice managerial leadership styles that are not in keeping with those of their superiors. Why is this not always necessarily so? Give some examples.
2. What are some of the reasons why the study of modern management theory can be of value both to experienced fire service officers as well as to those fire service officers who are either new in such positions or who aspire to them?
3. Write, in your own words, definitions for the words "management" and "supervision" that explain the differences between the two. Include an example of each.
4. In outline form, present some of the guidelines needed for an officer to become established as a competent manager once the transition has been made from fire fighter to officer.
5. Explain the importance of long-range planning, including in your explanation the titles of those members of the fire service most directly involved in long-range planning. Also include the particular roles these persons play in such planning.
6. As you have learned in this chapter, new supervisors have a tendency to see their roles and functions in a somewhat different perspective than their superiors do. Why might this be? What might be some of the results of such differences in perspective?
7. Briefly outline some of the basic communications skills that managers should continually strive to improve in order to further increase their competency as managers.
8. There are many areas where newly acquired management principles can almost always be applied, such as one's personal life. Explain how you feel your personal life might benefit from the application of good management techniques.
9. List some of the requirements that a useful management theory must satisfy if it is to be practical.
10. An important management skill that overlaps all other managerial skills is decision making. Explain the importance of decision trees and decision matrices as helpful techniques in decision making. Include in your explanation some of the advantages and disadvantages of each.

BIBLIOGRAPHY

[1] *Fire Protection Handbook*, 14th Ed., NFPA, Boston, 1976, p. 9–9.

[2] Flesch, Rudolph, *The Art of Readable Writing*, Harper & Row, New York, 1949.

[3] ———, *The Art of Plain Talk*, Collier Books, New York, 1951.

[4] Norwood, J. E., *Concerning Words and Phrasing*, Prentice-Hall, Englewood Cliffs, NJ, 1956.

[5] Garn, Roy, *The Magic Power of Emotional Appeal*, Prentice-Hall, Englewood Cliffs, NJ, 1960.

[6] Hayakawa, S. I., *Language in Thought and Action*, Harcourt, Brace & World, New York, 1964.

[7] Brockway, Thomas P. (ed.), *Language and Politics*, D. C. Heath, Boston, 1965.

Chapter Two

Management Theory —

Its Roots and Growth

INTRODUCTION

This chapter and the next three introduce the four areas that are generally considered as comprising modern management theory. These areas are: (1) management science, (2) the management cycle, (3) behavioral science, and (4) management by objectives. Management science, which developed in answer to a specific need — and some of the background that precipitated this need — is introduced in this chapter. Also presented herein is the management cycle.

THE NATURE OF WORK

Prior to the Industrial Revolution in the late 18th century, work was governed by tradition. Sons traditionally followed the work patterns of their fathers; daughters followed the work patterns of their mothers. People were generally born into their lifetime work situations and had little or no choice concerning them. Work followed a pattern, not a plan. For example, the work involved in planting fields, shaping metals, and maintaining households was performed according to work patterns passed down from previous generations. In such an environment there was little need for "management theory" as we understand the term today.

In Early Times

Even in those early times, competent managers and some type of management theory existed. This can be evidenced by the pyramids of Egypt, the Great Wall of China, and the magnificent cathedrals of Europe — all of which attest to the competency of the skilled managers of the times. The successful construction of the pyramids — the planning efforts, the methods for moving the huge blocks of stone, the supervision of the thousands of men and women who toiled directly and indirectly in the construction work itself and in the supply of tools, materials, and food — could never have been realized without the efforts of many knowledgeable managers. Unfortunately, comprehensive records of the techniques these managers used to guide their work forces are not obtainable. Little is known about the managerial techniques used in such historical events as the coordination of people and animals when maneuvering the huge blocks of stone into place during the construction of the pyramids.

Despite the tremendous size of some of the projects that required managerial skills, most of the management functions that were performed in the early days of civilization were performed on a small scale. There were no mass production assembly lines, and technology was uncomplicated. Coordinating and bringing together the knowledge of many specialists to accomplish a task was not necessary because there were few specialists and relatively few tasks that required the skills of such specialists.

Then, as now, individuals managed their personal activities by themselves. However, few people thought of this as management. For example, farming was not considered to be management of an enterprise because most of the production went for personal use. It was a job that people knew how to do — a job that followed a pattern and was much less complicated than it is now because there were no complex machines to worry about, no special fertilizers, no pest control chemicals, and no bank loans or multi-page tax forms.

Although there were some people who might be considered to have functioned as managers, they were few. Noblemen often employed the services of tax collectors (similar in function to today's credit and collection managers) to collect goods, rent, or taxes from tenants. (From time to time, obtaining "contributions" from tenants and serfs required more than the physical arm-twisting of delinquents.) This, however, can hardly be thought of as management as we know it today. In early times there was not even much in the way of careful management needed to turn a profit from trade with faraway places because such trade was primarily barter.

During the Industrial Revolution

With the advent of the Industrial Revolution came many changes that affected the work patterns of the average person. Hand looms faded from existence and were replaced by textile mills. Potters gave up their wheels and went to work in the pottery factories. The small crafts and guilds, the people working at home in their cottages, and the little shops that previously turned out cooking utensils, clothing, needles, and other necessities were replaced by something new to civilization — the mills, plants, and factories that came into being during the Industrial Revolution.

This transition brought with it a different type of existence for human beings, as well as entirely new types of work relationships for working people. Workers lost their individuality and no longer functioned on their own. They became part of the organizations that made up the work forces of the mills, plants, and factories; such organizations needed managers.

As in earlier times, not too much was recorded about the management theories ·of the day. This was primarily because few people could read, fewer could write, and the general public had little or no knowledge of scientific subject areas beyond rudimentary arithmetic.

ADAM SMITH, ECONOMIST AND OBSERVER OF MANAGEMENT TECHNIQUES

One of the first persons to record his thoughts about the way our work patterns affect our lives was the Scottish economist Adam Smith. In 1776, in his book titled *An Inquiry into the Nature and Cause of the Wealth of Nations,* Smith pointed out how the division of labor could help enrich a society. Smith believed that greater wealth could be derived from any system or method that helped produce more goods with the same amount of effort as required by previous methods. His· famous example was that of a pin factory:[1]

> To take an example, therefore, from a trifling manufacture; but one in which the division of labour has been very often taken notice of, the trade of the pin-maker; a workman not educated to this business (which the division of labour has rendered a distinct trade), nor acquainted with the use of the machinery employed in it (to the invention of which the same division of labour has probably given occasion), could scarce, perhaps, with his utmost industry, make one pin in a day, and certainly could not make twenty. But in the way in which this business is now carried on, not only the whole work is a peculiar trade, but it is divided into a number of branches, of which the greater part are likewise peculiar trades. One man draws out the wire, another straights it, a third cuts it, a fourth points it, a fifth grinds it at the top for receiving the head; to make the head requires two or three distinct operations; to put it on, is a peculiar business, to whiten the pins is another; it is even a trade by itself to put them into the paper; and the important business of making a pin is, in this manner, divided into about eighteen distinct operations, which, in some manufactories, are all performed by distinct hands, though in others the same man will sometimes perform two or three of them. I have seen a small manufactory of this kind where ten men only were employed, and where some of them consequently performed two or three distinct operations. But though they were very poor, and therefore but indifferently accommodated with the necessary machinery, they could, when they exerted themselves, make among them about twelve pounds of pins in a day. There are in a pound upwards of four thousand pins of a middling size. Those ten persons, therefore, could make among them upwards of forty-eight thousand pins in a day. Each person, therefore, making a tenth part of forty-eight thousand pins, might be considered as making four thousand eight hundred pins in a day. But if they had all wrought separately and independently, and without any of them having been educated to this peculiar business, they certainly could not each of them have made twenty, perhaps not one pin in a day; that is, certainly, not the two

hundred and fortieth, perhaps not the four thousand eight hundredth part of what they are at present capable of performing, in consequence of a proper division and combination of their different operations.

It is important to note that the methods of production described by Smith came into being long before he wrote about them, and that they gave evidence of extensive application of management theories. Smith's writings helped explain how the changes brought about by the Industrial Revolution helped bring about greater wealth.

Division of Labor

In the late 1700s, division of labor existed in fire fighting as well as in industry. Undoubtedly, at first, those people who demonstrated exceptional ability to throw water accurately onto a fire, or who could throw it further, were those who got to throw the water during a fire. Others carried the water. If there were enough people, water was handed from person to person. Thus, because not everyone had to walk to the well to get the water and because more buckets of water could reach the fire scene with the same number of persons working, the fire service, as it existed in those days, benefited from the division of labor.

As fire fighting became more sophisticated, tub pumps came into existence. Large wooden tubs on wheels were filled with water and brought to the fire scene. Hand pumps (similar to the hand pumps used on old wells) were located at the tops of the tubs. Water was pumped from the tub pumps into hoses, thus supplying fire fighters with somewhat erratic streams of water. (See Fig. 2.1.)

Fig. 2.1. Division of labor was reflected in the operation of early tub pumps as "runners" were needed to pull the pumpers, "relay people" were needed to supply the tub pumps with buckets of water, "pumpers" operated the hand pumps on the tub pumps, and "hosemen" handled the hose. (From Library of Congress)

The division of labor was reflected in this operation in that "runners" were needed to pull the pumpers, relay people were needed to supply the tub pumps with buckets of water, "pumpers" operated the hand pumps on the tub pumps, and "hosemen" handled the hoses. Eventually there were "laddermen," and when horses replaced the "runners" there were "out-riders," "drivers," and "tillermen." When steam pumping engines came into use in the mid-1800s, there were "stokers."

Today, although the scope and complexity of the work of the fire service differs from the early days, the division of labor can be evidenced in the areas of specialization required by properly staffed fire departments. This specialization of work includes fire fighters, fire officers, secretaries, teachers, ambulance drivers, radio operators, apparatus operators, building engineers, personnel directors, mechanics, accountants, experts in emergency first aid, and emergency medical technicians. Such specialization is continuing as the functions of today's fire departments become even more complex.

Complex Apparatus Takes Over Many Tasks: Today in the fire service, much of the division of labor has been reflected in the design of different apparatus. Apparatus has been designed to effectively fulfill many specific functions. As in today's industry where machines exist that can perform the operations of many people at once and require only a single operator, so the modern fire fighting apparatus has combined many functions and automated them. Today, one highly trained apparatus operator can perform the specialized functions of many people. For example, with a modern pumper, a skilled operator can:

- Move more than 1,000 gallons of water per minute; it would take hundreds of fire fighters with buckets to move that much water.
- Apply the water much more effectively in full streams or in dispersed streams.
- Apply water from the ground, or from elevated positions.
- Send messages faster than many messengers.
- Climb steep hills that would have required many "runners."
- Carry ladders and equipment.
- Perform the work of many horses in getting the fire fighters to the scene more rapidly, so that fewer fire fighters are needed to accomplish the task of extinguishing fire.

Complex Skills Required: With the advent of more complex equipment came the need for higher skills and greater knowledge on the part of fire fighters. Today's skilled fire fighter is a specialist who must be knowledgeable in many areas, including the following:

- Hydraulics and pump operations.
- Building construction.
- Flammability of materials.
- Rope work.
- Search and rescue.

- The use of complex respiratory protection equipment.
- The use of communications equipment.
- How to minimize losses by salvage work.
- Mathematics for metric conversions, flow rates, etc.
- Chemistry, for recognizing burning materials and the most effective means for extinguishing such materials.
- Emergency medical services.

Knowledgeability in these areas is necessary in order for fire fighters to function effectively at the fire scene. Also included in the specialized knowledge required of today's fire fighter is an awareness of such areas as inspection and preplanning, building construction, fire prevention, codes and standards, public and community relations, and public education.

MANAGEMENT SCIENCE

The height of the Industrial Revolution in England took place while the United States was in the throes of the War for Independence, and its aftermath. It wasn't until the late 19th Century that a similar economic revolution took place in the United States. The change, like that in England, was a gradual one. Due to the introduction of machines, profit farming slowly replaced subsistence farming and factories slowly replaced small trade shops. However, it was not until the United States underwent its economic revolution that a science of management really began. The next several sections of this chapter discuss the works of Frederick Winslow Taylor, Henry Lawrence Gantt, Frank and Lillian Gilbreth, Henri Fayol, and Chester Barnard — each of whom helped establish the groundwork for scientific management.

Gradually increasing specialization brought the development of machines that replaced people, and the recombining of jobs as the machines took over the work itself. Sometimes the more sophisticated machinery simplified the work to the point that one little girl could (and often did) tend many machines.

Behind the little girl, however, was an industry of highly skilled craftsmen who designed and built the machines, and groups of equally skilled mechanics who kept the machines running. Organizing the mechanized work process required far more skill than the more cumbersome hand processes that had existed earlier. Even the small pin factory that Adam Smith described clearly required the planning, the coordinating, and the supervising effort of at least one competent manager. Similarly, as the complexity of work in all other fields grew and increased, more and more managers were required to coordinate the increasingly specialized activities. When one person cuts and sews a complete dress by hand, very little management is required. A single manager could employ hundreds of people if all that has to be done is to provide a place to work and the cloth to use. However, when cutting is done by people with one type of machine and sewing is done by people with several different types of machines — and all the machines must be selected, purchased, and maintained, and the work effort of these people coordinated — then a hundred working persons require many managers.

As the need for managers arose, more managerial activity came about and management came to be thought of as a science; gradually, the theories that comprise modern management emerged. As mentioned in the introduction to this chapter, management science is one of these theories. The focus of management science is on performance with the least amount of effort. How could the maximum amount of output with the least amount of input be gained? Persons concerned with such matters are often thought of as regarding people simply as machines.

There was an interest in making work most effective in terms of output, but not necessarily at the expense of people. Management scientists, recognizing that people became fatigued, were concerned about making work as easy as possible without sacrificing output. Much of their concern centered around the following questions: What kind of devices could be used? What kind of methods could be followed? How could wasteful steps — or activity that did not contribute to increased production — be avoided?

FREDERICK TAYLOR, THE FATHER OF MANAGEMENT SCIENCE

One of the first to write about management concepts was Frederick Taylor. In the early 1900s Taylor, a Philadelphia steel mill superintendent who had developed a carefully thought-out system for managing work, saw around him a lack of detailed attention to the way work could best be organized. There were wasted steps and wasted motions. He reasoned, quite correctly, that such waste required effort, and if that effort could be used to produce more, everyone would gain. Taylor was not working on a theory: he was working to produce more steel at less cost in order to increase profits for his company. A brilliant engineer, he approached the problem methodically.

Unlike other managers of his time, Taylor was interested in the well-being of his employees. Well-being, however, had a different meaning in those days. While some employers looked upon employees in a paternalistic way and were honestly concerned for the people who worked for them, such concern was less far-ranging than it is today. To a competent manager of Taylor's time, the well-being of employees merely meant increased profits. Business was business, and an employee was an employee. The employer decided what was to be done, and when and how — and the employee obeyed.

Workers accepted this role of the boss as the decision-maker and regarded the shop or office as a place where one was supposed to work. They accepted, without question, the right of employers to change the nature of the work environment without consulting them. Of little concern was the modern expectation of employees for a voice in the way work is or isn't done. However, that some employees did consider this possibility is evidenced by the rise of the trade unions around the turn of the 20th century.

Aside from those who spearheaded the trade unions, most of the people who worked in Taylor's time did not expect any greater reward for their work than to be paid for it. They worked for money. Although they expected to be treated decently, they did not expect their employers to care whether or not they liked their work, whether or not they were content in their work, or whether or not they were comfortable in their work.

It is no wonder, then, that Taylor was not particularly concerned about the psychological needs of his workers. Instead, he was solely interested in how to increase the financial rewards that he considered to be the all-important element for leading employees to greater production and to greater efficiency. Later in the 1900s, managers were to become more aware that there were many other incentives that were even stronger than monetary rewards. They came to realize that "Man does not live by bread alone." (This subject is examined in detail in Chapter Three, "The Impact of Behavioral Science on Modern Management," which includes Taylor's feelings concerning human beings as "living machines.")

Such was the environment for Taylor's work. All around him could be witnessed a lack of detailed attention to the way the work could best be organized. Taylor observed that few people, if any, worked steadily and energetically all day. He reasoned that if he could somehow scientifically determine what constituted a day's work, he could better tell employees what he expected of them. He felt that if he were reasonable about it, he was bound to obtain a greatly improved output. Therefore, through experimentation, he set out to develop standards for a fair day's work. Following is an excerpt from one of his reports:[2]

> The first impression is that this minute subdivision of the work into elements, neither of which takes more than five or six seconds to perform, is little short of preposterous; yet if a rapid and thorough time study of the art of shoveling is to be made, this subdivision simplifies the work, and makes the study quicker and more thorough.
>
> The reasons for this are twofold:
>
> First. In the art of shoveling dirt, for instance, the study of 50 or 60 small elements, like those referred to above, will enable one to fix the exact time for many thousands of complete jobs of shoveling, constituting a very considerable proportion of the entire art.
>
> Second. The study of single small elements is simpler, quicker, and more certain to be successful than that of a large number of elements combined. The greater the length of time involved in a single item of time study, the greater will be the likelihood of interruptions or accidents, which will render the results obtained by the observer questionable or even useless. There is a considerable part of the work of most establishments that is not what may be called standard work, namely, that which is repeated many times. Such jobs as this can be divided for time study into groups, each of which contains several rudimentary elements . . .
>
> There is no class of work which cannot be profitably submitted to time study, by dividing it into its time elements, except such operations as take

place in the head of the worker; and the writer has even seen a time study made of the speed of an average and first-class boy in solving problems in mathematics. Clerk work can well be submitted to time study, and a daily task assigned in work of this class which at first appears to be very miscellaneous in its character . . .

Taylor quotes as follows from his paper on "A Piece Rate System," written in 1895:[3]

> Practically the greatest need felt in an establishment wishing to start a rate-fixing department is the lack of data as to the proper rate of speed at which work should be done. There are hundreds of operations which are common to most large establishments, yet each concern studies the speed problem for itself, and days of labor are wasted in what should be settled once and for all, and recorded in a form which is available to all manufacturers.
>
> What is needed is a handbook on the speed with which work can be done similar to the elementary engineering handbooks. And the writer ventures to predict that such a book will before long be forthcoming. Such a book should describe the best method of making, recording, tabulating and indexing time observations, since much time and effort are wasted by the adoption of inferior methods.

Taylor's Method Analysis

What was Taylor really doing? First, he analyzed the work to see what changes could be tried to find methods that would be most productive. Next, he taught these methods to employees. Finally, he timed the people doing the work to see what they could produce if they worked steadily without exerting themselves, and set that as a standard on which their pay was based.

Steps and procedures of time studies today stem from Taylor's work. The first step is analysis to find the best method. Opinion varies as to what should come next. Some hold that standards should be set, and training should follow. Others advocate training first, and then setting standards. In any case, Taylor's work set the stage for the development of increasingly better work methods. And in many instances, a foundation was created for machinery to take on an increasing share of the workload. Much of the automation that supports today's high standard of living is based on the work of Frederick Taylor and his followers.

METHODS IMPROVEMENT IN THE FIRE SERVICE

Methods improvement in fire fighting began in the late 1700s with the division of labor described early in this chapter. (See earlier section subheaded "Division of Labor.")

Hand Pumpers

When the tub pumpers were developed, they at first had only two persons pumping — one at each end of the pump handle. However, this did not pump enough water, nor did it pump water fast enough. The pump handle became a treadle that was worked up and down by a person standing at each end, as with a seesaw.

After this, the ultimate in hand pumpers came along. This model featured two long wooden bars called brakes, one on each side of the pumper. Fire fighters lined up — as many as ten on a side — their combined strengths pumping up and down on the brakes. Some pump teams could hit a rate of 140 strokes a minute — a rate that was so exhausting that team members could rarely keep up the pace for more than a minute. There were even backup teams to take over and alternate when a team of pumpers became exhausted. (It should be noted that in early competitions with steam pumpers, these hand pumpers often actually out-performed the steam pumpers by shooting a stream of water more than 160 feet into the air.) These hand pumpers were pulled to the fire by teams of fire fighters, two abreast. There were usually ten to fourteen of these fire fighters, or "runners," although often there were as many as there was room to grab onto the ropes and pull. When the fire gong sounded, volunteer runners in various kinds of disarray would grab the ropes while other volunteers, often attired in bedclothes during night alarms, joined along the way.

These runners were a remarkable lot. They often had to pull a pumper a mile or two at a steady trot, through the heat of summer and the snow of winter. Some fell by the wayside, while others joined in along the way. In the great Boston fire of 1872, a hand-tub company from the town of Wakefield pulled its pumpers twelve miles to Boston and then joined in to fight the fire.

Fig. 2.2. Horsepower replaced "runners" for pulling steam pumpers. (From Baltimore Fire Department, Baltimore, Maryland)

Horse-pulled Pumpers

The next efficiency improvement started around 1830 when some of the pumper companies began to use horses to pull the pumpers. Many of the runner companies resisted the change because they considered it "soft" to use horses. They also felt that on short runs people could still out-perform horses and get the pumpers to the fires faster. Not until the 1860s — when the big heavy pumpers came into use, some weighing eight tons — did horsepower generally replace humans for pulling pumpers. (See Fig. 2.2.) Even then there were some holdouts with lightweight steam pumpers still being pulled by men.

Gasoline Engines

Early in the 1900s the advent of the gasoline engine marked the next major improvement in fire fighting methods. As originally used by the fire service, the gasoline engine was a tractor-type contraption hooked to the front of a pumper in place of the horses.

By this time the members of the fire service had become as attached to the system of using horses to pull pumpers as they had been to the previous system of using human "runners." Many fire companies thought there was no way that this new gasoline contraption could ever measure up to horsepower in speed and efficiency in pulling apparatus to a fire. And oddly, at first, they were right. It actually took a fire company longer to crank up the fire engine and get it started than it took a crack horse company to get the horses hitched up and out of the fire station. And the early engines broke down more often than horses.

The "methods" people of their time were management scientists, of sorts. As a tribute to their work, some horse companies performed their methods and drill so well that they could get the horses from their stalls, harnessed, and out of the fire station in the almost incredible time of eighteen seconds. And many pumpers were pulled by horse teams having horses three-abreast. The fire horses were as eager and ready to go as the fire fighters. Once out of the fire station, the horse-drawn fire apparatus could go as fast as the primitive gas engines that had top speeds of fifteen miles an hour.

Next came the "self-starter" and improved gas engines, which eventually were built right into the fire apparatus. Finally, in the early 1900s, this apparatus replaced horses in the fire stations all across the country. Thus, the method of movement of fire apparatus to a fire has progressed from two or more human "runners" to from two and sometimes several horses to, finally, our modern pumpers with their hundreds of horsepower capacities and complex capabilities.

Examples of Taylor's Influence

Although Taylor's studies really applied directly to improving production in the steel mills, they can be used as a basis for analysis in other areas. For example, modern fire fighting equipment design reflects the concept of saving time in order to increase efficiency. Conveniently located preconnected hoses and mouth nozzles, instruments and valves in ready-to-use positions, easily accessible ladders, and quick-change couplings are only a few examples. Breathing apparatus that used to be in compartments is now frequently positioned to enable the fire fighter to jump off the truck with the equipment ready for use.

Ladders now come in sections so they can be extended to the necessary height. Truck beds have partitions so that two or even three hoses can be laid at one time, and hose-packing procedures allow much more rapid evolution of hoses with less chance that they will become snagged on ground obstructions.

There are other ways methods study can continue to help bring about further improvements in fire fighting. Availability of larger hose diameters, for example, brings new questions. That is, is it more effective to use one 2½-inch hose that can deliver as much water as two 1½-inch hoses, or are the two hoses better? To be considered when determining the answer to this particular question is that it often takes more people to reposition one 2½-inch line than it does to move two 1½-inch lines and, as the fire comes under control in one area, the second 1½-inch line can be moved to attack the fire elsewhere. However, a 2½-inch line can often deliver more water at higher pressure than two 1½-inch lines can. Only careful methods study — evaluating the fire flow as well as personnel requirements in the various probable situations the company is likely to face — can help to answer such questions.

Despite the many benefits resulting from Taylor's work there existed flaws that brought about major problems in the actual practice of scientific management. One such problem was the fear among employees that they, by working harder and more efficiently, would work themselves out of their jobs, thus causing many of them to be laid off. Employees were also afraid that higher and higher standards would be set, and that this would gradually lead to their having to work harder for the same money.

The concerns of employees were not the only significant problems brought about by the application of scientific management. Other problems involved such matters as the imperfections in the flow of information and of material, which often created wasted time. This waste was considered to be as serious as slow work or poor methods. Henry Gantt, one of Frederick Taylor's successors as a management scientist, addressed that problem.

THE WORK OF HENRY GANTT

Like Taylor, Henry Gantt was also concerned with the problems involved in increasing steel mill production. Gantt recognized the answers to some of the problems Taylor had failed to solve, and concentrated most of his research on how to avoid problems that occur when:

1. A machine breaks down and people all along the production line have to stand idle.

2. A worker or one operation takes longer than necessary, and everybody's work connected with that operation is necessarily slowed down.

3. A needed part does not show up at the right time.

Work Flow

The problem of work flow was as frustrating to employees as it was to managers. For example, an employee on piecework could lose both production time and wages on a given day due to a work interruption caused by any or all of the following: (1) a lack of material, (2) an absentee on the line, (3) a slow worker on the line, (4) a machine breakdown. Such loss, of course, was clearly unfair, and resulted in many complaints from employees. In like manner, employees who were paid by the day could show up for work only to find that because something had gone wrong, there was no work. These employees, made to bear the loss of the company, also complained. All of the problems that resulted in slowing down the flow of work and production caused a financial drain on business and were constant sources of dissatisfaction to employees. Many of these problems contributed to the bitter struggles between management and labor that occurred from time to time.

Gantt became involved in devising a system that he felt would harmonize the interests of both employers and employees. He believed there were two approaches to solving the problems of the slow-ups and losses in production time that resulted in lost revenue for employers and lost wages for employees. These approaches were: (1) the Gantt Charts, and (2) the Task and Bonus Plan.

The Gantt Charts

Gantt created in chart form detailed schedules of a type that is still in use today. Called "Gantt Charts," these schedules indicated what work-related functions were to be done, and when they were to be done. The schedules often showed how the work was to be "routed," or where the semifinished batch of work was to be taken after a specific part of it was finished. In this way, it would be ready for each following person or persons to work on it.

The Task and Bonus Plan

Gantt was also concerned with the problem of employees who were unfairly penalized by loss of pay because of things that went wrong over which they had no control. To help solve this problem, Gantt devised a "Task and Bonus Plan." In simple terms, Gantt's plan meant that when an employee was assigned a "task" (based on a predetermined amount of piecework that could be used as a standard for a day's work, or on a day's work as such), the employee would be paid for that work even if, due to some uncontrollable circumstance, the standard could not be met. On the other hand, if the employee exceeded the set standard, an extra "bonus" — calculated at an even higher rate — would be forthcoming for all that was accomplished above the standard. This gave the employee protection against undue loss of pay while still maintaining the incentive to do even better than the standard.

Gantt was aware that at times standards could be set that were out-of-line with what employees could reasonably be expected to do, and that there were many unforeseeable circumstances and situations that could disrupt any schedule. He also realized that there had to be some leeway, some room for revision, and greater flexibility than Taylor had allowed for.

THE WORK OF FRANK AND LILLIAN GILBRETH

Two outstanding contributors to the study of management were Frank and Lillian Gilbreth. Frank, whose family wanted him to go to college, decided he could make more money faster if he went to work. The work he chose was bricklaying. (It is of interest to note that many of the innovators in management theory placed heavy emphasis on making a good living for themselves as well as for others.)

Gilbreth soon found that bricklaying, as it was done in the 1880s, was a very inefficient business. Bricks were dumped in no specific order into a pile near the bricklayer. The bricklayer would walk to the pile, pick up an arbitrary number of bricks, and return to the wall that was being built. At the wall the bricks were put down, spread with mortar as needed, picked up again, and finally placed in location. Gilbreth asked several bricklayers for their opinions on the best ways to go about their jobs. Each one came up with a different answer. Gilbreth's trying to find a "better way" to do the job resulted in his devoting the rest of his life to the business of finding a "better way" to do things.

Early Method, Time, and Motion Studies

Gilbreth became absorbed with the business of trying out different ways to work more efficiently. He experimented with all kinds of ways to eliminate wasted motion. For example, he found that bricklayers could work much faster when bricks were neatly arranged in right-side-up positions and located as closely as possible to the bricklayers.[4] If the bricks were within arm's reach, time was saved in reaching out for them. If the mortar was conveniently located, it saved time and motion scooping it up and troweling it on. And, if the bricklayers could learn to spread the mortar with two sweeps instead of three, one-third of the time of that function would be saved. Gilbreth designed better scaffolding, better rigging, and better hods to carry the bricks. To eliminate fatigue caused by stooping, he designed scaffolds that moved upward as the work progressed. Because of his success at finding more efficient ways to work by saving time and motion, Gilbreth advanced from apprentice bricklayer to owner of a construction company within a period of ten years.

Gilbreth called his system "speed work" (not to be confused with "speed-up"). Speed work was not a system based on a faster pace; rather, speed work was based on the principle that performing a task more efficiently would eliminate wasted time and would improve the quality of the work. For example, Gilbreth found that by applying his methods to bricklaying, some 2,800 bricks a day could be placed in location instead of 900. Therefore, his system combined quality with quantity in order to gain the greatest productivity from a task.

Gilbreth's wife Lillian also became interested in methods study and time and motion study. As Gilbreth and his wife became more and more involved with their discoveries, they began to look at smaller and smaller motions. They even began to use motion-picture cameras in order to capture the exact movements involved in a particular piece of work as it was being done. Their motion-picture films even contained special clocks showing the exact amount of time for each motion.

The Gilbreths labeled seventeen basic elements of job motion with titles such as "search," "find," "select," and "grasp," through "wait-unavoidable," "wait-avoidable," and finally, "rest" and "plan." Their work led to the establishment of performance standards so precise that they were put into books of standards where industrial engineers could look up just how long it would take to perform a particular job function. For example, to find out how long it should take an employee to punch two holes in a piece of metal with a certain machine, one could look up the standard time for each of the motions required to accomplish such a function and merely add them up. The Gilbreths thus worked in more detail and in finer measure than Taylor.

Flow Process Charts

The Gilbreths also developed "Flow Process Charts." These charts provide a picture of the sequence of functions involved in a job so that wasted handling or backtracking can be identified and avoided. The sequence follows a product (or document) through all the steps that need to be performed on it before it can be completed. Each function shown is performed on a separate machine.

A similar analysis could be made of the work of an individual performing a job function, or a series of job functions. Entries under "details of method" in such a flow chart would be: waiting for assignment, receiving orders, walking to storage, retrieving material, performing the operation, etc.

The symbols used on the Gilbreth Flow Process Charts have the following meanings:

1. Operation — where work is being done; shaded circles represent work being done that changes the material being worked on (it includes entries on papers that are being processed); empty circles stand for preparatory (make-ready or set-up) work, and for cleaning up or putting away tools or other things that help with production.

2. Transportation — something is being moved from one place to another.

3. Storage — when material is kept idle while waiting for the next step or operation.

4. Delay — idle time caused by a bottleneck; unplanned storage.

5. Inspection — this would include proofreading, checking, or measuring.

6. An activity not covered by any of the other symbols.

Lillian Gilbreth worked with her husband for many years in research and writing, and then specialized more in the human engineering side of management. She successfully managed the household and her husband's business during his life and after his death. The Gilbreths raised twelve children, two of whom wrote the book *Cheaper by the Dozen*. Frank B. Gilbreth, Jr. and Ernestine Gilbreth Corey describe, in their book, how their mother and father organized and managed a household of fourteen members. Each child had an individual job, and each kept a plan and "job description" in full family view. Lillian Gilbreth's contributions to running a "managed" household are of great significance.

Differences Between Gilbreth and Taylor

Taylor, Gantt, and Gilbreth distinguished three basic elements in their work: (1) methods study, (2) motion study, and (3) time study. Methods study deals with how work can best be arranged and what portion of the work could be eliminated. Motion study concentrates on the individual motions to see how they can be simplified or shortened. Finally, time study determines how long the improved methods should take, and what, therefore, makes a reasonable performance standard. It analyzes how much time should be allowed for fatigue, how much for rest, how much for fumbling, etc. (*i.e.*, how much time a particular job function should take considering all of the many factors involved).

A basic difference between the studies of Taylor and Gilbreth is that Taylor was concerned with large segments of work — the putting of five or six pieces of material together, the moving of materials ten or twenty feet, the repeated walking back and forth, or the lifting, carrying, and placing of materials to more convenient locations. Gilbreth worked with much finer units of work — reaching six inches and grasping, the turning of a screw with repetitive motions that took only split seconds. Taylor, on the other hand, was concerned with operations that took five or ten minutes or more.

Fire Fighting Drills as an Example of Gilbreth's Work

Fire fighting drills are an example of how the careful elimination of waste motion can lead to better job performance. For example, a team of fire fighters practicing a strategy can perfect it, and then — with constant repetition — refine it down to the fastest possible time with the least amount of fumbling and error. While this constant repetition can be monotonous and unpleasant in many ways, it can also be beneficial. Although at times it might seem that an individual has become a piece of a machine, there can be no doubt that a well-drilled fire team will get the hoses laid and the ladders mounted more effectively and faster than a team that has not drilled thoroughly.

Drill is a detailed matter, and is as precise as a Gilbreth motion study plan. However, drills have diminished in importance because so much of the routine of all work is accomplished through good organization on the truck rather than by the individual fire fighter. That is, the fire apparatus operation of today is so well organized that fire fighters practically step off the trucks ready to take the hose line into the fire. Despite such organizational perfection, the drill is still an important function in the fire service. The best and fastest companies are those that are well-drilled and that understand and utilize, or have a good sense of, methods and motions.

Not all of the psychological aspects of drill are negative. There can be great satisfaction in being a member of a smoothly operating team. Routine drill, practicing one operation over and over, need not be demotivating. As any member of a successful athletic team knows, there is a great thrill of accomplishment in executing a perfect play; generally, the thrill of accomplishment more than pays for the monotony of having practiced over and over.

THE MANAGEMENT CYCLE — BACKGROUND

So far this chapter has discussed only the way management science gradually grew to match the complexity of the task that managers had to perform. Management *science*, however, is only the first phase of management *theory*. It concentrates on the efficiency of the work processes and on the way the individual worker or employee performs tasks.

There are three other components of management theory. These three components are:

- The behavioral sciences.
- The management cycle.
- Management by objectives.

The focus of each of these three components of management theory is as follows:

1. The focus of the *behavioral sciences*, which started considerably later than *management science*, is on the way people behave in their work involvements and on the influence their behavior has on the amount and quality of work output.

2. The focus of the *management cycle* is on an entirely different aspect of management. It steps away from analyzing the employee and concentrates on the manager's task — on how to make the manager's work more effective so that the people who report to the manager will achieve improved results.

3. The focus of the *management by objectives* concept — or management with goals — is an outgrowth of the *management cycle*. It is a significant refinement of, and in some major ways supersedes, the *management cycle* although many managers today still see these two as separate, independent concepts.

As more and more managers were needed to help manage tasks and people, and as management teams developed, more thought had to be given to the work of managers themselves. In developing the roots of scientific management, Taylor, the Gilbreths, and Gantt were concerned with the techniques of doing work better, improving work methods, and the performance of the detail jobs that all employees have to do. Their major area of concentration was on the employee; that is, how could the employee do the job efficiently and increase output? Little concern was given to the job of the manager and to the job of management.

HENRI FAYOL'S WORK —
THE BASIS OF THE MANAGEMENT CYCLE

Of all the people who studied how a manager's work should be organized, few showed greater understanding or wrote about it more clearly and intelligently than a French mining director named Henri Fayol.   Fayol spent his entire business career (over 50 years) as the industrial manager of a coal mine. He used the same scientific, rationally reasoned methods of attacking management problems as Taylor and Gantt, but in an entirely new area.

In his book titled *General and Industrial Management* (written in French in 1916; translated into English in 1949), Fayol outlined what managers should do, how they should do it, and how they should relate to each other.[5] Fayol saw the role of management as a cycle that keeps repeating itself — going around and around a specific set of functions that gradually leads every project or task to a satisfactory completion.

Management Skills

Fayol divided a manager's duties into five primary functions: (1) planning, (2) organizing, (3) commanding, (4) coordinating, and (5) controlling.   These functions, as Fayol saw them, form a cycle of management — a cycle because they blend in with one another to form a total concept of management. (See Fig. 2.3.)   Other theorists who have studied and written about a manager's duties have used various other terms to overcome the misunderstandings and problems that Fayol's original definitions sometimes created.   For example, planning and organizing are commonly used for the first steps.   However, some theorists follow with labels such as "executing," "implementing," "staffing," "leading," and "follow-up" — all words that essentially describe the same set of functions.   To a new manager some of these terms and their use may seem confusing and not to have much meaning.   However, such terms usually take on more meaning when a manager actually has to face job-oriented problems and decisions.

The many terms that are used by different people to describe the management cycle indicate, to some extent, one of the difficulties of working with the cycle concept.   The skills a manager needs for each step are not easy to define, thus making it more difficult to train people to become more proficient.   Because different theorists have emphasized different terms and approaches, a certain amount of confusion has developed about the specific elements of the cycle. The total concept of the management cycle, however, is an important one that every manager should understand.

The definitions of the steps in the cycle that are used in this text refer to Fayol's definitions — partly because it is useful to know how a concept originated, and partly because the terms are appropriate for the fire service.

Planning: Planning sets the aim and charts the course.   Anything that is done haphazardly without a plan is likely to be less satisfactory, whether it is

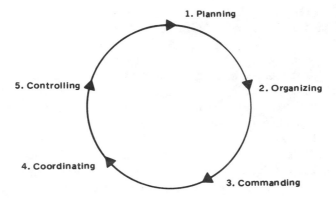

Fig. 2.3. Pictorial representation of Henri Fayol's management cycle.

painting the kitchen, managing a business, or attacking a fire.

Fayol saw planning in three time ranges: (1) long-range planning, (2) medium-range planning, and (3) short-range planning. Long-range planning involves decisions that will have a major effect on reaching goals far in the future, often up to five, ten, or even twenty years from the present. Personal long-range plans can set the course of an entire lifetime. For example, they can involve the choosing of a career or the choosing of a marital partner. In business, long-range plans concern the products the business will offer, the geographic areas it will serve, or the markets it will penetrate. By comparison, long-range planning in the fire service involves matters such as the number and location of fire stations, the planning of water supplies, and sometimes the purchase of major apparatus.

Because long-range planning generally deals with large-scale major decisions that can have major consequences, this type of planning is primarily done by top management. Long-range planning is one of the most difficult functions of management because there are so many options open and so many courses of action a manager can take. There are many different concerns to take into account, and the consequences of management decisions are vitally important.

Medium-range planning requires skillful foreseeing and forecasting, but the projects are generally not as large nor as distant as those involving long-range planning. As a rule of thumb, the medium-range plan is usually for goals that have been set to be accomplished from one to ten years in the future. Buying an automobile would probably be a good example of medium-range personal planning. A yearly schedule of inspections or the yearly budget are examples of medium-range planning in the fire service.

Short-range planning covers all of the planning that will have a more immediate effect, such as planning a party or planning a week's work schedule. The needs of short-range plans are more immediate and directly necessary. For example, should next week's work schedule not be prepared, people might stand around and waste time. Such failure to properly manage can help instill a strong incentive for making short-term planning a habit.

As Henri Fayol saw it, planning is like looking into both the near and the distant future and then laying out a course of action that best leads to the accomplishment of the established goals of a person or organization.

Planning is often considered difficult and unrewarding because few plans materialize exactly as constructed, and usually there are many adjustments that have to be made in plans as time progresses. Planning, therefore, is sometimes looked upon as a waste of effort and, because there usually are many other seemingly more urgent and important things to do, planning is often badly neglected.

Organizing: After planning, the next step in a manager's work is organizing — the putting together of all the pieces necessary to carry out the plan. Organizing and planning are closely related. Fayol felt that of all managerial activities, good organization and good selection are the most difficult. Planning can be compared to the work of the architect, and organizing can be compared to the work of the builder. To Fayol, organizing means "a place for everything, and everything in its place; a place for each person, and each person in his place." Implicit in organizing, according to Fayol, is order, and to Fayol order was more than a matter of neatness. As an example, Fayol presented the case of a yard full of carefully and neatly stacked steel ingots. All of the ingots were evenly stacked, thus giving an impression of orderliness. On closer inspection, Fayol discovered that ingots of six different sizes for several different uses were mixed together. In like manner, the spic-and-span fire station can be said to not always be the best way to organize a station for quick response when an alarm sounds.

As an example of the difference between planning and organizing in the fire service, the painting of a fire station can be used. The planning of the paint job may have to be started approximately a year in advance because it may need to be budgeted. However, the actual painting of the fire station is a job of organizing. The paint, brushes, and rollers have to be purchased and work assignments made. For good organization, the paint, rollers, and brushes have to be made available at the right time, and the right people have to be assigned to the right tasks. Important questions have to be answered, such as: Will four inexperienced persons be able to do the job more quickly and as well as two more experienced persons? Without good organizing, few plans will be followed. Accordingly, not only is much of the planning effort wasted when planning procedures aren't organized, but much less will be accomplished.

Commanding: One of Fayol's principles of command was that each person have only one superior giving orders. When two different people are telling one person what to do — or how to do it — confusion is created. He alluded to the uneasiness that then surfaces and increases the disorder. Fayol thought, therefore, that keeping within the proper lines, or chain of command, was of the utmost importance.

This principle of "unity of command" — one person in charge — is absolutely essential during emergencies. That is why the concept is so meaningful in the fire service and for troops engaged in battle. However, when there is no emergency, this same principle has disadvantages as well as advantages. For this reason the "unity of command" principle has lost popularity as work has become increasingly more complicated. Currently, a large number of specialized experts are needed to advise an organization in the performance of various aspects of its work.

For example, although some fire officers might be highly knowledgeable in fire and arson investigation, it is usually difficult for the company officer to direct the fire fighters in such an investigation. Thus, when it is necessary to conduct an investigation that requires the work of several fire fighters, the officer in the department who is most knowledgeable may be called in to provide technical direction — even though the company officer is still in charge of the fire fighters.

In business, more than in the fire service, this type of situation is becoming more and more prevalent. An example is the type of business in which the home office, rather than branch offices, has the ultimate responsibility for the marketing of the various product lines. Sales people for the various product lines usually communicate directly with the home office and only report to territorial managers on those matters that require an intermediary.

With this type of management, the decision not to adhere to the unity-of-command principle during nonemergency periods is not a bad decision. Although it costs the managers some loss of control, direct communication between salespeople and the home office brings with it the benefit of a more instantaneous sharing of the home office's expertise.

Coordinating: As Fayol saw it, coordinating is the force that pulls together all the people and their work into a common cause. Coordinating is what makes a real team, and an organization or business or government or fire service cannot function effectively if its parts are working at cross purposes.

In any organization there are separate areas, separate specialists, different departments, layers of command, levels of communication — all sorts of groups, policies, ideas, and even orders — that can rub against one another and set off sparks. When this happens, the unity of purpose is lost.

The need for the segments of the work to proceed in harmony (or in a unity of action) was Fayol's keynote. Fayol found that lack of coordination was usually caused by one or a combination of three possible situations:

1. If each segment of an organization is not interested in and knows little or nothing about the other segments.

2. If each unit works in too much isolation from other units.

3. If people do not have sufficient regard for the general interest.

In the fire service, lack of coordination rarely happens. However, there have been instances — especially where the lines of jurisdiction between several volunteer companies are not clarified — when problems have occurred. Fayol's suggested remedy for lack of coordination was weekly conferences of department heads to keep in touch with the latest developments and to coordinate plans of action. Unity of action is the objective of coordinating, and some managers have found that weekly conferences are not sufficient in helping to achieve harmony and unity; thus, even closer coordination of effort is required on some matters.

Controlling: Controlling, as Fayol saw it, is a verifying process in which weaknesses and errors are found and rectified, thus preventing them from recurring. It is making certain that prescriptions and orders are carried out, and that the job actually gets done.

In the previous example of the organizing of the painting of the fire station, suppose the paint begins to peel? This is a control problem. The reason for the peeling has to be found. To be considered are answers to the following: Was it the fault of the paint? Was it the fault of the wall surface? Was it the way the paint was applied? After the reason is established, the proper means of correcting the problem and preventing recurrence must be put into operation.

An important application of controlling as it relates to the fire service is in the area of training. In this particular area any errors or omissions during previous emergencies can be analyzed and, through training, skills for improved procedures can be developed.

THE WORK OF CHESTER BARNARD

Chester Barnard, for many years vice president of the New Jersey Bell Telephone Company, theorized that the personal objectives of the people in an organization must be coordinated with the overall objectives of the organization. This recognition of the importance of objectives and of the need to satisfy people was something new and important in management science.

In many organizations the individual objectives (the goals) of the employees and the overall objectives of the organization aren't clearly spelled out and understood. Generally, although methods have been improved, when an organization has not clarified exactly what its objectives are, the application of even the best management methods can be of little consequence.

Barnard concluded that it was most important for a manager to have the ability to weigh all the strategic factors intelligently and thoroughly in order to achieve proper decision-making in the selection of objectives, and that the making of proper decisions was the core of effective management. The more knowledge a person picks up in life, the better that person is able to weigh these factors because alternatives constantly change. What is a good decision today could be a bad decision tomorrow. Barnard emphasized the necessity for keeping objectives clearly in mind as decisions are made in order to be able to cope with changing conditions.

ACTIVITIES

1. (a) Why was Adam Smith's description of workers in a pin factory important from an economic point-of-view?
   (b) From a management point-of-view?

2. For the following jobs, determine whether management functions are needed. Defend your reasoning by listing the managerial functions you feel would be necessary for each job. Give an explanation for those jobs you feel do not require management skills.
   (a) The owner of a small business.
   (b) A short-order cook in a chain restaurant.
   (c) A truck driver delivering produce to the east coast.
   (d) The lead dancer in a theatrical production.
   (e) A cello player in an orchestra.
   (f) The publisher/owner of a weekly newspaper.
   (g) An arson investigator.

3. (a) In what ways does management science differ from the behavioral sciences?
   (b) Of the two, which theory do you think is more applicable to the fire service? Why?

4. Consider the reasons for the evolution of the division of labor in the fire service. Then answer questions (a) and (b):
   (a) Do you feel that the fire service is becoming too specialized in its division of labor? Explain why or why not.
   (b) Do you feel that the division of labor has made the job of fire fighting more successful? Explain.

5. Following are five of Frederick Taylor's theories of scientific management. Explain how at least three of these theories can be applied to the fire service.
   (a) Elimination of wasted steps and wasted motions will increase productivity.
   (b) Employees work for money; they do not care for job satisfaction.
   (c) The employer decides what is to be done and the employee obeys.
   (d) Standards can be developed for a fair day's work so employees will not become tired.
   (e) One job takes a specific amount of time.

6. How was Taylor's influence reflected in the fire service in the evolution of hand pumpers to gasoline engines? In what other ways was the fire service influenced by Taylor?

7. From what you have learned in this chapter about the Gilbreth's Flow Process Charts, explain how the following six chart symbols could be used to describe specific tasks in some fire service activity.
   (a) Operation.
   (b) Transportation.
   (c) Storage.
   (d) Delay.
   (e) Inspection.
   (f) An activity not covered by any of the other symbols.

8. If fire fighters were paid only for the fires they fight and not for the time they spend preparing for fires, how might the Task and Bonus

Plan provide more monetary reward?
9. (a) Explain how time study, motion study, and methods study can be applied to managing work in the fire service.

(b) Which study do you feel is most beneficial to the fire service? Why?
10. From the following list of duties, determine which category in Henri Fayol's management cycle is described:

(a) Drawing up plans for a new communications center in a fire station.

(b) Organizing rescue procedures during a high-rise fire.

(c) A department meeting to discuss an inspection group's findings on hotels in the municipality.

(d) Determining the efficiency of existing apparatus and existing station locations.

(e) Seeking answers to why fire department response time has increased by two minutes.

BIBLIOGRAPHY

[1] Smith, Adam, *An Inquiry into the Nature and Cause of the Wealth of Nations*, W. Strahan and T. Cadell, London, 1776; reprinted as *The Wealth of Nations* by Modern Library Giants, New York, 1937.

[2] Taylor, Frederick W., "Time Study," *Management: Analysis, Concepts, Cases*, Prentice Hall, Inc., Englewood Cliffs, NJ, 1964, pp. 248–49.

[3] ———, "A Piece Rate System," *Shop Management*, Harper & Row, New York, 1947, pp. 176–177.

[4] Gilbreth, Frank B., "Motion Study," *The Writings of the Gilbreths*, Richard D. Irwin, Inc., Homewood, IL, 1953, pp. 55, 63, 65.

[5] Fayol, Henri, *General and Industrial Management*, Pitman Publishing Corp., New York, 1949.

Chapter Three

The Impact of Behavioral Science
on Modern Management

HUMANS VERSUS MACHINES

At the start of the 20th century, industry's increasing production capabilities became a serious problem for workers. As more high-speed machines were invented to help produce more goods in less time, workers had to increase their work paces in order to keep up with the machines. Many workers became "slaves" to the machines they operated, and the question of treating humans like machines became a moral issue. For example, although Henri Fayol's principles of management and Frederick Taylor's techniques of efficient work helped bring about advances in technology with resultant gains in productivity and wealth, critics of their ideas felt that the techniques employed in scientific management were basically inhuman — even antihuman — in their application.

Rather than fulfilling career goals for workers or creating more pleasant working conditions, scientific management had converted many work situations into meaningless, repetitive small tasks and movements. As each new machine was built to handle a particular step in an overall process, the workers tending such machines became mindless automatons. Work, the critics charged, was becoming fragmented, repetitive, oversimplified, mind-deadening, and dead-ended. Workers were losing pride and interest in their work. Work, even at the higher wages paid for it, had grown steadily less responsive to human needs for satisfaction, growth, and recognition. Working situations were controlled by owners who were impersonal and distant, and the workers began to protest.

Such protests marked the beginning of another major step in the development of management theory. While scientific management concerned itself mainly with material operations and increased output through greater precision of movements, new behavioral theories were concerned with the ways in which workers — the most important element in an organization — could become more effective. These new theories were not simply a matter of seeking ways to increase worker happiness instead of productivity. In the long run, behavioral management theorists argued, peak organizational performance could be attained only by a matching of the organization's goals with the personal goals of the employees. It was theorized that an organization would be most effective when its employees found satisfaction in the work itself as well as in the overall importance of their particular tasks; productivity would improve as employee satisfactions improved.

IMPROVEMENT OF WORKING CONDITIONS

History often draws too sharp a line between contrasting movements such as scientific management and the behavioral, or "human relations," approach to management. Even in the earliest days of the factory system and long before the first writings on management theory appeared, common sense recognition of human needs and human growth possibilities was evident in the actions of at least a few owners of companies.

The Work of Robert Owen

In the early 1800s in Scotland, Robert Owen, son of a saddlemaker, demonstrated that concern for working people and concern for profits were not necessarily in contradiction. Owen began work in the textile business at the age of ten. By the time he was 23 he owned a successful cotton mill in Manchester, England. Six years later he bought other mills in New Lanark, Scotland, which he rebuilt into a model community for his workers. The working conditions and community facilities in Owen's model community were outstanding for their time. In 1813, in his "Address to the Superintendent of Manufactories," Owen urged his fellow industrialists to follow his lead:[1]

> Since the general introduction of inanimate mechanism into British manufactories, man, with few exceptions, has been treated as a secondary and inferior machine; and far more attention has been given to perfect the raw materials of wood and metals than those of body and mind.... A well-directed attention to form the character and increase the comforts of those who are so entirely at your mercy will essentially add to your gains, prosperity, and happiness; no reasons except those founded on ignorance of your self-interest can in the future prevent you from bestowing your chief care on the living machines which you employ . . .

Owen believed in the perfection of human beings through the perfection of their environment and the development of a cooperative society. In later years he used up most of his amassed fortune in a largely unsuccessful effort to spread his ideas in England and the United States (where he attempted to form the utopian community of New Harmony, Indiana, in 1825).

The Work of Frederick Taylor

A century later in Philadelphia, Frederick Taylor (the father of management science), like Owen, was also concerned about benefits for the "living machines" (a term he employed to describe workers) through the simpler and direct consequences of higher pay.

Taylor maintained that:[2]

> Scientific management was developed entirely with the idea of getting better wages for the workmen . . . so as to make them all higher-class men — to better educate them — to help them live better lives, and, above all, to be more happy and contented . . .

Taylor believed that the main outcome of his ideas would be a "mental revolution" in which workers would come to see their personal goals and the goals of their companies intertwined. Like his predecessor Owen, he was doomed to disappointment when he discovered that his ideas had been misapplied or only partially applied, and nowhere fully realized.

Although scientific management did lead to greater productivity and higher pay scales, it was practiced with almost total emphasis on efficient operations and with little or no regard for the feelings, needs, or general well-being of working persons.

In its precise observations and measurements (aimed at finding what Taylor called the "one best method" of doing each task), scientific management had a tone of authority that tended to reinforce traditional ideas of control: work, as ever, was simply what had to be done, and done without question. The worker stood at the bottom of a chain of command. In return for wages, the worker was supposed to unquestioningly accept whatever controls and job conditions managers established.

Despite his expressions of higher intentions, Taylor helped reinforce these traditional views with many of his detailed case studies. One of the most famous was his story of Schmidt, a laborer who worked at loading pig iron into railway box cars. Taylor described Schmidt as "a man of the type of the ox . . . a man so stupid that he was unfitted to do most kinds of laboring work." Part of Taylor's instructions to Schmidt were as follows:[3]

> Well, if you are a high-priced man, you will do exactly as this man tells you tomorrow, from morning till night. When he tells you to pick up a pig and walk, you pick it up and walk, and when he tells you to sit down and rest, you sit down. You do that right straight through the day. And what's more, no back talk.
>
> Now a high-priced man does just what he's told to do, and no back talk. Do you understand that? When this man tells you to walk, you walk; when he tells you to sit down, you sit down, and you don't talk back to him. Now you come to work here tomorrow morning and I'll know before night whether you are really a high-priced man or not. . . .

Schmidt, according to Taylor's account, almost quadrupled his daily production (from 12½ tons to 47½ tons), and earned 60 percent higher wages (from $1.15 a day to $1.85 a day). This was small consolation to the labor leaders and social reformers who bitterly attacked Taylor's ideas.

EFFECTS OF SCIENTIFIC MANAGEMENT

The basic ideas of scientific management were effective from an organizational viewpoint. By standardizing materials, machines, and processes, scientific management aided in creating organizations that were large and complex. The formation of the "mechanized" assembly line — the symbol of this standardization — gave individual workers much smaller tasks as production became more accelerated. The craftspersons of former times, who often made total assemblies or products substantially on their own terms, now found themselves doing smaller segments of work to exact specifications. The new automobile industry, having created a major consumer demand, also became a primary user of the assembly line. Hundreds of workers, each contributing a small performance, created finished automobiles in record time.

However, while scientific management aided industry, the well-being of workers was still not a foremost consideration, and those individuals who were familiar with constructing an entire product, or who used to contribute to a product's formation in a large way, had to settle for still smaller and smaller responsibilities. If workers protested by intentionally or unintentionally slowing down or failing to meet production quotas or quality standards, management usually responded by imposing further controls on workers and by further subdividing work responsibilities.

The development of scientific management continued without interruption through the decades. One of its results was automation — the complete abandonment of people as a vital working force in many production operations. Today, the idea of total automation faces formidable economic and social obstacles. To most people, the possibility of a world in which work is taken over by self-operating machines would seem to be more of a nightmare than a dream. Sometimes, however, even dedicated humanitarians applaud when machines are designed to replace human beings at particularly dull, degrading, dehumanizing, and hazardous jobs.

The basic logic of scientific management, with its objective measurements and increased production gains, seemed unchallengeable at the start. It is difficult to imagine that a highly technological society such as that in the United States could have been established and sustained without precise organization and scheduling of productive resources on a grand scale.

Dissatisfaction with Scientific Management

Foundations were developing, nevertheless, for still another major step in the development of management theory. This step was not necessarily intended to overrule scientific management, but was formed to augment, moderate, and refine it. A significant number of managers, for example, were bothered by the clash between the need for large-scale efficiency and their personal beliefs in individual independence, personal dignity, and equal opportunity. In the 1920s and after, many managers attempted to pay their debts of conscience by establishing humanitarian programs for workers. For example, the physical surroundings of many plants were brightened and improved. Some companies hired social workers to help employees with personal or family problems, and others built cafeterias and initiated educational, recreational, and health programs for employees. Often, while such programs helped offset the stresses of work, they did not affect the nature of the work itself. In many cases, such changes were consciously introduced by managers expecting direct payoffs in good will and productivity. Thus, some workers, suspecting that they were supposed to work harder or to stop asking for pay increases in return for welfare advantages, often resented such improvements.

In total, scientific management created unprecedented change, growth, and prosperity. Yet it also caused great dissatisfaction among whole classes of American workers. Economist Robert Heilbroner reasons, as follows, that progress can cause discontent rather than high morale and contentment:[4]

> Development is apt to be characterized by a growing gap between expectations and achievements . . . by an increased awareness of insufficiency and a decreased tolerance of both poverty and privilege. For the underlying masses, development is apt to be a time of awakening hostilities, of newly felt frustrations, of growing impatience, and dissatisfaction.

Scientific management had the effect of creating changes that brought about rising and unfulfilled expectations. This happened in several ways, as explained in the following paragraphs.

Changes and Unmet Expectations: Once introduced to the possibilities of change, workers were likely to want more change. Manual laborers, for example, found their work systematized and then mechanized. The shift from "bull worker" to machine operator often meant that the worker could produce more and earn higher pay, and perhaps feel like the "higher-class man" that Taylor talked about. The sense of change was still greater for the farm people and immigrants who were drawn to American cities by the vast increase in industrial work. (From 1890 to 1920, urban population grew from less than one-third to more than half the total population.) However harsh factory conditions might have been, they were preferable to the generally dismal conditions of life on the typical small farm of the time.

Having once experienced such changes, workers were likely to be disappointed to find they were supposed to stay put for a lifetime at one routine task. As concentrated industries grew larger and larger, it became less and less possible for workers to think of rising to the top or even talking to managers at higher levels. Workers began to voice dissatisfaction among themselves, and soon discovered that there could be "power in numbers." Workers, with the aid of social reformers and labor leaders, began to organize to give themselves a collective voice.

However, effective union organization was generally confined to specialized areas like the building trades and clothing manufacture. The successful organization of industrial unions in the biggest mass production companies was to take many years.

Demand for Increased Educational Opportunities: Educational opportunities expanded tremendously to meet both the problems and promises of industrial growth. In turn, education created expectations that industry could not seem to meet. Industrialists, unions, and social reformers joined in the demand for public education, each group for its own reasons. In 1913, in Syracuse, New York, New York City superintendent of schools William H. Maxwell expressed his concern about:[5]

> . . . the agitation with which the educational world is now seething for the introduction of industrial or trade teaching in the public schools. That agitation, as everyone knows, originated with the manufacturers. They had practically abandoned the apprenticeship system of training workmen. No longer training their own mechanics, they have found it difficult to obtain a sufficient supply of skillful artisans. . . . Out of this dilemma the exit was obvious — persuade the State to assume the burden.

Labor leaders also sought opportunities for school training in the skills that industry needed. Even the most menial factory jobs might now demand at least a minimum of reading and arithmetic. Workers had to be educated (it had never seemed important before) to run machines such as typewriters, addressographs, and duplicators, and to keep records for management. Others had to be educated to work with stopwatches, time-and-motion graphs, and production flow charts — all of which were important in scientific management. Unions also fought to bring about an end to child labor, which could be abolished by making it compulsory for children to attend school. Social reformers also saw compulsory school attendance as an antidote to the street delinquency of children whose parents were working long hours in the factories.

Such forces combined to bring about a great increase in educational opportunities. From 1896 to 1918, the number of five- to seventeen-year-old children attending school more than doubled. The number of urban evening schools and free public high schools tripled, and enrollment increased six times. Many farm families moved to cities in order to obtain better educations. College enrollments also climbed from three percent to eight percent for the eligible age group, and students took part in such new courses as chemical, electrical and mechanical engineering, corporate law, and business administration.

The increasing numbers of people attending school found their horizons broadened at the very time that work was becoming more compartmented, more monotonous, and more impersonal. "Getting ahead" was becoming much more difficult than legend said it was.

Worker Reaction to Mass Production: Technological developments and industrial growth created a flood of new consumer goods, comforts, and conveniences. Simultaneously, workers faced a growing gap between what they wanted and what they could afford. Almost at once, Americans became equipped with wondrous tools of entertainment, comfort, communications, and travel. Such new conveniences reduced time spent in the home and allowed more leisure time for the growing population. However, not everyone could benefit from the results of this accelerated consumerism without making other sacrifices. Some consumers utilized installment plan payments, loans, and credit to such an extent that many found themselves hopelessly in debt. Others were continually involved with the dilemma brought about by frustrations concerning what they wanted and what they could afford.

White and blue collar workers were especially torn in this "buying" society. At their jobs, many workers produced goods that they could not afford at home. Although from 1898 to 1918 worker salaries increased by almost fifty percent, the higher cost of living eliminated much of their gain.

BEGINNINGS OF HUMAN RELATIONS THEORY OF MANAGEMENT

Office and factory workers began to feel that all of the miraculous changes provided by mass production helped to prove the old saying that "the rich get richer and the poor get poorer."

Although many doubts and dissatisfactions were evident, they lacked a focus, a vocabulary, and a set of methods and research results to compare with the theories of scientific management. The possibility of a response was present, however, in the newly developing behavioral sciences like psychology and sociology. In 1923 the following was suggested by Dr. Robert Yerkes of the National Research Council:[6]

> The whole of history is a record of human behavior. Man has always been interested in himself, always observant of his acts. But mostly his descriptions are impressionistic, colored by the purpose and bias of the writer, inaccurate and incomplete. The science of psychology has undertaken to supply carefully controlled and accurate descriptions of behavior, based upon objective measurements of what man actually does in certain definite circumstances . . .
>
> With increasingly safe and abundant knowledge of man's mental traits and capacities, we shall intelligently, instead of blindly and by guess, help to fit ourselves and others into the social fabric. . . . We stand on the threshold of a new era . . .

Despite such fervent declarations, the behavioral sciences had little impact on management theory of the time. Such impact, when it finally came about, was undeliberate and virtually unexpected, and was mostly an outcome of the Hawthorne Experiments, a series of landmark studies conducted between 1927 and 1932. Researchers from the Harvard Graduate School of Business Administration conducted the experiments at the Western Electric Company's Hawthorne Plant in Chicago. The original intention of the Hawthorne Experiments was to verify the various scientific management theories that concerned the effects of physical surroundings, rest periods, and wage incentives on increased worker productivity.

The results of many of the experiments in the Hawthorne Studies were startlingly different from the researchers' original hypotheses. In the most famous of the experiments, six young women were detached from a department where hundreds of workers assembled a simple telephone relay component. Working in a separate room under extremely careful observation and friendly attention from the researchers, they were given rest periods of differing durations at various times in the working day. As predicted, their work output began to increase. However, when the rest periods were eliminated, the work output *continued* to increase dramatically and kept rising almost without interruption with every change in working conditions — whether the changes were favorable or unfavorable.

The Work of Elton Mayo

Dr. Elton Mayo of Harvard interpreted the Hawthorne Experiments in a series of papers and books that made him famous as the founder of the human relations theory of management. According to Mayo, experiments like the one involving the telephone component assembly workers demonstrated the importance of informal social groupings that were often more meaningful to workers than the formal organization of a company, changes in physical surroundings, or money incentives. The young women assemblers, he explained, increased production because of the friendship and trust they developed among themselves and because of the special recognition given them as a group when they were singled out for the experiment. They felt special, and acted that way. Mayo also pointed out that some of the other informal groups observed in the experiments operated to limit production and to fight controls even when better effort would have brought about higher pay. The reasons, Mayo suggested, lay in the suspicion and distrust these groups felt toward management, and the need they felt to build barriers and intra-group rules for their own protection.

Mayo's broadest conclusions were highly controversial. He disturbed many readers with his sweeping view of the informal group as the workers' last refuge in a cold, inhumane society. His prescriptions for management, involving tactics by which managers would identify and control informal workers' groups, angered many liberal observers who interpreted these ideas as anti-union. Whatever the arguments against Dr. Elton Mayo, he had managed to publicize a remarkable series of experiments that included more than 20,000 individual interviews with workers and their supervisors — thus emphasizing a psychology and a sociology of work.

Management theory had been extended beyond physical movement and wage-hour questions to a study of noneconomic questions concerning how workers behave and why. The study of management had thus grown in one leap to embrace a large segment of behavioral science inquiry into motivation, communications, the nature of leadership, the social characteristics of organizations, and the best conditions for employee development and career growth.

Scientific management and industrial engineering had by no means been displaced by the human relations school of management. Extensive follow-up on the findings of the Hawthorne Experiments was delayed many years by the higher urgencies brought about by the Great Depression and then World War II (a span of time during which the term "human relations approach" gradually declined in use and the more frequently used term "behavioral science approach" became preferred).

Experiments on Total Work Environment

The end of World War II in 1945 marked the beginning of a period of wide exploration into the individual employee's total environment.   Social and psychological needs were observed in carefully designed experiments, some of which were as painstaking as Taylor's observations of worker's physical actions.   The reasons for such research and the expected results of it are summarized in part by Saul W. Gellerman, as follows:[7]

> Most recent research indicates that we are overmanaging our enterprises to the point where initiative and ingenuity are too often driven to seek outlets outside. . . . The majority of employed people at all levels continue to have little leeway for exercising their own judgment at work. . . . Management will move toward greater flexibility and individual responsibility because there are more efficient principles than the traditional chain of command.

During the 1960s, the development of the behavioral science approach to management evolved from a number of key theories and experiments. Several of these theories are described in the remainder of this chapter, and can be categorized as follows:*

- Theories that emphasize the general characteristics of the individual worker.
- Theories that emphasize the matching of leadership style and the characteristics of subordinate workers.
- Theories that emphasize the matching of leadership style, characteristics of subordinates, and various situations.

THEORIES ON MOTIVATION
AND POTENTIAL FOR SELF-DIRECTION

A number of theories presented during the period following World War II cast new light on the nature of the worker by suggesting that the individual's motivation and potential for self-direction and growth might be far higher than traditionally assumed.

The Work of Abraham Maslow

People Have Basic Needs for Survival and Security, But Also Express Other Social and Personal Needs of a Much Higher Level

---

*These categories are somewhat arbitrary, and mainly chosen for convenience in exposition. Most of the theories summarized pay due attention to all three elements, but differ in primary emphasis.

Psychologist Abraham H. Maslow concerned himself with the total range of human mentality and relationships. His "Hierarchy of Needs," from *Motivation and Personality*, first widely published in 1954, has had a major influence in the development of current management theory.[8] In simple form, his conceptualization can be diagrammed as shown in Figure 3.1.

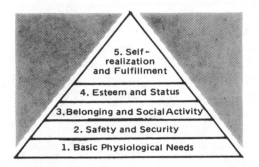

Fig. 3.1. Simplified diagram of Maslow's conceptualization of the five levels of basic human needs. (Adapted from "Hierarchy of Needs," *Motivation and Personality*, by A. H. Maslow)

The five levels of needs identified by Maslow are organized according to the following priorities:

Basic Physiological Needs: Needs that are primarily related to bodily survival; the need for food and water to maintain life, and the need for clothing and shelter to protect the body from harsh environments.

Safety and Security: Needs that are concerned with safety of body and security of provisions; the need for self-preservation, and the need to ensure future security. (These needs are closely related to the needs in No. 1, Basic Physiological Needs.)

Belonging and Social Activity: The need to belong to a group, to have some means of group identification, to receive and give affection, and to participate in some form of social activity. These needs should be met at work as well as away from it.

Esteem and Status: The need to have, to receive, and to give esteem and status (both of which are essential to human dignity); self-respect and respect for others are important in a modern industrial society because the previous three needs are, to a large degree, satisfied.

Self-realization and Fulfillment: The need to become all that one is capable of becoming; when this need exists, work becomes a challenge and provides greater satisfaction.

To some extent, Maslow portrays a pattern of human growth and suggests a human tendency to continually strive for even higher objectives. To illustrate this, consider as an example the person who is trapped at the lowest level of physiological needs and thus has to devote all thought and energy to the struggle for food, clothing, and shelter. Once these needs have been satisfied, such a person will usually require the assurance that in the future these same needs will continue to be satisfied. Given this assurance, the person will then usually want the society of other people, probably including the pleasures of friendship and group effort. From this stage grows the need for recognition by others and, finally, the need for inner knowledge of personal competence and worth (a quality that Maslow also calls self-actualization). This highest level, in particular, represents questions that were largely unexplored in management theory during Maslow's time.

A simplistic visualization of Maslow's theory is to imagine a person climbing up the "pyramid" illustrated in Figure 3.1, one step at a time. However, it is also important to visualize *all* of the needs represented by the steps of the pyramid as operating to some degree at the same time. For example, a fire fighter rookie, while still seeking a feeling of "belonging" within a fire department, may simultaneously be looking forward to a time of promotion and to a time when complete self-confidence and personal satisfaction is realized concerning the choice of a career with the fire services. In some exceptional circumstances, a person may be seeking higher level needs while ignoring others. An example of this would be the dedicated artist to whom painting the "right" picture is more important than food and housing.

The Work of David McClelland

Achievement, to Many People, Is Its Own Reward

Psychologists have identified more than twenty basic human motives that are present in almost all human beings, and which are shaped and accentuated by each person's lifetime experiences. Beginning in the late 1940s, Dr. David McClelland of Harvard University, in conjunction with associates, carried out a series of studies concerned with achievement motivation — the need people feel for doing something particularly well. McClelland's studies were developed using as a basis people from many fields (including business and industry) who seemed to demonstrate a high need for achievement. In particular, these people were studied regarding their ways of expressing thoughts about achievement as compared to their ways of expressing thoughts about affiliation (the need for companionship or friendship and for helping others) and power (the need to control or lead other people).

McClelland's studies disclosed a pattern of high achievement characteristics that was unexpectedly different in some ways from traditional views of how successful people behaved. The studies indicated that people who required a high degree of achievement enjoyed moderate risks and challenges that were neither too easy nor too hard—risks and challenges that offered an approximately fifty-fifty probability of accomplishment. These people also wanted steady feedback about how they were doing, and they readily accepted help when it was useful to them. Their fear of failure and enjoyment of success were more intense than were similar feelings in others. Money and other material benefits were important to the high achievers to the extent that these rewards helped prove that goals had been achieved. Many high achievers were happiest competing against their own previous best efforts.[9]

The Work of Douglas M. McGregor

Given the Opportunity, People Will Direct Their Working Behavior Toward the Best Goals and Interests of the Organization

Professor Douglas M. McGregor of Massachusetts Institute of Technology, a social psychologist, suggested that most organizations operated under certain traditional beliefs. McGregor called these beliefs Theory X and described them as follows:[10]*

> Management is a function which demands tight control over every aspect of the productive process. This is necessary because workers are naturally inclined to work as little as possible, to shirk responsibility, to be indifferent to organizational needs, and to resist change. Workers must be regulated by "hard" methods of strict discipline, or seduced by "soft" methods which offer extensive benefits and constant efforts to achieve harmony.

Theory X did not really work, McGregor maintained, because it ignored some genuine basics of human nature. He proposed that managers would be able to see their subordinates more clearly in terms of beliefs that he called Theory Y:[10]

> People do not have an inherent dislike of work. They have motivation to work, a willingness to assume responsibility, and a readiness to help the organization reach its goals. . . .
>
> . . . the essential task of management is to arrange organizational conditions and methods of operation so that people can achieve their own goals *best* by directing *their* own efforts toward organizational objectives.

McGregor pointed out that with Theory X, management takes both a hard and a soft line. He explained that the hard line — tight disciplinary measures when needed — is met by employee antagonism and leads to many forms of resistance. He described the soft line as including such benefits as vacations, pensions, and recreational programs. However, he went on to explain, these benefits are only enjoyable *off the job*, and each of them tends to encourage passivity on the job.

Theory Y, McGregor argued, would give workers a greater personal stake in their own work. They would be encouraged to use all their knowledge, skills, and ingenuity in accomplishing the organization's objectives. This would present a difficult challenge, McGregor allowed, but could be started in one way by the process of job enlargement (making workers responsible for larger and more complex parts of the production process).

The Work of Frederick Herzberg

The Most Effective Work Incentives Are in the Job, Where They Are Least Often Provided

---

*From *Human Side of Enterprise*, by Douglas M. McGregor. Copyright © 1960, McGraw-Hill. Used with permission of McGraw-Hill Book Company.

In the 1950s, a group of researchers led by Frederick Herzberg of Case Western Reserve University began an extensive survey process in which engineers and accountants were questioned concerning those aspects of their work that made them feel especially good, and those aspects of their work that made them feel especially bad. Using the answers to these questions as a basis, Herzberg developed the "motivation-hygiene theory of job attitudes" which has since been tested at all levels of work throughout the world.

Herzberg and his associates discovered a number of factors that were frequently listed as dissatisfactions, but rarely as satisfactions. These factors included a surprising number of conditions that had generally been regarded as work incentives (or motivators), such as salary, fringe benefits, and vacation and recreation policies. When these factors were deficient, they caused dissatisfaction. But when they were present, they did *not* represent important job satisfactions.

Herzberg called these factors the "hygiene elements of work," or "dissatisfaction-avoiders." He considered them as a type of preventive medicine that helped keep people from being unhappy. However, they did not do much to make workers happy or to motivate them.

Virtually all the factors listed by workers as satisfactions turned out to be directly connected with the jobs they did. These "satisfiers" included the nature of the work itself, achievement in a work project, recognition for the work, responsibility for a job, and advancement to greater responsibility.

After repeated studies, Herzberg concluded that most company-wide efforts to improve workers' attitudes and motivation had little effect. These included reductions in working hours, increased wages, improved fringe benefits, friendlier supervision, and company efforts to improve communications about policies. Much of the costs of these expensive programs, Herzberg proposed, should be shifted to job-enrichment programs designed to make jobs more challenging and to give employees greater on-the-job opportunities for initiative, responsibility, recognition, and personal growth.

Herzberg further explained his hygiene factors by comparing them to dog biscuits used to attract a puppy's attention. He explained that the food did not "motivate" the puppy; instead, the puppy's owner was motivated to attract the pet's attention. The dog biscuit offer would have only temporary effect and would have to be used over and over again, perhaps with greater frequency. Herzberg suggested that most off-the-job benefits work the same way, and also proposed that what is needed to turn on a person's "internal generator is truly important work which makes possible genuine achievement."[11]

THEORIES ON LEADERSHIP STYLE

The preceding theories deal largely with the human nature of people as employees. Another important set of theories deals with leadership style and the ability of managers to affect organizations in many different ways.

The Work of Rensis Likert

Demanding Production Is the Least Effective Way to Get Production

In the 1950s and 1960s, University of Michigan researchers conducted an extensive series of experiments in which they observed the output of departments headed by supervisors who were "employee centered," and the output of other departments headed by supervisors who were "production centered." One typical experiment focused for a long period of time on the clerical departments of a major insurance company. The lowest production levels were consistently found in departments headed by supervisors who placed a major emphasis on production, who exercised strict controls over employees, and who frequently intervened in the work process. When the production-centered supervisors were transferred to departments that previously had employee-centered supervisors, production fell off.

Rensis Likert, who summarized the experiments for publication, characterized management as falling into four types: (1) exploitive-authoritative, (2) benevolent-authoritative, (3) consultative, and (4) participative.[12] The participative type was probably best, he theorized, because employees actually worked in self-disciplined groups which, in order to be productive, required little or no pressure. The most effective role for the supervisor, Likert concluded, was to provide information, materials, organizational support, and to "stay out of the way." Likert allowed, however, that authoritative control appeared to be necessary in certain exceptional crisis situations.

The Work of Robert Blake and Jane S. Mouton

Managers Can Balance Concerns for People and Production in Many Ways

With the publication of their *Managerial Grid* in 1964, Drs. Robert R. Blake and Jane S. Mouton offered a model that they felt appropriate to the realities of organizational life.[13] The grid took into account a fact that many behavioral science researchers had noted earlier: high morale among workers did not necessarily equal high productivity. Ideally, they suggested, managers should move the organization to work equally toward maximum concern for people *and* maximum concern for production (Point 9,9 on the *Managerial Grid*® shown in Fig. 3.2).

The Blake and Mouton *Managerial Grid* thus acknowledges that some organizations can survive under extreme leadership conditions. For example, at Point 1,1 on the *Managerial Grid*, work went on despite the fact that supervisors shunned responsibility or blame, and might be almost totally out of contact with both higher management and subordinate workers. A Point 9,1 (Sweatshop Management) approach was considered possible if workers were uneducated and highly submissive to authority. A Point 5,5 position could be sustained only with constant compromises between production needs and human needs, with little satisfaction of long duration in either direction. Though

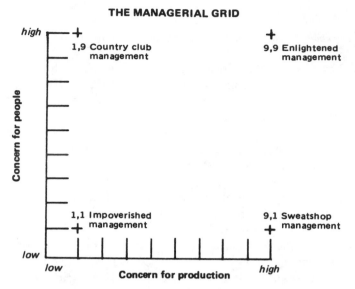

Fig. 3.2. *The Managerial Grid.* (The Managerial Grid figure from *The Managerial Grid*, by Robert R. Blake and Jane Srygley Mouton. Houston: Gulf Publishing Co., Copyright © 1964, page 10. Reproduced with permission.)

it accommodated these realities, the *Managerial Grid* also suggested a "road map" for organized leadership to guide toward circumstances considered better for the long-range effectiveness of the organization.

The Work of Chris Argyris

Rigid Structure Threatens the Mental Health of Workers and Organizations

Professor Chris Argyris of Yale used a parent-child analogy to describe problems between organizations and workers. On the one hand, he observed, while most employees come to the job lacking experience, many begin to develop mature characteristics as people and workers. They are able to develop more self-control, more patience, more ways of behaving, the ability to give and take directions, and higher self-concept. On the other hand, he suggested, most organizations are like unbending parents who refuse to recognize growth and try to keep their "children" childlike and immature; mature workers become frustrated and angry under such management controls.

Argyris contended that these frustrations generally arise because organizations believe they must be committed to one unchanging management style. He felt that managers believe they are obliged to press their authority at all times, even when it may not be required, and that they believe they must direct activity at all times, even if such direction throttles ideas and suggestions. Argyris also proposed that managers believe that managerial controls, whether in the form of restrictions or incentives, cannot be changed.

For the sake of their own survival, Argyris argued, organizations must learn to adopt a variety of management styles with workers contributing ideas to the development of such styles. Otherwise, he suggested, the mental health of both the workers and the organization would be threatened by a vicious cycle: controls designed to make workers "manageable and spiritless" would cause workers to become more dependent. This, in turn, would demand still more controls, thus continuing the cycle.[14]

The Work of Clare Graves

The Behaviors of People Are Not Easily Changed;
Organizations Must Change to Get the Many Types of Workers and Managers Needed

Professor Clare W. Graves of Union College is clearly less optimistic than other behavioral scientists about the capacity of *all* workers and managers to mature as people in uniform ways. It is more realistic, Graves stated in an article titled "Deterioration of Work Standards," to recognize that adults may progress steadily in behavior, may stabilize or become fixed at certain levels of behavior, and may sometimes slide back to lower levels of behavior.[15] Every level of workers' behavior, Graves suggested, demands an appropriate style of managerial behavior. According to Graves, if a worker matures in behavior and the manager does not, there will be a likelihood of conflict and declining productive effort. On the other hand, there will also be conflict if the manager changes and the worker wants to be managed in the previous way.

Graves concluded that such conflicts may signal the need for "constant reorganization" designed to match managerial control systems to workers' levels of behavior. Among the seven levels of worker behavior outlined by Graves are: (1) the sociocentric type in which the worker takes part enthusiastically in group efforts but does not care about personal achievement or gain, and (2) the aggressive-individualistic type in which the worker accepts management goals but is determined to get to these goals in a highly productive and creative, yet highly personal way. Each of these types needs its own kind of manager, and trouble ensues if either type is put under control of a prescriptive, hard-bargaining type of manager.[15]

The Work of Raymond Miles

Managers Often Adopt Two Different Models of Participation —
One for Themselves and One for Subordinates

When Raymond E. Miles of the University of California at Berkeley interviewed hundreds of middle-level and upper-level managers in business and governmental organizations about participative decision-making, he discovered what he claimed was "a great deal of confusion." Miles based his studies on two models, which he described as follows:[16]*

Human Relations Model: The key element in the human relations approach is its basic objective of making organizational members *feel* a useful and important part of the overall effort. This process is viewed as the means of accomplishing the ultimate goal of building a cooperative and compliant work force. Participation, in this model, is a lubricant which oils away resistance to formal authority. . . . The manager "buys" cooperation by letting his subordinates in on departmental information and allowing them to discuss and state their opinions on various departmental problems. He "pays a price" for allowing his subordinates the privilege of participating in certain decisions and exercising some self-direction. In return he hopes to obtain their cooperation in carrying out these and other decisions for the accomplishment of department objectives. Implicit in this model is the idea that it might be easier and more efficient if the manager could make departmental decisions without involving his subordinates. . . .

Human Resources Model: This approach . . . focuses attention on all organization members as reservoirs of untapped resources. These resources include not only physical skills and energy, but also creative ability and the capacity for responsible, self-directed, self-controlled behavior. . . . In this model the manager does not share information, discuss departmental decisions, or encourage self-direction and self-control merely to improve subordinate satisfaction and morale. Rather, the purpose of these practices is to improve the decision-making and total performance efficiency of the organization. The human resources model suggests that many decisions may actually be made more efficiently by those directly involved in and affected by the decisions. . . . In fact, it suggests that the area over which subordinates exercise self-direction and control should be continually broadened in keeping with their growing experience and ability.

Miles reported some of his findings as follows:

Which approach to participative management do managers actually follow? . . . Managers' views appear to reflect both models. When they talk about the kind and amount of participation appropriate for their subordinates, they express concepts that appear to be similar to those in the human relations model. On the other hand, when they consider their own relationships with their superiors, their views seem to flow from the human resources model. . . . They see themselves as reservoirs of creative resources. Moreover, the fact that they frequently view themselves as more flexible and willing to change than their superiors suggests that they feel their resources are frequently wasted. Correspondingly, they expect improvement in organizational performance to result from greater freedom for self-direction and self-control on their part.

Miles expressed his personal preference for the human resources model on grounds that "managers up and down the organizational hierarchy believe their superiors should follow this model." Some contributions to management theory stretch to include a total view of subordinates' style, leadership style, and varied situations.

The Work of Robert Tannenbaum and Warren Schmidt

Leadership Style May Change to Suit the Needs of People and Situations

In 1958, Professors Robert Tannenbaum and Warren H. Schmidt of the University of California in Los Angeles published a simple, but now classic, diagram of leadership behavior called the "Continuum of Leadership Behavior" (see Fig. 3.3).[17] The problem they addressed was the difficulty managers find in trying to be "democratic" while simultaneously maintaining authority and control. The solution they proposed was an ability to operate effectively along the whole continuum from boss-centered to subordinate-centered leadership. This challenge is one which can be met if the leader pays attention to key questions about self, subordinates, and the situation. Some of their questions are summarized as follows:

- **Leader:** What are my own values and convictions? Do I have confidence in my subordinates and a desire to see them grow and advance? Do I feel secure in uncertain situations?

- **Subordinates:** What sort of behavior do they expect from the leader? Do they need independence and want responsibility? Do they feel the problem is important, and do they have the technical knowledge needed to discuss the problem? Do they trust the leader in various styles?

- **The Situation:** What are the demands of organizational policy? What are the time pressures? Is there a need to keep some information confidential?

Such questions may help to clarify the leader's decisions about how to lead at any given time and may, in fact, confine leadership style to a particular

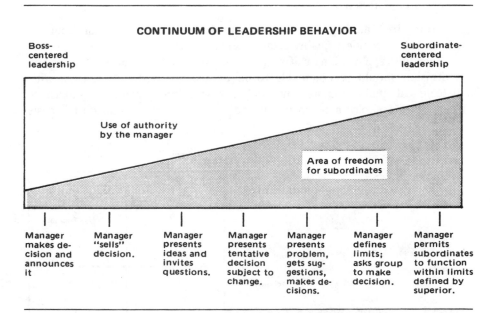

CONTINUUM OF LEADERSHIP BEHAVIOR

Boss-centered leadership

Subordinate-centered leadership

Use of authority by the manager

Area of freedom for subordinates

| Manager makes decision and announces it | Manager "sells" decision. | Manager presents ideas and invites questions. | Manager presents tentative decision subject to change. | Manager presents problem, gets suggestions, makes decisions. | Manager defines limits; asks group to make decision. | Manager permits subordinates to function within limits defined by superior. |

Fig. 3.3. Continuum of Leadership Behavior. (Harvard Business Review, Copyright ©
1958 by the President and Fellows of Harvard College; all rights reserved.)

segment of the "Continuum of Leadership Behavior" diagram (as may happen, for example, when *both* leaders and subordinates do *not* wish decision-making to be shared). At least two points are considered essential by Tannenbaum and Schmidt:

1. The leader should never shirk responsibility for the decision, however it is made.

2. The leader should always make clear what style of leadership is being used; there should be no attempt, for example, to trick subordinates into thinking that the leader's decision was their decision.

The Work of Norman Maier

Participative Decision-making Requires Skilled Judgment

Norman R. Maier of the University of Michigan designed a grid based on leadership and decision-making considerations (see Fig. 3.4). Maier's grid, which is simple in appearance, is rich in complex questions concerning the technical and acceptance quality requirements involved in decisions. These qualities can be summarized as follows:

Technical Quality Requirements are the kinds of specialized knowledge and the amounts of such knowledge needed to reach an effective decision.

Acceptance Quality Requirements are the considerations of the amount of acceptance for the decision to be effectively implemented by all of those who are, or will be, affected.

According to Maier's grid, a decision with high acceptance quality requirements and low technical quality requirements might involve the reassignment and rescheduling of working shifts. (For example, see "A" of Fig. 3.4.) The best decision should be acceptable to all people involved. A decision with high technical quality requirements and low acceptance quality requirements might involve a choice between two brands of a similar chemical on the basis

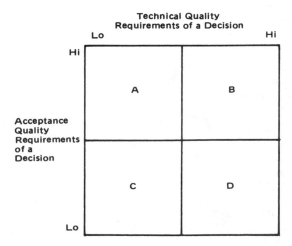

Fig. 3.4. Simplified leadership and decision-making grid. (Based on the work of Norman R. Maier)

of elaborate scientific specifications. (See "D" of Fig. 3.4.) Only one specialist may have the knowledge to make the choice. Most difficult, perhaps, is a decision with high technical quality requirements *and* high acceptance quality requirements. (See "B" of Fig. 3.4.) Members of a fire company, for example, may need to choose one course from a listing that offers ten training courses. In such a case, all or several members of the fire company may have to do their best to become "experts" about various courses and the qualifications of instructors.

Maier proposes that participative decisions can be effective because:[18]

> There is more information in a group than in any of its members. Thus, problems that require the utilization of knowledge should give groups an advantage over individuals. Even if one member of the group (*e.g.*, the leader) knows much more than anyone else, the limited unique knowledge of lesser-informed individuals could serve to fill in some gaps in knowledge. For example, a skilled machinist might supply information on how a new machine might be received by workers.

Maier points out, however, that a strong leader may be needed to function as the group's "central nervous system" even when participation levels are highest. The leadership skill in this case involves the ability to keep discussion open, balanced, and fair.

ACTIVITIES

1. Explain how Robert Owen and Frederick Taylor attempted to deal with the protests of workers who felt dehumanized by increased mechanization. Why do you think their theories weren't widely accepted by the general public and industry?

2. What changes resulted from workers' dissatisfaction with scientific management? Why do you think workers' attempts at effective union organization were not successful at that time?

3. A major result of automation was the creation of a smaller amount of work for the individual. Increasing automation became a threat to workers who felt they would be replaced by machines.
   (a) Although fire departments have many machines to help prevent and control fires, fire fighters must do a great amount of work on the job. Discuss and list the fire fighter's work from the moment an alarm is received until the time the fire is extinguished.
   (b) If your community's fire department were to become automated, what types of machines would be needed to perform your duties as a fire fighter? With automation, how would your duties be different from those listed in part (a) of this activity?

4. Identify the researcher(s) who proposed each of the following theories on motivation and self-direction. Since each of these theories proposes distinctly inherent workers' needs, discuss with your classmates

the role you think management should play in order to complement
these needs.

(a) The need people feel for doing something particularly well.
(b) Employee-centered departments *vs.* production-centered depart-
     ments.
(c) People do not have an inherent dislike of work.
(d) Motivation-hygiene theory of job attitudes.
(e) High morale among workers does not necessarily equal high
     productivity.
(f) Every level of workers' behavior demands an appropriate style
     of management behavior.
(g) Participative decision-making.
(h) There is a parent-child relationship between organizations and
     workers.
(i) Managers find it difficult to be democratic and, at the same time,
     authoritative.

5. (a) Why did the sciences of human behavior and psychology play such
        an important role in human relations studies?
   (b) How did the initial studies of human behavior of workers help
        form the theories of human behavior in management?
   (c) How do you feel that the results of psychological studies con-
        ducted on members of the fire services might be most beneficial?

6. Consider Maslow's five levels of basic human needs. Then, with a
   small group of your classmates, discuss what you feel are a fire fighter's
   basic human needs on the job. Next, compile a list of your group's
   thoughts on examples of a fire fighter's human needs that differ from
   Maslow's. Use your list as the basis for a general class discussion.

7. (a) Why was there an increased educational demand for workers in
        the 1900s? In your opinion, was the upgrading of the workers'
        educational requirements a good change? Why or why not?
   (b) Why do you think increased educational requirements for mem-
        bers of the fire services are continually demanded?

8. Your fire company has been informed that the chief has compiled a
   list of decisions that must be made in the department. Some of these
   decisions should be made using high technical quality requirements *and*
   high acceptance quality requirements. What types of decisions would
   involve these requirements?

9. How might David McClelland's theory of human behavior be applied
   to members of the fire services?

10. With a group of your classmates, discuss the philosophies of scientific
    management and of the human relations theory of management. The
    group should then be divided into two sections, with each section
    choosing either a pro-scientific management "platform," or a pro-
    human relations theory "platform."   To "debate" their platforms,
    the following steps can be used by the sections as a general guide:

(a) The members of each section should compile a list of the strongest and most positive aspects of their particular platform.

(b) A spokesperson should be appointed by the members of the section who will use the group's list as a basis for the points of the debate.

(c) The spokespersons representing each section should decide who the first speaker will be.

(d) Each spokesperson will speak to the entire group for no more than three (3) minutes on the positive aspects of the particular platform that section has taken. The spokespersons' goal should be to emphasize and thereby to prove that one system of management is better than the other.

(e) At the end of the two speeches, each member of the group should vote on the "better system" by writing why the positive aspects of one platform were better than the other.

BIBLIOGRAPHY

[1] Owen, Robert, "Address to the Superintendents of Manufactories," *Classics in Management*, American Management Association, New York, 1960, pp. 24–25.

[2] Copley, Frank B., *Frederick W. Taylor: Father of Scientific Management*, Vol. 2, Harper & Row, New York, 1923, pp. 237–238.

[3] Taylor, Frederick, *The Principles of Scientific Management*, W. W. Norton & Co., Inc., New York, 1911, p. 47.

[4] Heilbroner, Robert L., *Great Ascent*, Harper Torchbooks, New York, 1963, p. 18.

[5] Maxwell, William H., "On a Certain Arrogance in Educational Theorists," *Educational Review*, Vol. 47, Feb. 1914, pp. 175–176.

[6] Yerkes, Dr. Robert M., "Testing the Human Mind," *Atlantic Monthly*, Vol. 131, No. 3, Mar. 1923, p. 366.

[7] Gellerman, Saul W., *Motivation and Productivity*, American Management Association, New York, 1963, p. 95.

[8] Maslow, A. H., *Motivation and Personality*, Harper & Row, New York, 1954.

[9] McClelland, David C., Atkinson, J. W., Clark, R. A., and Lowell, E. L., *The Achievement Motive*, Appleton-Century-Crofts, New York, 1953.

[10] McGregor, Douglas, *Human Side of Enterprise*, McGraw-Hill, New York, 1960.

[11] Herzberg, Frederick, "One More Time: How Do You Motivate Employees?," *Harvard Business Review*, Vol. 46, No. 1, Jan.–Feb. 1968, pp. 53–62.

[12] Likert, Rensis, *Human Organization: Its Management and Value*, McGraw-Hill, New York, 1967.

[13] Blake, Robert R. and Mouton, Jane S., *Managerial Grid*, Gulf Publishing Co., Houston, 1964, p. 10.

[14] Argyris, Chris, *Personality and Organization*, Harper & Row, New York, 1957.

[15] Graves, Clare W., "Deterioration of Work Standards," *Harvard Business Review*, Vol. 44, No. 5, Sept.–Oct. 1966, pp. 117–128.

[16] Miles, Raymond E., "Human Relations or Human Resources?," *Harvard Business Review*, July–Aug. 1965, p. 148.

[17] Tannenbaum, Robert and Schmidt, Warren H., "How to Choose a Leadership Pattern," *Harvard Business Review*, Vol. 36, No. 2, Mar.–Apr. 1958, pp. 95–101.

[18] Maier, N. R. F., "Assets and Liabilities in Group Problem Solving: The Need for an Integrative Function," *Psychological Review*, Vol. 74, No. 4, Apr. 1967, pp. 240–241.

Chapter Four

Modern Management Concepts

THE ADAPTABILITY OF MODERN MANAGEMENT CONCEPTS

The foundation of modern management theory has been discussed in the earlier chapters of this text. From the complexity of this theory, it is apparent that for today's competent managers there is more to its application than just good leadership style. In most managerial situations there is generally more work and the necessity for greater attention to detail than some managers care to accept.

An early definition of management still holds true: Management means getting things done with and through people. Not too long ago this was believed to mean that a manager who skillfully delegated work had little involvement in the details of that work. Today it is realized that there is more to modern management than merely delegating workloads from a position of authority. Today's managerial functions include providing support and helping direct subordinates, making effective decisions, being competent in planning and organizing, being highly perceptive in recognizing the needs of subordinates, and determining solutions to problems that are beyond the capabilities of, or resources available to, subordinates. Thus, even with skillful delegation of authority, there is much that today's competent managers have to do.

Although modern management concepts set particular standards for effective management, these concepts can be adapted to a particular manager's needs. Because each organization wants to achieve different goals, and because each employee has an individual personality, each manager should vary modern management concepts to suit both the organization's needs and the needs of the employees. Within these larger variations there may be smaller variations for particular situations. For example, although a manager may employ democratic decision making most of the time, situations often arise in which an individual decision is the most effective decision. This is particularly true in the fire service. Often, in decision-making situations involving functions such as fire station cleaning schedules, the chief will allow the fire fighters to determine the best solution. However, in other situations such as when the fire alarm has been received and the engines are speeding to the fire scene, the employment of democratic decision making is inefficient.

In recognition that one form of management or one specific type of leadership is not always applicable for all situations, modern management concepts allow enough flexibility for managers to vary their leadership techniques. Modern management concepts also allow flexibility in the decision-making process, depending upon the goals of the organization and the employee capabilities. There are three factors, however, that influence the decisions that managers have to make. These are:

1. **The Situation:** Is there an emergency? What technical knowledge is required for a decision? What information relevant to the decision is available? Who are the people who have to implement the decision or who are otherwise affected by it? How much do these people care about the decision?

2. **The Leader's Style:** What is the natural behavior of the manager or leader? What are the manager's capabilities? What is the reaction of subordinates to these styles?

3. **The Competencies of the Subordinates:** What is their knowledge? What is their level of maturity? What are their needs?

When all three factors are considered, it can be seen that a leader needs to use a wide range of leadership techniques ranging from highly participative to highly autocratic. Yet the leader's techniques depend greatly upon the leader's technical competence, and planning and organizing ability. A leader must also be able to recognize the technical competence of the individuals who have to work with the leader. A fire chief or a training officer would know that, with a group of veterans, less time will have to be spent on training procedures than is necessary to spend with a group of rookies. In such a situation, leadership style would vary from one of less visibility with the veterans to one of close guidance with the rookies. This, of course, is a fairly obvious example. However, in the day-to-day activities of a fire officer, far more subtle distinctions have to be made and more accurate guidelines are needed than those that have been offered by the management theories of the past.

Modern management concepts, with behavioral science principles as their basis, help guide managers and other organizational leaders so they are better able to utilize available resources. This chapter describes, in a fairly general way, a comprehensive modern management concept that provides some clear management guidelines. It is called the linking elements concept. Originally conceived by Erwin Rausch, President of Didactic Systems, Inc., the concept has been expanded and refined to become a guide for modern managerial actions. The following chapters will apply this concept to the various functions of management in the fire service. They will also describe how better understanding of the principles of the linking elements concept can help fire service management personnel perform their managerial functions more effectively.

THE FOUNDATION OF THE LINKING ELEMENTS CONCEPT

The foundation of the linking elements concept is described in Figure 4.1. Beginning at the top of the organizational unit (be it an entire fire department, a fire station, a company, or a shift), the main goal of the organization is performance. The word performance can have many meanings depending upon the field of activity.

In the fire service performance could mean quick response to a fire alarm, a high level of efficiency in delivering water and extinguishing materials onto the fire, an excellent record in rescue operations, a high level of competence in fighting fires in different environments, careful prefire planning and inspections, etc.

Organizational Basis

The diagram in Figure 4.1 describes how an organizational unit can achieve the highest level of performance that can possibly be attained in the environment within which the organizational unit exists. Performance for any organization depends greatly upon three requirements: (1) control, (2) technical competence, and (3) morale.

Control: Control includes four main areas that dictate the overall performance of an organizational unit. First and foremost, control means a sense of direction. The organization must know where it is going and how fast it wants to get there.

Modern management concepts call this sense of direction the goals for the organization. These goals for the organization depict achievement and standards of performance to provide everyone concerned with a plan of action for the achievement of these goals.

The second area of control is discipline. In the conceptual sense, discipline does not mean punishment, but rather a training or a sense of direction that ensures that every individual in the organization: (1) recognizes the needs of the organization, and (2) is willing to forego personal interests for the sake of achieving the goals for the organization.

Thirdly, an organizational unit needs coordination as a part of control. Coordination means that everyone involved knows what to do to achieve a

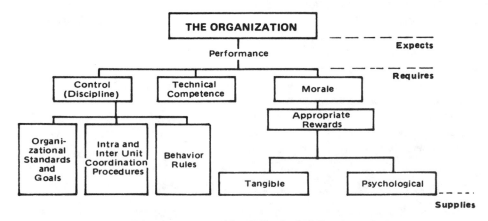

Fig. 4.1. The organizational basis for the linking elements concept.

goal, and that attainment of a goal means working in conjunction with others. In a fire department, the goal of laying hose lines as quickly and efficiently as possible when apparatus arrives at a fire scene depends greatly upon the co-ordination of all apparatus personnel. If coordination is lacking, hose laying will become time consuming and confusing. A well-drilled, tightly disciplined team can lay hoses and connect them much faster than a team that does not have such excellent coordination, and can thereby achieve the performance necessary to accomplish the goal.

Finally, the fourth area of good control includes behavior rules for the individual that establish what the unit can expect from an individual. These rules, in turn, tell the individual what is expected and what work must be accomplished.

Technical Competence: In addition to control, an organizational unit must have high technical competence if it expects to achieve a high level of performance. Technical competence means having the necessary capabilities — knowledge and skill — to efficiently perform the assigned tasks. For example, if a fire department's goal is to drastically reduce the response time in arriving at the scene of its community's fires, then the department must be thoroughly knowledgeable concerning its city's streets and all the possible routes to a fire in any given area within its district.

Morale: If individuals are motivated towards their work and if the type of leadership that they are shown is equivalent to their work capabilities, then a high level of work will evolve. Satisfaction from work — either tangible or psychological — will result from morale and will be evidenced in efficiency and quantity of work evoked. An organization must therefore provide the tangible and psychological rewards that are the foundation of high morale.

Employee Basis

An organization can achieve a high level of performance through control, technical competence, and morale only if the employees in that organizational unit have the characteristics and abilities that are needed to accomplish goals, and only if they are willing to devote themselves to the goals of the organization. Figure 4.2 shows what individuals bring to an organization.

Personal Performance Standards: Individuals usually come into an organization with personal performance standards and a willingness to work. These contributions may or may not match the effort needed by the organization from its employees in order to achieve its goals. If the willingness to work on the required tasks and assignments is equal to the organizational unit's needs, then the manager or officer has little to do in linking the organization's needs with the abilities of the employee. If, on the other hand, the standards of each are not equal, the manager must work to gain greater willingness from the employees in working towards organizational goals. A rookie in the fire service may have a personal performance standard of working as quickly as possible to accomplish the task at hand. However, if the rookie's quantity of work does not have the necessary quality, then the fire officer must work with the rookie until the department's standards and the rookie's standards meet.

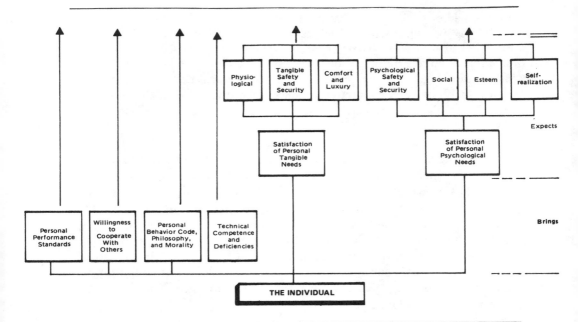

Fig. 4.2.   The employee basis for the linking elements concept.

Willingness to Cooperate with Others: The coordination that an organization requires for all its subunits to move towards the goals in an efficient manner requires cooperation and coordination among its employees.   People must work smoothly with each other and with other subunits to accomplish these goals; for good coordination, people must contribute a willingness to cooperate.

When individuals are cooperating with each other, the manager or fire officer need not intervene.   However, many obstacles to cooperation may occur between individuals and subunits because of personality differences or insufficient coordinated training.   The manager or officer must be prepared to intervene in such situations and must be able to handle all difficulties that might arise between individuals.

Personal Behavior Code, Philosophy, and Morality: An individual brings attitudes, a philosophy of life, and a morality into an organization.   Sometimes these attitudes may be matched to all the rules that are in existence in a particular organization.   At other times the individual may "revise" personal attitudes and moralities to meet requirements in an organization.   However, many individuals may feel that some rules are wrong or should not be applied in a particular situation.   When this happens a manager or an officer faces a difficult decision.   Sometimes privileges may be granted by waiving the rules temporarily; other times, adherence to the rules must be demanded.

A manager or an officer should first determine that all the rules that are in existence for an organization are understood and that they are respected. Yet the leader must also ensure that the rules are fair for the individuals that work within them. If, for example, a fire department has a special rule about wearing of dress uniforms on many occasions where they may not be necessary, and the fire fighters are clearly unhappy about the rule, the officer should work towards obtaining a change in the rule.

Technical Competence and Deficiencies: Not all employees who join an organization have the appropriate knowledge for the task that has been assigned. Usually the hiring of an individual means that the skills are present or that the individual can be trained for the job. Individuals usually start working at lower level jobs and obtain the necessary skills and training that are needed for higher level positions.

It is a manager's task to try to eliminate the deficiencies that exist in competence in order to let the individuals develop themselves in the directions for which they will be most effective for the organization. This type of "on-the-job" training is particularly apparent in the fire service. A rookie will enter a department with certain basic skills, but surely not with enough experience for fighting every single type of fire with no guidance. The training officers and the fires that are fought will give the rookie the skills needed to accomplish the job and to gain the experience needed to move to higher-level positions. Training is also necessary for experienced fire fighters to upgrade skills and knowledge and as preparation for promotion.

Satisfaction of Personal Tangible and Psychological Needs: Every individual expects the satisfaction of a complex set of needs in the organization. These needs comprise both tangible and psychological desires. Tangible needs include the monetary rewards, such as salary, which satisfy the physiological needs such as those for food, clothing, shelter, and security. The tangible rewards also reflect a certain amount of desire for comfort and luxury.

These tangible needs are greatly related to the psychological needs of an employee, such as the need to feel secure, the need to belong, and the need to "find" oneself in one's work. Satisfaction of psychological needs also requires that managers recognize dissatisfaction within employees, and are able to deal with any emotional aspects of the workers. The job of fire fighting, in particular, places a tremendous emotional strain upon fire fighters who must deal with deaths and with serious injuries such as burns. Fire officers must be aware of the job's psychological effects, and must then have the ability to help their people cope with the stresses that exist. How a manager or an officer can help provide the linking elements needed in an organizational unit is discussed in the following paragraphs.

THE LINKING ELEMENTS CONCEPT

Linking elements are the skills that a manager needs to apply so that the organization's needs and the rewards that it must provide achieve the greatest possible alignment with the characteristics and the expectations of its subordinates. Figure 4.3 depicts the linking elements concept by showing the relationship between the organizational unit and what the individuals bring to an organization. The upper portion of the figure shows the organizational requirements for performance as they relate to employee needs for performance. The arrows extending down from the major subheads under "The Organization" align with the individual's characteristics. Extending upwards from these individual traits are arrows that align with, but do not meet, organizational characteristics.

The area between the sets of arrows is denoted as "Linking Elements." Each set of arrows depicts the need for competence in at least one specific managerial skill — the linking element. Linking elements are, then, the managerial skills needed to make the arrows from the organizational unit unite with the arrows from the individual. When this union occurs, the manager is employing management techniques to unite the strongest abilities in both the organization and its employees in order to achieve the highest performance level possible in a joint effort to meet the goals.

The leadership techniques employed in deriving the greatest performance, however, are not easily attained. The leader needs to consider each employee

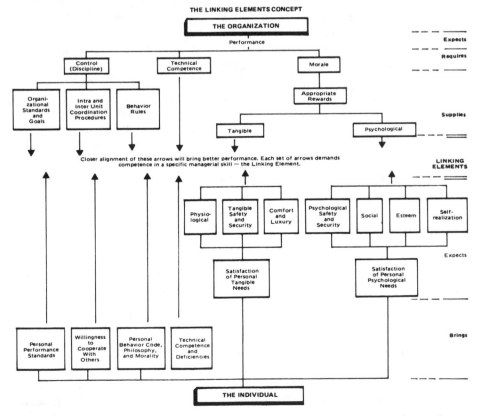

Fig. 4.3. The linking elements concept. Note the relationship between the employee and the organization.

and that individual's personality in order to effectively join the employee and the organization. The manager must then supply the five linking elements in order to evoke a high level of employee performance. These five elements link the: (1) personal performance standards, (2) willingness to cooperate with others, (3) personal behavior code, philosophy, and morality, (4) technical competence and deficiencies, and (5) personal tangible and psychological needs, to the organization's matching characteristics.

The Applicability of the Linking Elements Concept

Although linking elements are considered a modern management concept, it is interesting to compare much of the management theory discussed in Chapter Three, "The Behavioral Sciences and Management," with this chapter's discussion of uniting the individual with the organization. What the behavioral sciences began, modern management concepts are continuing and employing. The experimentation undertaken by the early behaviorists has now become applied knowledge for the modern manager. For example, the theories by Maslow on worker's needs have become the basis of the linking elements concept of satisfying personal tangible and psychological needs. Further, experimental work on motivation and employee reaction to varying levels of disciplined leadership now serve as a basis for improving coordination and cooperation between employees and management.

The evolution from scientific management to the behavioral sciences to, finally, modern management concepts (and to managing by objectives, discussed in Chapter Five) has placed a considerable amount of responsibility on the modern manager. Today's manager must not only be concerned about production and profit: today's manager must be concerned, and aware of, all facets of a particular field of activity. Today's fire chief is not only concerned with extinguishing a raging fire; rather, the fire chief must recognize the need for budgets, prefire plans, training in hazardous chemicals, etc.

In order to achieve the necessary level of performance in an organizational unit, managers must consider methods of dealing with employee standards and needs. These managerial methods, or skills, are applied to the five linking elements areas previously discussed. In order to satisfy organizational goals, managers must: (1) satisfy both personal tangible and psychological needs of the employee, (2) achieve technical competence from their employees, (3) improve coordination and cooperation between employees and the organization, and (4) align rules of the organization with personal behavior codes. (Refer again to Fig. 4.3 for illustration of the relationship between the organizational unit and what individuals bring to an organization.)

SATISFYING TANGIBLE AND PSYCHOLOGICAL NEEDS

Chapter Three, "The Impact of Behavioral Science on Modern Management," described Maslow's conceptualization of a hierarchy of human needs. Though it has survived for many years as one of the best explanations of human needs, there are a number of questions it raises:

1. **What exactly is the role of money?:** As most managers and fire officers know, people seem to think that money motivates. There is certainly ample evidence to show that people will come to work when they are paid; however, they also work as volunteers on projects they like when they are not paid. Yet people talk a lot about money needs, and it is common to hear someone say: "If you want me to do that, then pay me for it."

Maslow's diagram, however, is mute on the question of money and its relationship to employee needs, which may be one of the reasons why managers do not see Maslow's theory as a practical concept to be applied in an organization.

Frederick Herzberg's studies at Case Western Reserve University (discussed in Chapter Three) proved that money is relegated to a secondary position by workers. The conclusions he reached stated that although the promise of a raise or the prospect of a raise seems to have a positive effect on worker motivation, the effect is_only temporary. Workers will most generally revert to their preraise motivations if their job and environment remains essentially unchanged. However, the fact still remains that people respond to money because of the necessities and luxuries purchased by money.

2. **What is the relative importance of satisfying esteem and social needs?:** Considerable research that has been done to validate Maslow's hierarchy of needs seems to indicate that the two lower levels — the physiological needs and the security needs — are indeed valid, fundamental needs. There is, however, considerable question about the definition, the meaning, and the relative relationships of esteem and social needs. For example, it would seem that there are many people who place the satisfaction of esteem needs above the satisfaction of social needs. For these people, it is more important to be recognized as individuals and to be valued for particular strengths and characteristics than to be members of a group.

Other people, however, feel that being part of a group is more important. They want to be liked or to feel the security of a group, which is more valuable to them than being esteemed. Wanting to be part of a group may be the result of upbringing and culture, or it may be a natural need for the security that a group provides. Whatever the reason, there are many people who prefer the warmth that a group can provide rather than the recognition of personal worth for outstanding characteristics.

3. **What is self-realization?:** For those people who clearly understand what they want to do during a part of their lives or with their entire lives, there is no doubt that self-realization is the highest level needed. For other people, however, self-realization is a somewhat nebulous concept. During certain periods of their lives, people seem to gain exceptional joy and satisfaction from doing certain things. These periods have a tendency to change, however, during the course of one's life and one's career. The many types of self-realization raises questions about what self-realization really is, and how a manager or officer can help employees in the department find some of it or

help in realizing it fully. In the fire service there is a considerable amount of self-realization and challenge to finding self-realization in fire fighting. However, when fires are not frequent, there is less of this feeling because fire prevention work or drills do not bring about the same challenging level of involvement as in fire fighting.

Despite the questions inherent in Maslow's theories, the basic framework of his hierarchy of needs can be retained because of the evidence available that attests to its validity. Maslow's diagram can become a practical tool for managerial decisions even though it has areas under question, for it places the important needs of individuals into perspective. Although many managers do not particularly like to work with theories because of their abstractness, without good theories technology could not have advanced as far as it has and will not advance further.

Managers are aware of the accomplishments of theory but may doubt their application to the management of people. There is some justification to this belief because behavioral theories are not as precise or as exact as the theories in the physical sciences.

The following paragraphs will explore the linking elements that are concerned with the satisfying of tangible and psychological needs, and will suggest answers to the preceding three questions.

The Role of Money in the Maslow Hierarchy

Physiological Needs: In order to clearly show money's role in the hierarchy of needs, a separation between psychological and physiological needs must be made. Although some physiological needs are free (such as air), most physiological needs are supplied by the salary from working. Clearly, food, clothing, and shelter can be obtained only through purchase.

Safety and Security Needs: Many safety and security needs are satisfied with money, especially those that reflect the physiological needs of food, shelter, and clothing for the future. Safety and security for these items can be obtained through organizational pension programs, hospitalization insurance, and other insurance programs. Other ways of ensuring safety and security needs are through business contracts such as a union contract or a tenure agreement. Both ensure the safety of an individual's job and the security of knowing that a salary will be received for an agreed period of time.

However, there are psychological matters that also contribute to a feeling of security on the part of employees. These are primarily the attitudes and beliefs about an organization and its managers. People who work for an effective organization that has competent management and trustworthy supervisors feel secure. On the other hand, people cannot feel secure when they work for an organization that is unstable, or for a manager who is unreliable or untrustworthy. Therefore, a manager or officer who is competent and at the same time honest with employees is more likely to create a positive motivational climate than one who has shortcomings in either area. Figure 4.4 shows the separation of safety and security needs into physical and psychological ones.

Fig. 4.4. Modification of the Maslow diagram, which shows the separation of safety and security needs into tangible areas (white) and psychological areas (shaded).

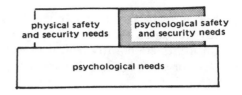

Esteem and Social Needs: Although Maslow diagramed esteem and social needs as two separate entities, there seems to be mixed feeling (as stated earlier in this section) as to which need is more important. Therefore, for the purposes of this text, both will be shown together as one step in a hierarchy of needs. (See Fig. 4.5.) Although these two needs are depicted in Figure 4.5 as psychological, there is also another side to these needs. Many people obtain gratification of social and esteem needs by mimicking someone whose lifestyle they admire. "Keeping up with the Joneses," however, requires monetary reward in order to obtain their (the "Joneses") particular view of social and esteem needs.

Even though many people obtain some measure of esteem and social satisfaction from things that money buys, segments of these needs still remain that must be satisfied in other ways. Policies and procedures of an organization that evoke greater cooperation and assistance between workers create more social and esteem needs satisfaction than policies and procedures that lead to friction and conflict. In addition, managers or officers can stimulate social interaction between the members of their group during personal emergencies or can stimulate mutual support at other times.

In the fire service, periods of inactivity can occasionally be used for social activities by an officer who is capable of stimulating friendly interaction between shift members or groups that work together.

While social needs depend greatly upon group interaction, esteem needs are more difficult to satisfy because esteem is usually received on an individual basis. Few officers or managers go out of their way to find actions for which fire fighters can be commended, or seek imaginative ways of providing recognition. One of the greatest tools for creating a more motivated climate — the

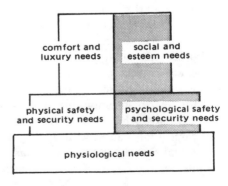

Fig. 4.5. Modification of the Maslow diagram, which shows social and esteem needs as one psychological entity, and comfort and luxury as a complementary tangible one.

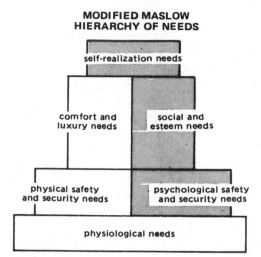

**MODIFIED MASLOW
HIERARCHY OF NEEDS**

self-realization needs

comfort and
luxury needs

social and
esteem needs

physical safety
and security needs

psychological safety
and security needs

physiological needs

*Fig. 4.6. Modification of the
entire Maslow diagram, which
shows the physiological needs
(white) and the tangible needs
(shaded). Note how the diagram shows that both tangible
and psychological needs are required to progress to self-realization needs.*

use of praise — is one of the least utilized ones. The result is that few fire fighters
or other workers receive individual recognition from their superiors.

There are many legitimate reasons why few managers or officers use praise
as much as they should. One is the difficulty in finding avenues of praise.
Because of this, many managers avoid being untruthful in order to praise an individual for something that should not be praised. However, if praise can be
given deservedly and sincerely, then it should be given. Besides evoking a feeling
of esteem, praise also shows a friendliness that has a favorable influence on
worker cooperation and motivation.

There are many other ways besides praise that can be utilized to bring about
a feeling of greater esteem. They include such things as a manager asking
for a subordinate's advice, writing commendations, and employing many
forms of formal recognition, including awards for exceptional bravery or unusual devotion to duty. Unfortunately, most of these awards are restricted
to distinguished action during fire fighting and very few, if any, are given for
outstanding or exceptional work on fire prevention or for reliability. The
armed forces, by contrast, awards medals not only for valor in the line of
duty, but also for meritorious service in daily routines.

From an understanding of social and esteem needs come many opportunities
for officers and managers to provide greater satisfaction of these employee needs.
Leaders can create an environment that provides more job-related satisfaction
even if they cannot add to the luxury and comfort needs of the employees.
Creating a climate that satisfies social and esteem needs is especially important
when considering the psychology of self-realizations. (See Fig. 4.6.)

Self-realization: Self-realization is a concept that is difficult to define because few people, including fire fighters and fire officers, recognize early in
life that they have a strong professional preference for their work. Some artists,
scientists, and renowned individuals have always had strong inclinations towards

their work. However, people in other fields of activity have also achieved self-realization in their work. There is a true case about a pot washer in a New York City hospital who apparently was so devoted to his job that one could say that he had found his self-realization. He reported to his kitchen happily every morning and continued to be content as long as his pots and pans were not mishandled by others. On the few occasions when he was absent from work and another individual took care of the pots, he was clearly disturbed when he returned to work to find the pots neglected.

While this individual may be a rarity, there are other people from all walks of life and jobs who are happy with their work because they enjoy it. Their day passes quickly with interesting things to do; they enjoy going to work in the morning, and they often leave with the feeling of accomplishment. Even when unpleasant events have occurred during a day, they have the feeling that the next day will be better — and it usually is.

People who find such enjoyment in their work are fortunate because it makes for a much more pleasant life to find satisfaction in work. Yet not every individual who works long hours is a "workaholic." Some enjoy their work as well as, if not more than, socializing or watching television. People who feel joy in striving for the difficult and attaining it are compensated for the extra hours they have to devote to what other people call "work." They regularly gain the same exhilarating sensation from seeing projects near completion as fire fighters who experience the feeling of conquering a stubborn fire.

Other people rarely find pleasure in their work. Their work may be dull or strenuous or their supervisors may be lacking in competence, both of which contribute little pleasure to their work. For most people, however, the enjoyment of work comes despite the fact that they have no special preference for their particular occupation. They may have drifted into it because their first real jobs gave them the necessary experience, or a college professor may have told them that enjoyable careers existed in a particular field. However, these people would know little about self-realization in work. They would know that there may be activities that they prefer such as hobbies, sports, or social activities. Yet they may have difficulty in indicating the work activities that would retain their most interest or effort for the majority of the time.

Whether a person has achieved self-realization or not, there still exists a certain level of motivation. A person who works apathetically on the job may work enthusiastically, without pay, during off-hours in a community or social organization. What is it, then, that makes one person find greater satisfaction from work than another? What conditions must be met by employer or employee in order for work to be more rewarding?

Small teams of participants in hundreds of seminars were asked the following question about their motivation:

> If you think back to positions you have held in the past, or if you look at your current position, what actions could your superiors take, or have taken, and especially your direct supervisor, without spending any money, that would bring, or have brought additional job satisfaction to you?

The following list of things the supervisors could do were made from these responses:

- More information about what is happening in the job.
- More freedom to do the job the way I want to do it.
- Being brought into decisions at an earlier time.
- More guidance.
- More recognition.
- Honest feedback about my work.
- No promises that can't be kept.
- My boss should know more about what I'm doing.
- More interesting assignments.
- Less overseeing.
- More support when needed.
- More confidence in me.

The list is interesting in that all items do not refer to any specific type of work. If people found self-realization in specific tasks, there would seem to be requests such as "let me do exactly this," or "let me do exactly that." However, this does not occur. People are not asking for more technical work, more supervisory duties, or more specialized assignments. Even the general statement "more interesting assignments" is exceedingly rare. To some extent people are in jobs that appeal to them more than other jobs; nevertheless, one would expect many statements about the specific work that the boss could give them, or has given them.

The picture that emerges from these answers is that people believe that they could obtain much greater satisfaction from their existing jobs if their managers treated them differently. They want to know more about what is happening in the organization and they want a bigger voice in decisions that affect them. They want to be freer to do the job the way they believe it can best be done, but they do want guidance and training to ensure successful completion. Most important of all, it seems, people want to be recognized for their accomplishments. The fascinating part of these results is that self-realization lies not so much in specific work, but rather comes from the environment. People are, in effect, saying: "The work may not be the greatest, but it can come much closer to giving me some self-realization if the boss would provide more safety and security (by being honest, fair, and open), and more esteem satisfaction (by providing recognition and participation in decisions)." Even though self-realization is a nebulous concept, the supervisor, manager, or officer can indeed do a great deal to help subordinates find a larger amount of self-realization in their jobs.

Improving the Motivational Climate: There are three specific strategies that managers can take to improve the motivational climate in an organization. They require considerable effort, but they can gradually lead to a climate in which there is a higher motivation and more satisfaction of psychological needs.

Managers sometimes rarely see their organization and the work involved from the point of view of their subordinates. Even though the managers experience the usual number of negative and unpleasant impulses that occur in working periods — detailed reports, the machinery or gadgets that require repair, lengthy meetings, and mounds of routine paperwork — they rarely realize the responsibilities they might have to eliminate the negative feelings.

If there were less tension and less frustration in a working environment, people could accept a work environment where there are only few pleasant events. In the modern world, though, a manager has an important responsibility to balance the negative impulses by providing satisfying moments or pleasant impulses. Some of the balance can come from employees, but much comes from the work, from success, from doing things well, and from pride in an accomplishment. To achieve this balance, in a fire department as well as in any other type of work, a manager or officer can apply three strategies to improve the motivational climate: (1) short-run strategy, (2) intermediate strategy, and (3) long-run strategy.

The short-run strategy, which is the left column in Figure 4.7, starts with the recognition that few managers or officers commend their people for as many actions as they should. Short-run strategy concerns the steps that a manager can take by spending a few minutes, several times each week, thinking about and listing the actions that subordinates could receive recognition for, and the ways that recognition could be shown. Managers who are new to their position may find few items to list; however, as managers acquire greater practice and experience the lists usually become longer. There are many ways that a manager can commend a job well done to all employees, not only the outstanding individuals.

For example, a fire officer can commend individual fire fighters or subordinate officers for an infinite number of actions in fire fighting, yet can also give similar commendation for other duties such as fire prevention activities. For every specific job that was done well — helping others, making worthwhile contributions during a training session or drill, or taking initiative with something that needs to be done — some form of recognition can be given. However, it is important that recognition goes not only to a few outstanding company members, but also to others who contributed to the best of their own abilities. Not all members in a fire company are equal in ability, and commendation for even minor improvements in an individual serves to elevate motivation. It is important that the manager or officer provide all members of a unit with positive moments that are related to the work.

The short-run strategy is based solely on the manager personally providing more recognition and other pleasant work-related events for an employee. The emphasis here is on "work related" because compliments or other nonwork-related friendly words are not likely to have the same impact on the motivational climate. They lead more toward the "country club" atmosphere of the 1,9 supervisor (see Chapter Three, Fig. 3.2).

Figure 4.7 shows that a manager who wishes to take full advantage of the opportunities that the short-run strategy can give will begin to use more media (newspapers, bulletins, letters, informal notes, various verbal forms, etc.) to

CLIMATE IMPROVEMENT STRATEGIES

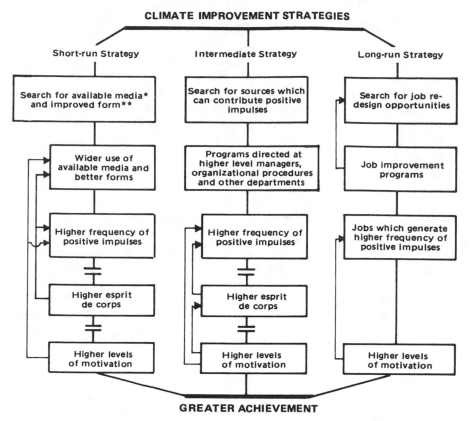

Short-run Strategy	Intermediate Strategy	Long-run Strategy
Search for available media* and improved form**	Search for sources which can contribute positive impulses	Search for job re-design opportunities
Wider use of available media and better forms	Programs directed at higher level managers, organizational procedures and other departments	Job improvement programs
Higher frequency of positive impulses	Higher frequency of positive impulses	Jobs which generate higher frequency of positive impulses
Higher esprit de corps	Higher esprit de corps	
Higher levels of motivation	Higher levels of motivation	Higher levels of motivation

GREATER ACHIEVEMENT

*Media are the ways in which motivational impulses can appear. Positive ones include such things as challenging assignments, supportive statements, routine reports, tie pins, certificates, etc. Negative ones are reprimands, reject notices, mistakes, etc.

**Form is the style that influences the impact of the motivational impulse. It can be the way the award is presented, the words which are said during the telephone call, or facial expression, place, timing, etc.

Fig. 4.7. A representation of the three strategies used by management for improving the motivational climate for employees.

bring more frequent instances of pleasant experiences for the fire fighters. That, in turn, may lead to a higher job interest and greater esprit de corps — the common spirit existing in the members of a group and inspiring enthusiasm, devotion, and strong regard for the honor of the group. There is a limit, however, to the effect that this short-run strategy can have because there are just so many times in the course of a week or month that a fire officer can give direct recognition to a fire fighter. That is why there is a break in the line between "higher frequency of positive impulses" and "higher esprit de corps," and again before "higher levels of motivation." More is needed than just the short-run strategies to add to the instances when a fire fighter experiences a pleasant feeling from a work-related occasion.

The intermediate and long-run strategies bring the additional positive impulses that are needed. For the intermediate strategies the fire officer could involve those who command other platoons and other companies — possibly the chief, public officials, and even the public — to provide pleasant work-related experiences for the fire fighters. Such pleasant experiences could include a reminder to the chief to commend one of the fire fighters for something that has occurred recently, commending people in other companies or on other shifts whose officers might respond in kind, or stepping aside and letting fire fighters accept the thanks of citizens for saving lives, preventing injury, protecting property, or being helpful during an inspection.

The distinction between short-run strategy commendation and intermediate strategy commendation is that the positive impulses do not come from the immediate superior, which serves to show to the fire fighter or lower level officer that others recognize the work performed.

Steps taken to anticipate and prevent friction between members of a group or another group can also add to a more pleasant job-related environment by increasing the satisfaction of social needs in order to prevent them from being decreased. Activities such as these on the part of the officer will add to the likelihood that the fire fighters will obtain greater satisfaction from their work, resulting in a higher esprit de corps.

The higher esprit de corps that results from the positive impulses of short-run and intermediate strategies may then lead to higher levels of motivation. Although the positive impulses mentioned have come from people, positive impulses that come directly from the job itself can also be present. Long-run strategy employs the types of job improvement programs as those recommended by Frederick Herzberg. Herzberg recommended what he called job enrichment as a major approach to enhance motivation (see Chapter Three, section titled "The Work of Frederick Herzberg"). Jobs that are shifted or revised in such a way that the job brings satisfying sensations result in a more continuous work flow, which leads to an even higher level of motivation to work on the job and to achieve job-related goals. The officer, in trying to develop a satisfying atmosphere, directly reinforces the work that subordinates must do in order to create a smoothly operating goals program — one that makes goal achievement a way of life. Joint goal setting that includes not only operational goals, but also self-development goals will satisfy many of the psychological needs presented by linking elements by providing regular opportunities for the subordinate to:

- Explain solutions for problems that exist on projects, or which may exist in the future, that are being used in order to know whether the leader is in agreement with the solutions used.
- Obtain help with difficulties that are presented.
- Report on accomplishments that the subordinate takes pride in.
- Discuss aspirations for the future, particularly those involving preferences for various aspects of the work.
- Voice problems and complaints.

This linking element — providing for the satisfaction of the psychological needs of employees — can help considerably in creating an achievement-oriented climate in which the needs of the employees, as well as those of the organizational unit, are satisfied extensively.

ACHIEVING TECHNICAL COMPETENCE

The road to a higher level of technical competence for a department or a company starts at the selection of new personnel or in the promotion of competent individuals to higher positions. Ability to learn and interest in learning should be important criteria in this choice. The selection process itself requires technical competence by the selector in order to recognize enthusiasm and ability. A lack of technical competence that results in hiring individuals who have insufficient knowledge and motivation will make it difficult, if not impossible, to develop high technical competence in the new individuals.

Selection

Careful initial selection of fire fighters and equally careful observation of new recruits during their probationary period enables fire officers to devote more time to basic training and application needed in a "green" recruit. Chapter Eleven, "Personnel Management," will discuss the process of candidate selection and promotion in detail; for this chapter's scope, the *Fire Protection Handbook* briefly outlines fire service candidate requirements:[1]

> It is the responsibility of fire department management to notify the personnel agency of vacancies which exist in the organization and to request the number of persons needed to fill these vacancies. In connection with recruitment, fire department management has three responsibilities. The first is to recommend to the personnel agency appropriate recruitment standards. So that staffing will consist of competent persons such as those recommended by NFPA 1001, *Standard for Fire Fighter Professional Qualifications*, . . . , qualifications in the standard should be followed in order to obtain persons physically and mentally qualified to do the work. The second is to provide the basic training necessary for the new personnel so they can properly perform their assigned duties. The third is to certify after providing the basic training that the new members are ready for appointment as permanent fire fighters, or where individuals prove unable to perform satisfactorily, to recommend that their services be terminated before permanent appointment.

Position Management

Once employees have remained on a job long enough to exhibit their performance strengths and weaknesses, the manager is then able to explore how to improve strengths for the organization's effectiveness and how to correct weaknesses. A manager may rearrange work schedules or delegations of tasks to incorporate a new member. If the new member is a part of a unit such as a fire fighting platoon the workload for the entire platoon may be rearranged to some extent. The changes can simply concern minor rearrangements to accommodate work preferences of the new person, or they can be more extensive and involve the desires of several team members. Such changes do not have to take place immediately, but can evolve gradually as members discuss with each other the adjustments they would prefer; on the other hand, the leader can consciously guide changes to take into account the needs of the organizational unit as well as those of its members.

Whatever changes occur within an organizational unit — by the manager or by employee suggestions — the needs of the organization and its members guide the formation of a change. The work that has to be done should be analyzed and broken into clearly definable tasks. These tasks must then be arranged into positions that fit the capabilities and interests of persons who have to follow them. The new arrangement of tasks can then lead to: (1) high productivity, (2) good quality work, (3) ability of the team to quickly and effectively respond to changing demands of clients, customers, or public, and (4) highest possible level of needs satisfaction for the team members.

If the arrangement does not result in achievement of these four requirements, tasks must then be rearranged until they are adequately satisfied. Even though, in an existing organization, workload and delegations have always been completed, rearrangement of workloads and trial periods for these arrangements is a continuous process that is especially important whenever a new person joins an organization. A competent manager will usually look at the positions of members in an organization in the same way a football coach would look at the players to decide who should do what during the next play for the best performance. A fire officer will do essentially the same thing at a fire scene by assigning tasks on the basis of the capabilities of the individuals. The engine would most likely be attended by a fire fighter skilled in hydraulics or in the operation of the pump.

However, an organizational unit must also have backup members capable of handling each task that may come along. As much as possible every fire fighter should be able to perform each one of the tasks that are required. With the thorough training of each fire fighter, fire officers will be better able to choose those that do extremely well in particular areas to take advantage of the strengths. Nonemergency work also needs constant review to see whether the existing arrangement leads to the best possible combination of productivity, response capability, and needs satisfaction of team members.

The appropriate selection of people for tasks and assignments in keeping with their strengths can achieve the highest technical competence of the team, but only for the moment. For the long run it is an error to use a particular group of fire fighters over and over again on those tasks that they can do best; this may make the entire unit heavily dependent upon that group. In the absence of the group the entire unit may become incapable of performing tasks normally delegated to a group of individuals. Good technical competence means flexibility and the ability to adapt to many different environments; for every task, several fire fighters must be available that know the task. Because of this, good technical competence also means continuous analysis of deficiencies in knowledge and skills by management in order to take steps to eliminate these deficiencies.

Careful selection of people and assignment of tasks on the basis of strengths and weaknesses, as well as on interest, is of similar importance at higher levels. When deciding on selection or promotion to available positions, the chief has a wide range of experience with individual fire fighters' and officers' performance to draw on. Once a new officer has been chosen for a position, the assignments still have to be reviewed in order to view the skills of the officer in relation to the new position.

For example, an officer who has been in charge of fire prevention may not be particularly interested in such work, or may not be considerably qualified for it. The addition of a new officer who has considerable experience and significant aptitudes for fire prevention work may make it advisable to place that officer in charge of fire prevention, and to reassign the officer who was previously responsible for the function in order to elicit the strongest performance.

Training and Development: Good selection and position management are not enough to ensure high technical competence. Continuous training and development is essential even if experienced, competent people are selected and job assignments take full advantage of their strengths:[2]

> Fire Fighter I, at the first level of progression, has demonstrated the knowledge of and the ability to perform the objectives specified for that level, and works under direct supervision. Fire Fighter II, at the second level of progression, has demonstrated the knowledge of and the ability to perform the objectives specified for that level, and works under minimum direct supervision. Fire Fighter III, at the third level of progression, has demonstrated knowledge of and ability to perform the objectives specified and works under minimum supervision but under orders.

On-going training, whether in the fire service or in another organizational unit, allows for a continuing improvement in existing competence and knowledge. In the fire service, on-going training is necessary because:

- Continuing changes in technology create a need for frequent updating of knowledge and skills.
- A training that includes learning the tasks of others educates all for smoother communications.
- Every fire fighter and officer is more knowledgeable and skilled in some areas than in others. Considerable training is needed to eliminate, or at least reduce, any deficiencies as much as possible.
- Career development for those who aspire to higher level jobs, or more specialized ones, can only occur through broadened knowledge and continuous development activities.
- Knowledge and skills that are not in continuous use begin to fade. Continuous training refreshes areas not in daily use, and prepares the fire fighter for the time when a situation does occur.

The benefits of a thorough and continuous training program can sometimes result in the achievement of the appropriate level of technical competence needed in a particular organizational unit. (Training techniques and training methods, as well as how training applies to the fire service, are discussed in detail in Chapter Twelve, "Training as a Management Function.")

Yet training, no matter how complete, may not always result in the desired level of technical competence. Other problems may exist that stand in the way of a particular achievement, which may block any amount of training. Figure 4.8 represents a performance analysis model that can be used by a manager or leader to identify whether a blockage to achievement of technical competence is related to training, ability, or performance.

Analyzing Performance Problems: In order to investigate the cause of a performance problem, managers should recognize first that an individual comes into an organization with personal performance standards, which are measured by: (1) a willingness to work, and (2) abilities, which are reflected by an individual's knowledge and skill. The individual's personal performance standards must be able to coincide and unite with the organization's performance needs in order for an employee's work to be satisfactory. Many times an employee requires a small amount of training in order to fulfill organizational performance standards. However, some individuals may require more extensive training, and others may need a solution to a particular performance problem that training cannot solve. Figure 4.8 diagrams several questions that should be asked by a manager when employee performance standards must be rectified. These questions and their answers may lead to possible avenues of solutions that will help to link the individual with the organization.

In the fire service, more time is devoted to training than in other occupations; however, many personal performance problems exist despite the overwhelming training. Therefore, fire chiefs and officers need to distinguish between those performance problems that can be rectified by training and those that are the result of nontraining causes. Fire department managers can use Figure 4.8 in first determining, if there is a performance problem, whether or not a knowledge/skill deficiency is involved. If that is the case, the next question should be whether or not the respective fire fighter or subordinate officer used to be able to do the work that is revealing an unsatisfactory performance. If the answer is no, training should be arranged. If, on the other hand, the individual has satisfactorily performed the task in the past, it is likely that a knowledge/skill deficiency is not involved. Retraining can be arranged to determine whether the problem goes away or whether other causes must be found.

If the officer must answer the question "knowledge/skill deficiency?" negatively because the fire fighter or subordinate officer knows how to do the task, then the problem is not one that can be solved by any amount of training or retraining. The fire chief or officer must then ask four questions to pinpoint the crux of the performance problem:

1. **Is the performance punishing?:** Tasks may be performed poorly if the fire fighter views these performance tasks as "punishing." Even during a quiet

day a fire fighter may find that an inspection announced at the last minute is "punishing." Frantic cleaning and pressing of a uniform before the inspection allows little time for the fire fighter to view the task with enthusiasm; therefore, the performance that results will most likely be less than what the individual usually is capable of. Training will not help in this situation.

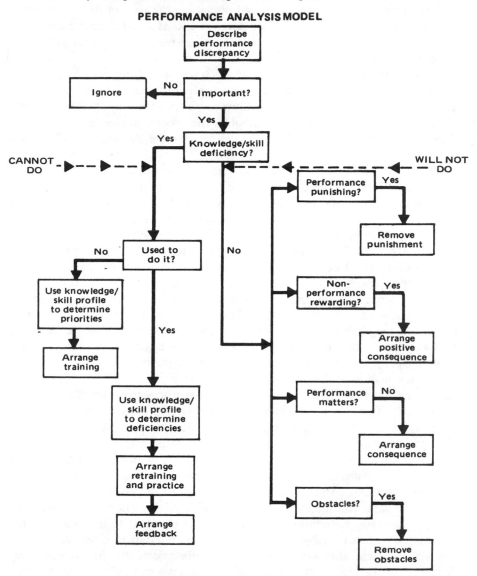

Fig. 4.8. Performance analysis model that aids a manager in determining whether an individual's lack of performance is related to training or to performance problems. (Adapted from Analyzing Performance Problems; or, You Really Oughta Wanna, *by Robert F. Mager and Peter Pipe.)*

Inadequate knowledge for a task such as an inspection can also make performance punishing. Fire fighters are frequently asked questions they should be able to answer during inspections; often, inadequate knowledge and insufficient time to prepare for the task may make the fire fighter associate inspections with punishment.

By speaking with the fire fighter and discussing the root of the performance exhibited, the fire chief or fire officer can then take steps to eliminate the "punishment" of the inspections. Only after that has been done can training bring the desired beneficial results.

2. **Is nonperformance rewarding?**: Sometimes an officer may require less work when fire fighters object, may call for a rest period when overhaul is being handled haphazardly, or may allow more time for housekeeping because of complaints from fire fighters. Although the officers in charge may feel that they are helping the fire fighter, in reality they are damaging performance standards because they are rewarding their subordinates by less work. Less work for the fire fighter may tend to lead to more requests for a decreased workload, and may result in increasing disfavor for required work.

In all these cases, training can help only after there are appropriate rewards for good performance and negative consequences for failure to perform.

3. **Does performance matter?**: A lack of attention on the part of superiors to some aspect of the fire fighter's work gives the impression that performance does not matter. Fire fighters and subordinate officers may come to believe that their superiors do not care whether or not a specific job or task is completed properly. For example, if someone is asked to help prepare a report and no one asks whether that report has been prepared, or if a goal is set to perform a certain number of inspections and no one checks to see that they have been made, then performance motivation may be dampened. The message from above appears to say that it really does not make any difference whether or not the task is performed well or at all. Here, too, training can improve performance only after there is evidence that performance does matter.

The lack of attention evidenced in these examples clearly reflects a lack of organization in the fire department. Since the officer is responsible for the smooth operation of the organizational unit, steps must be taken on that level to rectify the lack of attention. By solving this problem at the root of the cause, performance standards of the subordinates should rise.

4. **Do obstacles exist?**: Many obstacles to good performance may exist within a department in addition to the items already mentioned. For example, a fire fighter may be required to perform a simple task, such as cleaning the fire station's kitchen facilities. However, if the materials to clean the facilities are not available, this would constitute an obstacle to the fire fighter's performance of the task. Other more serious obstacles can exist such as the lack of a budget to guide performance or the lack of tools necessary to accomplish an assignment. Adequate instructions to carry out the specific task will be of use only after the obstacles have been removed.

Achieving the highest possible technical competence in an organizational unit involves four skills that the competent manager should constantly strive to improve:

1. Good selection of a new staff member.

2. Careful monitoring of positions to ensure that they are the best arrangement for achieving high levels of productivity, quality of service, response flexibility, and employee needs satisfaction.

3. Review of performance problems to ensure that all obstacles to improved performance are removed.

4. Appropriate training and coaching (see Chapter Twelve, "Training as a Management Function").

The four questions presented in this section, although representing major sources of performance problems, certainly do not represent all causes of performance problems. Many nonperformances can result from other needs of the individuals. One such need is coordination and cooperation with coworkers and with the organization.

IMPROVING COORDINATION AND COOPERATION

A willingness to coordinate and cooperate with other members in an organization is reflected by an individual's ability to work with the other members of the subunit or the organization towards the organization's goals. In the fire service, coordination and cooperation is particularly vital because of the uniqueness of the job of fire fighting:[3]

> Fire fighting requires a major degree of physical strength, and an important factor is the interdependence of fire fighters on each other in fire suppression and rescue operations. If there is a great disparity of physical strength and endurance between members of a crew, then an unreasonable burden and strain is placed on those with most strength and stamina. This is not only dangerous to the fire fighter, but also adversely affects performance in the protection of the public.

According to the linking elements concept for modern management, the manager or fire officer has two primary responsibilities for achieving efficient coordination and cooperation: (1) setting up coordination procedures, and (2) achieving cooperation of subordinates with these procedures.

An example of a coordination procedure for the fire chief or fire officer would be the determination of the delegation of duties for subordinates when responding to an alarm. After this has been determined the officer then must obtain cooperation in order for the fire fighters or units to work efficiently within their assigned share of the activities and to eliminate interference with the work of other units. Coordination may require that members of one company relieve those of another company at the nozzles. Inefficient coordination between the two units may result in time-consuming confusion that could mean the loss of life in a fire.

The coordination and cooperation between shifts in a department is just as important as the effective relief of nozzle personnel. During a shift change the company officer's responsibilities include coordinating with the other shift to ensure that the other officer understands the procedures of the first shift, whether it concerns how the kitchen is to be left at the end of the shift or whether more serious matters are involved. After the coordination procedures have been clarified, however, the company officer has the responsibility to obtain the cooperation of the fire fighters. At the higher levels the need to coordinate and achieve cooperation is even greater since several companies or different bureaus may be involved.

Coordination, therefore, requires many skills from the competent officer. Not only is it necessary to schedule carefully and to communicate the schedules appropriately, but the officer must also keep an ear carefully tuned to any indications of unhealthy friction between various members of the subunit or others in the department.*

However, it is not always easy to distinguish when conflict is potentially troublesome and when it is not. Competition for best performance is a form of conflict, yet one would not consider it undesirable until the competition becomes so intense that one team obstructs the work of another team rather than concentrating solely on perfecting its own activities. Similarly, it is not easy for an officer to recognize what statements are gripes, or when subordinates air their dissatisfactions. Every organization, at one time or another, has dissatisfied an employee in some small way. Gripes are then aired, and work continues as before. It is important to distinguish these from the more serious indications of conflict with other people or units that may lead to detrimental actions, such as open or hidden refusals to cooperate.

Creating an Open Communications Climate

Many officers have not had training in counseling, and therefore may be reluctant to start a private discussion with a fire fighter or a subordinate officer when trying to change attitudes on a conflict or some other matter that may be important to that person. Other officers may step in too abruptly or bluntly and accomplish more harm than good. A good counselor, for the purpose of achieving coordination, need not be a trained psychologist; rather, an officer can easily become a good counselor by sharpening a few basic skills. These same skills, incidentally, are also useful during goals reviews (discussed in Chapter Five, "Managing by Objectives"), grievance handling, and on other matters that relate to employee achievement and motivation. They include:

- Creating an open climate where communications can proceed smoothly.
- Providing feedback.

---

*Scheduling is an activity that rarely involves the company officer except for the simple personnel schedules that may be required for vacations or other special occasions. Officers working in some of the specialized bureaus in larger departments sometimes have to use sophisticated scheduling techniques for major maintenance, renovation, or building projects. All officers, however, should be aware of modern scheduling techniques.

- Therapeutic listening.
- Empathetic listening.
- Using transactional analysis concepts.
- Using questions.

The Johari Window: Figure 4.9 is a depiction of the Johari Window, developed by Joseph Luft and Harry Ingham ("Johari" is an acronym combining the first names of the inventors). This diagram can be useful in increasing one's skill for achieving more open communications between two people. Each square of the window results from two overall considerations: (1) there are some things that one knows about one's self, and some things that one does not know; and (2) there are things that other people know about an individual's self, and there are things that other people do not know. Area 1 is an area of open activity that represents those subjects, topics, and character-

JOHARI WINDOW

(The name JOHARI reflects the originators, Joe Luft and Harry Ingham)

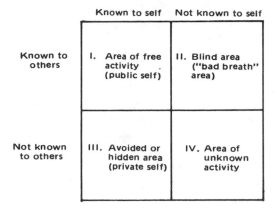

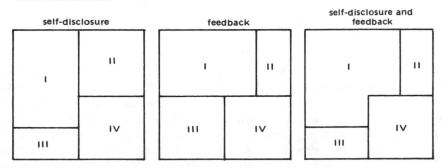

Under conditions of:

Fig. 4.9. The Johari Window, which is helpful in achieving an open communications climate. (From *Group Processes: An Introduction to Group Dynamics* by Joseph Luft, by permission of Mayfield Publishing Company [formerly National Press Books]. Copyright © 1963, 1970 by Joseph Luft.)

istics that are known to the self and to others. If a fire officer has trained a fire fighter in pump operations, the fire officer and the fire fighter know that this job is understood and is an area they can discuss freely. They can talk about how the fire fighter has learned the subject and how the officer can help in solving any problems with this subject.

Area 2 is an area of closed activity that represents items that are known to the self, but not known to others. For example, a fire fighter may know that some of the assignments that have been delegated from the officer are not pleasing. Yet the individual may feel that there would be difficulty in discussing this displeasure with the officer. In Area 2 are all the topics that are not easy to discuss in the existing environment, which include matters that a fire fighter knows about other members of the team, but are considered confidential. Even if the fire fighter knows that an officer is not aware of these matters, but should be, difficulties in communication with superiors or adherence to personal morality may inhibit an open discussion.

Area 3 is an area that is not known to the self, but is known to others. This definition could be described as a "bad breath" area, but it does not contain only unpleasant things. These are things about the other person that one does not want to tell that person, or does not think about telling. This includes negative information, such as bad breath, as well as positive information such as words of appreciation that were neglected, or sincere compliments that can be given.

Area 4 represents those matters that are neither known to the person nor to others. It is a totally hidden area that becomes apparent only if new events bring a new awareness about that person. This area could indicate a hidden ability in a fire fighter that is unknown to the self and to the officers in the department. A chance happening or a series of events could aid in revealing this ability to the individual and to the department.

For example, because of an illness the department's official photographer may be absent from a particularly spectacular fire. A fire fighter may happen to volunteer to photograph the fire operations, and both the fire fighter and the other members of the department may learn that the individual has a hidden talent for on-the-scene photography.

In a less happy situation, a fire fighter in Area 4 may be subconsciously dissatisfied with the job, but would not know this and would not be able to let the department know this. In either instance, the hidden area is the most difficult area for good communications because, to both the self and to the department, there is nothing tangible that can be communicated. In this area, time and an ability to be in touch with one's self are the most important factors for eliminating hidden problems or revealing hidden abilities.

Self-disclosure and Providing Feedback: There are two methods of providing an open communications climate. The first is self-disclosure, which means that an individual is willing to disclose some feelings about the work assigned, job problems, or about another person. The second is feedback, which will help to open up an opportunity for a free discussion of topics.

Feedback can sometimes lead to self-disclosure. For example, if the officer points out that the fire fighter seems unhappy about some of the assignments that have been delegated, the fire fighter may respond by admitting dissatisfaction and revealing why. If both parties in a discussion are aware of the Johari Window and wish to achieve a better understanding on some subject, then both can practice reasonable self-disclosure and provide useful feedback. The discussion can then be carried to a successful conclusion for both sides. But even if only one person understands the Johari Window well, more open communications can result than if neither is aware of it. Although many officers are apprehensive about even limited self-disclosure to a subordinate because of a fear of losing a leadership role, some amount of self-disclosure may help in relaxing the subordinate so open communications may start or continue. Once communications proceed smoothly, feedback can then be given in an open climate.

However, providing feedback is not easy. What is meant as constructive criticism can be delivered too abruptly or bluntly, and can therefore result in intimidation of the individual receiving the feedback. On the other hand, feedback can be delivered too subtly or unclearly and can result in misunderstanding.

There are a number of recommendations that are useful to follow in delivering effective and successful feedback:

- Feedback should be as factual as possible. This means that it should be based on specific occurrences that can be referred to for illustration.
- Feedback should be timely. To say: "Three months ago you did so and so and that was not the best way to go about this," accomplishes very little in recommending improvement. Rather, feedback that is given immediately has more impact and more meaning to the person receiving it, and will serve in eliminating future errors.
- Feedback should be only about things that are under the control of the other person. If a fire officer tells a fire fighter: "You really have a lot to learn about water specifications," this feedback offers little in the way of a recommended improvement for the fire fighter. However, if the fire officer said: "You really need to learn more about water specifications. Here are two books that will help you. When you're done, we can discuss any questions you have," this offers a definite method of improvement for the fire fighter.
- Feedback should be given calmly. Feedback that is given in an excited way is often perceived as a reprimand or criticism. During a discussion when one person attempts to open communications, criticism may cause the other person to become defensive and less willing to share thoughts or feelings. Feedback that is delivered in a calm, steady pace allows time for discussion and reflects to the individual that the problem that needs to be solved can be dealt with in a calm, steady manner.

Therapeutic Listening: Therapeutic listening helps the other person "get things off the chest," and thereby relieves burdensome feelings so that the discussion about a problem can proceed with fewer emotional interferences.

During effective counseling sessions the counselor does more listening than speaking, for persons being counseled must have an opportunity to open up feelings to someone who can, and is, willing to, understand them.

A good counselor must keep tight control over individual conclusions until the other person has completed the verbalization of feelings. After the opening-up process, questioning by the counselor interspersed with a few direct statements will usually be far more effective than telling the other person what to do. Good counseling requires that the person who is being counseled sees the advantages of looking at the situation from an entirely different perspective with the aid of the counselor.

Empathetic Listening: Empathetic listening shows the other person that there is a genuine desire to understand that person's point of view, and therefore encourages open explanation and participation by the speaker. Empathy can be combined with a sympathetic attitude for the other person's point of view; however, one can be empathetic and wish to fully understand the other person without necessarily agreeing.

Use of Transactional Analysis Concepts

Transactional analysis is a technique for analyzing human behavior and communications between people that is an excellent way to see emotional involvement in the transmittal of messages. The transactional analysis theory states that a person has, at all times, three ego states that vary in strength.

The first ego state is the parent ego state, which is made up of all the things that people have been taught by their parents, teachers, and others they have encountered in life. The parent is the righteous segment of one's personality that says work hard, stay pure, and follow the rules and laws that have been set. The parent is usually stuffy, self-righteous, usually knows it all, and has an answer for everything.

The second state — the child ego state — is the emotional, happy-go-lucky, rebellious part in people that is almost the opposite of the parent. The child rushes into things; likes to play "explore" and "create," likes to enjoy life and

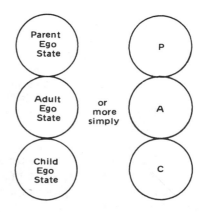

Fig. 4.10. A representation of transactional analysis ego states.

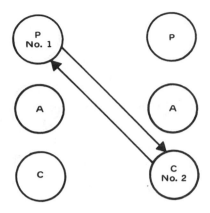

Fig. 4.11. *A representation of a complementary transaction.*

be happy, but also is free to express anger as well as many other generally subdued emotions. The child in a person is relatively weak and insecure, but can also be stubborn and unreasonable.

The third ego state, the adult ego state, is the rational and factual part of people. The adult ego state makes decisions based on information it receives from the child, the parent, and the world in general. The adult is logical, reasoning, helpful, understanding, responsive, etc. These three ego states are often depicted as shown in Figure 4.10.

Transactional analysis starts by defining each communication between people as a transaction. If one person says "hello" to another person, that is a transaction. If the other person answers, that is another transaction. If the other person does not respond that is also a transaction, though of an entirely different kind. The friendly greeting is a positive transaction; a refusal to return the greeting is a negative transaction.

Transactions, of course, have to start from some ego state. If at any one moment the parent ego state is dominant in a person, then the parent ego will be heard when that person speaks. If the child ego state is dominant at the moment, it will be the child that is speaking when that person says something. Sets of transactions can come in three different ways:

1. **They can be complementary:** These transactions occur when the message comes from an ego state and receives a response from the ego state that it addressed in the other person (see Fig. 4.11):

> Fire fighter No. 1 to fire fighter No. 2: "You are doing this all wrong. Let me show you how to do that." (Parent addressing child.)

> Fire fighter No. 2 to fire fighter No. 1: "When I need someone to show me how to do it, I'll call you. Otherwise, mind your own business." (Child to parent.)

2. **The transactions may be crossed:** These are the result of an unexpected response made to a statement (see Fig. 4.12):

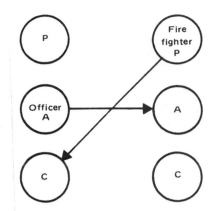

Fig. 4.12. A representation of crossed transactions.

Officer: "What did you do with that nozzle?" (Adult addressing adult.)

Fire fighter: "I gave it to you. Did you lose it?" (Parent addressing child.)

A crossed transaction does not often lead to easier and friendlier communications. At the extreme, this kind of transaction could almost immediately lead to a heated exchange that could only be rectified by a better communication between complementary ego states.

Crossed transactions can occur easily because either the child or parent ego states are often the dominant egos. The officer who has the responsibility, to lead a task often starts a conversation from the parent state because the officer is in a "parental" role. The result is a minor crossing of transactions; if that is recognized, it becomes easier to lead communications to complementary transactions. More work, of course, is accomplished by adult-to-adult complementary transactions. By communicating on an adult level, situations can be reviewed and the actions that should be taken can be discussed in a calm and factual manner.

3. **Transactions can be hidden:** These have an unspoken meaning that is somewhat like a double message. When such a message is sent it is usually disguised behind a socially acceptable transaction. For example, fire fighter No. 1 and fire fighter No. 2 may be sitting in the fire station's kitchen. They have just battled a blaze in a three-decker house. During the blaze, fire fighter No. 2 tried to save the life of a young child overcome by smoke, but was unsuccessful. Fire fighter No. 1, in order to alleviate the depression of fire fighter No. 2, might say:

Fire fighter No. 1: "Bet I can beat you in a game of gin rummy." (Child to child; see Fig. 4.13.)

Fire fighter No. 1, although speaking from the child ego state, is really hiding a communication from the adult ego state. The hidden meaning could really be saying, "We know you did all you could to save the child, so why don't

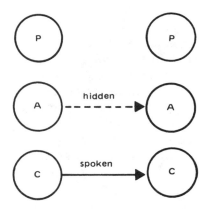

Fig. 4.13. A representation of a hidden transaction.

we play a game of gin rummy to get our minds off it?"

Recognizing ego states and understanding transactions are the most important transactional analysis skills for a manager or officer to master. They can help maintain calmness when the other person is temporarily dominated by the child or the parent. By doing so, it is therefore easier for an individual to remain in the adult state because the adult state is the more mature one, and the person remaining in the adult state has the satisfaction of knowing that. That awareness helps considerably in maintaining one's own equilibrium, and thus helps to gradually bring the other person to the adult ego.

There are three other concepts in transactional analysis that are of value in communicating with superiors and subordinates. They are: (1) life positions, (2) strokes, and (3) stamp collecting.

Life Positions: Four life positions come from Dr. Thomas A. Harris' book, *I'm OK-You're OK.*[4]

1. **I'm OK-you're not OK.** In a general way, this is the position of the parent who has to tell the other person what is right and what is wrong.

2. **I'm not OK-you are OK.** This shows the position of the child who understands that full maturity has not yet been reached or feels a little guilty about self actions. This position, however, could also indicate a mental health problem that is more serious than just a temporary child ego state.

3. **I'm not OK-you're not OK.** This position is definitely one that is assumed by people who have moderate to serious mental health problems.

4. **I'm OK-you're OK.** This is a position that the adult person assumes. The adult sees that every individual has certain strengths and weaknesses, but is otherwise fundamentally sound. The I'm OK-you're OK position includes the three ego states, and concludes that any of these ego states can be the dominant one at the moment; however, this life position also acknowledges that in every person there is a strong adult. There are times when the child ego should be allowed to enjoy itself, and there are times when it is necessary for the parent ego to show itself. But in the I'm OK-you're OK position, the adult ego should always be in control.

Strokes: In every transaction there is a stroke. If what is said or done gives the other person a pleasant feeling, then it is a positive stroke; if what happens gives a negative feeling, then it is a negative stroke. A friendly greeting is a positive stroke; an unfriendly greeting is a negative stroke. A failure to return a greeting is a negative stroke; unfair criticism is a negative stroke. A commendation or praise is a positive stroke. Strokes can come from people or they can evolve from work. In general, what was discussed as positive impulses in the three climate improvement strategies are positive strokes.

Stamp Collecting: Stamp collecting is based on strokes. In a relationship between two people, or between a person and a job, no stamps are collected if the positive and negative strokes are balanced. If, however, one person provides a series of positive strokes to the other person, the latter person is collecting positive stamps; sooner or later, those stamps are likely to be "cashed in" by reciprocating in a pleasant way. On the other hand, if one person collects many negative strokes from another person, sooner or later some argument or negative reaction will take place.

The Use of Questions: Questions can be excellent tools in helping to achieve agreement on an issue when they are used properly and in moderation. Three types of questions can be used in obtaining information about an issue: (1) open questions, (2) reflective questions and statements, and (3) directive questions. All three types of questions serve to open areas for discussion because they cannot be answered with a simple "yes" or "no." Open questions are intended to start the other person talking, and generally begin with phrases like: "How do you feel about . . .?" or "What do you think of . . .?"

Reflective questions and statements, on the other hand, merely repeat the last point that the other person has made without adding anything significant. Instead, they reflect what has been said in different words in order to encourage further explanation and lead to new information. For example, the listener may question: "What you think, then, is that Officer Jones has not been fair in assignments given to you?"

Directive questions are questions that help expand the area of agreement by leading to further explanation of a particular point. Directive questions could start with phrases like: "May I ask why you like . . . ?" or "Am I correct if I say that you agree . . ."?

There are many benefits that good questioning and listening skills can bring:

- More accurate knowledge about the other person's needs.
- More information about the problem.
- Greater opportunity to recognize potential areas of agreement.
- Greater confidence that the counselor is handling the situation correctly.

It is important to recognize the differences between a meaningful interview and an interrogation. An uninterrupted series of questions (including reflective statements, which are often viewed as questions) can form an interrogation. The best way to prevent an interrogation or an impression of one is to allow enough time between questions for the other person to answer at length and to restate or summarize, from time to time, to show that the other person's position has been understood. In that fashion, a steady stream of questions is interrupted and a more meaningful two-way communication is established.

In order to achieve alignment of the coordination requirements of an organization with the willingness of people to cooperate, there are two clusters of skills that an officer must sharpen in order to do the best possible job:

1. To coordinate the work of different people or of different units, the technical skills of planning, scheduling, and organizing are necessary to ensure that good coordination procedures exist and are appropriately communicated in order for people to work smoothly with each other.

2. To achieve the best possible cooperation between people and units, an officer has to keep close watch on potential occurrences that indicate that some people or some units are not willing to work with others. When such an occurrence is noted, it is important to discover the cause of the problem so that effective action can be taken to eliminate it. This requires counseling skills in order to establish an open communications climate that allows people to talk openly about frustrations and emotions that stand in the way of effective resolution of the problems.

ALIGNING RULES AND PERSONAL BEHAVIOR CODES

The third linking element involves aligning the organization's behavior rules with the employee's personal behavior code, philosophy, and morality. A simple example of the alignment of an organization's rules with employee behavior codes is the working hours of a business. When an employee joins an organization, it is the employee's responsibility to work during the designated business hours. Although an employee may personally be accustomed to waking at 10 AM, if the employee's job begins at 9 AM, the employee will have to meet organizational rules by conforming to the starting time.

However, alignment of organizational rules to employee codes is not solely an employee responsibility. Management is also responsible for "rules-to-code" alignment in four ways. They are:

1. Clarity: ensuring that all employees clearly understand the rules.

2. Conciseness: ensuring that all necessary rules are in writing, but that the set of regulations does not grow to unwieldy proportions.

3. Enforcement: enforcing rules with compassion for the needs of individuals while keeping in mind at all times that every privilege granted can become a precedent, which other people may demand as a matter of right.

4. Reviewing: judging the appropriateness of the rules for the organizational unit, changing those that can be changed directly, and working towards changing those that require the agreement of higher levels of management.

Communicating Rules

Rules exist so that every person in an organization is aware of the correct and incorrect forms of behavior that are required for effectiveness of an organization. In order to ascertain that all organizational members conform to a set of rules, managers or officers must ensure that all rules are explained and understood by either oral or written communication. Until people are aware of rules they cannot abide by them; therefore, it is important that everyone clearly understands the rules.

Written Rules: Many small organizations may communicate their rules orally to their small staff. However, larger organizations commonly issue a written set of rules and regulations — a guidebook or a handbook — detailed to reach their large numbers of employees. However, a guidebook sometimes creates more problems than it solves. Individuals may associate a written set of rules as a complete set of requirements for an organization; therefore, any rule that is not clearly spelled out may be open to individual interpretation. Employees may feel that they can do what they believe is right in an unwritten situation because if there had been a rule for that particular situation, it would have been in the guidebook. Therefore, attempting to obtain control by trying to compile a strict, written set of rules requires considerable insight into all avenues of possible interpretation, and also requires considerable effort.

However, a small number of written rules can be highly desirable on the most important policies applicable to a particular organization, for they set the tone and provide the background for everyone to visualize the rules of reasonable behavior. Beyond that, maintaining an open climate in which problems can be discussed and decisions can be made in fairness to all concerned is the best policy. The manager will set the overall motivational climate by either adhering fairly strictly to a minimum set of rules or by allowing frequent privileges with the rules that exist.

Enforcing Rules: Every manager or officer knows that once privileges are granted, they are difficult to take away. As soon as others learn that one person has been granted a privilege, they expect the same benefit. Granting of privileges to one person and not to others is a situation that any leader does not want to create, for such an action can give a leader the reputation of playing favoritism or of discriminating against some people. If employees are unionized this situation becomes even more important; if one person is granted certain privileges, the union can use this as a reason to demand that the same privileges be extended to all employees either informally or through a change in the contract.

Officers and managers can avoid problems of special privileges and their consequences by employing wise decision making and constructive discipline. Many officers or managers do not realize how wide the range of choices is for resolving rule problems or problems related to requests for privileges. Decision making in such situations may seem to be a matter of saying either yes or no; however, the manner in which decisions are made allows for a few steps in between yes and no. For example, an officer could approve a request in such a way that it clearly makes it very difficult, or impossible, for the person making the request to ask for another privilege in the future; *i.e.*: "I will make an exception in this instance, but only in this instance." Or an officer can deny a request in such a way that the person requesting the privilege feels that the officer has been very fair and has given the request the most favorable consideration; *i.e.*: "After much thought, I've come to the conclusion that I cannot allow you to do such and such. I'm sorry that this could not be possible." Wise decision making means that, before making a final decision on a request, an officer can carefully analyze the choices that are really available to make a decision while keeping in mind that granted privileges are difficult to take away.

A manager can also use constructive discipline in a situation where an expected privilege is requested. An approval of the request could be given in exchange for some sacrifice. This would allow the organization to offer the same privilege to others who request it, provided they are willing to accept the same sacrificial consequences. To illustrate this method, an example may be useful of an industrial plant that operated two shifts: day shift and night shift. Few people liked the second shift despite the slightly higher earnings that were offered on that shift. One of the night shift employees requested a change to the day shift because of an invalid mother who required full-time care. The employee's relatives and neighbors helped to care for the mother during the day, but the employee could not afford to hire someone to stay with her at night. Despite the employee's circumstances, the company felt that it could not allow the transfer because others who were not fond of the night shift might request a similar privilege. However, because of the employee's circumstances, the company did suggest that the employee find someone to exchange shifts.

When the employee could not find anyone to change shifts the employee again appealed to the company for help. After lengthy deliberation and discussion, the company came up with a solution that employed constructive discipline: compassion for the employee, respect for rules, and granting of a major privilege in such a way that it would not set a precedent for others. The company offered the employee an open position on the day shift, which was available at significantly lower pay and gave the employee no assurances that another opening at the employee's current salary would be available in the foreseeable future. The employee made the sacrifice, and both the company and the employee benefited from the method of privilege. Six months later a position at the employee's previous wage opened up for which the employee was qualified; thus, the entire matter was resolved to everyone's satisfaction. (For further information on enforcing rules, see Chapter Nine, "Fireground Command Management Functions," section titled "Enforcement of Rules.")

Review of Rules: A manager who wishes to create the positive motivational climate that linking elements represent must keep in mind that rules that are considered unreasonable or arbitrary will not receive unquestionable employee support. Because of this, the manager should review rules that do exist for their applicability and relevance to organizational needs and goals. Innumerable instances exist where unreasonable or obsolete rules are either being maintained or ignored at a considerable sacrifice for worker's motivation and enthusiasm. A regular review of rules would give the manager the ability to change those rules that are unfair or outdated, and would allow a manager time to change rules that are detrimental to employees or to the organization. (For further information on reviewing rules, see Chapter Nine, "Fireground Command Management Functions," section titled "Review of Rules.")

ACTIVITIES

1. Describe how a leadership style influences the motivation of employees.
2. What skills could a supervisor or officer apply to help achieve a high level of technical competence from employees?
3. (a) In what ways have the theories of the behavioral scientists influenced the development of the linking elements concept?
   (b) Write an explanation describing how you think the application of the linking elements concept can best be utilized by fire service management to help increase efficiency.
4. (a) Describe the two factors management can use for measuring personal performance.
   (b) What questions can a leader use to determine the basis of a personal performance problem?
5. (a) Why is the on-going training of personnel necessary in the fire service?
   (b) How does the fire service determine the levels of ability of its fire fighters?
6. (a) Outline the positive and negative aspects of: (1) a written set of organizational rules, and (2) an oral set of organizational rules.
   (b) Explain how you think a fire department's rules can best be communicated to: (1) a new recruit, and (2) a newly appointed officer.
7. You have been asked to conduct a two-day seminar on your municipality's hydrant locations and color coding in order to improve familiarity and response time. This seminar is intended as a training course for the newer members of your department, and as a refresher course for the experienced members. Two hours before you begin the seminar a registrant asks to be excused, stating: "I know it all already."
   (a) Based on what you have learned about the transactional analysis theory described in this chapter, determine the registrant's dominant ego state.
   (b) What transactions are available for use in answering the registrant's statement?
   (c) What do you think would be the best transactional response to the request? Why?
8. For each of the following situations, what steps could a fire service officer take to assure that there will be good coordination and cooperation?

(a) Performing assigned departmental tasks.

(b) Laying hose at the fire scene.

(c) Bickering among members of a subunit.

(d) Competition between two subunits.

9. The following methods can be used to improve the motivational climate of fire departments. Identify whether each method is a short-run strategy, an intermediate strategy, or a long-run strategy, and explain why.

(a) Special recognition by the municipality's mayor for a subunit's inspection work.

(b) Preparation of a certificate of commendation to a fire fighter by the immediate superior for outstanding work in fire prevention.

(c) Formation of a softball league for the fire department members.

(d) Revision of work assignments related to departmental goals.

(e) A local newspaper article describing the steps taken by the fire department in a recent dwelling fire.

(f) Individual sessions with fire fighters to discuss their career aspirations.

10. Identify the linking element(s) that would be most applicable for helping to solve each of the following situations:

(a) An animosity develops between two fire fighters in the same subunit.

(b) A previously capable apparatus operator is not performing as well as in the past.

(c) A new member of the fire department returns from inspecting residential dwellings in the community with insufficient data on the inspection forms.

(d) Over a three-month period, required fire apparatus maintenance work by assigned fire fighters is consistently three days late.

(e) After fighting a particularly tragic fire, an experienced fire fighter's motivation seems to decrease.

BIBLIOGRAPHY

[1] *Fire Protection Handbook*, 14th Ed., NFPA, Boston, 1976, p. 9–9.

[2] ——, p. 9–10.

[3] ——, p. 9–10.

[4] Harris, Thomas A., *I'm OK-You're OK*, G. K. Hall & Co., Boston, 1974.

Chapter Five

Managing by Objectives

PURPOSE OF MANAGING BY OBJECTIVES

Goals represent specific targets. As such, they can give direction and can serve as a basis for the planning steps necessary to achieve a specific target. Individuals and organizations set goals for much the same reasons — in order to provide direction. It is generally agreed that it is better for individuals and organizations to work with a clear view of goals than it is to work without them. How goals are set, and how management can obtain employee cooperation and/or desire to achieve goals is the subject of this chapter.

In an article in *MBA* magazine, Stephen Singular explained that organizational goals programs often appear under different names.[1] According to Singular, these programs are most frequently called "Managing by Objectives" ("MbO" or "MBO"), "Managing by Objectives/Results," or are hidden behind labels such as "Performance Appraisal" or "Performance Objective" programs. The different names are used because the words "goal" and "objective" have different meanings in different organizations.* Whatever the label, Singular cites research that estimates that less than half of *Fortune Magazine*'s list of the largest 500 industrial companies manage their businesses with systems that can be termed "Managing by Objectives" ("MBO") based. This, according to Singular, is in spite of the fact that:[1]

> . . . It (MBO) is a technique based on real planning and thought and is, most agree, the best theoretical management program ever conceived.

Also, according to Singular, of these 500 companies:

> . . . less than 10 percent of those 500 corporations — somewhere between 36 and 50 companies — have MBO-based programs that are considered a success. And only 10 companies, or 2 percent, have programs that are considered "highly successful."

---

*For purposes of this text, the words "goal" and "objective" are used synonymously; the valid distinctions that exist between their various meanings are covered later in this chapter in the section titled "The Hierarchy of Objectives."

Managing by objectives, hereinafter referred to in this chapter as **MBO**, is a refinement of the venerable, universally accepted management cycle previously discussed in Chapter Two, "Management Theory — Its Roots and Growth." The cycle of planning, organizing, implementing, and follow-through is the same as MBO. A goals program (by whatever name) that is operating properly, automatically plans. Thus, setting goals is planning; and organizing, too, is primarily planning. Carrying out the plan is implementing, and the reviewing stage (actually an evaluation of progress towards the goal, at which time it is decided what new steps need to be set and undertaken) is follow-through.

Objectives for Individuals

Everyone has goals. Even people who lead very simple lives have some vague, general idea about where they would like to be sometime in the future. With many, this is just daydreaming or wishful thinking. But for people who think seriously about the future and expect to accomplish something in life, goals are not merely guesses about the future: they are real and meaningful targets to strive for.

Consider, as a simplified example of a goal, a high school student with a part-time job who wants to buy a stereo system by a certain date. This is a very clear and direct goal, and the student realizes what must be done to obtain the stereo set. First, a budget should be planned so that a specific amount of money can be put aside each week. Then, assuming that no emergency will arise that would necessitate the money being used for other purposes, the student should be able to pick up the stereo set on a particular day. The student's goal is a comparatively easy goal to achieve. It is specific, it is clear, it is direct, and it is relatively short term.

However, not all goals are as simple or as quickly accomplished. And many goals are not as specific about the date they can be reached, or even about what is to be achieved. For instance, consider the example of the fire fighter whose career goal is to become a fire officer — possibly a chief. This goal is fairly clear, but not as specific as the student's goal in the preceding example. This goal does not state exactly when the fire fighter wants to become an officer, nor where, nor whether the goal expectation is to become a fire officer or a chief. Unlike the purchaser of the stereo system, the fire fighter cannot be specific and can only hope to achieve the goal at some time in the future. This example of a long-range goal is not as easy to plan for as was the stereo system goal: to become a fire department officer or chief involves many more complex and intangible factors, including years of study, specialized training, work experience, and the development of pertinent abilities. Although all of these factors might be accomplished, there is still no guarantee that this long-range career goal will be reached because of possible competition from more qualified candidates applying for high-level positions when such positions become available. There are many factors, some of them unforeseeable and uncontrollable, that might be involved in realizing long-range personal goals.

Objectives for Organizations

As with individuals, organizations set out to accomplish goals for many of the same reasons that individuals do — to provide direction and to get everyone involved in working toward the same purpose. Organizations set goals to satisfy the mission, to improve products or services, to increase sales, to speed up deliveries, and so on.

The bulk of this chapter concerns itself with what goals mean to well-managed organizations such as government agencies, school systems, businesses, and fire departments. The chapter explores the process of setting goals, presents reasons why goal-setting systems can be beneficial to organizations, contains a detailed analysis of why some goal systems fail, introduces some of the principles that can be used to overcome the various problems involved in using goal-setting systems, and also discusses some of the obstacles that prevent such systems from becoming a way of life that helps organizations become better places to work and better sources of products and services.

To become a way of life, a goal system should not become an elaborate set of procedures that attempts to cover all facets of all activities. Such extensive and detailed planning usually turns out to be cumbersome and impractical, and often includes excessive amounts of undesirable paperwork. Conversely, goal systems cannot be superficial if they are to be roads to better performance. To be totally successful, goal systems require good management practices throughout the organization. For example, in the fire service this means that in order to achieve increasing levels of competence for the entire department, officers at all levels must constantly strive to improve their skills as leaders and managers. A goal system for a single organizational unit such as a company can work quite well, even though the department as a whole does not have a working goals program. All that is needed is for the company officers to understand and practice the necessary skills. Although the basic principles involved in goals systems are similar in all organizations, the process of goal setting takes different forms in every organization.

Objectives for Fire Departments

If the chief of the department believes the organization should have a program for managing with objectives, the process for starting it could follow that outlined in the NFPA *Fire Protection Handbook*. The NFPA *Handbook* presents the following information on fire department objectives:[2]

> The foundation of any organization is a set of sound objectives that provide both purpose and direction to the organization. Fire departments, as organizations, are no exception, and must establish valid objectives in order to perform effectively. The traditional objectives commonly accepted by most fire departments are:
> 1. To prevent fires from starting.
> 2. To prevent loss of life and property when fire starts.
> 3. To confine fire to the place where it started.
> 4. To extinguish fires.

These objectives, whether documented or implied, are likely to be the only objectives of many fire departments. All four are presented here as broad, general statements that are not definitive in terms of achievement or performance. To be more meaningful, objectives should be performance oriented.

Each fire department, regardless of size, should develop a set of performance objectives that specify goals to be achieved, the results expected, and the period of time required for achievement. The following material explains a system for developing performance objectives and their related enabling objectives. The procedure for developing objectives and the examples given are a brief overview, given for illustrative purposes. . . .

Developing Performance Objectives: The first step in developing performance objectives is to determine the purpose of the organization and why it exists. This should be done not only for the department as a whole, but for each operating division or section. When determined, these items should show the relationship between the department and each of its operating divisions, and the relationship between the divisions. An example of how this may be done is to make lists with standard headings such as: "The Fire Department exists for the purpose of," "The Fire Suppression Operations Division is currently responsible for," "The Fire Prevention Division is currently responsible for," etc.

The next step is to develop a list of responsibilities. Each operating division should be asked to develop a list of its current responsibilities and activities. The responsibilities listed should be specific. Once complete, this list should indicate where there is overlapping or where there are deficiencies in areas of responsibility. This information may be listed in tabular form, as in the following example. The example shows only two operating divisions. Additional headings should be provided for each operating division within the department.

The Fire Suppression Operations Division is currently responsible for:	The Fire Prevention Division is currently responsible for:
1. Suppressing Fires	1. Fire Prevention Code Administration
2. Rescue	2. Building Plans Review
Current Activities Are:	Current Activities Are:
1. Prefire Planning	1. Public Fire Prevention Education
2. Training	2. Inspections of all Educational Occupancies

The third step is to write a series of statements that describe desired goals. These statements should be expressed in terms that describe definite and measurable goals, and should describe in detail what the department or division would like to achieve. It is important that the statements developed be realistic and achievable. Statements that extend beyond the scope or resources of the department may be meaningless unless they are properly labeled as long-range goals. Most departments or operating divisions should prepare not one, but a series of statements. Following are two examples of such statements:

1. Fire Suppression Operations Division — Each company will conduct an inspection of all target hazards in their first duty area.

2. Fire Prevention Division — Design and develop a fire prevention curriculum and resource material for implementation at the third grade elementary level.

Once the divisions have determined their desired goals, an evaluation should be made by comparing what is currently being done with what has been proposed. This comparison might indicate the need for a decision concerning present status and desired goals. Perhaps the extra effort needed to achieve the desired goals may not be productive, and in many cases there might be gaps between present and desired levels of performance. It is in these areas that priorities should be assessed in order to establish realistic objectives. For example, in the Fire Prevention Division example, the stated goal is the designing and developing of a fire prevention curriculum for third grade elementary school students. Assuming that there is currently a fire prevention program at the third grade level and that there are other goals desired by the Fire Prevention Division, it may not be feasible to channel resources into this effort at this time; the third grade curriculum might well be terminated or set aside as a long-range goal.

In the example for the Fire Suppression Operations Division, the stated goal is that all companies will conduct inspections of all target hazards in their first due area. Are the companies currently doing this? If not, and if it has been decided that all companies will accomplish this goal, then enabling objectives that explain *how* to achieve this goal must be established in order for it to become a performance oriented objective.

Enabling objectives must be measurable, a standard of performance established, and a definite period of time set. If the enabling objectives are not expressed in quantitative terms, they will be of little value since there will be no means of measuring the performance necessary to achieve the overall objectives or goals.

The chart that appeared earlier in this excerpt illustrates one method of listing the steps for the Fire Suppression Operations Division to achieve its desired objective, and shows how objectives are subdivided when more than one division is involved.

Management by Objectives: Once specific objectives have been established, consideration should be given to the possibility of developing a more functional operating system than the current one. This requires that the specific steps necessary to achieve results must be identified, the problem areas determined, details of what is going to be done must be planned, and a time sequence programmed. It is important that time deadlines be set at various points so that programs and procedures may be monitored and schedules met.

To establish a possibly more efficient operating system, it should first be determined whether or not the present system has the capacity to do what is desired. Based on this decision, changes in the present system may be necessary. For example, using the previous Fire Suppression Operations

Division as an example, if it has been decided that all companies are to conduct inspections of target hazards in their first due area, the following questions might be asked:

1. Does the present system have the capacity to do this?
2. Have the fire fighters been trained in inspection techniques?
3. If not, what training is required?
4. Does the training division have the time and resources to conduct this training?
5. How long will the training take?

The answers to the preceding questions will help fill any existing gaps in the present system, and will help to identify key areas that need to be improved.

Next, specific enabling objectives for any changes and improvements should be written. The enabling objectives should be expressed in terms of how these changes and improvements are to be accomplished, and should be used as the basis for revising the present operating system or for establishing a new system.

Before the overall program can be completed, objectives for individual positions within the system must be developed. These objectives must also be specified in terms that are performance oriented, measurable, and a time limit should be established for their completion. In this way, each individual will know what is expected and the amount of time allowed for completion.

Examples of two individual objectives for the Fire Suppression Inspection Project involving more than one division are as follows:

1. Fire Suppression — Each company officer will arrange for and ensure that the target hazards in each first due area are inspected starting in January of the next calendar year. Each company will submit weekly progress reports on the inspections completed, and the completed inspection forms. All inspections will be completed prior to the last day of March.

2. Training — The training officer will design and develop a training course for suppression personnel on the techniques of inspecting target hazards. The training course will include all items necessary for the identification of potential hazards and recommendations for their elimination based on the fire prevention code and nationally recognized good practices. Progress reports on course development will be submitted on a weekly basis to the chief of training. All work will be completed prior to the last day of October.

Finally, it is necessary to continuously monitor results at timed intervals as specified in the objectives. Monitoring provides an opportunity for evaluation, and shows what is happening. There may be instances during evaluation when it becomes evident that some of the objectives that have been established are not realistic and may require change. Also, because some objectives may be above or below the capacity of the department, they may require change.

The process of managing an operating system by the use of performance objectives is not static. If good objectives are established, the process is dynamic and continuously changing. Constant feedback, realignment, changing, and adding objectives is required.

This is a fairly comprehensive process and will lay the foundation for a goals program that starts at the top. The company officer who wants to bring a goal-oriented way of life to a company when the department does not have a program can do so to the company's benefit by starting such a program on a more informal basis.

AN OVERVIEW TO SUCCESSFUL MBO PROGRAMS

A question that frequently arises in organizations using goal-setting systems is, "Why haven't MBO programs been more effective?" Stephen Singular's research includes two possible reasons for failures: (1) adoption in ignorance and (2) implementation in haste.[1] As noted in Singular's magazine article, to be successful, the goal-setting process in any organization requires new forms of cooperation and communication throughout the organization. Therefore, any successful goal-setting program must not only satisfy the needs of the organization, but also must simultaneously take into account the needs of each individual employee so that he or she will feel an interest in the organization's objectives and thus gain satisfaction from helping to achieve them.

Many goals programs concern themselves only with the goals of the organization — with what the organization seeks to accomplish — thus ignoring the personal needs of the employees. Such programs can never gain the same full and enthusiastic support that more soundly based programs can achieve.

A goals program that ignores the desires and needs of the individual employee is often considered to be a device for getting people to work harder without providing benefits for them. Such benefits need not be in the form of additional money, but must be present in some form because the purpose of an MBO program is not efficiency as an end in itself, but greater overall effectiveness. This is not a play on words, because effectiveness has a broader meaning than efficiency. A manager who strives for greater efficiency only usually has to look toward getting more work and effort from people. A good MBO program seeks better output for the short run from smarter approaches — not from greater effort. It also seeks to improve conditions for the future so that the organization can enjoy greater long-run success. As summarized by the noted management consultant Peter Drucker, ". . . usually only twenty percent of a manager's work brings eighty percent of the desired results."[3] The key to effectiveness lies in that twenty percent of the manager's effort that involves planning and organizing for the near and far future.

Thus, a successful MBO program helps avoid duplication of effort, helps prevent wrong starts and purposeless drifting, and instead provides better planning, better direction, and better coordination at all levels within the organization. Also included in the results of a successful MBO program are less wasted effort and significantly better overall decisions as more of the people who can contribute useful information and expertise become involved in decision-making at all levels.

Although it might seem as though successful MBO programs involve extensive planning procedures plus all of the accompanying paperwork, this is only true in situations where, previously, planning was inadequate. However, this is not the case with most organizations. A successful goals program will usually bring better planning by concentrating the planning effort in those areas where such effort will do the most good at a particular time. This kind of planning requires much more skill and judgment than planning with less attention to priorities.

There are no instant solutions that help make MBO programs successful — nor are there any pat formulas available, or answers that can be suitably adopted to any and all organizational situations and structures. To help make organizations more effective by bringing about significant improvement in performance and in job satisfaction for employees, MBO programs must provide satisfactory answers to the eight questions presented at the end of this paragraph. In the case of a fire department, for example, only when all staff members understand the deeper meaning of these eight questions and find satisfactory solutions to the problems involved, can a goals program come close to achieving its promise.

1. How many goals should be set for any one person?

A fire department must decide how many of the ongoing or special responsibilities of each officer, or possibly even of each fire fighter, should be given special emphasis during the coming months, quarter, or even year.

2. How can quality of goals and goal statements be judged?

Is it enough to agree that during the coming year the company will prepare additional prefire plans, or continue a thorough fire inspection program, or renovate the kitchen area? Are such statements adequate?

3. How extensively should a manager be involved in the way in which direct subordinates work toward goal achievement?

How often should the chief check and discuss with the respective officer how well the drills are being performed, or when the hose-drying program starts, or what inspection schedule is planned? Or how often should the captain check into the way an individual fire fighter works out an assignment?

4. How frequently should progress toward goals be reviewed and new goals be set?

How often should an officer meet with individual subordinates to discuss what has been achieved since the last time goals were set? What goals should be revised, what ones can be dropped, and what new ones should be considered? What help do subordinates need from the officer?

5. How should performance with respect to goal achievement be evaluated?

On how many goals were achieved? On some other basis? What should be the relationship to achievement of goals? What really is it that an officer should be held accountable for beyond the accomplishment of routine duties? What about fire fighters? If goals are agreed upon with fire fighters, what should be expected from them?

6. How much influence should subordinates have in setting goals?

Who should be involved in the first place? At what point in time? For instance, if a new piece of apparatus is going to be purchased, who should be asked to contribute ideas, at what point in the decision, and how much weight should be given to their opinions? What about in deciding on the drill schedule and drill topics, or the inspection program?

7. What should be the role of performance appraisal in MBO?

If there is a performance appraisal system in the department, how should it relate to the MBO program? Separate and independent? Some common ground?

8. Where do personal development of subordinates and career planning belong in an MBO program?

What goals can be set for individuals so that they will gain greater satisfaction from their work and from the direction of their careers?

THE HIERARCHY OF OBJECTIVES

Most people who work with goals realize that there is a wide range in types of goals. For example, goals range from the long-range type that spell out the general direction in which an individual or organization wants to move, to the more immediate short-term types that need to be achieved within days or weeks if they are to be reached at all. As presented earlier in this chapter, the career goal of the fire fighter who hoped to become fire chief is an example of the former, and the goal of the student who hoped to purchase a stereo set by a certain date is an example of the latter. Obviously, these types of goals differ not only in the time it takes to achieve them, but also in terms of the importance, or complexity, of the achievements they describe. The career goal of becoming a fire chief is more complex in that it requires far more effort, ingenuity, and conquering of obstacles. Time, as well as quality, also distinguishes the two goals. (See Fig. 5.1.)

In Figure 5.1, "Time" refers to date of achievement and "Scope" refers to the complexity. Reading down on both scales indicates a lower level for each. Thus, reading down on the "Time" branch in Figure 5.1 means a shorter time frame, and reading down on the "Scope" scale means a less complex accomplishment. In a general way these two scales parallel each other, except that philosophical goals lack a date when they will be accomplished while the others do not. Strategic goals generally take longer to achieve than do oper-

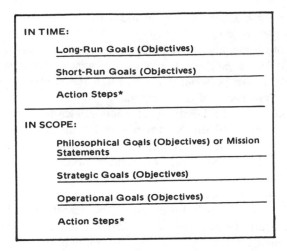

IN TIME:

    Long-Run Goals (Objectives)

    Short-Run Goals (Objectives)

    Action Steps*

IN SCOPE:

    Philosophical Goals (Objectives) or Mission
    Statements

    Strategic Goals (Objectives)

    Operational Goals (Objectives)

    Action Steps*

*Action steps are not goals; their significance will be explained later in this chapter in the section titled "Action Steps — The Working End of a Goals Program."

Fig. 5.1.   Hierarchy of objectives.

ational goals because every strategic goal is supported by one or more operational goals. Nevertheless, the time relationship is not a direct one. Some operational goals take years, while some strategic goals can be accomplished in months.

Philosophical Goals — Mission Statements

In the hierarchy of objectives, philosophical goals (mission statements) for organizations represent the highest level goals. They are really never achieved because they include such qualifying words as "best," "fastest," or "most"; philosophical goals aim forever towards the future. For example, as one of its mission statements a fire department may state that: "With the resources provided by the community, the department will strive to achieve the fastest possible response time to all fires in its area." Obviously, this goal can never be achieved since improvements will always be possible. Philosophical goals describe in the broadest terms possible the usual aim of an organization or sub-unit. Thus, the term "mission statements" is often considered to be an accurate definition of philosophical goals. Individuals are seldom directly concerned with an organization's philosophical goals because the individual manager or employee can never achieve them: as previously stated, an entire organization cannot completely achieve philosophical goals since improvements to them will always be possible. However, individuals work on strategic and operational levels; and, as the goals at these levels are being achieved, the entire organization is simultaneously moving closer toward the realization of its mission statement.

Although philosophical goals are rarely considered as direct guides for action, they do, primarily, offer a vague sense of direction. Frequently they do not appear in writing, and exist only in the form of a general consensus upon which most people would agree.

Individuals, of course, also have personal mission statements toward which they strive. To be an excellent fire officer is such a statement. Individuals work toward their own personal goals through the strategic and operational goals within the framework of their careers.

To help explain how the hierarchy of goals relates to a fire department, a fictitious department called the Anytown Fire Department will be used. The Anytown Fire Department has two fire stations with three companies each. It is a department having eight paid fire fighters and four paid officers in each station. The other members of the department are volunteers. For purposes of this example, it should be assumed that the department has decided that it will operate with a formal MBO program. The department's first step was to agree, at a departmental meeting, to establish a steering committee and to charge that committee with guiding the installation of the MBO program. The committee was asked to recommend the basic philosophical goals that would become the foundation for all other goals the department's organizational units would adopt.

The steering committee reported proposed philosophical goals at the next department meeting. These were goals for fire suppression, fire prevention, building location and size, apparatus requirements, personnel policies, etc.

The fire prevention mission statement that was adopted at the department meeting read: "The department will establish, follow, and periodically update fire prevention policies and procedures to prevent all fires that could have been anticipated and prevented." (For this example, this fire prevention mission statement is the only one that will be used. Examples of mission statements and of strategic goals for fire department functions other than fire prevention will be discussed in later chapters in this text.)

Strategic Goals

Strategic goals are the specific big goals toward which every department, division, company, platoon, bureau, or office is working. If a goals system exists, every member of the organizational unit is aware of the strategic goals for the unit and all officers are responsible for their shares of such goals.

The strategic goals are allocated to the various sub-units in such a way that the organization's strategic goals will be accomplished if every sub-unit achieves its assigned goals. How this allocation of goals takes place, and how the decisions are made concerning who gets what to do was discussed in Chapter Four, "Modern Management Concepts."

Sub-units do not work on the goals themselves — it is the individuals in the unit who work on them. This means, then, that if the employees in a sub-unit achieve a specific set of strategic goals, then the sub-unit will achieve its strategic goal. And if all sub-units achieve the related strategic goals, then the unit will achieve its goal and so on up to the departmental goal. Figure 5.2 illustrates this relationship.

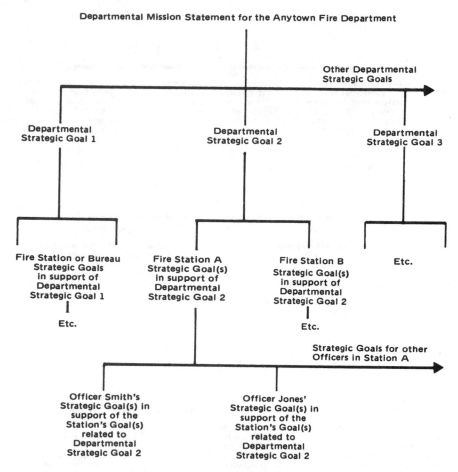

Fig. 5.2. *Partial general goals diagram.*

As shown in Figure 5.2, the departmental mission statement is supported, first of all, by one or several departmental strategic goals. Strategic goals set for Station A, and the same or similar strategic goals for Station B, are needed to achieve each departmental strategic goal. If other stations exist, they would probably also need strategic goals in support of the overall departmental mission statement.

Every strategic goal for an organizational unit requires that individual managers be assigned a share of the particular goal. (Again, for referral, how these assignments should be made to achieve best performances was discussed in Chapter Four, "Modern Management Concepts.") Figure 5.3 is a diagram of some of the Anytown Fire Department's strategic goals related to the fire prevention mission statement.

The first strategic goal for the Anytown Fire Department concerns inspection of specific buildings. It would be supported by fire station goals calling for inspections at appropriate intervals for a defined size area. The second stra-

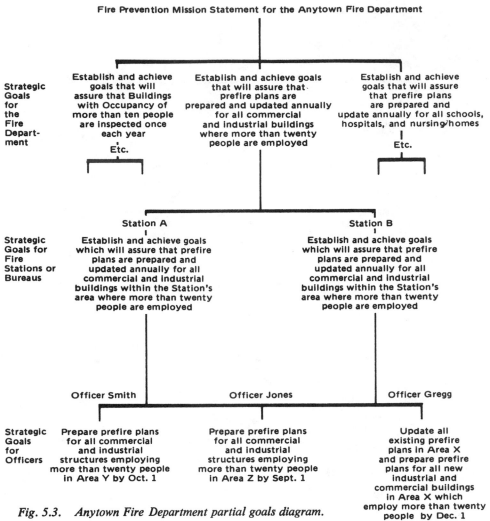

Fire Prevention Mission Statement for the Anytown Fire Department

Strategic Goals for the Fire Department

Establish and achieve goals that will assure that Buildings with Occupancy of more than ten people are inspected once each year

Etc.

Establish and achieve goals that will assure that prefire plans are prepared and updated annually for all commercial and industrial buildings where more than twenty people are employed

Establish and achieve goals that will assure that prefire plans are prepared and update annually for all schools, hospitals, and nursing homes

Etc.

Strategic Goals for Fire Stations or Bureaus

Station A

Establish and achieve goals which will assure that prefire plans are prepared and updated annually for all commercial and industrial buildings within the Station's area where more than twenty people are employed

Station B

Establish and achieve goals which will assure that prefire plans are prepared and updated annually for all commercial and industrial buildings within the Station's area where more than twenty people are employed

Officer Smith

Officer Jones

Officer Gregg

Strategic Goals for Officers

Prepare prefire plans for all commercial and industrial structures employing more than twenty people in Area Y by Oct. 1

Prepare prefire plans for all commercial and industrial structures employing more than twenty people in Area Z by Sept. 1

Update all existing prefire plans in Area X and prepare prefire plans for all new industrial and commercial buildings in Area X which employ more than twenty people by Dec. 1

Fig. 5.3. Anytown Fire Department partial goals diagram.

tegic goal for the department concerns prefire planning of all hazards over a certain size; the matching station goals cover the specific geographical area within the jurisdiction of the particular fire station. Other strategic goals could call for investigation of all fires, and for taking all necessary steps to reinforce strategies one and two. This includes communication of all findings and appropriate recommendations to the community and the officials involved.

It should be noted here that the strategic goals of the respective stations are identical in wording, and differ only in geographic areas to which they apply. The strategic goals of individual officers, which support that station's strategic goals, are not the same. In the example, only one is in different terms. In the real world, it is highly likely that substantially greater differences would exist between the strategic goals of the individual officers.

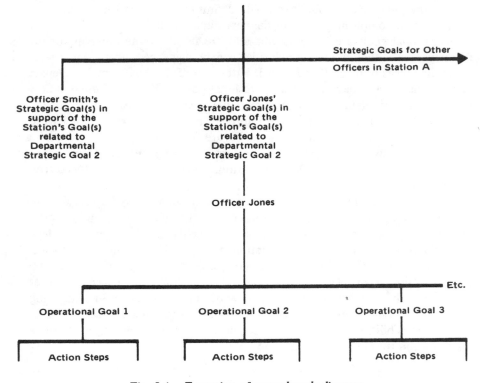

Fig. 5.4.   Extension of general goals diagram.

Not all departmental strategic goals have to be assigned to stations. In larger departments the responsibility for achieving strategic goals in fire and arson investigations, for instance, could be concentrated in a headquarters group. If so, a particular station may not have any responsibility with respect to that goal — or only a very limited routine responsibility that would not require a specific goal. However, somebody or some unit within the total department would have one or several goals with respect to that specific responsibility.

Operational Goals

Operational goals are primarily for people. These are goals that can be expressed in terms of specifics; they are directly measurable in scope and time factors, as can be seen from the extension of general goals diagram shown in Figure 5.4.

Although the general direction of an organization is set by the philosophical goals at the top, most sub-units and individuals reach the major goals by working on the lower ones. Achieving lower-level goals automatically means arrival at the goals of the next higher level. Thus, if all operational goals are met, strategic goals will be realized.

Similarly, if the strategic goals are accomplished, the organization is moving toward the philosophical objectives. (By definition, reaching the goals of any level means accomplishing those of the next higher level.)

Operational goals are fairly specific and are usually quite different for different people, although some similarities can be evidenced when people work on similar types of jobs. (See Fig. 5.5, Extension of the Anytown Fire Department Partial Goals Diagram.) The operational goals in Figure 5.5 are quite different for the different officers. For example, because the Anytown Fire Department has initiated the use of an improved new set of symbols for its prefire plans, the first operational goal in Figure 5.5 may concern familiarizing all fire fighters with this new symbol system in order to enable them to prepare better prefire sketches. Other operational goals could be developed from those shown in the Figure.

As shown in Figure 5.5, Officer Jones has the responsibility for carrying out one or more of the specified operational goals. If Officer Jones and all other officers carry out their assigned operational activities, the overall strategic goal will be accomplished by Fire Station A. And, if the other stations also accomplish their parts of the strategic goal, collectively they will achieve the Anytown Fire Department's mission statement. It should be kept in mind that, simultaneously with executing various operational goals for pre-fire planning, the respective officers may also have responsibilities in other operational areas. Such responsibilities might require that goals are set for working inspections, for drills and training, for maintenance, etc.

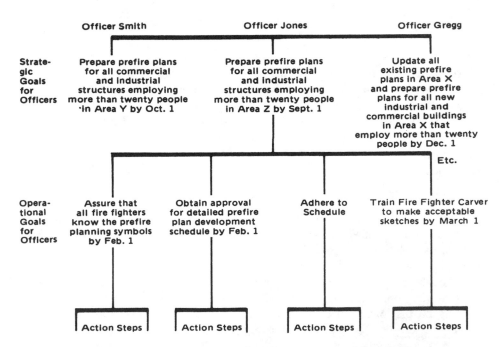

Fig. 5.5. Extension of Anytown Fire Department partial goals diagram.

There are both long- and short-range strategic goals, and long- and short-range operational level goals. For example, in Figure 5.5 the operational goal of "Adhering to Schedule" is a longer-range goal than the strategic goal "Preparing prefire plans by September 1." Usually, it is not necessary to have a clear picture of the line that separates strategic goals from operational goals. Sometimes that line is very fuzzy, and other times it is unimportant. What does count, though, is that all operational goals are clearly established with a specific completion date and a clear statement of the quantity, or quality, of the final outcome. If these can be stated, the goal is probably an operational goal regardless of the length of time required to obtain it. It is not as simple to determine a specific date and quantity for a strategic goal. An easy way to distinguish between the two is to ask the question, "Are there other goals that have to be set to achieve this goal?" If the answer is yes, then the goal is a strategic one. However, before this question can be answered, it is important that the distinction between operational goals and sub-unit of activity (action steps) is clear. Although this distinction might seem to be merely theoretical, this is not the case. There are major differences in the ways managers should look at action steps, and such differences have implications of great significance in the success or failure of goals programs.

Action Steps — The Working End of a Goals Program

As previously explained, goals are basically statements that describe ends to be achieved. At the operational level, goals should always be measurable, attainable, and significant.

Action steps, the specific steps that are necessary and desirable in order to come closer to accomplishing a goal, can be characterized as follows:

> The most distinguishing characteristic of action steps is that they are always under the control of the persons or group assigned or responsible for carrying them out. Therefore, action steps can be completed. Thus, the individual or group can be held responsible for the completion of the action step.

Goals, because they are also subject to external and uncontrollable events and circumstances, may never be achieved even if appropriate action steps leading to them are planned and will be taken. In the earlier example of the student who wanted to buy a stereo, the action steps of the student were "to lay aside money from every pay check." These action steps would lead to the student's goal only if the student did not get laid off. Action steps can be large or small, short or long term: the length of time or the size of the task is not the key factor. What is distinctive is that the action step itself is clearly achievable by the person or persons involved. Further clarification of what action steps are can be obtained by referring to the examples of action steps contained in the Anytown Fire Department goals program diagrammed in Figure 5.6.

Following is a listing of some possible action steps leading to the Anytown Fire Department's operational goal of assuring that all fire fighters know the

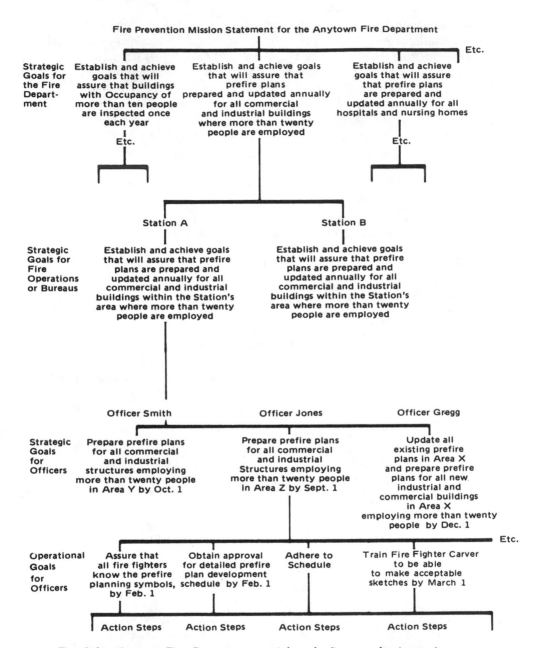

Fig. 5.6.   Anytown Fire Department partial goals diagram showing action steps.

prefire planning symbols by February 1. Rarely is there the need to prepare a formalized listing of such action steps because competent officers are usually well acquainted with the action steps that are necessary to achieve any specific operational goals.

1. To set up a training session for all fire fighters next Monday.

2. To prepare copies of all symbols and to distribute them before the training session.

3. To discuss all symbols at the training session.

4. To give practice samples at the session.

5. To give tests at the training session.

6. To meet with each fire fighter individually to discuss the results of the tests before the end of the week.

7. To administer additional practice assignments to those fire fighters who had difficulty with the tests within two weeks.

MAKING MBO PROGRAMS SUCCESSFUL

Due to the relative simplicity of the MBO concept, it might seem that the problems involved in the setting and carrying out of goals could be easily resolved, and that all MBO programs should be successful. But, obviously, the real world of MBO programs is far more complicated. There are no easy answers, and no quick solutions. MBO programs within fire departments are no exception. The problems attendant in goal-setting programs are the same in any organization — whether that organization is a private company, government agency, school system, or hospital.

The remainder of this chapter explores the eight problem areas that usually arise in MBO programs, and discusses how these particular areas might apply to the managers and individuals (*i.e.*, fire service officers and fire fighters) in a fire department.

The eight problem areas can be summarized by the anagram EQIFAPPO, as shown in the potential problems chart presented in Figure 5.7. Fire service officers need to know how to cope with these problem areas if they wish to achieve not only smoothly operating goals programs, but the higher morale and better performance that can result from successful goals programs.

Extent of Goals to Be Set

In order to determine the number of goals to be set at the various departmental levels, it is necessary for fire service officers to have a thorough understanding of the meaning and value of goals and a knowledge of how to establish them at the respective levels. Two of the problems involved in determining how many goals to set are:

- The setting of too many goals, thus enmeshing the entire process in a maze of paperwork that can prevent the MBO program from generating the enthusiasm it needs to become a way of life.
- The setting of too few goals, thus establishing a program that does not involve people sufficiently enough to challenge them, or to help them to realize the benefits that can result from a successful goals program (such as greater success and higher job satisfaction).

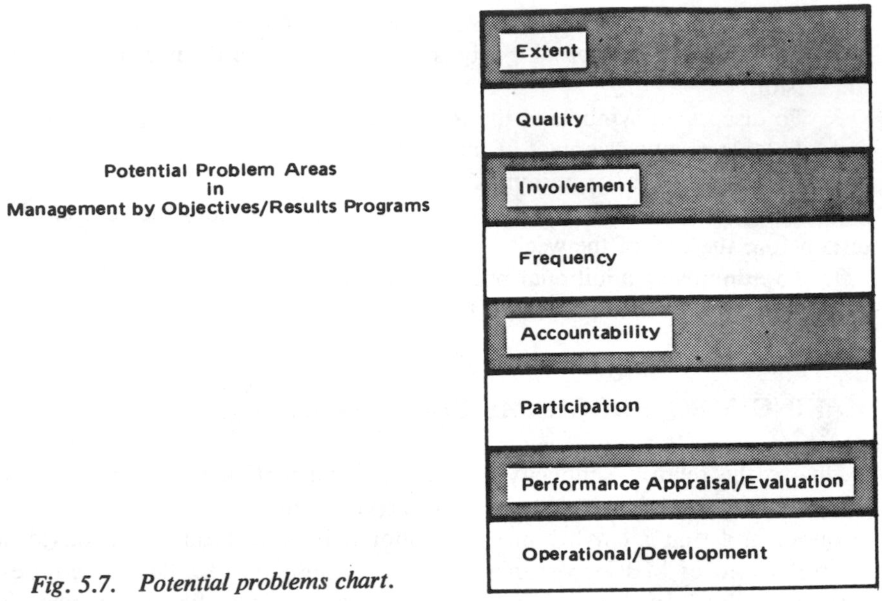

Potential Problem Areas
in
Management by Objectives/Results Programs

| Extent |
| Quality |
| Involvement |
| Frequency |
| Accountability |
| Participation |
| Performance Appraisal/Evaluation |
| Operational/Development |

Fig. 5.7. Potential problems chart.

For every time period, departmental officers must determine how many programs or activities the main thrust should be focused on. Accordingly, officers at the various levels can then help each immediate subordinate prepare separate, individual, personalized goal lists. These are in addition to proper discharge of all regular duties. In the example of the Anytown Fire Department, the operational objectives called for Officer Jones to develop a certain number of prefire plans by a specific date (see Fig. 5.6). The preparation of these plans was in addition to Officer Jones' routine duties and responsibilities as an officer in the department.

When setting goals, it is possible to become too detailed and thus defeat the intended purposes by setting too many goals. For example, an individual officer or fire fighter might be expected to achieve goals for inspections, for prefire planning, and for training — all while attending to regular duties, so that there is not enough time to accomplish all these duties. The purposes of a goals program can also be defeated when those involved become overwhelmed by too much detail or record keeping so that a considerable amount of time is wasted with what might seem to be unnecessary "busy work." Basically, determining how many goals to set for any one person can be considered as being as important as determining who should set the goals.

Quality of Goals to Be Set

All goals must be relevant to the overall organization's mission and the individual's purpose. Operational goals should be clear and measurable in order for superiors and their subordinates to know to what extent an operational goal has been accomplished. So that they add to the motivational aspects of the environment, goals, while being realistic, should be demanding and challenging for the specific individual involved. To be measurable, operational goals must not only specify what is to be accomplished, they must have a built-in time factor — a date for completion. For example, a goal that states:

> "We will prepare three prefire plans"

is not definite enough even though the quality of the work is clearly implied. Such a goal statement is inadequate because it lacks a specific time reference as well as reference to the amount of work to be done (some plans involve a great deal of work, while others are very simple). Even if the completion date were indicated in the goal statement, the quality of the plan is not spelled out. Considerable misunderstandings can result when goals are inappropriately stated.

A more appropriate goal statement would be more specific, such as:

> "We will prepare a prefire plan for block such and such by such and such a date"; or ". . . on these specific buildings by such and such a day."

So stated, the goal is measurable if everyone clearly understands what details should be shown on a plan. It is clear and specific. Whether it has been successfully accomplished can be readily determined. A further example is the vaguely stated goal:

> "We will train all fire fighters in prefire planning."

This goal statement doesn't indicate specifically *what* subject is to be mastered or *how* it is to be achieved. It could mean only that each fire fighter has to sit through a lecture on the topic for the goal to have been accomplished, even if the fire fighters understand very little about prefire planning after such "training." But, if the goal statement included the following specifics, it would then be measurable and easy to determine whether or not it had been achieved:

> "By the end of June, every fire fighter in the company will be able to draw a sketch of a one-story building with all pertinent sections noted and with the proper symbols prescribed by the procedure."

Involvement

This problem area concerns the amount of involvement by the supervisor in the way the subordinate works to achieve a goal. It is closely related to another problem area — the subordinate's role in the setting of goals, which is examined later in this chapter in the section subheaded "Participation in Decision-making Process." It is sufficient to note here that any well-conceived MBO program recognizes that there are very specific responsibilities at all levels. For example, if a battalion chief's time has been committed to the supervision of a specific number of building inspections during a particular year, such inspections will need to be divided amongst the subordinate units. In turn, these subordinate units could then set their own goals for carrying out this particular job by determining how many inspections they would do in a specific month and in what order, who would perform the inspections, and all of the other specific operational steps needed to complete the job.

The following questions involve the confidence and trust in, and extent of the work loads imposed on, the units. They are important in determining to what degree the battalion chief should be involved in seeing that the job is being done:

1. How frequently should the battalion chief check? (Some superiors — at all levels of command — check more frequently than do others.)

2. How detailed is the checking that is necessary?

Whether or not an MBO program is successful is often determined by the type and amount of involvement by a superior. For example, many supervisors give their subordinates the impression that they are constantly being watched and that they are not permitted the freedom to think creatively enough to do the job the way the subordinate feels it should be done. At the other extreme is the problem of the supervisor who is rarely available for questions or help when needed.

Determining how often those in managerial positions should check the progress of their subordinates in the attainment of established goals is not easy, but it can have great impact on the popularity of the goals system with those who are most involved — the people at lower levels. Closely connected are the equally thorny issues of how frequently new goals should be set and how often old ones should be revised.

Frequency of Reviews in Goals Programs

This problem area involves the need for regular reviews. In order for an MBO program to be successful as a managerial technique, regular reviews are necessary. However, what is considered as being "regular" for one individual may not be "regular" for another, depending on each individual's competency, experience, needs, maturity, and so on. For example, most people would probably agree that daily reviews are too frequent, and that yearly goal reviews might not be frequent enough at any level.

There is no question that reviews should be well-planned; they are important, two-way communication tools that allow both sides to know what is going on. Reviews enable the subordinate to inform the supervisor of any areas of difficulty encountered when striving for achievement of goals, and of the kinds of problems that exist so that the supervisor can provide the additional support needed for the completion of the job. At the same time, the review provides a direct method that enables the supervisor to keep informed of the status of the situation at all times.

Other advantages to regular, built-in reviews include the following:

1. Reviews help to overcome complaints from subordinates that supervisors do not really know what the subordinates are accomplishing, or contributing, to the achievement of the organization's goals.

2. Reviews provide evidence that goals programs are serious in intent, that the managers support goals programs, and that goals programs aren't merely eye-wash for still higher-level managers.

3. Reviews are opportunities for supervisors to obtain additional knowledge about the capabilities and potentials of subordinates, thus enabling the supervisors to help subordinates develop greater competence and success.

In addition to reviewing the progress of the goals to date, a review should include any changes in the action steps that may be required to meet the organization's needs during the period undergoing review. The review should also help determine what assistance the manager should provide in support of the work of the lower-level manager or employee.

To be as effective as possible, reviews should be carried out on a one-to-one, face-to-face basis. Regular written reporting or correspondence procedures can be incorporated, should such procedures be considered helpful.

Accountability

This problem area is concerned with: (1) what a supervisor can reasonably expect from a subordinate; (2) what a subordinate can be held responsible or accountable for; and (3) the extent to which people can be held accountable for the accomplishment of goals if outside interferences become roadblocks (*i.e.*, can a subordinate be held responsible if expected support for working on a goal does not materialize, or if unexpected emergencies pop up anywhere along the route?). For example, in the event that during the year an unexpected and extensive rash of fires and emergencies required much more time than had originally been anticipated, to what extent might Officer Jones be considered accountable or not accountable for fulfilling a goal? Might it be considered that Officer Jones did a good job during this period by completing one-half of the prefire plans, or might it be considered that Officer Jones did a poor job by completing only one-half of the prefire plans?

Accountability involves the extent to which an individual can be expected to achieve a goal, as well as how performance can be judged if the goal is not reached. Most goals programs fail, in part, because they are not able to deal with this specific problem area. More simply stated, accountability is concerned with the following questions:

1. Whose fault is it when goals are not achieved?
2. Who should be held responsible, and to what extent?
3. What is considered fair, and what is considered objective?

These questions are closely related to the concerns that are discussed later in this chapter in the section subheaded "Performance Appraisal and Evaluation," which deals with the relationship between a goals program and a performance appraisal program, where one exists.

Participation in Decision-making Process

This problem area is closely related to the "Involvement" problem area. It is generally agreed upon that subordinates should participate in the setting of goals (a type of decision-making). However, there is considerable disagreement on the amount of leeway that should exist, or just what the appropriate level of participation should be.

Participation in the making of *all* goal decisions is certainly not necessary or even desirable. For example, a fire scene is an emergency situation at which there is little time for formal joint decision-making. At a fire scene, the ranking officer takes command and assumes a dominant role in all decisions.

In most other decision-making situations, the answers to the important considerations are not as clear: (1) What persons should participate? (2) To what extent should those persons be involved? and (3) At what point in the process should they participate? There is a great deal of misunderstanding concerning these matters on the part of managers everywhere. It should be clearly understood that the concerns that apply to participation in the setting of goals apply to all decisions affecting people. Goal setting is just one specific type of decision.

In some decision-making situations, all of the persons who will be affected by the decision can — and should — take part. In other situations, the persons who should take part in making decisions should only be those persons who have expertise in the particular topic with which the decision is concerned. Sometimes it is preferable that everyone participate right from the beginning; in other cases such involvement might be included only at a certain time, or for a segment of the total decision such as with the implementation aspects of a decision when that phase begins.

There are many levels at which people can participate in the setting of goals. For example, an officer might ask: "We're going to prefire plan this whole block. Where shall we start?" Or, "What should we preplan?" Or even, "How should we organize ourselves to do this preplanning?" It should be noted that each successive question requires a broader and more significant level of participation. Because there are many kinds of levels and possibilities, the question of participation in the decision-making process is a complicated and widely misunderstood one, and will be discussed in detail later in this text.

Performance Appraisal and Evaluation

Most employees, including fire fighters, are concerned with what their supervisors think of them and of the quality of their work. They want to know how they are progressing in relation to their own future and in terms of their contribution to the overall success of the organizational unit. Information about performance or specific assignments should be made available to subordinates on a regular basis and should cover both positive and negative aspects of the subordinate's progress. From time to time, however, there should be a formal review that: (1) clarifies how the manager perceives the subordinate's overall performance, (2) suggests ways in which the subordinate's performance can be improved, and (3) explains how the manager can help the subordinate reach personal work and career goals. Such reviews are usually called performance appraisals or performance evaluations.

A major concern of many managers involved with the preparation of performance appraisals is how to keep such appraisals on as objective a basis as possible. Supervisors need to be as factual as possible in their evaluations of people, even though they may have personal preferences for certain strengths and personal dislikes for certain weaknesses. The approach of establishing clear accountabilities based on goals — and even more on action steps leading to the goals — can help to overcome many of the obstacles that arise when one person evaluates another. An objective and fair evaluation can usually be based on the key activity of the action steps; this avoids many of the difficulties encountered when goal achievement is the basis on which performance is evaluated. Because action steps are under the control of the individual while goals may not be, action steps are a more realistic basis for evaluation. Goal achievement can be blocked, whereas action step achievement is always possible.

Operational Vs. Developmental Goals

As stated earlier in this chapter, operational goals are for people (see section titled "Operational Goals"). Developmental goals, like operational goals, are also for people, but in a more personal way. Developmental goals are concerned with the professional development of the people who work on the organizational goals.

The professional development of personnel through training is an important concern for all organizations. Such development enables personnel to become more competent in their current jobs and to become better qualified to accept the responsibilities of higher-level positions when openings occur. An organization made up of skilled and competent personnel who are continuing to develop themselves toward even higher levels of competency is more likely to achieve its goals than is the organization that has little or no concern for the professional growth of its personnel.

A fire department in which all of the fire fighters and officers are competent and strive for ever higher levels of performance can be compared to a ball team that wants to win every game. It presents a spirited atmosphere in which it can be a pleasure to work. Thus, the training of all persons to the limits of their abilities and personal desires is an important consideration in goals programs.

In some work situations the people involved are satisfied with the kind of work they do, but not necessarily with their own competence. Often, such people would prefer to become more proficient and thus obtain more satisfaction from their work. Developmental goals can usually help satisfy much of this need. Goals programs that include serious approaches to helping personnel develop in ways that enable them to obtain more satisfaction from their work aren't one-sided programs; and as such they have a much better chance of enlisting the support of all the members of an organization. In such programs it is necessary to establish the procedures that will assure that the personal goals of people will also be considered when the goals of the organization are planned and implemented.

Multi-unit Goals

While not generally considered equal in importance to the eight problem areas summarized in the anagram EQIFAPPO, a problem often encountered at organizational levels concerns multi-unit goals that cut across departmental or divisional lines. This problem occurs when several units in an organization share a common goal that cannot be accomplished without the combined efforts of the units involved. Multi-unit goals are of concern to the fire service when departmental goals are set that affect all units — divisions, battalions, and companies — within the overall organization.

Although multi-unit goals should be the primary responsibility of a higher level, this is not always practical and the problems inherent in them must then be solved at lower levels. Only when the goals process is thoroughly understood by an organization can such problems be easily resolved. One solution is to charge a manager with leading and coordinating the efforts of the different units involved. In such a case, the manager helps plan out the action steps needed by each unit in order to help the organization accomplish the goal. The manager also works directly with all of the personnel involved so that the plan can be changed and adapted as needed to suit the requirements of the various participating units within the organization.

ALIGNING GOALS AND PERFORMANCE STANDARDS

One management process that an officer can use to ensure that the company or platoon will improve its performance is competent goal setting. The emphasis is on "competent" because many managers and organizations do set goals. They do not, however, obtain the benefits from doing it because they overlook too many of the subtle, yet important, things that are part of competent goal setting.

Goals programs and the problems that prevent them from becoming very successful have been discussed in the first part of this chapter. In this section, the same eight problems will be reviewed, but this time with some suggestions on how they can be overcome. Emphasis will be on the way the theory can provide practical suggestions to an officer on how to make better decisions in all these areas.

As illustrated in Figure 5.7 earlier in this chapter, the eight potential problem areas in goal setting are:

1. The extent of goal setting.
2. The quality of goals and goal statements.
3. The involvement by the officer in the way fire fighters and lower level officers work towards their goals.
4. The frequency of goals reviews.
5. What subordinates are held accountable for.
6. The voice that subordinates have in the goal-setting process.
7. The way performance appraisals are handled in relation to the goal-setting program.
8. How developmental goals for individuals fit in with the operational goals of organizations.

At the very beginning of this book, and in various other places throughout it, it has been emphasized that all decisions that an officer makes have to be guided by the following three considerations:

- The officer's own capabilities.
- The capabilities and competence of the subordinates.
- The particular situation.

Guidance by these three considerations is especially true with respect to all the aspects of goal setting.

Extent of Goal Setting

Record Keeping and Goal Setting: There are many industrial managers who believe that goals should be set on all activities. Other managers will set goals on all those activities that they consider important enough so that the expected results should be specified. Often they expect these to be in writing, together with summaries of plans for achieving them. Very often the attempt to make the goals program so comprehensive brings a heavy load of paperwork and may be self-defeating. People are inclined to see such goals programs as nothing else but just another task that must be done so-and-so often. A goals program can thus lose the opportunity to become a "way of life" that sees the achievement of goals as a primary part of the job.

Capabilities of Subordinates: With some subordinates, an officer can agree on several or many goals because the people are competent enough to work on several goals at the same time. There are other subordinates with whom only one single goal can be set.

No matter how many goals are set, every subordinate still has to work on all the duties that are part of the job. However, during any one period there should also be one or several tasks or responsibilities that deserve greatest attention. These tasks deserve greatest attention because they are the ones where maximum improvement is especially important during coming weeks or months. These are the ones on which goals are set.

It is therefore important to look at the capabilities of subordinates when determining how many goals to be set and, of course, how to set these goals.

The Life Cycle Theory of Leadership: Drs. Paul Hersey and Kenneth Blanchard, professors at Ohio State University, developed a theory of leadership that is diagramed in Figure 5.8. In this diagram, the two coordinates — the vertical and horizontal axes — can represent an organizational unit. The horizontal axis depicts the extent to which an officer or a manager assigns tasks. If the manager or officer assigns very few tasks, the coordinate would be near the left end of the horizontal axis. If the leader assigns most or all of the tasks, the coordinate would be near the right end of the horizontal axis.

The vertical axis of the diagram represents the leader's concern for establishing a good work relationship. If a point is plotted at the bottom of the diagram, the leader has little concern about how well the subordinate likes the

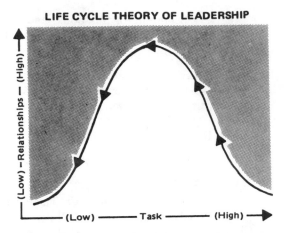

LIFE CYCLE THEORY OF LEADERSHIP

Fig. 5.8. A representation of the life cycle theory of leadership. (Reproduced by special permission from the February 1974 *Training and Development Journal.* Copyright © 1974 by the American Society for Training and Development, Inc.)

decisions that are made. If a coordinate is plotted at the top of the diagram, the leader has maximum concern about the way the decisions or work arrangements are accepted by the subordinate.

To illustrate all possibilities of coordinates, a child's growth to an adult can be examined. Following the diagram from left to right as the curve indicates, it can first be seen that an infant requires very high task assignment by the parent. There is little need by the parent to be concerned about whether or not the child likes the decisions that the parent makes. As the child grows older, the curve progresses very little as the parent is still an "authoritarian" figure. If a child is told not to cross the street or not to touch a hot stove, the parent usually is not concerned whether the child is happy about these instructions or not.

But as the child begins to mature and becomes more aware of decisions and reasoning, the parent must be more concerned about explaining reasons for decisions to the child. This is shown by the way the curve rises on the vertical axis.

As the child moves into adolescence and becomes more independent and more knowledgeable about the world, the parents must relinquish some of the decision making for their offspring, but at the same time they must still be slightly authoritarian in the tasks they assign. However, as the offspring moves to college or to a job and on to an independent life, parents can no longer be deeply involved in making decisions for the offspring because they are no longer in close or continuous contact. The offspring must now accept more of the responsibility for individual choices.

What is true for the child as it matures is true for an employee who enters and becomes established in a new job. In the fire service, a rookie must be introduced to the job, the rules of the organization, the procedures and evolutions that are being practiced, etc. The rookie must accept these rules and requirements without a part in the decision making. However, as time and experience help the rookie become acquainted with the job the fire officer will find it necessary to explain the reasons for decisions if the fire fighter is to perform well in emergency situations. Depending upon previous experience and personal capabilities, a new fire fighter may move up the curve more or less rapidly as the fire officers relinquish more and more of a specific assignment of tasks and, instead, increase their concern for the relationship they establish with the individual as the fire fighter reaches higher capabilities or higher positions. However, each child and each fire fighter is different; the speed at which relinquishment of total guidance occurs depends upon individual capabilities.

Although their superiors must train the fire fighters in combating all types of emergencies, fire officers cannot be expected to constantly oversee operations as a result of the nature of their work. Because of this, fire fighters are located primarily on the left side of the curve: They are capable of accepting assignments in more general terms as they usually make more of the decisions about what they should do, when it should be done, and how it should be done. Fire fighters usually establish their own goals in consultation with their superiors, and they work independently toward the achievement of these goals.

Goal Setting in the Life Cycle Theory: The life cycle theory and its curve suggest conclusions to the extent of goal setting that can be done by managers, depending upon the location of an individual on the curve. For example, with a new fire fighter or one who is limited in potential for personal development, only very few goals can be set. However, with more experienced, competent, and mature individuals several goals can be set at one time.

Setting Priorities in the Life Cycle Theory: The life cycle theory primarily concerns the influence that the competence of subordinates has on the extent of goal setting. The officer's capabilities and the situation on hand are also involved when setting goals and the priorities for these goals. If only a few goals are to be set, the manager would most likely choose the most important of these goals to attend to first. In making such a choice, the manager or officer must decide what tasks are most important and would deserve the highest priority. However, all goals cannot be set solely by priorities because of unforeseeable complications.

For example, when an alarm sounds all fire fighters must respond by abandoning any other activity, no matter how important. But more than just a response is occurring in the mind of the officer. The officer must make a series of decisions that involve priorities on the way to the fire scene: placement of apparatus, deployment of fire fighters, preparation for mutual attack, etc. Rescue usually comes first on the scene of a fire, but if there is an exceptionally dangerous exposure the second priority could be to protect the exposure rather than to direct attack on the fire. Four factors are usually considered when setting priorities for goals:

1. **The urgency of the goals.** Although an organization may have many important goals to accomplish, there are times when the urgency of one particular goal necessitates that it be accomplished more promptly than others.

2. **The importance of the goals.** Sometimes several tasks may occur at

the same time that would all require a particular action or response and that would all be a part of one goal. For example, returning administrative telephone calls would be a part of the major goal of good departmental communications. If many telephone calls have been received in one day the task of answering these calls would be set by priorities, as the most important call would be handled first. A call from an irate citizen concerning a blocked exit would demand utmost attention since the fire department serves and exists for its taxpayers. Of secondary importance may be a call from a union president concerning a grievance. Finally, a call from a fire apparatus salesperson would have priority after the two previous telephone calls.

3. **How quickly the particular goal can be completed.** There often is a desire to complete those goals that can be finished quickly in order to simplify scheduling and to allow full concentration on those goals that are more time-consuming. However, the time-consuming goals may be of utmost importance, which would therefore mean they must be accomplished first.

4. **The relationship between the completion of one goal with the completion of another.** If a series of inspections have to be made during a particular time frame and, in the same time frame, the goal of drawing up prefire plans must be fulfilled, the inspections should be done first so that prefire plans can be based on the results of the inspections.

Although the priorities of goals are usually weighed by the urgency needed in their achievement, there may arise situations where important, but not urgent, goals are postponed longer than they should be, resulting in crises at a later time. Figure 5.9 depicts an importance/urgency diagram that may help in remembering important goals that have been postponed. The diagram is divided into four blocks that represent the priorities of goals. Area B represents those goals that are the most urgent and therefore receive first priority.

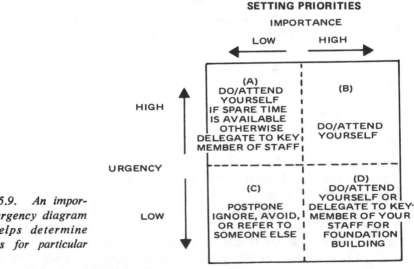

Fig. 5.9. An importance/urgency diagram that helps determine priorities for particular goals.

Area D represents second priority goals that are important, but not as urgent as the goals in Area B. The goals in Area D should be accomplished after the goals in Area B, but they should not be delayed for a lengthy period of time as postponement may require more work and less time for this work.

Areas A and C represent goals that are not of primary or secondary priority rating. Area A's goals are still urgent, but they are not as important as Areas B or D. In a fire department Area B may indicate the goal of faster response time because of a major road's reconstruction in a city; therefore, this goal would be of utmost importance. Area A may designate the tune-up of all major pieces of apparatus in the department. This goal would be important, but not as pressing as Area B's goal.

In relation to the goals in Areas B and D, Area A represents goals that are of lesser importance, but which still need to be fulfilled. A goal in this area may be housekeeping for the kitchen and washing facilities in the station. This goal would require urgency, but would be done after goals B and D have been or are being accomplished.

Finally, those goals that are neither important nor urgent are located in Area C. Such a goal might be reading fire service magazines that are received by the station. This goal would be accomplished only after the goals in Areas A, B, and D have been achieved. In instances where A, B, and D contain pressing goals, the goal(s) in Area C may have to be indefinitely postponed. When Areas A, B, and D have no pressing goals, Area C would become the "important" goal until the time arises when it must be temporarily or permanently abandoned.

Quality of Goals and Goal Statements

There are several requirements of goals and goal statements that are needed to achieve the appropriate quality from them. First, goals must be in line with the mission. As previously discussed, little is gained by setting goals on all activities and functions. Since only a few goals are set for any one period, they must concern only those matters that are important to the mission of the organizational unit.

Second, goals must be challenging. This means that they must be set high, but not so high that they are beyond achievement. To set a goal of a response time that would mean traveling at excessive speeds is clearly unrealistic. On the other hand, to work toward a reduction in turnout time by ten percent or even twenty percent may be challenging, yet realistic.

It is important to understand that goals are based on forecasts or estimates of what can be accomplished. Forecasts, of course, can never be accurate; the best that can be done in setting goals is to reach for something that appears achievable. For instance, if it appears as though ten inspections a month are possible but difficult, then that could be a realistic goal for a company. Yet, if it is clear that ten inspections have never been accomplished even during the best periods, then that goal may not be realistic and may be too high. When goals are clearly set too high, they are not challenging because people either do not take them seriously or they are discouraged by them. On the other hand, if a goal is certain of accomplishment without extra effort, it is hardly worthwhile to spend time on setting it.

Officer Involvement in Ways Subordinates Work Towards Goal Achievement

In deciding how deeply to become involved in helping subordinates or in checking how they approach their assignments, an officer should keep the life cycle theory in mind. Those subordinates who either have limited experience or limited capabilities usually require fairly careful checking to see that they are approaching their assignments in a competent way.

In fire departments, company officers usually work closely with the fire fighters in jointly carrying out goals. This is particularly true of the goal of fire fighter training and education. If it is decided that a fire fighter will enroll in a tactics course in a community college, the company officer would become involved to ensure that the fire fighter will gain the most from the course. With a highly motivated and mature fire fighter, only minimal officer involvement may be necessary to discuss how the course is progressing. With an individual who is less motivated or less capable of learning, much more involvement would be required. The officer, in addition to inquiring about the course's progression, may also provide assistance in reiterating areas of confusion in the fire fighter's mind. It might also be necessary after every class to briefly review the lesson.

Detailed involvement with the more competent fire fighter, however, could be interpreted as interference and may dampen motivation. On the other hand, less competent individuals would appreciate this assistance, thereby increasing motivation.

Frequency of Goals Reviews

Goals review sessions have four primary purposes:

    1. To review where the manager should provide additional help or support so that those goals that are in danger can be achieved, and to discuss what form such support should take.

    2. To keep the manager informed of progress on those goals where work is proceeding smoothly.

    3. To review what goals should be set for the upcoming period.

    4. To review which goals have become unrealistic as a result of events, and should therefore be modified.

Of these, probably the most important purpose is to determine how the manager can help a subordinate with the achievement of those goals that could be reached if additional help in the form of advice or resources were available.

There are few hard and fast rules to guide the number of times a year that goals review should be held. However, many organizations who have reasonably effective goals programs require their managers to hold goals reviews with each subordinate at least once every three months. Within that requirement, however, it is possible to hold a review even more frequently, such as biweekly or weekly. With highly competent subordinates who can work on several goals at the same time, a monthly review is beneficial for there is relatively little need for detailed discussions about how the goals are being approached.

If there is relatively little involvement by the manager in the way the subordinate works toward achieving the goal, then there may be a need for frequent goals review sessions. In these sessions progress towards goals is explored, and the subordinate has an opportunity to call on the skills and capabilities of the manager to assist with the difficult problems. At the same time, the manager receives an update on the status of the various projects that are in progress.

Goals reviews can be less frequent with subordinates where the manager has to be deeply involved in the way they work toward achievement of goals. These subordinates are constantly in need of help or guidance with the steps that have to be taken. With such subordinates a manager can hold formal goals reviews once every three months because of the constant supervision and knowledge of the project. Similarly, quarterly reviews would be adequate for a manager who works continuously with a small team of subordinates.

In a fire department, the chief might hold goals review sessions with officers who report to the chief once each month. On the other hand, the company officer who works regularly with each fire fighter might review goals quarterly to see which are worth setting for the coming period, and what changes should be made in existing goals that have not yet been achieved.

One problem that often confuses managers about goals programs — particularly when there is discussion about goals review once every few months — lies in the fact that many goals are of very short duration. They may be on tasks that can be accomplished in a few weeks or even a few days. These short-run goals are, of course, only steps toward long-run goals. For instance, to complete a certain number of inspections in the course of a week is part of a goal to complete a much larger number in the course of a year. Similarly, a goal to make a revision in hose bed layout is part of a larger goal to achieve a more efficient apparatus. Goals, however, do not need to be set on every activity; if it is an accepted routine to inspect a given number of call boxes in the course of every week, there is no need for a goal.

Holding Subordinates Accountable

Since goals are primarily forecasts and since goals may not be achieved even with the most careful planning and sound implementation, it does not seem useful to hold individuals responsible for the actual achievement of goals. It is meaningless to observe that eighty percent of a goal has been achieved, or to note that the goal has been achieved on schedule, a few days earlier than scheduled, or two weeks or a month later than scheduled. The original goal may have been totally unrealistic and impossible to achieve, or it may have been very easy.

In either case, to measure in some numerical way what percentages of goals were achieved does not represent a useful way to judge a subordinate's performance. On the other hand, there are many things that a subordinate can and should be held accountable for:

Setting Challenging Goals: Participation by subordinates is desirable when setting goals; however, goal setting is meaningful only if subordinates are sincere in helping to establish goals that are both realistic and challenging. If a subordinate is forced to play a game to obtain the lowest possible goal so that the least amount of effort is required to achieve it, then mutual goal setting is not effective. Managers therefore need the cooperation of the subordinates in helping to set challenging and realistic goals.

If a goals program exists and the manager wants it to become a way of life rather than a paper program, then obviously the manager cannot expect people to set challenging goals if they are punished when they do not achieve them. A manager who requires that subordinates set challenging goals must be prepared to look at goals as predictions of achievement, and to expect serious efforts to be made to attain them. Some goals, however, may not be achieved even with the best action program and the most untiring effort. If a manager accepts this fact, then subordinates can be held accountable for setting realistic goals that are also challenging.

Action Steps: Another aspect for which a manager can hold subordinates accountable is the thoroughness with which action steps support all goals. A person working on goals should always be aware of what action steps are necessary to come as close to the achievement of that goal as possible, and should have those action steps fairly clearly in mind. Even though a manager would not frequently ask competent subordinates what progress is being made towards the accomplishment of a goal or what actual steps are being taken, the subordinates would know what these steps are. That does not mean that these action steps need to be in writing, nor does it mean that there need to be very many of these action steps. However, they should be of the quality that helps to achieve the mission, and the subordinate should be fully aware of what they‘are. The manager can, therefore, hold subordinates responsible to have appropriate and adequate action steps for their goals.

Planning: A manager can also hold subordinates responsible for good planning and for the thoroughness with which their planning occurs. A competent person, working against goals, will think of goals at all times. A less competent person will forget about goals during certain periods. The least competent people will remember goals only when they know their managers will ask about them.

Quality of Effort: When looking at the action steps that the subordinate takes, the manager obviously must evaluate them to see whether they are the best that can be taken. A subordinate who regularly takes action steps that show improvement certainly deserves to be commended; one who takes inadequate action steps should be held accountable. If inadequate steps are being taken, performance should be viewed against the training that the subordinate has received. A lack of quality could be related to training.

Schedule of Results: If a subordinate agrees to complete a certain action step by a certain time and does not accomplish it in that time even though it was possible, the subordinate should be held accountable. The same is true of all action steps leading to goals. Fire fighters or fire officers, once they commit themselves to a plan of action, should implement that plan as decided and should be deterred from it only by matters beyond their control.

Viability of Action Steps: When someone accepts responsibility for a goal, develops a set of good action steps, and takes those action steps, it may sometimes become apparent that the action steps will not lead to achievement of the goal. When that happens, the person working towards the achievement of the goal should be expected to immediately reconsider the action steps and take any additional steps that may be desirable to come closer to reaching the goal.

Notification for Unachieved Goal: Once an organization understands how to work with a goals system, everyone knows that it is essential to notify the manager as soon as it becomes clear that a goal will not be achieved. This gives the manager an opportunity to decide whether to: (1) provide additional resources, or help to see that the goal can be achieved, or (2) change the goal if it appears that all has been done to achieve it, yet it cannot be achieved with the effort or the resources that are being devoted to it.

For example, a fire officer may have the goal of investigation of hose evolutions. The officer has been committed to completing the trials by a certain date but, as time progresses, finds that more urgent matters have come up and the tests cannot be completed in time. At that point, the officer can let the goal slide, or can inform the superiors that the goal will not be achieved unless more time is allocated to the goal, or unless others can be assigned to assist with the goal. If there is still time for the goal's achievement, the superior then has the opportunity to rescue the goal or to let it be completed at a later date.

If everyone in an organization accepts the responsibility to provide timely notification when a goal is in trouble, then there is greater likelihood that goals will be achieved on time.

Relationship with Others: There is one more aspect of goals programs for which subordinates can be held accountable; this is the relationship with others. Subordinates can be judged on the extent to which they are able to obtain cooperation from others with the achievement of goals and on the help that they, in turn, are willing to give to others.

All these things for which subordinates can be held accountable for are, of course, far more complicated than just simply checking how well they have achieved their goals. Nevertheless, this is a far more effective way to evaluate the performance of subordinates. Holding people accountable that way will bring a much better chance that subordinates will accept goal setting as a useful process.

Participation

The most important step in bringing satisfaction to subordinates concerns the amount of participation that subordinates have in the goal-setting process.

Every individual wants an opportunity to influence the decisions that will affect life in the present as well as in the future. This includes the things that have impact on individual working conditions, as well as on the work itself.

Obviously an organization cannot permit everyone to have equal influence on goals, for an organization must perform many functions that are a requirement because they are part of the mission. These goals, therefore, require no participation in the setting of the goal. A fire department, for example, must run inspections, must ensure that the alarm boxes are checked regularly, and must remove snow or obstacles in front of hydrants. None of these goals is subject to discussion because they are basic to the very existence and effectiveness of the department. Their performance, therefore, is done regardless of the wishes of individual fire fighters.

It should be clarified here that goal setting and decision making have a great many things in common. The setting of any goal requires at least one and possibly many decisions. Therefore, almost anything that applies to decision making automatically applies to goal setting.

Because of the importance of participation in goals, and in other decisions affecting the work, behavioral scientists have devoted considerable effort to investigating the way participation should be used. The more important of these theories will be discussed here and related to the goal-setting process, and will be used as limited guidelines to action for the officer who wishes to create the best possible motivational climate. The more important of the theories was Tannenbaum's and Schmidt's "Continuum of Leadership Behavior" (refer to Chapter Three, Fig. 3.3). From this diagram, it was explained that an officer must choose the level of participation for every decision or for the setting of a goal that is correct for that particular situation and for the capability and competence of the subordinate. The manager who can make good decisions on how much participation to allow will establish a much better relationship with the subordinates and will help to provide the climate that motivates them to greater achievement.

Selecting the Best Level of Participation: Tannenbaum's and Schmidt's diagram poses a difficult question: What point along the range of possible participation choices should the manager select for a specific situation? There are two general guidelines that can be used. First, participation depends upon the competencies and capabilities of subordinates. The more competent and capable a subordinate is, the more likely participation will lead to favorable results. Second, Miles' human resources model (see Chapter Three) provides another guideline. The model says, in effect, that the manager has to decide on that level of participation that will lead to better decisions. If better decisions are made, then more success is achieved; success leads to greater satisfaction, and subordinates gain both in the satisfaction of having participated and in the satisfaction of seeing a successful outcome.

Thus, the manager or officer should decide what level of participation is most likely to lead to success before setting a goal or before making a decision. For instance, an officer may have been asked by the superior officers to do everything to assure that a certain task is completed by the end of the week. If it is important that the task indeed be completed by the end of the week, then this is not a decision that should be resolved participatively. On the other hand, the questions of how the job should be accomplished or how the assignment should be implemented could very well involve the fire fighters.

One way to decide what level of participation would be best is to follow Miles and ask the question: What level, timing, and intensity of participation will bring the highest level of success? To answer that question, more specific guidelines are needed for there are no simple rules that can be used to help a manager or officer here. The issues that are involved are far too complex to permit the use of a simplistic formula. They do, however, lend themselves to more detailed analysis, which then allows a more accurate selection of the participation level and timing.

Issues Related to Characteristics of the Subordinate: When a manager or officer is able to use employee participation, consideration is usually given to three characteristics of the subordinate in determining the amount or quality of participation: (1) attitudes and maturity, (2) willingness or interest in becoming involved, and (3) knowledge of subject matter related to a goal.

Attitudes and maturity concern the extent to which an individual is willing and able to accept responsibility and to devote extra effort when required; the level of judgment that the person can apply; the willingness to accept the direction in which the goal takes the group, etc. If a person generally makes decisions based on emotional rather than factual considerations and does not analyze the facts carefully, then that person cannot participate at the same level, or in the same manner, as someone who has a more objective, rational, and careful approach.

In addition to emotional maturity, the level of participation should take into account the extent to which the subordinate wants to be involved. There are many reasons why a subordinate may not wish to participate in a particular goal. One reason includes the attitudes that the subordinate may have toward the goal. If a subordinate thinks that the manager or officer merely wants participation in order to have others share responsibility, then there might be a negative attitude towards participation. Similarly, if subordinates believe that a manager asks for participation only on a token basis and does not really want opinions or help with a decision or a goal, then subordinates often do not want to participate in the goal or in the decision of the goal.

Finally, a thorough knowledge of the subject matter involved is required. If the subordinate has little technical knowledge in the subject of a goal, then it would not be wise to give that subordinate a large voice in the decision related to that subject. A fire fighter who knows little about apparatus requirements could not contribute significantly in the selection of new auxiliary apparatus; furthermore, it is possible that this fire fighter would not want to be involved in the decision because of embarrassment at the lack of knowledge. Often lack of knowledge may not be based on education or experience of subordinates, but rather on the amount of information about the decision that is available, or can be made available, to them. Without such background data and perspective on the situation surrounding a decision or goal, the contribution by subordinates often cannot be a large one. Managers can also use the life cycle theory discussed previously in determining the extent of participation that a subordinate is capable of.

Issues Related to the Situation: There is another point that needs to be considered in deciding the level of participation. It concerns the requirements of the decision or the goal itself. In order to make a decision or to set a goal in the best possible way, two things have to be considered: (1) the technical quality requirement, or the knowledge that is required to make a successful decision or to set a high quality goal, and (2) the acceptance quality requirement, or the extent to which successful implementation of the decision or achievement of the goal requires acceptance on the part of the people who are affected. (See Chapter Three, section titled "The Work of Norman Maier," and refer to Fig. 3.4.)

What participation level to use is easiest to decide when technical quality requirements are highest and acceptance need is lowest. These decisions are made and then announced or explained to subordinates. The selection of a new piece of apparatus could be an example of this type of decision.

Decisions that require neither high technical knowledge nor widespread acceptance are rare, yet they are generally decisions where nobody really cares which way they are being made. Although a fire station's facilities must be kept clean, not many fire fighters would like to make the decision as to who should take out the garbage on a specific day, as long as that work assignment is a fair one. However, it is a decision that must be made that requires little technical quality and acceptance quality.

Decisions that require high acceptance for success could include increasing drill time or training time, running more inspections, or preparing more pre-fire plans. Most matters involving a significant amount of effort would be in this area, except for those decisions or goals where, in addition to acceptance, high technical knowledge is also required. For example, a decision to hold more drills does not require technical knowledge. Everybody knows what is involved if more drills are held. That does not mean that everybody can hold the drills, but everybody knows what the implications of the decision are and to what extent it would affect the people involved. Any goal or decision that requires employee contribution and that affects employees directly requires a high level of participation. Good skills are needed by the manager to lead the group to a joint decision so that there will be no resentment and so that all will exert the greatest effort toward making it successful.

Finally, goals and decisions where many technical problems are involved and where high acceptance is needed also require the greatest skill on the part of the manager. A goal to reduce the time required to lay a specified amount of hose and to charge it may require considerable technical knowledge to set it realistically; for successful implementation, a high level of acceptance is also necessary. In another example, a fire department may have decided that it wants to improve its attack time. One officer has been asked to investigate and recommend hose bed layout for the 2½-inch hose that would allow most rapid straight and reverse lay of 250 feet, and to comment to the chief when the recommendation will be completed. If accepted, the best time would be set as a goal for all companies that would be converted to the layout. To forecast how long it will take to make the studies and to make an estimate of the evolution time requires considerable knowledge about time studies and how to make them, as well as about the time that is required for various types of evolutions. On the other hand, to successfully implement the tests and to get accurate time values while the tests are being run requires the cooperation of all of the fire fighters involved.

Decisions of this type are most difficult. Technical knowledge on the part of the decision maker, and a high degree of acceptance on the part of those who have to implement the decision are necessary. They require the greatest skill on the part of the manager or officer involved in them. Yet by following three important guidelines, the manager will be able to decide on the best level of participation when setting any goals or making any decisions:

1. Before making a decision, or discussing a goal, a manager or officer can ask the question: What level of participation will lead to greatest success? This automatically ensures that the choice of participation level will receive serious consideration.

2. Looking at the technical quality requirement as well as the acceptance quality requirement of the decision or of the goal helps to narrow the choice of participation level and provides direction when approaching the goal or decision.

3. Looking at the capabilities and other factors related to the subordinate or subordinates — emotional maturity and attitudes, willingness to participate, and knowledge of subject matter — helps to pinpoint the best level of participation.

After determining the answers to these guidelines, a manager or officer is then able to follow through on the conclusion and can apply a wide range of leadership styles. A manager should neither be seen as autocratic nor as democratic; rather, a manager should select from the many dimensions of leadership styles those aspects that fit the needs of the situation and the subordinate. At one time a manager could rely on others to supply answers and decisions, or the manager could inform subordinates of a decision; at another time, the manager could be highly supportive and provide help, or may insist on strict compliance with previous requests without offering any additional resources. Such flexibility to adapt to the needs of the situation may easily be mistaken for unreliable behavior if the manager does not base reasons for decisions and choices of leadership style on careful thinking and practice and the ability to communicate decisions to subordinates. Consistency and reliability of leadership do not mean rigidity and a limited number of approaches; rather, leadership style relies upon the soundness of the underlying principles that guide the manager's actions and the ability to communicate these principles.

Relationship of Performance Appraisal to Goals Reviews

Almost every fire fighter or other subordinate wants to know, and should be kept informed about, how superiors feel about performance for three reasons: (1) most fire fighters or subordinates want to do the best they can do within the limits of their capabilities, and therefore need to know where they stand; (2) if superiors keep their subordinates informed on some regular basis, they will be more factual in the way they look at performance and will rely less on personal preferences and aspirations; and (3) if deficiencies in knowledge and skills are to be corrected, these must first be identified; a goals review session provides excellent opportunities for finding these deficiencies.

At one time performance appraisals were based primarily on the personal opinion of the superior; they were judgments about the subordinate's ambition, initiative, general reliability, loyalty, and so on. The supervisor would also evaluate quantity and quality of the work, punctuality, and other aspects of the subordinate's work that were somewhat more measurable. Very often, though, these were not based on facts but mainly on feelings, and therefore were heavily influenced by how much the boss liked the subordinate. Gradually there came greater awareness that appraisals of that type were grossly unfair to many people and especially favorable to those who managed to establish a friendly relationship with their bosses. As a result they often were resented and contributed to poor morale and controversy.

Many voices were raised, therefore, asking that performance appraisal be based on achievement. The best way to measure that, many people felt, was with goal accomplishment. However, this too turned out to leave a lot of freedom to the manager to use personal opinion in deciding whether the subordinate had good and acceptable reasons for missing a goal. Since many difficult goals are not achieved and many "easy" goals are exceeded, there is still a great deal left to personal feelings and to the opinion that a manager has about any one subordinate. Obviously, there will never be a system that can completely eliminate these defects. But a performance appraisal system that is based on the accountabilities discussed previously has the greatest chance, at the moment, to be fair to the organization and to the individuals involved. It concentrates on the effort that people devote towards the achievement of goals and on the quality of that effort.

If performance appraisals are to support a goals program they must be based on accountabilities, and they must provide an opportunity for the subordinate to participate in the process. The best performance appraisals are joint activities in which both the manager and the subordinate complete the required forms and then discuss any differences in the way they perceive the subordinate's performance in each accountability. Such comparisons, of course, require considerable skill on the part of the manager; even more important, the manager needs to establish and maintain a close personal acquaintance with the way the subordinate performs the work.

These performance reviews also serve as an excellent foundation for deciding what knowledge or skills a subordinate needs for better performance and as preparation for possible promotion. These knowledge and skill items can then become the basis for learning goals or for practice goals that the subordinate would strive to achieve.

One question that often arises about performance appraisal concerns the similarities and differences with goals reviews. The two are similar because both are detailed contacts between a manager and a subordinate. Both provide an opportunity for the manager to learn more about the interests, views, and aspirations of each subordinate. However, during a performance appraisal session the relative position between manager and subordinate is synonymous to their positions: the manager does the evaluating; the subordinate is evaluated. In a well-conducted performance appraisal the subordinate's views receive a full hearing; the evaluator /evaluatee relationship remains, and the effect on income and career is direct, though possibly not immediate.

During a goals review — if it is conducted in the spirit that will make it most effective — the discussion is between two people, both of whom have something to contribute to the achievement of the goal. The discussion does not center about what was done well and where there were shortcomings. Instead, it concentrates on what else is needed to achieve goals that have been set, what new goals should be set, what goals can be dropped, and, most important, how the manager can help with the subordinate's problems.

Including Developmental Goals in a Goals Program

A goals program that covers only operational goals that are concerned with performance objectives is not complete. Employees need to see that the manager or officer will include some goals that are intended not only for the organizational unit, but also for the subordinate. Such personal goals can involve personal development toward a career goal, assignments that provide satisfaction to the subordinate, or help with job problems that exist. A manager or officer who attempts to create a workable goals program has many opportunities to determine what the personal needs and aspirations of subordinates are, and what specific knowledge or skills would most help them improve their performance. Developmental goals thus become a regular part of the goals program, and provide chances for officers to be totally supportive. Thus, the organization and the manager prove they do not consider the goals program a one-way street toward greater output, but rather as a way to fulfill employee needs and the quantity and quality of the work to be done.

Motivational Impact of Goal Setting on Employees

Many managers believe that their function is to "motivate" their subordinates, and many believe that they can do so by being "good leaders." However, leadership — no matter how good or bad — cannot motivate the individuals who have an aversion to any form of work. These people rarely gain satisfaction from work because of their negation of it.

Most people, however, cannot be "motivated" by the qualities of their leader. Leadership, in whatever form it takes, usually proves too artificial to deal with the humanity of motivational feelings. Therefore, modern management concepts desire a management approach that creates a climate that will allow employees to *find* motivation.

There exists no clear formula for a manager to instill within an employee the desire to accomplish greater goals. Rather, motivation results from a combination of employee traits, manager actions, and the nature of the work. A manager or officer who tries to provide for many needs of workers and tries to help them attain greater satisfaction from their work usually finds that people are more motivated. Individuals vary greatly in the extent of motivation even if all individuals are experiencing the same type of leadership.

Yet most individuals are motivated to some extent by managers who are competent and who display their competency. The motivation that these individuals reach is evidenced in better performance. The more competent the manager is in providing job satisfaction for employees, the more employees will feel a happier job outlook. A well-operating goals program can help to bring a climate in which people can find motivation through most of the steps that make the program a good one in many ways:

- If the appropriate number of goals are set that properly challenge the subordinate, and if the priorities are selected so that they satisfy the desire to accomplish something worthwhile.

- The quality of goal statements contributes to the motivational climate because it removes uncertainties and questions about what is really expected and because good quality eliminates much confusion. Good goals give a feeling of direction that anyone can share. The goal to win the next game is a highly motivating one to every ball team, if it is within reach. In the work environment, goals are rarely as challenging or as motivating, but if they are equally clear they do have some of that challenge quality.

- The climate of motivation is enhanced if a manager exercises good judgment in providing help when needed, and refraining from becoming involved when subordinates would rather accomplish a goal independently.

- A manager who reviews progress on a fairly regular basis and who, during these reviews, explores what help the individual unit members need to achieve their goals provides the kind of support and the kind of secure feeling that can add substantially to job satisfaction.

- A manager who holds people accountable for the things they can achieve, and does not place blame or give credit for things they have no control over, adds a feeling of confidence that contributes to job satisfaction.

- The right amount of participation in goal setting brings many job satisfactions. If a manager or officer allows the proper amount of participation in those matters that affect subordinates, they gain the feeling that they have influence over their work and their future, and they know that they have a voice in deciding the way the work is to be done. That knowledge contributes greatly to the satisfaction they have in their work and to the confidence that they have in their organization and in their managers.

LINKS BETWEEN LINKING ELEMENTS

After discussing the linking elements concept in Chapter Four and devoting this chapter to managing by objectives, several ways in which goals/performance standards and the linking elements coexist in an organizational unit arise.

1. **Goals/Performance Standards and Coordination/Cooperation**

   • Goals reviews provide considerable information about where coordination problems may exist.
   • In eliminating coordination/cooperation problems, goals may have to be set if important matters are involved.
   • Goals can be useful in the establishment of improved coordination procedures.
   • Self-development goals for the officer may be involved pertaining to knowledge and skills of scheduling, preparing plans, and organizing for coordination.
   • Counseling skills are necessary in both areas.

2. **Goals/Performance Standards and Rules**

   • Goals reviews can provide information on which rules are inappropriate.
   • Goals can be set that pertain to the way a fire fighter adheres to rules.

3. **Goals/Performance Standards and Technical Competence**

   • Goals reviews provide information about developmental needs of subordinates.
   • Goals should be set to eliminate competence deficiencies.

4. **Goals/Performance Standards and Tangible Needs**

   • Career goals lead to satisfying the tangible needs.
   • Guidance in setting career goals occurs during goals reviews.
   • Competent goal setting on the part of the fire fighter or an officer can lead to greater respect by superiors, and thus help with the achievement of career plans.

5. **Goals/Performance and Psychological Needs**

   • In joint goal setting, the subordinate has an opportunity to influence the shape of the work.
   • Through effective goal setting the subordinate gains information about what occurs in the organization.
   • The open communications that must come from meaningful joint goal setting leads to a much more open general climate.

- Effective goal setting provides meaningful factual feedback on performance.
- When goal setting is done properly, the subordinate knows that superiors are aware of the individual's contributions to the organization.
- In goal setting the subordinate receives considerable guidance with career plans for personal development.
- With proper goal setting, performance appraisals are factual and fair, and subordinates are not held responsible for matters over which they have little control.

ACTIVITIES

1. Describe the purpose of the following terms in relation to managing by objectives:
   - (a) A goals program.
   - (b) Organizing.
   - (c) Follow-through.
   - (d) Implementation.
   - (e) Reviewing stage.
   - (f) Planning.
2. (a) You have decided that your individual long-run goal is to become a fire service specialist in the field of extinguishing systems. What short-run goals and action steps would you need to take to accomplish this goal?
   - (b) How would these steps differ from those needed to achieve a goal such as the preparation of a twenty-page research paper that has been assigned for completion in one month?
3. Do you feel an emergency situation should require joint decision making, authoritarian decision making, or a combination of the two? Explain your reasoning, and describe some of the problems that could occur should a fire officer feel that extensive joint decision making is highly desirable at the fire scene.
4. (a) Explain why it is necessary that, in order to be successful, a goal-setting program must satisfy both the needs of the organization and the needs of the employees.
   - (b) What are some of the general guidelines that an organization can make use of to fulfill the needs of both the organization and the employees within the organization?
5. Describe the differences between operational goals and developmental goals, and explain why it is important for organizational leaders to provide both types within a goals program.
6. (a) Explain the advantages of regular built-in reviews in a goals program.
   - (b) What are the most effective ways of carrying out these reviews?
7. In addition to your routine duties, you and your fellow fire fighters have been assigned the goal of completing a six-month physical fitness program. After six months, only one-half of the program has been completed.
   - (a) What factors should your superior consider when determining the

accountability for the goal not being fulfilled?

    (b) If you were the only fire fighter who had not completed this goal, what factors might your superior consider in reviewing your performance?

8. Following are hypothetical goals — some for a fire department, and some for its personnel. Determine whether each goal is philosophical, strategic, or operational. Then present a written explanation for each decision.

    (a) The department will extinguish fires as quickly as possible.

    (b) All manufacturing plants that make or employ hazardous materials will be inspected twice a year.

    (c) All fire fighters will participate in a physical fitness program beginning December 31.

    (d) I will be the best Emergency Medical Technician possible.

    (e) The community's radioactive materials plant will receive the best possible fire protection this department can offer.

    (f) I will make sure that I am well qualified in order to be considered for a promotion in the next year.

    (g) All training officers will instruct fire fighters in the handling of radiation emergencies by July 1.

9. Review the eight problem areas most often found in MBO goals programs. Then, with a group of your classmates, discuss the particular problems that could arise in the process of attaining each of the following goals and, for each goal, prepare a written summary statement that explains how your group of classmates thinks it could best alleviate these problems.

    (a) The preparation of two prefire plans.

    (b) Maintenance of station facilities.

    (c) Reduction of total response time.

    (d) Inspection of all one- and two-family dwellings during the next three years.

10. Explain how each of the following factors can be used to create a climate in which employees can find enhanced motivation for goal achievement.

    (a) Number of goals.   (d) Goals reviews.

    (b) Quality of goals.   (e) Accountability for goals.

    (c) Assistance with goals.   (f) Participation in goals.

BIBLIOGRAPHY

[1] Singular, Stephen, "Has MBO Failed?," *MBA; the Master in Business Administration*, MBA Communications, Inc., Oct. 1975, pp. 47–50.

[2] *Fire Protection Handbook*, 14th Ed., NFPA, Boston, 1976, pp. 9–4, 9–5.

[3] Drucker, Peter, *Management: Tasks, Responsibilities, Practices*, Harper & Row, New York, 1974.

Chapter Six

Management Functions
in the Fire Service

ORGANIZATION OF A FIRE DEPARTMENT

The first segment of this text (Chapters One through Five) primarily concerned itself with the essentially universal fundamental concepts and principles of modern management theory. The second segment of the text emphasizes fire service managerial situations. Thus, this chapter is intended as a "linking element" between the previously discussed fundamental concepts and principles of modern management theory and the application of these concepts and principles to specific functions in the fire service.

In Chapter One, "Introduction to Modern Management," mention is made of the uniqueness of the fire service and of its management needs. By presenting a brief history of the development of public fire protection and a discussion of a fire department's organization, areas of management responsibility, and the management roles of a department's administration, this chapter provides both an overview and the foundation for further detailed treatment of management functions unique within the fire service. Included in this in-depth treatment in the remaining chapters of the text are such topics as management of fire prevention activities, fireground command management functions, management of physical resources, fire service personnel management, and training as a management function.

The foundation of any organization is a set of valid objectives that provide both purpose and direction to the organization. Fire departments are no exception and must establish valid objectives in order to perform effectively. The NFPA's *Fire Protection Handbook* states that the traditional objectives commonly accepted by most fire departments are:[1]

1. To prevent fires from starting.
2. To prevent loss of life and property when fire starts.
3. To confine fire to the place where it started.
4. To extinguish fires.

However, the scope of these objectives has changed over the years since individuals realized the necessity for communal and organized fire fighting. In addition, the scope of responsibilities within the fire department has also changed. Highly trained medical professionals in fire departments have broadened responsibilities to include saving lives in disasters other than fires, such as airport crashes or automobile accidents. Today's fire chiefs and officers are no longer only fire scene leaders: they must also know how to train personnel, how to manage both physical and economic resources, and how to effectively manage an entire fire unit. All of these changes in roles and in fire department responsibility have evolved from years of increased technological development in the fire sciences.

History of Fire Departments

In 1648, New Amsterdam appointed five municipal "fire wardens" who had general fire prevention responsibilities; this is often considered to have been the first public fire department in North America. Thirty-one years later, Boston experienced a devastating conflagration that destroyed 155 buildings and led to the establishment of the first paid municipal fire department. Boston obtained for its department a fire engine from England, and employed twelve fire fighters and a fire chief. From its inception, the department used municipal fire fighters on a call basis; by 1711 fire wardens were appointed to respond to fires, and by 1715 Boston had six fire companies complete with English-manufactured engines. The concept of mutual aid also had its beginning in Boston: affluent citizens banded together to assist each other in salvaging valuables from fires in their businesses and homes.

In the latter half of the 19th century, fire departments developed further techniques for reducing water damage and increasing salvage from fires. Technological advances in manufacturing methods led to such improvements as the development of more effective fire hose, automatically raised ladders, progress in the area of hydraulics, and increased use of mechanized apparatus. In turn, such improvements led to the need for specific organizational and training techniques within fire departments. Thus, in 1889, Boston established a drill school; in 1914, New York City established a "Fire College." In 1976 a National Fire Academy, under the aegis of the federal government, became a reality. Some further developments that helped increase the efficiency of fire departments, as detailed in the NFPA *Fire Protection Handbook,* are as follows:[1]

> Two of the most significant advances since World War II have been the widespread adoption and use of adjustable spray nozzles and radio communications.
> Fire attack techniques have been improved through the use of preconnected attack lines and turret nozzles. Larger water tanks on pumping apparatus, and larger pumper-tankers have increased the efficiency of departments operating in locations that are remote from water sources. . . .
> More recent developments include: the use of computers for record

keeping, plotting, and assisting in dispatching; pumpers designed to allow nozzle operators to control the rate of flow from the nozzle; telescopic booms mounted on standard pumpers; and water additives that reduce friction loss in hose streams, . . .

Although developments and improvements in apparatus and fire fighting techniques can elevate a department's overall efficiency, a department cannot effectively employ such developments without proper organization. Although fire departments had small and simple beginnings, their early years reflected the need for internal organization. For example, in 1711 Boston fire wardens had, as their main duty, the supervision of citizen bucket brigades. Even though the fire fighting equipment used in colonial times seems simple when compared to present equipment (see Fig. 2.1 of Chapter Two, "Management Theory — Its Roots and Growth"), all "fire fighters" had to have an overall organizational plan or a leader to provide direction.

A fire department, like any other organization, is comprised of a group of people working together to achieve a common set of objectives. For any organization to function effectively, there should be some form of external structure for that organization; in addition, there should be an internal structure, usually in the form of ranks or roles of the individuals within that organization, in order to achieve the purposes of the organizational unit.

Organizational Components of a Fire Department

To help distinguish the differences between the organization of the fire service and the organization of businesses, it is helpful to consider the primary purposes of a fire department. NFPA 4, *Organization for Fire Services,** recommends three areas of fire department purpose: (1) control of combustibles and fire prevention work, (2) fire fighting and emergency services, and (3) governmental purpose. NFPA 4 describes these areas as follows:[2]

11. CONTROL OF COMBUSTIBLES AND FIRE PREVENTION WORK

11.1. Control of the Community Complex of Combustibles.

11.11. Purpose. Control of the community complex of combustibles should be undertaken by the fire department in furtherance of its fundamental purpose of protecting life and property from fire. The department program should be aimed at keeping the complex of combustibles with which man surrounds himself within reasonable limits. . . .

11.12. Inspection Program. The fire department should have a program under which its manpower should be constantly examining every part of the community where a fire problem may develop. . . .

11.13. Prefire Planning. One purpose of an inspection program should be the evaluation of the fire conditions it finds and planning how the fire department is to deal with these conditions. From data collected in in-

---

*A revision of NFPA 4 is up for adoption at the 1977 NFPA Fall Meeting. If adopted, it will also be renumbered to NFPA 1201.

spections, prefire study should determine how fires are likely to start and spread. Plans should be developed as to how fires are to be fought specifically, rather than in a general way. Decisions should be made on response to be provided, positions the fire companies will take and on all phases of manpower operations at fires. . . .

11.14. Law Enforcement. Another purpose of the inspection program should be the enforcement of community ordinances for the prevention and control of fire and the preparation of recommendations on situations which the ordinances do not cover. . . .

11.2. Consultation and Education.

11.21. Fire Department Consultation Service. The fire department should be prepared to consult with individuals who have fire problems and help in their solution. . . .

11.22. Education. The fire department program should include education of the public by all possible means so that individuals can achieve safety from fire in their homes and businesses.

12. FIRE FIGHTING AND EMERGENCY SERVICES

12.1. Scope of Services.

12.11. Purpose. The fire department should be organized to perform fire fighting and emergency services to protect life and property from fire.

12.12. Other Services. Other services demanded of the fire department, because the fire department force is available and because it has specialized training, should be undertaken only to the extent that they do not interfere with the department's basic purpose and that they are activities justifiably related to it.

12.2. Fire Fighting.

12.21. Capability. A fire department should be capable of preventing the small fire from becoming large and also be prepared to deal with a large fire. . . .

12.3. Emergency Services.

12.31. Potentially Dangerous Situations. A fire department should provide emergency services to avoid a fire or explosion situation and to safeguard life in a great variety of situations where prompt action is needed. Such situations then should be turned over to the appropriate utility or commercial service agency or to another city department. . . .

12.32. Fire Department Should Limit Emergency Service. Fire departments should not handle regularly situations for which there are other agencies available. Persons calling for such services should be asked to use other agencies with the equipment needed which is not, like fire department equipment, on standby for emergencies.

12.4. Rescue Work.

12.41. Fire and Emergency Rescue. Rescue work should be a primary responsibility of the fire department in connection with fires and emergencies. Departments should also be prepared to do rescue work and care of the injured in connection with traffic accidents, train wrecks, aircraft crashes, floods, windstorms and earthquakes. The fire department should handle the emergency phases of such situations, turning the injured over to doctors and hospitals as promptly as possible. . . .

12.42 Ambulance Service.   Fire department ambulance service should never be performed by the same manpower needed for fire prevention and fire fighting service. . . .

13. GOVERNMENTAL PURPOSE

13.1. Municipal Government.

13.11. Fire Department Should Perform a Municipal Function.   The fire department should perform a municipal or similar local government function. . . .

13.12. Fire Department Should Use Municipal Services Available.   The fire department should draw on administrative services of any municipality with which it is associated in connection with financial and personnel management, purchasing and similar matters. . . .

13.2. State-Municipal Relationships.

13.21. Statutes Affecting Fire Department.   Fire department purpose should reflect the provisions of statute law. . . .

Once an organization establishes its purpose, the "building," or framework, of the organization needs to be constructed.   As stated earlier in this chapter, this construction comes in the form of external and internal organization.

External Structure of a Fire Department: The external organization of a fire department shows the relationship between the operating divisions of the total organization.   Although this relationship is not intended to outline how to manage a fire department, it is a relationship that can be used to show the ways management can be utilized.   Figures 6.1, 6.2, and 6.3 show typical examples of the organizational structures of small, medium, and large fire departments.

Internal Structure of a Fire Department: Two components can be used to illustrate the internal organizational structure of a fire department.   One is the organizational principles, and the other is the roles of the individuals within the organization.   The latter component will be discussed later in this

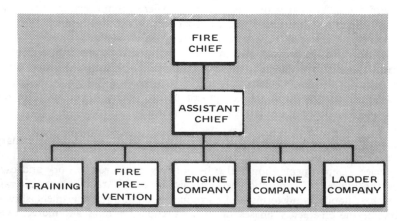

Fig. 6.1.   Typical organizational structure of a small fire department.

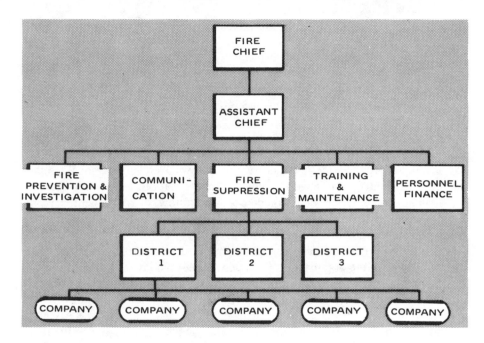

Fig. 6.2.   Typical organizational structure of a medium-sized fire department.

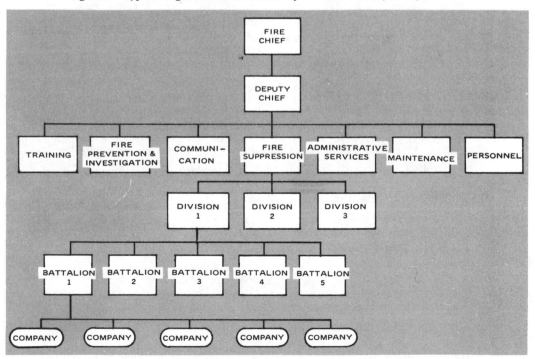

Fig. 6.3.   Typical organizational structure of a large fire department.

chapter in the section subtitled "The Role of Fire Service Officers in MBO Programs" (see text page 161).

The most basic organizational principle for a fire department is the division of work according to a well-arranged plan, both among the individuals in the organization and in the operating units. The plan should be based upon the functions that must be performed according to the fire department's purpose and duties, such as fire prevention, training, communications, etc.

Another organizational principle is the increased need for coordination as the department increases in size and complexity. A small department usually has a simple organizational structure that allows frequent personal contact among individuals, thus ensuring efficient coordination. However, because the structure of a larger department does not allow such frequent personal contact in order to achieve the department's objectives, more extensive coordination of the operating units is necessary.

Still another organizational principle is that lines of authority must be established. A simple line organization for a department would show an individual's relationship to the total organization. A more detailed line organization would show each operational unit or division with its relationship to the total organization. The principle of lines of authority also includes the extent of an individual's input into the decision-making process, and the individual's independence when working on assigned tasks. In many cases, individuals are given the responsibility of performing certain tasks, but are not given the authority to make some of the decisions necessary to complete the tasks. This tends to restrict the performance of the organization since these individuals will constantly need to consult their immediate supervisors when decisions have to be made. (See Figs. 9.3 and 9.4 in Chapter Nine.)

A final organizational principle is the unit of command in departmental structure. The delegation of conflicting orders from several superiors can result in confusion and inefficiency for the employee. On the other hand, an individual who receives orders from only one superior can usually perform more efficiently. Likewise, similar situations can occur to supervisors who guide too many individuals. In such instances the leaders can sometimes tend to commit a major portion of their time to supervising subordinates, thereby ignoring other important managerial duties.

AREAS OF MANAGEMENT RESPONSIBILITY

As stated in the excerpt from the NFPA *Fire Protection Handbook* on the first page of this text, the fire service has many unique management problems that range from the requirement of a distinct team spirit to the need to deal with the public in both minor and major crisis situations. Despite its unique problems, the fire service has generally performed well for many years. Over a 50-year period, only about twenty percent of the fires dealt with resulted in a loss exceeding $500, and only about 500 out of one million fires extended to a loss exceeding $250,000: these facts are significant testimony to the effectiveness of the fire service and its management.[3]

The operation of a fire department is normally a function of local government (in the case of a fire district, possibly the only function), which supports the service and is responsible for the level of service rendered. According to the NFPA's *Fire Protection Handbook*, the operation of the fire department involves three major areas of responsibility for the governing body:[3] (1) fiscal management, (2) personnel management, and (3) productivity. In general, fiscal management practices follow those used by the government agency supporting the department and include budgeting, cost accounting, personnel costs including payroll, and purchasing or procurement costs. Fire department personnel management is involved to some degree in the recruitment, selection, and promotion of personnel needed to fill various positions in the organization. In general, these matters are governed by law, by personnel agencies (including civil service authorities), by direct decisions of the governmental agency operating the fire department, and by codes and standards such as NFPA 1001, *Standard for Fire Fighter Professional Qualifications*. (See Chapter Eleven, "Personnel Management," for more detailed discussion of personnel management functions in the fire service.)

Productivity is the most difficult function in the fire department for management to measure. The basic objective is the protection of life and property, which involves two major activities: (1) control of hazards to minimize fire losses and to prevent fires, and (2) dealing with actual fires and emergencies to keep suffering and losses at a minimum. It is difficult to assess the number of fires and the suffering that have been prevented by fire department activities; likewise, the fact that most fires are suppressed with minimum losses and injuries does not indicate conclusively that an adequate level of fire department service has been provided. Often, major fires and emergencies arise from combinations of circumstances beyond the immediate control of fire department management. Therefore, productivity can also be concerned with maintenance of reasonable standards of organization based upon local and national fire loss experience. Fire department management is responsible for maintaining highly trained and efficient operational units to perform assigned tasks both in the prevention and suppression of fires.

Fiscal Management

As stated previously, fiscal management refers to the economic factors involved in the operation of a fire department. Although it can easily be seen that accounting and budgeting are involved in fiscal management, there is also a great degree of planning and research that is involved in assessing current and future developments and needs before budget proposals can be formulated. After the actual budget is submitted, fiscal management further includes the wise purchasing of equipment and supplies, and the storage of these supplies.

Planning and Research: The responsibility for planning in a fire department varies. In some jurisdictions, all department heads are required to submit estimates of projected capital equipment needs for five years in advance. In rapidly developing communities, some of the larger fire departments have planning staffs to assist in the planning of new fire stations, the replacement and possible relocation of old stations, and also for replacement of apparatus. However, in the vast majority of communities, planning is far less sophisticated. City administrations may approve citizens' demands for better protection of areas remote from existing fire stations, and the fire department may merely be consulted as to a suitable location. Outside consultants may also be employed to recommend relocation and consolidation of fire stations, or fire department annual reports could be used to recommend various improvements. Whatever method is used for department planning, the NFPA *Fire Protection Handbook* describes some recommendations for planning sessions as follows:[4]

> It would appear desirable for all fire departments to have regularly scheduled planning sessions presided over by the fire chief or the executive assistant, with participation by officers responsible for the various staff services. . . . most municipalities have a planning board or other official planning agency which often has considerable resources, including federal funds and information, that could be of value to the fire department planning effort. Regular contact should be maintained by the fire department administration and the planning agency. . . .

Good planning, however, relies heavily upon research that reveals needs for planning or budgeting in particular areas. Few departments, however, are adequately staffed or financed to support significant research activity. Limitation in research is largely due to the fact that most fire departments are relatively small organizations that do not have sufficient personnel to meet their on-going obligations for furnishing fire protection. True research into such areas as efficient equipment design or improved turnout equipment is generally beyond the capability of most fire departments.

Research can be the major factor in effectively pinpointing needs; therefore, fire department management should conduct research in both general and specific areas, as suggested by NFPA 4, *Organization for Fire Services:*[5]

> . . . The fire chief should be concerned with two areas of planning. One of these involves operations of the fire department itself. The other involves the relationship of the fire department with other city departments and the overall community growth. The chief should be intimately aware of the overall planning for community development. . . .

There are many avenues to use for fire department research. One could be compiling tables, flow charts, or graphs in order to discern areas of need or expansion. Table 6.1 shows a percentage breakdown of fire department calls and a classification of fires that could be used for apparatus planning and procurement, or for allocation of resources for inspection into properties that are fire risks in the community.

Table 6.1 Example of Statistical Research for
Fire Department Management*

Fire Department Calls	Percent	Classification of Fires	Percent
Fires	38.0	Dwellings	35.2
Emergencies other than fires	23.6	Other buildings	10.2
Rescue calls	9.5	Rubbish outdoors	10.8
Ambulance calls	21.0	Trees, brush, grass	21.0
False alarms	7.9	Miscellaneous fires outdoors	5.0
	100.0	Vehicles	17.5
		Aircraft	0.2
		Ships and boats	0.1
			100.0

*NFPA 4, Organization for Fire Services, NFPA, Boston, 1971, p. 4–6.

NFPA's *Fire Protection Handbook* recommends other research sources that are available to fire department management. One is utilizing a fire record program such as *Uniform Fire Incident Reporting System* (UFIRS), developed by NFPA in cooperation with a selected group of fire departments.[6] The NFPA's research division also can be of direct help and benefit to fire departments. In addition, the International Association of Fire Fighters (IAFF) operates a research department that is available to assist its local affiliates with problems on request.

Accounting and Budgeting: The second area of management responsibility in fiscal management is accounting and budgeting. Accounting is the detailed description of money spent and money earned from a budget. According to NFPA 4, *Organization for Fire Services*, accounting involves two main areas of management responsibility: (1) system of accounts, and (2) bookkeeping:[7]

> **51.11. System of Accounts.** The fire chief should set up a system of accounts for financial administration. The system should keep a record of funds received by the department and funds expended. Furthermore, the system should enable the fire chief to constantly analyze how the money is spent to show how, if necessary, to change the department's operations to get better results for the money. . . .
>
> **51.12. Bookkeeping.** The system of accounts should include books of original entry and ledgers. Books of original entry should include a general journal and register for cash receipts, purchase vouchers, contracts, material issued, and payroll. Ledgers should be a general ledger and subsidiary ledgers for revenue, appropriation expenditures, stores, bank funds, and property.

Budgets are the work programs for fire departments expressed in dollars and cents. One part of the budget lists the services, activities, and projects for the department with the appropriate or projected expense of each. The other part lists the income to be used to meet the total expenses. Chapter Ten, "Management of Physical Resources," can be consulted for further, more extensive treatment of the accounting and budgeting process.

Purchasing and Storing: The final area of management responsibility in fiscal management is purchasing and storing, which includes records of procurement of budgetary needs and the authorized storage of the acquisitions. The NFPA *Fire Protection Handbook* states that procurement of fire department equipment and supplies is usually done through purchasing departments.[8] Common items are usually requisitioned from the purchasing agency and charged to the appropriate fire department account. Items of a specialized nature, however, require the preparation of purchasing specifications by the fire department, approval from the purchasing department, and advertisement for bids. The fire chief, with the advice of the apparatus and equipment superintendent, should determine whether or not proposals submitted by bidders adequately meet specifications.

When emergency purchases must be made, most departments require estimates from several suppliers. If the expenditure is small and if funds are available from the budget, the chief can authorize the expenditure. If funds are not available in the budget, authorization and funds must be obtained from the municipal management or finance officer.

After items are purchased, procedures for storage of the supplies can be followed, as recommended by the NFPA *Fire Protection Handbook:*[8]

> . . . All fire department supplies are inventoried and kept under lock to be issued only on requisition by the supply officer. Some large fire departments have a supply department. More commonly, office and fire station supplies are kept in a headquarters storage area, and maintenance supplies are kept in a stock room in the fire department shop. Regular annual inventories are required from fire officers covering all items issued to the various fire companies and fire stations. Usually a senior captain is designated as station officer or station commander responsible for all station supplies and equipment.

Management of Fire Department Personnel

In order for a fire department to operate effectively and efficiently, personnel should be selected who meet the appropriate standards. Normally, recruitment of personnel is seldom a paid fire department responsibility except in those cases where there is no local governmental personnel agency. NFPA 4, *Organization for Fire Services*, recommends that the fire chief function as the personnel officer, and that personnel standards and procedures be established at that management level.[9] The department's chief may choose to delegate authority in order to provide specific direction and control of department members. For example, in some departments the chief may decide that an assistant chief should specialize in personnel matters in order to become department personnel officer. The specific personnel activities that might be conducted by a fire department, however, may depend on the scope of personnel services provided by municipal or state personnel or civil service agencies. State, provincial, and civil service commission legislation may set specific standards of pay, hours, working conditions, working schedules, and other features of personnel policy that would limit the authority of the municipality and the fire department. (See Chapter Eleven, "Fire Service Personnel Management," for a more detailed description of the effect of authority as it relates to personnel matters.)

Personnel Standards: The personnel standards of a fire department should be designed to establish and maintain a competent and well-trained force by recruiting highly qualified individuals and by providing an interesting and useful career from recruitment to retirement. After recruitment has been accomplished, there are various areas where personnel standards apply, as summarized from NFPA 4, *Organization for Fire Services:*[10]

- Attendance and departmental duties.
- Annual physical examination.
- Safe working conditions.
- System of ranks.
- Disciplinary action.

Selection, Recruitment, and Promotion: A detailed discussion of the selection process for management, including procedures for management responsibility from the initial interview to salary administration, training and development, and career development, is contained in Chapter Eleven, "Fire Service Personnel Management," in the section subtitled "Personnel Management Functions." For the scope of this chapter, management's responsibility can best be summarized as the selection of the most qualified candidate for the fire department's most effective operation.

Promotion within the department's ranks should also be accomplished with the same overall objective as selection. NFPA 4, *Organization for Fire Services*, suggests that the following steps could be used by the chief in a promotion program in a department.[11] These are summarized as follows:

- Preparing lists of members for promotion.
- Arranging assignments so that promotion candidates may have a variety of duties and experience in various staff work.
- Requiring supervisors to report on the aptitudes and attitudes of candidates to aid in evaluating qualifications for promotion.
- Requiring candidates to successfully complete an in-service training program.
- Arranging assignments for education at accredited schools.

Management of retirement procedures is the final area of responsibility in personnel management. A compulsory retirement age should be established that would include age and ability, rather than length of service. Ideally, a sound retirement system would provide for retirement on the basis of age, years of service, and physical and mental condition of members as related to the members' duties.[11]

Productivity Management

As previously stated, productivity is an area of management responsibility that is difficult to measure or define. Productivity can encompass not only the effectiveness of the fire department, but also the public image of the department. Therefore, management's area of responsibility in obtaining the productivity essential to successful fire department operation is to ensure that a department operates as efficiently and effectively as possible in spite of any limitations in personnel or equipment, or any obstacles that exist while responding to fires in a municipality. Although this may seem a difficult task, there are many ways a fire department manager can ensure high productivity, including those outlined in the following paragraphs.

Records and Reports: According to the NFPA *Fire Protection Handbook*, a record system should be provided to supply the fire chief and the officers with data that indicates the department's effectiveness in preventing and fighting fires. The record system would provide data on fire department activities that the chief can use as a basis for making recommendations to city officials and to the public, and would provide a statistically accurate summary of fire department operation. (See Table 8.2 of Chapter Eight, "Loss Prevention Activities — Prefire Planning and Related Functions," for typical fire department management records and reports.)

Water Procedures: In order to ensure adequate water supplies for fire fighting, NFPA 4, *Organization for Fire Services*, suggests that a chief assign a water officer to help maintain regular contact with the managers of public and private water systems, and to keep the department informed about water available for fighting fires. Additionally, it is recommended that each company in the fire department maintain a water resources map of its first-due area that would indicate:[12]

- Location and size of mains in public or private water systems.
- Indications of any sections where insufficient flows or pressures will require special operations.
- Locations and capacities of hydrants or insufficient systems, data on location, and capacity of auxiliary water supplies.

A department training program might include information and instructions on available water sources or field exercises that would educate fire fighters in hydrant locations for fighting possible fires.

Operating Procedures: All operating procedures of the department, such as duty requirements of its members and response procedures for fires and emergencies, are recommended by NFPA 4 to be published and circulated to all members of the department. To ensure the most effective results, these regulations should be enforced and revised where necessary.

Fire Investigation: According to NFPA 4, the investigation of fires is basic to good fire department management since it results in bringing to light factors that can be used to lessen the number and severity of fires in the future. The findings from these investigations can also be used as a basis for fire prevention work in educating the public and in inspecting municipal properties.[13]

Training: Chiefs, chief officers, and training officers can be used in formulating, guiding, and evaluating a department's training program. Training sessions could be used to discover capabilities and deficiencies of department members, and could cover such topics as:[14]

- Company management.
- Instructor training.
- Fire prevention techniques.
- Fire cause determination.
- Communications procedures.
- Maintenance practices.
- Tactical operations.

Communications: Communications for a fire department involves not only emergency calls from the public, but also en route and fireground communications between fire department personnel. Additionally, alarm and signaling systems from individual properties and street box alarm signals are included. Regular testing and inspection of all means of communications can ensure adequate response time for effective fireground activity. (See also Chapter Ten, "Management of Physical Resources," section subtitled "Communications Equipment" for a more detailed discussion of this topic.)

Equipment and Buildings: Chapter Ten, "Management of Physical Resources," gives considerable explanation of management's responsibility in assessing and providing adequate facilities and equipment for effective department operation. For the scope of this chapter, however, fire department management is considered as being responsible for evaluating and upgrading department facilities, apparatus, and personnel equipment in order to ensure good performance and safety on the job.

Public Relations: NFPA 4 suggests two main areas of responsibility in public relations for a fire department:[15] (1) promoting public awareness of the fire department, and (2) promoting public understanding of fire. Chapter Seven, "Fire Prevention Activity Management — Codes, Operational Tasks, and Inspections," provides greater examination of the relationship between the productivity of the fire department and public relations in the section subtitled "Fire Prevention Operational Tasks and Concerns."

ADMINISTRATIVE MANAGEMENT

As stated in the discussion of the internal organizational structure of a fire department, the roles of the individuals are vital for good organization. These various roles and their individual responsibilities ensure a division of labor in the fire service and a knowledge of a member's relationship with the department and with the management.   Chapters Four and Five have discussed the importance and scope of effective management organization authority and decision making; in the fire service, the same principles hold true. Just as business managers have assistant managers and department heads to aid them in their decision-making and leadership techniques, so the fire chief is assisted by officers and aides for the decisions that must be made in a fire department.   According to the NFPA *Fire Protection Handbook,* the chief of the fire department is usually assisted by three ranks of officers who have their respective roles and responsibilities: (1) chief officers, (2) chiefs' aides, and (3) fire officers.[16]

Chief Officers

At least one deputy fire chief who is responsible for the department in the absence of the chief officer and who assists in overall operational command at fires is needed in all fire departments.   In some small paid fire departments, the deputy chief is in command of one of the regular work shifts, while platoon captains are in charge of the other work shifts, thus performing dual roles as company officers and duty shift commanders.   A different arrangement in some departments would be making the platoon chief in charge of each duty shift. The platoon chief supervises the various fire companies through their officers, and responds to all alarms for structural fires and other working fires in a command car.   In addition, the platoon chief is also in charge of operations and has the authority to call off-shift help when needed, or to request additional mutual aid assistance.   The senior platoon chief or deputy chief is in charge of the department in the absence of the fire chief unless there is a higher ranking administrative deputy chief designated for this responsibility.

Chiefs' Aides

One of the positions most important to fire department efficiency is that of chiefs' aides or assistants.   Aides are experienced officers or fire fighters who are assigned to work directly as assistants to various chief officers rather than as members of a company team.   Aides are administrative assistants in the operation of the command; generally they operate the command car, handle and channel most fireground radio communications with the alarm center, and assist their chief in numerous other ways, including helping to size-up a fire and directing placement of fire companies as determined by the chief.   The assistant is essential to efficient management and operations since the chief officers they work for must prepare hundreds of fire, personnel, and inspection reports while also answering alarms and supervising the administration of companies in their districts.

Fire Officers

Every fire company or similar fire fighting unit should be under the supervision of a qualified company officer both when in quarters or when responding to alarms, or when making in-service inspections. In many fire departments company officers hold the rank of fire captain, and there is a fire captain assigned to each duty shift of each fire company. The captains are also used as relief chiefs when one or more of the chiefs on the duty platoon are absent, and is station commander and coordinator of operations in the absence of a chief officer.

Some fire departments also have a rank of "sergeant" for fire officers; actually, sergeants are third-grade officers who are in charge of work shifts in their assigned companies. While sergeants often function as lieutenants by doing the work of lieutenants, they rank below lieutenants in the chain of command both in quarters and on the fireground.

ROLE OF FIRE SERVICE OFFICERS IN MBO PROGRAMS

Chapter Five, "Managing by Objectives," detailed the goals and stages in MBO programs. This chapter will explore the roles of the chief, the intermediate level officers, and the company officers in a successful MBO program, and will form a basis for the detailed presentation of fire service management activities presented in the rest of the text.

The Chief

First and foremost, the chief of a department provides direction for the members of the organization and for the operation of the organizational unit. This means that the chief should, in conjunction with the community political structure, determine the long-range goals for the activities of the department. In order to do this, the chief must have the ability to foresee the future of the operation of the department by preparing for the problems and the needs that could occur in years to come. In this way the entire department can gradually take the necessary steps in anticipation of, and for laying foundations for, needed changes. For example, a new fire station may take decades to build from the time when the department recognizes the present need for the station. Or, a department may have to wait three to six years before large pieces of apparatus are delivered. The chief should therefore be able to plan for these needs and should be able to cope with deficiencies in the existing facilities or equipment in order to ensure stable department operation.

Setting Goals: Long-range planning obviously is not the only thing a chief has to do. Long-range plans become long-range goals, and long-range goals need short-range goals (or enabling goals) to support them.

These latter goals, however, often involve officers and fire fighters who may be several levels removed from the chief. To achieve the desired results, the chief should guide and lead the department members indirectly toward the establishment and achievement of these lower-level goals. The long-range goal of constructing a new fire station, staffing it, and equipping it with apparatus would require yearly strategic and operational goals. In the year during which the decision is made to seek approval for the new station, these goals might involve only the chief, who might obtain proposals from consultants for a study to determine where the new station might be located, and to recommend which consultant should be selected. Even at this early stage, however, there might be a need for a series of goals at the chief's level and at lower levels to acquaint the community with the reasons why another station is required and what the benefits to the community would be. Such goals might involve only a few officers, or they might lead to involvement of all companies; members could conduct fire station tours, maintain contact with the community through the news media, or direct personal efforts to neighbors, friends, and acquaintances. In later years, there would be other goals involving decisions about features of specific pieces of apparatus and for equipment to go in the new station, based on past and projected records of fire department activities.

Using Linking Elements: The chief's role in planning, organizing, and implementing through the goal-setting process requires familiarity and use of the linking elements concept discussed in Chapters Four and Five. It is the chief's role to ensure coordination and cooperation between the different divisions in the department, particularly if there are staff divisions that are concerned with matters affecting maintenance, equipment decisions, etc.

Alignment of rules to the organization is also of importance when they pertain to the maintenance and use of equipment and apparatus. These rules should be reviewed from time to time to ensure that they are still appropriate for the department's needs and for its members. The chief should take an active role in ensuring that such a review does take place from time to time, that any rule changes that are recommended are approved or revised, and in helping to see that all rules are observed while they are in force.

A third linking elements concept that the chief could apply would be the concern with the total development of the department's human resources. The chief's role to set policy with respect to training and to help the various units develop their training goals would be of importance when building and apparatus maintenance and the use of equipment are involved. The training should be done to ensure that each unit keeps abreast of the changes and developments in technology that have an impact on the decisions in these fields.

If apparatus, facilities, and equipment are concerned in long-range plans, there might seem to be a few ways to provide tangible rewards in the form of pay to the staff members of the department. However, hidden tangible rewards exist from the allocation of responsibilities for equipment among different fire stations and companies. New apparatus should be assigned to members of the department, and decisions involving re-equipping or obtaining new equipment should be made. The assignment and procurement of these materials can have a significant impact not only on an individual's tangible needs, but also on the morale of all personnel involved. The motivational climate in the department will be affected by the way decisions are made and by the "image," or pride, that is evoked from obtaining new equipment or a new building.

Intermediate Level Officers

Deputy chiefs, battalion chiefs, and officers in staff positions such as those in bureaus concerned with buildings or apparatus have important roles in helping the department achieve the goals it has set. These intermediate level officers should help provide direction and recommendations, and should perform their functions competently in order for a department to achieve the highest possible level of performance. This means that all deputy and battalion chiefs who are involved with the chief in all major aspects of a building program and the purchase of apparatus in their respective units should also apply the linking elements concept to their decisions and their leadership techniques. Not only should these officers be involved in some of the goals of the department, but they may also be deeply involved in coordination and in providing psychological satisfactions.

These officers, however, are of utmost importance to the chief's overall decisions. The chief can use these specialists for training sessions to acquaint officers and fire fighters with the facts, respective advantages, and disadvantages of equipment that could be considered. Officers and fire fighters would thus be better prepared to participate in the formation of decisions. The potential gains from this sharing of information can bring about an even greater exchange of ideas between staff and line, better decisions from participation by more fully informed staff members, and greater personal satisfaction from participation in the decision-making process as well as from the results of the better decisions.

Company Officers

The company officers have the task of translating some of the strategic goals and the operational goals into action steps. This applies not only to the operational goals on the specific aspects of the equipment and maintenance decisions, but also to the training and development goals. The specialists in staff departments, the training officer, and knowledgeable representatives of the equipment manufacturers can be brought in to help lift the knowledge level of the company's members so that they can gain the maximum benefit from new equipment, supplies, and from new techniques. Even the representatives of industrial chemical manufacturers can sometimes be very helpful in providing ideas that would stimulate desire for even better care and maintenance of facilities. At the same time there are major responsibilities for the line officer in finding ways to help fire fighters gain psychological rewards from their work on maintenance or housekeeping, and in the use and purchase of equipment and supplies. This may seem to be a difficult task, but opportunities for providing social and esteem satisfaction are widespread in allocating work assignments that are seen as desirable, in giving recognition through appropriate participation with decisions, and in giving the general public and special groups opportunities to inspect the station and equipment during Fire Prevention Week or on other occasions.

Officer Management of a Goals Program

Every fire department needs to accomplish different goals during any period and, from period to period, the goals change. To outline in this chapter a comprehensive set of strategic and operational goals that may have wide application is impossible. However, a hypothetical list of goals with their appropriate organizational level goals may help in detailing officer roles in MBO programs.

- **Examples of Department Mission Statements**

    1. To provide sufficient stations located to supply the best possible protection of life and to minimize damage to property.

    2. To provide the necessary apparatus and equipment for fire fighters to carry out their responsibilities in the protection of life and property.

    3. To minimize cost to taxpayers.

- **Examples of Chief's Strategic Goals**

    1. Establish and achieve apparatus and equipment performance goals.

    2. Establish and achieve goals related to location and structure of fire stations.

    3. Establish and achieve public information goals on need for apparatus.

    4. Establish and achieve stringent, but realistic, budgets.

- **Examples of Station Strategic Goals (for officer in charge of station)**

    1. Establish and achieve goals related to adaptation of apparatus and equipment to the district's needs.

    2. Establish and achieve goals related to reduction in turnout time.

    3. Establish and achieve building maintenance goals.

    4. Establish and achieve goals relating to budget input procedures.

    5. Establish and achieve goals relating to greater efficiency in attack preparation.

- **Examples of Chief's Operational Goals**

    1. Ensure that tests to evaluate alternative hose loadings and breathing apparatus mountings are completed by December 31.

    2. Obtain agreement of department officers on new apparatus to be requested by October 25.

    3. Arrange for three articles on equipment needs in local newspapers by July 1.

    4. Achieve agreement with municipal manager on department budgetary needs by end of next month.

    5. Ensure submittal of a report on the impact of the proposed new hospital on department fire protection capability by August 31.

- **Examples of Station Operational Goals (for officer in charge of station)**

    1. Obtain data and prepare specific recommendations on changes in the layout of the crew's quarters by September 1.

    2. Analyze available breathing equipment and recommend specifications by October 1.

    3. Reduce building housekeeping and maintenance time by ten per-

cent without reduction in cleanliness or building operation efficiency by October 15.

4. Obtain agreement on revised kitchen procedures by July 10.

- **Examples of Company Officer Operational Goals**

1. Make three time study tests of experimental hose layout changes by September 1.

2. Obtain fire fighter agreement or recommendations on changes in quarters by August 20.

3. Reduce turnout time by twenty seconds by July 1.

4. Set up quarterly goals review sessions with each company member to prepare developmental goals. First set of meetings will take place during the week of March 1.

5. Take course in Advanced Fire Tactics and obtain grade of B or better by July 1.

6. Ensure that Fire Fighter Smith thoroughly understands revised prefire planning symbols by May 1.

- **Examples of Company Officer Action Steps**

1. Write and submit report on time study tests by first week in March.

2. Meet with each company member individually by second week in March to gain personal feelings on desirable changes in quarters.

3. Meet with fire fighters on September 1 to prepare suggestions on ways to improve kitchen cleanup.

4. Have Fire Fighter Smith study prefire planning symbols on Wednesday afternoon. Prepare an exam, and set up another study session if at least eighty percent is not scored on the test.

5. Register for Advanced Fire Tactics class at an accredited college on January 12.

Officers would rarely write out a complete set of goals and action steps except possibly during the initial stages of becoming acquainted with the way a goals program works. Normally, only two or three goals might be in writing and only important action steps might be on a calendar or in a notebook. If working with goals is to be a way of life, the mechanical aspects must be informal and the paperwork minimal.

MANAGING THE OPERATION OF A FIRE DEPARTMENT

The discussion of the topics presented in this chapter — organization of a fire department, areas of management responsibility, and administrative management and roles of fire service officers in MBO programs — is intended to serve as an overview and basis for the presentation of materials contained in the remaining chapters of this text. What was briefly dealt with here will be discussed in greater detail in Chapters Seven through Twelve; however, to better understand the uniqueness of the management functions of the fire service, it is important to keep in mind the organizational principles of management and the development of various management concepts.

ACTIVITIES

1. In what ways have the traditional objectives of a fire department been revised and expanded?

2. Trace the historic development of fire departments by briefly describing some of the more significant advances during the following time periods.
    (a) The 1700s.
    (b) The late 1800s.
    (c) Post World War II.
    (d) The present day.

3. What are the primary purposes of a fire department?

4. Briefly explain the external and the internal structure of a fire department. How is each structural form important to the overall organizational structure of a fire department?

5. Identify the management responsibilities that would be involved in each item in the following list of managerial tasks:
    (a) Procurement of a new pumper.
    (b) Replacement of the existing fire station.
    (c) Retirement of a fire officer.
    (d) Formation of a budget.
    (e) Ensuring adequate water supplies.
    (f) Training a member of the department.

6. (a) Why is productivity management difficult to define?
    (b) In what ways can a fire department ensure high productivity?

7. What are the roles of chief officers? Of chiefs' aides? Of fire officers?

8. Using examples of your own, describe how a department chief could include the entire department in setting goals.

9. (a) How are linking elements used in the chief's goal-setting process in long-range goals?
    (b) How can intermediate level officers and company officers provide satisfaction of some of the linking elements?

10. You are the chief of a fire department in a rapidly expanding community. The growth of your community has necessitated that your department increase its personnel and facilities. Using what you have learned about areas of management responsibility from this chapter, briefly outline what you would do to ensure high efficiency as each of the following changes is made in your department.
    (a) The addition of ten new members to your department.
    (b) The need for two new pieces of fire fighting apparatus.
    (c) The construction of a new fire station.
    (d) The need for a revised budget that would include new members and new expenses.

BIBLIOGRAPHY

[1] *Fire Protection Handbook*, 14th Ed., NFPA, Boston, 1976, p. 9–4.

[2] NFPA 4, *Organization for Fire Services*, NFPA, Boston, 1971, pp. 3–9.

[3] *Fire Protection Handbook*, 14th Ed., NFPA, Boston, 1976, p. 9–9.

[4] ——, p. 9–20.

[5] NFPA 4, *Organization for Fire Services*, NFPA, Boston, 1971, p. 24.

[6] *Uniform Fire Incident Reporting System* (UFIRS), NFPA, Boston, 1977.

[7] NFPA 4, *Organization for Fire Services*, NFPA, Boston, 1971, p. 28.

[8] *Fire Protection Handbook*, 14th Ed., NFPA, Boston, 1976, p. 9–23.

[9] NFPA 4, *Organization for Fire Services*, NFPA, Boston, 1971, pp. 34–35.

[10] ——, pp. 35–37.

[11] ——, p. 40.

[12] ——, pp. 47–48.

[13] ——, p. 79.

[14] ——, p. 96.

[15] ——, p. 43.

[16] *Fire Protection Handbook*, 14th Ed., NFPA, Boston, 1976, pp. 9–17 — 9–18.

Chapter Seven

Fire Prevention Activities —
Codes, Operational Tasks,
and Inspections

OBJECTIVES OF FIRE PREVENTION

The major part of a fire department's resources — including personnel, equipment, facilities, and support services — is committed to fire suppression efforts. There are, however, additional tasks performed by fire suppression personnel that are not tactical operations, but are equally important. These are fire prevention activities, prefire planning, and training. This chapter discusses how management techniques are applied to fire prevention activities, and how fire departments perform the invaluable service of aiding in the fire prevention effort through enforcement of codes, inspections, and involvement in related operational tasks. Chapter Eight deals with loss prevention activities including prefire planning, and Chapter Twelve covers training as a management function.

The participation of fire suppression personnel in fire prevention activities is as necessary as their participation in tactical operations. Because the majority of the fire department's resources are committed to suppression activities and are systematically distributed throughout the protected area, it is important that these resources also be committed to fire prevention efforts.

Good fire department objectives can provide the proper approach for involvement in fire prevention activities. Departments that are committed to a comprehensive fire prevention and inspection program can utilize fire suppression personnel on a regular basis for routine inspections within their first due response area, and reserve fire prevention personnel for follow-up inspections, enforcement, and special technical inspections. The total involvement of all personnel, particularly those assigned to suppression activities, should not only decrease the incidence of fire, but should also demonstrate maximum utilization and competent management.

Fire department management is responsible for maintaining highly trained and effective operational units to perform tasks involving both fire suppression and fire prevention.* The degree of competency achieved by a department in these areas reflects the abilities of a department's management.

The 14th Edition of the National Fire Protection Association's *Fire Protection Handbook* describes fire prevention as follows:[1]

> Fire prevention encompasses all of the means used by fire departments to decrease the incidence of uncontrolled fire. The fire prevention methods employed by fire department personnel involve a combination of engineering, education, and enforcement. Good engineering practices can do much to provide built-in safeguards that help to prevent fires from starting; such practices also help to limit the spread of fire should it occur. Education is the method used to instruct and inform groups and individuals of the dangers of fire and its possible effects. Enforcement is the legal means of correcting deficiencies that pose a threat to life and property. Enforcement is implemented when other methods fail. In addition, fire investigation aids fire prevention efforts by indicating problem areas that may require additional educational efforts or legislation to correct deficiencies.

Beginnings of Fire Prevention

One of the first tasks of the early settlers in the Boston area was to build shelter against the harsh New England winters. Using local materials, they constructed wooden houses with thatched roofs similar to the ones they were accustomed to in Europe. The chimneys were made from wooden frames covered with mud or clay. Exposure to the elements dried the thatch and washed or blew away mud or clay that protected the wooden frames of the chimney stacks. Such structures invited catastrophe through fire; burning embers, drawn up the chimneys, ignited the roofs and set the houses ablaze.

Early Fire Laws: Recognizing these construction hazards, the town fathers of the Bay Colony outlawed thatched roofs and wooden chimneys. A fine of ten shillings (a large sum in those days) was levied on any householder who had a chimney fire. This encouraged people to keep their chimneys free from soot and creosote. In effect, the first fire law was thus established and enforced.

As the town of Boston grew in prosperity and size, so grew its need for new laws to protect it from the ravages of fire. The laws outlined the joint responsibilities of the homeowner and the authorities for fire protection. These new laws required every homeowner to have a ladder long enough to reach the ridge pole of the roof. They also required that homeowners have in their possession poles with swabs on the ends of them. When soaked in water, these poles were used to help extinguish roof fires.

The modern fire department can be said to have had its start when the town of Boston provided centrally located equipment and supplies to help home-

---

*The term "fire prevention" is used herein to include all of the activities necessary to help prevent the origin and spread of fires.

owners extinguish fires. Attached to the outside of the town meeting house were several ladders and a pole with a hook on it. The purpose of the hook-ended pole was to tear away the structure of neighboring houses and thus stop the fire from spreading. The need for a readily available water supply was recognized by the establishment of a cistern, and night patrols were formed to sound alarms.

The town of Boston enacted laws to punish those people who exposed themselves and others to fire risk. No person was allowed to build a fire within "three rods" of any building, or in ships tied up at the docks. It was illegal to carry "burning brands" for lighting fires, except in covered containers (there were no matches in those days). The penalty for arson was death.

Thus, several of the important elements of organized fire prevention and control existed in these early days: codes and enforcement for fire prevention, quick alarm, water supply, and readily available implements for control of fire. Despite such precautions, in Boston and in the other municipalities that were springing up, conflagrations were commonplace occurrences and it was necessary to enact more laws to govern the construction of buildings and to make provisions for public fire protection. Thus emerged a growing body of rules and regulations concerning fire prevention and control.

In early American cities buildings were usually thrown up in close proximity to one another, and construction was often started before adequate building codes had been enacted. The year before the great Chicago fire of 1871 the London insurance company of Lloyd's stopped writing policies in that city, so horrified were its officials at the way in which construction was proceeding. As often happens even today, many of the early laws came about as the result of tragedies. Other insurance companies had difficulty selling policies at the high premiums they had to charge. Even with these high rates they often suffered great losses when fires spread out of control.

The National Board of Fire Underwriters* realized that the adjustment and standardization of rates was a paper solution to an essentially technical problem. It began to emphasize safe building construction, control of fire hazards, and improvements in both water supplies and fire departments. New tall buildings constructed of steel and concrete adhered to controlled specifications that helped to limit the risk of fire. These were called Class A buildings.

In 1906 in San Francisco, while there were some of the new Class A steel and concrete structures in the downtown section, much of the city was still composed of flimsily built fire-prone wooden shanties. The National Board of Fire Underwriters was so alarmed that it predicted hazardous conditions would lead to a major disaster. It wrote, "San Francisco has violated all underwriting traditions and precedents by not burning up." That same year, the city of San Francisco did indeed burn up.

---

*In September 1964, the National Board of Fire Underwriters (organized in 1866) merged with the Association of Casualty and Surety Companies (organized in 1926) and the former American Insurance Association (founded in 1953) to become the new American Insurance Association. The basic objectives of the Association are to promote the economic, legislative, and public standing of its participating insurance companies.

However, although the contents of the new buildings were destroyed, the walls and frames and floors remained intact and could be renovated. After analysis of the fire damage, fire protection engineers realized that further improvements were necessary. For example, glass would have to be reinforced if it were not to shatter and deform under the intense heat of the fire, and auxiliary water towers on roofs would be needed to supplement the regular local water supplies. Furthermore, it was concluded that the vertical spaces such as stairways and elevator shafts in tall buildings would have to be enclosed in order to stop the vertical spread of fire.

With increasing awareness of the importance of fire prevention came further knowledge about the subject. Engineers began to accumulate information about fire hazards in building construction and in the manufacturing process, developing a new science to meet newly perceived needs.

In the United States the full value of fire prevention was not realized until fire departments and agencies began to compile meaningful information concerning the causes and circumstances of fires. Such information caused the more progressive departments to initiate more effective fire prevention efforts in addition to maintaining their fire fighting forces. Currently, the results of such efforts are being more clearly defined every year. In 1973, fire prevention received its greatest endorsement when the National Commission of Fire Prevention and Control reported on the fire problem in America. Throughout the report, top priority was given to the necessity for increased fire prevention activities in reducing fire loss.

Principles of Fire Prevention: From its studies of the San Francisco disaster and other major fires, the National Board of Fire Underwriters became convinced of the need for more detailed, comprehensive standards and codes relating to the construction, design, and maintenance of buildings. Regulations based on such codes could undoubtedly prevent most fires and reduce losses in the ones that did occur.

Codes in themselves obviously are only standards. If they are to be meaningful and fulfill the purpose for which they were created, regulations must be drawn up covering their enforcement. Thus, it is the responsibility of the fire department and the local authority to identify and order the removal of undesirable conditions. The local government has the power to do this through the enforcement of state regulations in support of codes where they exist and through the enactment of its own ordinances. The fire department, for its part, must see to the enforcement of these regulations and ordinances. If there have been changes within the district that make present codes inadequate (such as the development of mobile or trailer parks) it is the fire department's responsibility to voice the need for modification and to help develop new codes and regulations where they are needed. To be effective, regulations must be supported with inspections. This means that buildings in which large numbers of people work, live, or meet must be inspected to ensure that they are free from any known hazards; that they do indeed conform to the standards and codes specified in the regulations and ordinances.

Identification alone, however, does not always bring compliance. The owner of a building can refuse to remove the fire hazards or to renovate a building so that it conforms to the standards. To eliminate these possibilities, firesafety ordinances — regulations built around a model fire code — must not only outline inspection procedures, but they must also be capable of enforcement and carry penalties for violators. Violators may be fined, certificates of occupancy may be withheld, or permits for specific businesses or manufacturing processes withheld until compliance with the codes is obtained.

NATIONAL STANDARDS AND CODES

Fire prevention installations and activities are designed to prevent fires and loss of life, and to minimize damage to property by assuring compliance with fire codes. Fire department management is directly involved in the supervision of these installations and activities.

Regulations relating to firesafety are determined and subsequently enforced by the different levels of government. Although some of these functions overlap, federal and state laws generally govern those areas that cannot be regulated at the local level.

Role of the Federal Government

Under the Constitution of the United States, the legal authority of the federal government in fire matters is limited to those of an interstate of international character. The principal items covered by federal law therefore have to do mainly with transportation. They include the control of the shipment of hazardous substances by road or rail across state lines, and the enactment and enforcement of fire protection regulations aboard planes and ships. National parks and forests are under the jurisdiction of the Fire Service Division of the United States Department of Agriculture, which oversees the maintenance and utilization of fire prevention programs.

The federal government also makes a contribution to research on fire prevention and fire protection through its various agencies. This federal contribution is made, in particular, through the National Bureau of Standards, a part of the Department of Commerce in Washington, D.C. It conducts all kinds of fire research. Also under the umbrella of the Department of Commerce are the Fire Data Center and the National Academy of Fire Prevention and Control, which were set up under the provisions of the 1974 Federal Fire Prevention and Control Act. A research office evaluates fire equipment such as breathing apparatus, fire detectors, hose nozzles, portable pumps, smoke ejectors, and in-place fire prevention systems.

However, it is the nongovernmental organizations that have the greatest influence on the development of knowledge and standards relating to fire prevention. The most influential organization of this type is the National Fire Protection Association.

National Fire Protection Association (NFPA)

The National Fire Protection Association, based in Boston, was organized in 1896 "to promote the science and improve the methods of fire protection and prevention, to obtain and circulate information on these subjects, and to secure the cooperation of its members in establishing proper safeguards against loss of life and property by fire." The NFPA was originally organized by eighteen men drawn primarily from the insurance industry. Now the majority of members come from commerce, industry, and the fire service itself.

One of the NFPA's most important functions concerns the development of basic firesafety standards for processes, materials, and operations that involve a degree of fire hazard. Although these standards are often adopted and incorporated into state and local ordinances, the NFPA considers its status to be only advisory. The standards and codes are published in reference volumes, and cover a wide range of subjects — including flammable liquids and gases, electricity, building construction, and the installation of sprinkler systems. Two of the better-known codes are the *National Electrical Code* and the *Life Safety Code*. The codes are periodically revised to encompass updated construction techniques, processes, materials, and uses.

Preparation of NFPA Standards: NFPA technical committees are charged with providing reasonable standards for firesafety without prohibitive expense, interference with established processes and methods, or undue inconvenience. Each committee is a balanced working group made up of all the interests concerned with the standard in question. In general, committees include representatives of public authorities, owners of property, insurance interests, and other groups having interests in fire protection engineering.

Adoption of NFPA Standards: The Association makes every effort to give consideration to all individuals or groups interested in any standard, and such individuals or groups are given opportunities to present their views to the committee involved. Public interests always receive first consideration by all of the committees.

When a committee has compiled a proposed standard or a revision to an existing standard, such recommendations are included in a report that is printed in advance of annual meetings of the Association for distribution to interested members of the Association, to industries affected, and to the technical press. The committee's report is then acted upon officially at an annual meeting of the Association. If approved at the annual meeting, the proposed or revised standard is adopted. Annual meetings are open to the general public and afford further opportunities for individuals to present their views.

American Insurance Association (AIA)

A series of studies conducted by the American Insurance Association isolated the factors that contributed to the major conflagrations in our cities in the late 1800s and early 1900s. The AIA used this information and the basic NFPA standards to establish levels of adequacy for fire prevention in cities. AIA activities have brought about the development of the *National Building*

Code, a model code that has been adopted by many municipalities across the United States. The AIA has also suggested a *Fire Prevention Code* for cities. Both the *National Building Code* and the *Fire Prevention Code* are based largely on NFPA standards as well as on recommendations relating to various problems encountered by industries in their manufacturing processes.

Underwriters Laboratories

At one time the AIA also sponsored the Underwriters Laboratories (UL), a testing laboratory originally organized to investigate electrical hazards. UL is now a separate organization supported by fees from manufacturers who want their products tested and approved in follow-up inspections. The UL official label certifying compliance with nationally recognized safety standards can only be issued after these second stage follow-up inspections.

UL's current corporate membership is drawn from the following categories: consumer interest, public safety body or agency (responsible primarily for enforcement in the field of public safety), governmental body or agency (not responsible primarily for enforcement in the field of public safety), insurance, safety expert, standardization expert, public utility, education, and officer of the corporation. UL is managed by a Board of Trustees drawn from the aforementioned categories, plus an additional "at large" category. Only one officer of the corporation is included on its Board of Trustees.

Factory Mutual System

The Engineering Division of the Factory Mutual System (FM) also maintains laboratories for testing building materials and fire equipment and, like the UL, issues labels to indicate certain products that have passed its tests. The Factory Mutual Research staff of the Factory Mutual System consists of the Standards, Research, and Approvals Groups.

The Standards Group is made up of engineers in many fields who develop information and recommendations based on research and loss experience, and also are available to offer advice to Factory Mutual System members on specific loss prevention matters.

The Research Group consists of two groups of scientists: One group is a basic research group whose object is to secure information pertaining to the initial phases of fire, its detection, and growth patterns. The theories that they develop are expected to lead to new methods of loss prevention and control. The other group, an applied research group, is concerned with improvement in effectiveness of fire protection systems, fire modeling studies, rack storage and plastics storage fire tests, new suppression agents and systems, ignition and flammability of materials, and design and cost evaluation of effective fire protection systems.

The Approvals Group subjects equipment and materials to rigid tests to determine that devices submitted by manufacturers will operate dependably, and that materials can pass fire tests that indicate an acceptable low flammability. An approval guide is issued annually.

Other Groups Having Fire Protection Interests

There are also a number of other technical groups that prepare standards for specific manufacturing processes or for the risks they cover. Just as the AIA used the NFPA standards to prepare its own codes and grading schedule, so these groups representing various occupations or industries with fire protection interests prepare even more stringent codes, using NFPA and other standards as a base. Their purpose is to obtain lower insurance rates for those industries that comply with the tighter requirements and accept regular inspections by the group's inspectors.

State Regulatory Office

The principal instruments for implementing regulatory authority for fire laws at the state level is often the office of state fire marshal. Almost all states have an office of state fire marshal, and in most states enabling legislation gives the fire marshal the power to make regulations covering various hazards and, in many cases, such regulations have the effect of law. The responsibilities of the office of state fire marshal are in the following general areas:

1. Prevention of fires.
2. Storage, sale, and use of combustibles and explosives.
3. Installation and maintenance of automatic alarms and sprinkler systems.
4. Construction, maintenance, and regulation of fire escapes.
5. Means and adequacy of exits in case of fire in public places or buildings in which a number of persons live, work, or congregate (such as schools, hospitals, and large industrial complexes).
6. Suppression of arson, and the investigation of the cause, origin, and circumstances of fire.

In most states the fire marshal has the legal power to draw up rules and regulations covering various fire hazards. In many cases these rules and regulations have the force of law.

The precise responsibilities and organization of the fire marshal's office vary from state to state. The fire marshal's office is concerned with the maintenance of fire records, the investigation of suspected arson, and all matters related to fire. The office is sometimes associated with the state insurance department. In those states that do not have a fire marshal's office, responsibilities are divided among other state agencies such as the Attorney General's office and the State Police.

While the state fire marshal's office has legal authority for fire prevention, much of this power is delegated to the local fire departments and to local government. Fire departments may carry out inspection of private properties to determine if there are fire hazards or code violations on the premises, and local authorities are given the power — through "enabling acts" — to adopt their own regulations relating to fire prevention.

For further information concerning the fire prevention duties of the state fire marshal's office, see section titled "Organization for Fire Prevention" later in this chapter.

Local Codes and Ordinances

It is the local codes and ordinances that are of greatest interest for the fire fighters and officers. In them are incorporated many of the standards and codes set up by state and private organizations. Some states have adopted uniform codes in areas such as building construction. Such uniform codes may supersede any existing local ordinance.

Laws for local firesafety generally fall into two categories: (1) those relating to buildings, and (2) those relating to hazardous materials, processes, and machinery that may be used in buildings.

Local planners frequently disagree as to what should go into a building code and what should go into a fire code. In general, requirements relating to construction go into the building code and are enforced by the building inspector and the building inspector's department, and requirements relating to the safe operation of machinery or equipment are the responsibility of the fire department. Following is a general outline of what is usually covered under the building code, and what is usually covered under the fire prevention code:[2]

> Most municipal building codes cover, in general, the following items: (1) administration, which spells out the powers and duties of the building official; (2) classification of buildings by occupancy; (3) establishment of fire limits or fire zones; (4) establishment of height and area limits; (5) establishment of restrictions as to type of construction and as to use of buildings; (6) special occupancy provisions which stipulate special construction requirements for various occupancies such as theaters, piers and wharves, garages, etc.; (7) requirements for light and ventilation; (8) exit requirements; (9) materials, loads, and stresses; (10) construction requirements; (11) precautions during building construction; (12) requirements for fire resistance, including materials, protection of structural members, fire walls, partitions, enclosure of stairs and shafts, roof structures, and roof coverings; (13) chimneys and heating appliances; (14) elevators; (15) plumbing; (16) electrical installations; (17) gas piping and appliances; (18) signs and billboards; (19) fire extinguishing equipment.
>
> The principal provisions usually found in a fire prevention code cover the following: (1) administration, which includes the organization of the bureau of fire prevention and defines its powers and duties; (2) explosives, ammunition, and blasting agents; (3) flammable and combustible liquids; (4) liquefied petroleum gases and compressed gases; (5) lumberyards and woodworking plants; (6) dry cleaning establishments; (7) garages; (8) application of flammable finishes; (9) cellulose nitrate plastics (pyroxylin); (10) cellulose nitrate motion picture film; (11) combustible metals; (12) fireworks; (13) fumigation and thermal insecticidal fogging; (14) fruit-ripening processes; (15) combustible fibers; (16) hazardous chemicals; (17) hazardous occupancies; (18) maintenance of fire equipment; (19) maintenance of exit ways; (20) oil burning equipment; (21) welding and cutting; (22) dust explosion prevention; (23) bowling establishments; (24) waste material handling plants; (25) automobile wrecking yards, junk yards, and waste material handling plants; (26) manufacture of organic coatings; (27) ovens and furnaces; (28) tents; (29) general precautions against fire.

While there may seem to be some overlap in the administration of these requirements, closer scrutiny will show that the inclusion of the original fire prevention item (for example, duct, vent, exit, or sprinkler system) should be supervised by the building department, but the determination of its continuing adequacy should be the responsibility of the fire department.

The NFPA provides standards for both the building code and the fire prevention code. In spite of the establishment of these standards, confusion and rivalry sometimes exist between the departments of building and fire prevention as to who is responsible for which safety provisions, and for the enforcement of same. An article from the magazine *Fire Command!* points to this controversy:[3]

> Building code hearings find little or no effective input from fire officials, yet when a major fire occurs, the same fire officials are found on the front page of the local newspaper condemning the building officials. All too often, the fire department leaves code writing and enforcement (plan review, construction inspections, etc.) to a building official who does not have the background to evaluate and correct any fire code deficiencies. The fire experts are found sitting in the station waiting for the code deficiencies to provide their work load.

> The initial questions for each fire official are:

> 1. Are you aware of the intent of your local code?
> 2. Did a fire official provide input when the code was written?
> 3. Is your code compatible with local needs?

One might add to this: What can be done to change or modify an inadequate code?

In an effort to lessen some of the confusion about enforcement of fire codes, some states depend on model building codes such as: (1) the Basic Building Code[4] of the Building Officials and Code Administrators International, Inc. (BOCA); (2) the American Insurance Association's National Building Code; (3) the Uniform Building Code of the International Conference of Building Officials; and (4) the Standard Building Code of the Southern Building Code Congress. Each of these model building codes has an accompanying fire prevention code. The states that have adopted one of the model building codes may recommend that local governments also adopt its companion fire prevention code to provide a uniform functional separation of the building and fire departments. Since the codes are to be adopted in their entirety, the duties of each department are clarified in relation to the other.

Wherever problems exist, they can usually be lessened by a frank approach and open communication. When high-level officials from both departments meet on a continuing basis to discuss their responsibilities and mutual concerns, problems about conflicting jurisdiction can be reduced.

In some European countries this problem has already been eliminated. In Germany, for example, the question of overlap has been solved by making

Fig. 7.1. Fire fighter-inspector discusses building and fire code requirements with a local contractor. (Tracy Fire Department, Tracy, California)

fire department officials responsible for both building and fire codes. Some local governments in the United States have also elected to assign fire fighters to the work of inspecting for building and fire code violations at the same time. (See Fig. 7.1.)

FIRE PREVENTION OPERATIONAL TASKS AND CONCERNS

Some of the operational tasks and concerns directly related to effective fire prevention are: (1) plans review and prefire plans, (2) inspections, (3) public education, (4) seasonal activities, (5) special interest groups, (6) fire prevention codes, (7) public information, (8) consultation, (9) records and reports, (10) photography, (11) fire ignition sequence investigation, (12) water supply, and (13) legal aspects.

The following paragraphs briefly introduce these operational tasks and concerns as they relate to the fire service. Chapter Eight, "Loss Prevention Activities — Prefire Planning and Related Functions," presents more detailed information on their applicability in loss prevention programs.

Plans Review

This review of construction plans for various classes of buildings is now legally mandatory in many localities. It provides the fire service with its best opportunity to see that fire protection standards are met prior to construction. Plans review must be followed up with on-site inspections to ensure that the fire protection provided for in the plan is not overlooked in construction.

Prefire Plans

Prefire plans include detailed layouts of properties in the fire district (with the exception of one- and two-family dwellings) showing entrances, exits, stairs, fire walls, standpipes, areas covered by sprinkler systems, and the information pertinent to an attack. Sometimes outlines for attack preparation such as the positions of apparatus and initial hose layouts are also shown. Prefire plans are drawn up by fire fighters and their company officers. After they have been approved by the department, the prefire plans are usually carried on the apparatus so that they may be referred to on the way to the fire. Prefire plans can also serve as a base for simulation in company training drills. Prefire plans and inspections overlap in two areas: (1) they familiarize personnel with buildings where other than routine fires may occur, and (2) prefire plan surveys can sometimes uncover code violations, thus helping to support inspection work. Prefire planning is covered in detail in Chapter Eight, "Loss Prevention Activities — Prefire Planning and Related Functions."

Inspections

Local fire codes call for the inspection of several categories of hazards within the district served by the fire department. The recommended number of annual inspections generally depends on the type of occupancy. These types are:

1. One- and two-family dwellings (these are usually not inspected except on request of owner/occupant).
2. Three or more family dwellings.
3. Commercial office buildings.
4. Industrial (high, moderate, and low hazard).
5. Mercantile (high, moderate, and low hazard).
6. Public assembly complexes.
7. Institutions.

Institutions, places of public assembly, and high hazard mercantile and industrial plants are frequently designated as "target properties."

There are two kinds of inspections: (1) regular, and (2) technical. Fire fighters perform "company inspections" (or "field inspections" as they may sometimes be called). These are routine, regular inspections that check for compliance with the general regulations concerning access to standpipes and sprinkler valves, adequacy of fire extinguishers, lack of obstructions to emergency evacuation means of egress, and for the more obvious safety problems such as multiple connections from electrical outlets. Records of each building are maintained. Where code violations are found, violation notices are issued and follow-up visits are made to ensure that deficiencies are corrected.

Because most fire fighters are not trained in the complexities of modern manufacturing processes or operations, someone has to be especially assigned to perform technical inspections. These are detailed inspections of particular occupancies that ensure that the use of hazardous materials or processes are subject to definite safety precautions.

Businesses and industries using such materials require permits from the fire department and cannot start hazardous activities (or continue them) without such permits. The technical inspections are carried out before a permit is issued or renewed.

Public Education

Educational programs help to obtain the cooperation of the taxpayers the fire department serves. These may include publicity in the media, flyers, and special informational programs such as slide shows at special group activities and at schools.

Public education is a necessary tool in fire prevention. If the public is to take the initiative in helping to solve the fire problem, it must be made aware of the problem; should the fire service fail to provide adequate knowledge and motivation, lack of public concern may result. The purpose of the public fire service makes it a logical organization for helping to educate the general public. Also, individual organizations can provide effective campaigns that help to draw attention to particular problems.

Public education must be constantly updated and upgraded in order to maintain public interest and support. Failure to be up-to-date in an educational approach to fire prevention often results in the loss of excellent opportunities for communicating vital information to special interest groups as well as to the general public. More detailed information concerning public education programs is presented in the following Chapter Eight in the sections titled "Public Education Through Publicity," and "Public Education Through Programs."

Seasonal Activities

The four seasons of the year present a natural timetable that is often used as the basis for informative education programs of interest to the general public. Public education programs include National Fire Prevention Week, Operation EDITH (Exit Drills in the Home), and Sparky's Junior Fire Department Programs. Many materials supplied by the National Fire Protection Association are used in public education programs.

Special Interest Groups

In some communities, groups spring up spontaneously or are organized by the Fire Prevention Bureau to provide channels of communication between various segments of the community and the fire department.

Special interest groups with information needs similar to those of the general public, but different enough to require individual programs, include educational, industrial, institutional, residential, high-rise, civic, service, professional, and commercial groups. There are many ways to reach such groups. For example, the media looks for public service information that will be of interest to their viewers, readers, and listeners; educational groups are interested in lesson plans that can be added to study programs.

Fire Prevention Codes

Many well-meaning fire prevention recommendations receive voluntary public acceptance and compliance. However, a fire prevention code that has been adopted into law is essential for any successful fire prevention program. The major objective of any successful code is to provide a reasonable degree of safety to life and property from fire.

The Insurance Services Organization publishes its recommended fire code, and several building code organizations have written, or are in the process of writing, fire codes for use in conjunction with their own building codes. The National Fire Protection Association has also developed NFPA 1, *Fire Prevention Code.*[5]

Some states and local governments have adopted the *National Fire Codes* of the NFPA; these fire codes are often considered to be the country's most authoritative codes.

Public Information

At times there is certain information that the general public needs to know immediately, and time does not permit its dissemination by means of regular public education channels. It may be information about a particular fire problem that suddenly appears, such as hazardous toys or garments, a particular need of the fire service, or a large fire that is in progress and of concern to the public. Some departments have officers on their staffs who serve as public information officers; in the absence of such officers, information is usually handled by the fire prevention bureau.

Consultation

The general public looks to the public fire service for answers to its fire problems. Because fire prevention covers such a broad area and reaches so many people, consultation services are necessary. Fire prevention officers must be capable of explaining the fine points of fire codes to professional people such as architects and engineers who may be experiencing fire codes for the first time when they file their fire plans for review, as well as being able to explain to children the dangers of playing with matches.

Records and Reports

Records are essential for effective fire prevention. They may include the following:

1. Copies of violations, inspections, and follow-ups.
2. Prefire plans — maps and attack practices.
3. Statistical information organized into maps, charts, etc., for use in fire prevention planning.
4. Recommendations dealing with specific problems in certain occupancies or areas, or for decisions about future needs.

Records and reports of fire prevention activities should be clear and concise. Every time an inspector or fire prevention officer visits a location, information about that location is included in a record or a report. The occupancy file of each building visited should include a complete history of the building site, building plans, specifications (whenever this is possible), permits issued for the use, storage, and handling of various hazardous materials, inspection reports, and fire incidents.

Further information on the use of records and reports is contained in the following Chapter Eight, "Loss Prevention Activities — Prefire Planning and Related Functions." (See especially Table 8.2.)

Photography

The inclusion of photography in records and reports is invaluable. A photograph, properly taken and identified, is one of the best ways to fully illustrate conditions to persons such as the city attorney, owner of the building, chief officer, judge, or jury. Photographs and detailed reports can help eliminate much argument as to actual conditions at the time of exposure. Photography is also useful for educational purposes. Many departments have full-time photographers and complete camera and laboratory equipment and facilities.

Fire Ignition Sequence Investigation

All fires are investigated to determine their first ignition sequence. If arson is suspected, the police or state fire marshal's office may be contacted. Data compiled from such investigations is useful in providing ideas on how future fires can be prevented.

Most fire departments were organized to provide for the immediate urgency of fighting fires, and few were set up to develop and compile comprehensive, in-depth information on the number of fires occurring by location and occupancy, the fire ignition sequence or causative factors, the time of day or week of occurrence, the room or floor in which the fire occurred, and similar information that is basic to any effective evaluation of a fire problem.

While it has long been recognized that fire prevention is one of the major concerns of all fire department personnel, a point that has not been as well recognized is that comprehensive investigation of fires and all the factors influencing or contributing to the fire ignition sequence or communication of fire is the very foundation on which fire prevention is built. Without the extensive and detailed information obtained from these factors, it is impossible to develop the most effective regulatory codes, standards, inspection and suppression procedures, and similar actions designed to prevent or control fire. (See also Chapter Eight, section titled "Fire Ignition Sequence Investigation," for further information on arson investigation and the role of the company officer in investigations.)

Water Supply

The fire department is usually responsible for making recommendations to the local government about the adequacy of water supplies for fire fighting, especially when plans for the development of new industrial, commercial, or residential areas in the community are considered.

The Fire Prevention Bureau works with the local authority and water company in making a survey to ensure that there is a sufficient water supply to extinguish fires in the district. In such a review, the size of water mains is examined in relation to the size and density of buildings as well as to sprinkler systems and water towers (where they exist). The number, location, and maintenance of hydrants is also checked. (See also Chapter Eight of this text, section titled "Water Supplies and Systems as a Management Concern," for more detailed information on water supplies and systems as related to fire protection activities.)

Legal Aspects

The state, in most instances, delegates to local officials its police power to regulate persons and properties for the safety of the public. The courts rule on any conflicts that may develop in the interpretation of these regulations.

Accurate determination and reporting of the fire ignition sequence is in the public interest. This is indicated by the broad powers given most fire marshals in rights of entry for fire inspection and investigation, fire marshal's hearings, rights of subpoena of any records or persons who may have information as to the fire ignition sequence, etc. These powers have been upheld by most courts of law. Such powers are invaluable in establishing and corroborating ignition sequence of fire, and such authority should be honored when utilized by members of the fire service when performing their duties.

Such broad powers are not generally applicable, however, to criminal investigations, and since arson is a felony, these rights do not apply to fire investigation after the fire ignition sequence has been established as arson. These rights may also tend to become diffused when a recognized police agency conducts fire ignition sequence investigations in cases where the ignition sequence is not immediately established. For this reason, it is usually advantageous to maintain some distinction between civil actions involving fire ignition sequence and criminal investigations of arson.

ORGANIZATION FOR FIRE PREVENTION

In the Dominion of Canada there are provincial fire commissioners for the various provinces and a Dominion Fire Commission. In the United States, although certain branches of the federal government conduct research and gather data concerning the fire problem, no national governmental agency has been created to maintain a fire fighting or fire prevention force. Most states have offices at the state level to oversee certain phases of fire protection. The chief administrator at the state level is usually called the state fire marshal.

State Fire Marshal

The makeup of state fire marshal offices differs from state to state. Most receive their authority from the state legislature and are answerable to the governor, a high state officer, or a commission created for that purpose. In some states the fire marshal's office may be a division of the state insurance department, state police, state building department, state commerce division, or other state agency. Few are organized as separate agencies.

State or provincial agencies normally function in those areas that go beyond the scope of the municipal, county, or fire district organizations. Local fire protection organizations are sometimes granted the authority to act as agents for the state in stipulated areas of inspection, enforcement, and investigation.

Chief of Fire Prevention or Local Fire Marshal

The laws of the county, municipality, or fire districts delegate the responsibility and authority of fire prevention to the fire chief or fire department head. Provision is then made for that person to delegate this authority to an individual or division, depending on the size of the department. The individual or head of the division should be a high ranking chief officer and should also function as a staff officer to the fire chief. This division of the fire service is normally called the fire prevention bureau, and its top officer is chief of fire prevention or local fire marshal. Where size permits, the bureau is divided into subdepartments of inspections, investigations, and public education. These subdepartments are then headed by subordinate chiefs.

Fire Inspector or Fire Prevention Officer

The term fire inspector or fire prevention officer has different meanings in different departments. Sometimes the two titles are the same and denote the position responsible for conducting fire inspections assigned to the fire prevention bureau. In bureaus not large enough for three sub-departments, the fire inspector is also responsible for conducting fire investigations and performing public education duties.

Fire Protection Engineer

The complexity and magnitude of fire protection problems make the services of fire protection engineers very desirable. While most of their work is done on a consulting basis, some public fire protection agencies have recognized the need for full-time staff engineers.

Delegation of Responsibilities

How does a department organize itself to carry out all of its fire prevention tasks and concerns? In a large city department these functions may be separated and assigned to two or more distinct sections, with responsibilities for fire prevention and education in one and inspection, enforcement, and investigations in the other. Medium-sized departments might concentrate all of the fire prevention duties into one centralized bureau, assigning specific responsibilities to each officer.

In small departments the chief may conduct inspections with the assistance of fire fighters who are specially interested in this facet of fire department work. Generally, fire prevention personnel do not work in shifts. However, in every department, whatever its size, there should always be at least one person "on call" to carry out immediate investigations of specified fires that may have resulted in severe property damage or high loss of life, or that were considered to be of suspicious origin.

A fire fighter who has assumed fire prevention duties might receive compensation for the extra training. The fire fighter's additional responsibilities lead to greater competence and understanding of fire department activities. In addition, such broader perspectives enhance the likelihood of promotion when opportunities arise.

Alternative Organizational Patterns

Instead of keeping fire prevention solely as a "staff" function, some departments have modified their organizational framework by assigning fire prevention inspectors to shifts. Following are some of the advantages to this method:

1. Someone with special knowledge about specific buildings and their hazards is always on hand to provide additional information to the fire fighters.

2. An immediate investigation into the cause of the fire can proceed.

However, a major disadvantage to shift assignments is that very few technical inspections can be conducted at night. The result of this disadvantage is, of course, lower productivity.

Volunteer Departments

Volunteer departments may organize themselves to carry out fire prevention activities in various ways. Following are a few possibilities:

1. They may offer special training for those fire fighters who wish to assume fire prevention duties.

2. They may hire paid civilians on a full or part-time basis. Sometimes such personnel are retired fire department personnel.

3. The chief or deputy chief may assume fire prevention duties, sometimes in rotation.

PERSONNEL ASSIGNMENT AND FIRE PREVENTION PRIORITIES

To a certain extent, the personnel assigned to fire prevention duties reflect not only the size of the department, but also the department's financial resources and the degree of priority assigned to fire prevention by the chief, local government officials, and taxpayers.

The 1973 Report of the National Commission on Fire Prevention and Control recommended that local governments make fire prevention at least equal to suppression in the planning of fire department priorities. Nevertheless, few departments, if any so far, have committed fifty percent of their resources to this function. Under present conditions, it would be very difficult to give fire prevention that kind of attention. For example, massive changes in the way a fire department organizes itself would be required. Also, many of the jobs that are currently done during the day (such as inspections, the checking of apparatus, and housekeeping chores) would have to be performed at night.

Special facilities would have to be provided to accommodate such changes, and everyone, from the taxpayer to the fire fighter, would have to be willing to accept such an arrangement. Because society is generally unaware of the need to emphasize fire prevention, it is unlikely that such a change will occur in the near future.

Currently, several factors hamper the expansion of fire prevention activities.

Barriers to Expansion of Fire Prevention Activities

Inspections make up the bulk of fire prevention activities. If a greater proportion of available personnel were assigned to daytime shifts to carry out more inspections, a fire department might find its night shifts so depleted that it could not respond as effectively to some major emergencies. To offset this disadvantage, daytime personnel might be placed in rotating "on call" shifts to respond in the event of a serious fire.

There are approximately only eight hours in the day when most businesses are open. Regular day-shift personnel perform a full work load of duties that can only be carried out during the day. Such personnel might find it difficult to assume additional fire prevention duties.

In most departments there are not sufficient inspectors assigned to cope effectively with the present work load. Fire fighters conduct company inspections not only to familiarize themselves with the district, but also to enable the department to carry out the required number of inspections per occupancy. The hiring and training of additional personnel would necessitate additional resources at a time when local authorities are looking for ways to trim their budgets. Portions of existing funds would have to be reallocated from fire fighting activities to fire prevention — a highly unlikely step.

Ways to Expand Fire Prevention Activities

Although it might be too difficult to commit a greater percentage of available working hours to fire prevention, some departments could take advantage of the following:

1. Restaurants, bars, schools, etc., could be inspected in the evening.

2. Overcoming some of the obstacles involved in inspections might produce greater efficiency. (This will be discussed in detail later in this chapter in the section titled "Inspections.")

3. Good public education programs can reduce the incidence of fire and the need for any expansion of fire fighting capabilities. Such programs can help change the attitudes of public and government officials regarding their current financial allocations for fire prevention.

ROLE OF THE COMPANY OFFICER IN FIRE PREVENTION

As previously mentioned, fire prevention activities are those activities which, if allowed, could take up as much time as all other fire fighting activities combined. This is seldom the case, one important reason being that many officers and fire fighters look upon fire prevention activities as less than satisfying functions in the overall role of fire fighting.

From the viewpoint of the company officer, fire prevention can provide an opportunity to put meaning and greater job satisfaction into an important segment of a company's work — especially for those companies which, unlike some hard-pressed metropolitan companies, are not called upon to fight fires very frequently. Fire prevention activities can also present an opportunity for officers to stimulate a type of job enthusiasm that can spread to other activities as well. To do that is not easy. Such enthusiasm can, however, be instilled through creative leadership. For example, company officers might consider that:

1. Prefire plans can be used for simulating fires at various locations.
2. Command of the simulations can be rotated among the fire fighters.
3. Inspection trips can be used for interesting discussions of the processes being used at the location, the fire hazards they contain, and the implications for fire fighting.
4. While many people do not like to learn in an uninspiring environment, if the officer knows how to make training sessions more interesting the fire fighters will more likely enjoy the sessions in which they learn more about codes, inspection procedures, and fire investigations.

Goals for the Chief

As with other types of fire fighting activities, good management approaches to fire prevention functions start with good goals. A few sample goals for a chief in fire prevention functions could be:

Overall:
- Obtain budget and establish a fire prevention bureau by (date).
- Obtain budget and establish fire prevention capabilities for each shift by (date).
- By (date) establish a program that will provide for use of prefire plans and inspection results in training sessions.

With Each District or Individual Company:
- Jointly, with the commanding officer in each district, set goals for number of inspections to be conducted by each company during each month.
- Jointly, with each district commander, set goals for the number of prefire plans to be prepared or reviewed by each company during each month.
- Develop, jointly with the district commanders, a public education program by (date).
- Establish by (date) a citizen's committee to help with fire prevention.
- Ensure that all district commanders have plans for Fire Prevention Week ready by September 1.

Goals for Company Officer:
- Establish inspection schedule to be accomplished during the coming month by the 20th of the preceding month.

• Jointly, with the training officer, develop by (date) training programs on inspection procedures and other inspection-related knowledge/skills.

• By (date) establish the schedule of prefire plans to be drawn during the next quarter.

• By (date) begin to use prefire plans for simulations in training sessions.

• By (date) develop an improved method for checking alarm boxes in the district to achieve a five-percent reduction in time, without reduction in frequency, of inspections.

INSPECTIONS

Inspections are necessary for enforcement of the fire code. The degree to which codes are enforced is one of the factors considered by the Insurance Services Office in its evaluation of a fire department.

Fire department inspections fall into four general categories. Occupancies to be inspected in the first three inspection categories include places of public assembly, educational, institutional, residential (not interior of dwellings), mercantile, business, industrial, manufacturing, and storage. The four general categories are:

1. Inspections required by law are usually conducted by members of the fire prevention bureau. These inspections include all buildings and premises with the exception of the interiors of private dwellings. Inspections are made for the purpose of seeking out those conditions that violate the fire code, and that are liable to cause fire or endanger life and property. Emphasis is also placed on those conditions of interest to fire officers for prefire planning and training purposes. (See Fig. 7.2.)

2. Fire inspections conducted by fire companies that supplement inspections of the fire prevention bureau. Before performing inspection work, fire fighters should receive proper training and be granted the authority to conduct

Fig. 7.2. Inspection reveals fire department connection with access blocked by fence. (Michael W. Magee)

Fig. 7.3. Inspection of the building in the foreground would reveal the unsafe condition of the fire escape stairs. Most of the wood in this escape is rotted, and handrails have collapsed. (Amy E. Dean, NFPA, Boston)

inspections as fire prevention officers. These inspections are normally conducted in the fire company's first due area. The fire prevention bureau provides assistance where needed in obtaining compliance to company recommendations.

3. Inspections made by fire company personnel for the purpose of prefire planning and training. Emphasis is also placed on conditions that violate the fire code, and that are liable to cause fire or endanger life. Conditions that require more than on-the-spot correction are usually referred to the fire prevention bureau.

4. Home inspections conducted by fire companies. The fire fighters are received into the homes voluntarily by the occupants. The recommendations made are not mandatory. If definite code violations are found, an effort should be made to have the hazard corrected through proper department channels of authority. (See Fig. 7.3.)

In June 1967 the Supreme Court of the United States made a landmark decision affecting inspections and right of entry. This decision has not affected fire inspectors of public or private commercial establishments to a very large degree. The decision does point out, however, that in those rare cases where the owner of a business might insist on a warrant before the business can be inspected, it is best to obtain the warrant. (See pages 231–234.)

Objectives of Inspections

The functions that are performed during an inspection, and the compilation of the report resulting from the inspection are covered in detail in the *NFPA Inspection Manual.*[6] Major inspection objectives consist of the following:

1. Company and technical inspections to uncover code violations and potential fire hazards.

2. Company inspections to acquaint fire fighters with fire codes and also with OSHA (Occupational Safety and Health Act) building and safety codes as well. A knowledge of these codes will often help in actual fire fighting operations.

3. Company inspections to familiarize fire fighters with contents and construction hazards, thus making fire fighting operationally more efficient. For example, fire fighters gain an understanding of how a fire can spread through vertical openings (such as elevator shafts, stairwells, and the stairways of buildings), or they gain an awareness of where the primary potential sources of fire hazard are located.

4. Another objective of the company inspection is to make most efficient use of personnel assigned to fire prevention duties. Most fire departments try to inspect target properties at least four times a year, as suggested by the model fire code. Goals for moderate and low hazard occupancies are to inspect at least twice a year. This objective is sometimes accomplished by combining technical inspections with company inspections.

The inspectors from the fire prevention bureau might inspect target properties twice a year, especially when permits are due or when changes of occupancy or process require a more detailed inspection. This leaves only two for company inspection.

The Inspection Process

Whether inspections are carried out by fire fighters or by fire prevention bureau personnel, the basic process is similar:

1. Before conducting an inspection, all records related to the prescribed area and premises, or occupancies, are reviewed. An inspector needs to know what kinds of violations have been found previously, the owner's attitude toward correcting them, and the causes of any fire that might have occurred in the building.

2. An inspector should take along a comprehensive checklist in order to ensure that no items have been overlooked. While some large departments may have one checklist for each category of occupancy, fire fighters may sometimes be required to compile their own. Table 7.1 is a sample fire inspection report checklist for fire prevention inspectors.

3. Before entering the building an inspector should check the property to see where apparatus might be stationed, should check the location of fire escapes and their condition, and should check for obstructions of standpipes or emergency exits.

4. Upon entering the building, good public relations demands that the inspector announce to the person in charge of the building that an inspection is about to be made.

5. The actual inspection might begin at the roof where exposures and adjacent rooftops and parapets can be seen.

6. The inspection would then proceed down from attic to basement, from floor to floor, in a systematic fashion; each item would be checked off on the inspector's checklist, as applicable.

7. During a company inspection, special attention should be given to the way in which the building could be ventilated, to fire protection equipment, stairways and corridors, doorways and exits, heating and exhaust ducts, in-

Table 7.1   Sample Fire Inspection Report Checklist*

FIRE INSPECTION REPORT FOR			DISTRICT	
Street			Number	
Owner/Agent/Superintendent				
Address of above				
Class Construction	Roof		Stories	
Occupancy			Fl.	No. of Tenants
			DATES OF INSPECTIONS	
FIRE HAZARDS				
Heating System				
Clearances				
Heat Deflectors				
Condition of Flue				
Flue Pipe Fit				
Burner Controls				
Storage of Explosives				
Storage of Flammables				
CONDITION OF				
Fuses/Breakers				
Electrical Wiring				
Electrical Appliances				
Chimneys				
Vent Ducts				
Rubbish				
Storage of Ashes				
Air Conditioning				
Gas Appliances				
Miscellaneous				
FIRE PROTECTION				
Sprinklers	Wet	Dry		
Standpipes				
Second Egress				
Extinguishers				
Fire Doors				
Fire Escapes	W	M		
Aisles				
Halls				
Chutes				
STRUCTURAL DEFECTS				
Roofs				
Walls				
Floors				
Foundations				
Stairs				
Elevators				
Enclosures				
Stairway Enclosures				
LOCATION OF CUT OFFS				
Sprinkler				
Standpipe				
Gas				
Electricity				
Water				
LOCATION OF SIAMESE CONNECTIONS				
Sprinkler		Standpipe		
Inspector's Initials				
Violation Notice Issued				
Date Corrected				
REMARKS				

*Courtesy of Plainfield Fire Department, Plainfield, New Jersey.

sulation and wiring, storage areas, facilities for disposal of refuse, and general maintenance procedures.

8. Certain specific points must be checked. For example, the panic hardware on the exit doors may have been inadvertently removed and replaced with regular fixtures. Also, the door itself may be jammed or blocked. "No Smoking" signs may have become unreadable, blocked, or removed, and there may be a need to designate an area "Smoking Permitted." All exit signs must be visible from all approaches.

All conditions that are not in compliance with regulations should be noted; for the more important violations to the regulations, violation notices should be issued and the others should be recorded for checking during a follow-up inspection. (See Fig. 7.4.)

Private Dwelling Inspections: Inspections of residential areas should be carried out in much the same manner as the preceding. However, inspection of private dwellings is not required by regulation. Private dwellings are inspected only on request of the owner. Where personnel are available, and where public education programs have been successful, most residents will voluntarily participate in an inspection program. When inspecting private dwellings, inspectors might point out possible escape routes in the event of fire and provide information about fire detection equipment and small fire extinguishers.

Fig. 7.4. A dangerous arrangement of a lightly supported television antenna in the proximity of power lines would be noted in an inspection.

Fig. 7.5a. A mag-card type-writer (left) used to prepare violation notices. (Houston Fire Marshal's Office, Houston, Texas)

Fig. 7.5b. Example of a violation notice (below) that will clearly indicate the potential liability of the offending party. (Portland Fire Bureau, Portland, Oregon)

NOTICE OF VIOLATION OF CITY ORDINANCE

Name _____ Date _____ 19 _____

Location of Complaint _____ Occupancy _____

Notice is hereby given that you are violating Ordinance No.   and the following

corrections must be made _____

_____

_____

_____

_____

_____

_____

Failure to comply within _____ days will make you liable to prosecution in District Court. Should a fire occur from the condition mentioned above you will be liable to the City for the expense of extinguishing same, and for damage to property owned by others.

By _____
                             Fire Inspector

Reasons for Code Violations: People sometimes violate codes because it costs money to comply; it costs money to have enough fire extinguishers, to put in additional electrical circuits, or to add extra storage space. Sometimes people simply forget to be careful about fire hazards. They sometimes forget to check whether the fire escape is still in good condition, and whether the sprinklers are in workable condition. If there is not enough storage space for all the boxes, it is easy and convenient to pile them up in a corridor for a few days — just until more room for storage is found. But the required space often will not be found unless a fire inspection calls attention to the fact that obstructions in corridors and doorways are fire code violations.

Most inspections produce some code violations. When code violations are discovered, they should be corrected within the prescribed period of time. (See Figs. 7.5a and 7.5b.)

Correction of Violations: Where corrections of code violations involve a substantial amount of money, a discussion of how the owner might best rectify the situation can be helpful. If necessary, special technical advice could be sought from the fire prevention bureau.

A period of grace is allowed for violation corrections. It is up to the technical inspector or company officer to determine how many days to allow. This usually depends on whether the violation is a simple one like removing obstructions in doorways, or whether it is a comparatively difficult one like installing a fire escape.

In the case of industrial inspections, follow-up visits are needed to determine whether violations have been corrected. In the case of voluntary inspections of private dwellings, follow-ups are not usually made, except by request.

Inspections — Opportunity for Public Relations: When the company takes the apparatus along to the section of the district being inspected, the placards used by many departments for making their presence known can serve both to inform the public that an inspection is in progress, and to indicate that the company is in radio contact with the dispatcher in case of an alarm.

A well-groomed appearance — clean and pressed uniforms — will help promote a positive and professional image for the department.

As the inspection proceeds, the inspector (whether a fire fighter or a technical inspector from the fire prevention bureau) has the opportunity to emphasize the preventative aspects of the inspection work. The inspector who explains the implications of violations to the owner or employee of the premises being inspected helps greatly to enhance the image of the department.

The owner or person in charge should also have a copy of the inspection checklist or report, in addition to any notice of violation. It indicates that the inspector conducted an efficient, systematic inspection and shows that the fire department is competent and is approaching its job of protecting the community in a responsible manner.

Role of the Company Officer in Inspections

It is the responsibility of the company officer to integrate all aspects of company inspections into the general purpose and goals of fire prevention. This task is complicated by the fact that many fire fighters have negative feelings about conducting inspections. There are many reasons for this.

Fire Fighter Attitudes to Inspections: Some of the reasons fire fighters feel negative about conducting inspections are inherent in the nature of the work of a fire fighter and are difficult to remove. Others, however, are much easier to do something about if the company officer understands what can be done and how to do it. The first five of the following reasons might be included in the first category. Competent officers can often modify reasons six through eleven.

1. Most fire fighters joined the fire service because they wanted to fight fires. It is that aspect of the fire service that attracted them — not preventing fires from occurring.

2. Some fire fighters do not have outgoing personalities, thus making it difficult for them to relate quickly to the people they must deal with in inspection work.

3. To carry out inspections, fire fighters must change into clean, pressed uniforms. This either costs the fire fighter extra money, or necessitates a certain amount of extra effort.

4. During field inspections, fire fighters are restricted in their freedom of movement — much more so than when they are at the station.

5. Inspections often occur at inconvenient times for the building owner, such as when the owner is busy or the premises to be inspected are in full use. This can cause the fire fighter to feel uncomfortable.

6. Fire fighters often find it difficult to understand how inspections relate to their primary job of fire fighting.

7. When asked why they are conducting an inspection, fire fighters who have not been properly trained may have no response other than "I was told to do it."

8. To many fire fighters, it is frustrating to impose on people and to carry out some safety procedures that the public often only vaguely understands.

9. When asked questions, fire fighters may feel insecure about the accuracy of their responses, and may become frustrated when confronted with a questioner who assumes that all fire fighters know all there is to know about fire prevention.

10. The attitudes and reactions of the people whose premises are being inspected often make fire fighters feel unwanted.

11. Inspections often result in a longer work day.

There are several ways in which the company officer might begin to modify attitudes about inspection work so that fire fighters obtain greater satisfaction from this part of their work. Included in these ways are: (1) careful planning and scheduling, (2) better training, and (3) appropriate supervision.

Planning and Scheduling: The company officer is responsible for planning company inspections so that the entire area assigned to that officer's jurisdiction is covered within a prescribed period of time. To do this, the company officer must estimate how long it will take the available number of assigned fire fighters to conduct each inspection, as well as the number of hours needed to cover the entire area undergoing inspection.

Since inspections often result in a longer than average work day, the officer who wants to reduce any unfavorable impact carefully plans and schedules them so that they proceed properly within the allotted time. The company officer should ensure that all of the materials needed to carry out inspections are available, such as checklists, records, any maps that may be on hand, flashlights, rulers, pencils, and forms. The book of codes and regulations carried on the apparatus can provide easy reference when questions arise.

Training in the Understanding of Codes: Fire fighters better understand the importance of inspections and how they relate to their primary job of fire fighting and fire prevention if they understand codes and the purposes of inspections. Once such an awareness is gained, fire fighters are better able to impart some of this knowledge to the people whose premises they will inspect. This helps promote a more comfortable atmosphere for both parties involved. To a great extent, most people dislike being questioned in areas where they may not be able to provide an adequate response. Thus, fire fighters feel more confident if they are able to accurately answer many of the questions they are asked during inspections. To be able to do this requires training in the common codes and in answering the more popular questions.

Training in the Application of Codes: It is not sufficient for fire fighters to merely be aware of and understand codes and the purpose of inspections. It is also necessary that they be trained to apply this knowledge in order to distinguish code violations as distinct from a normal, safe environment. Skill is needed to analyze the conditions present in a building, and to determine how a fire might begin and spread. Competent fire fighters must also be able to check whether escape routes are adequate enough to ensure quick evacuation in case of fire or emergency evacuation. This type of skill involves more than simply knowing that electrical circuits cannot be overloaded, or that flammables must be stored in approved, self-closing containers, although these precautions are important parts of the codes. (See Fig. 7.6.)

Fire fighters must also be able to take the knowledge of firesafety accumulated over the years and embodied in the codes and apply such knowledge

Fig. 7.6.   Fire fighter applies training in fire prevention codes by inspecting the power generator in a community barn for possible electrical hazards. (L. Franklin Heald, Dept. Photographer, Durham-University of New Hampshire Fire Department, Durham, New Hampshire)

Fig. 7.7.   In the interests of good community relations, fire fighters should seek an owner's permission before inspecting property. (Seattle Fire Department, Seattle, Washington)

to the present situation. For example, if a floor or space is of substantial height, a fire fighter usually knows that there should be fire curtains so that when heat from fire rises it does not spread, but is contained. It is important that fire fighters either know, or can quickly find out, the answers to questions like: How should fire doors be hung, and when do they meet specifications? When are the windows an approved design? What is required so the fire escape is in compliance with the codes?

Training in Public Relations: The company officer must help fire fighters understand the importance of good public relations in order to gain cooperation from the community. For example, although regulations generally give an inspector the right of entry, it is often advisable to provide some type of advance notification of an inspection or, in certain situations, it is preferable to make an appointment. Upon arrival at the inspection site, an inspector should seek out the person in charge and request that person's permission to make the inspection.

In addition, the inspector should suggest the accompaniment of the owner or the manager during the inspection of the premises or, if this is inconvenient, should suggest that someone else accompany the inspector. (See Fig. 7.7.)

Providing Adequate Supervision: During fire prevention inspections, the company officer should provide close guidance to, and maintain frequent contact with, the members of the inspection team. Such contacts allow for spot checks to ensure that the inspections are being conducted thoroughly and that no important points are being overlooked. They also give the company officer a chance to observe areas in which additional training might be needed.

Follow-up procedures enable the company officer to evaluate the performance of fire fighters. Follow-up can provide information such as how knowledgeable fire fighters are in specific areas, and how seriously they take their work. Information obtained from follow-up procedures can also serve as a basis for determining areas in which further training is necessary. Often, opportunities present themselves for commending a fire fighter in the presence of others, thus adding to pleasant experiences in field inspections.

ACTIVITIES

1. Describe the meaning of fire prevention. Then list the three areas that are part of fire prevention, and explain what role each plays in fire prevention.
2. (a) How have past fires influenced the formation of fire prevention codes and laws that exist today?
    (b) How have past fires brought about the formation of fire protection agencies?
3. Explain the effect of the fire department's input concerning the formation of codes and regulations. How does the fire department enforce fire prevention codes?
4. Describe: (1) how each of the following fire protection agencies was formed, and (2) the purpose of each organization.
    (a) National Board of Fire Underwriters.
    (b) National Commission of Fire Prevention and Control.
    (c) National Fire Protection Association.
    (d) American Insurance Association.
    (e) Underwriters Laboratories.
    (f) Factory Mutual System.
5. Why is it important that fire department personnel participate in fire prevention activities as well as in fire suppression operations?
6. Explain how the following agencies formulate the national standards and codes.
    (a) Federal government.
    (b) National Fire Protection Association.
    (c) American Insurance Association.
    (d) Underwriters Laboratories.
    (e) Factory Mutual System.
7. If you were the company officer of a fire department that was experiencing a negative attitude towards fire inspections, how might you go about eliminating some of the negative feelings?
8. What is the role of each official in fire prevention?
    (a) State fire marshal.

(b) Chief of fire prevention or local fire marshal.

(c) Fire inspector or fire prevention officer.

(d) Fire protection engineer.

9. As the chief of fire prevention in your municipality, you have been called upon to discuss the inspection process for a local fire department training seminar. Prepare an outline of the inspection process, including in your outline a brief summary of the four types of inspections.

10. With a group of your classmates, discuss the tasks and concerns related to effective fire prevention. Next, compile your answers into a list. Then, divide the items on the list equally among the group. Each group member should write a summary of the assigned tasks and concerns, including in the summary:

(a) The importance of each task and concern in the overall program of fire prevention.

(b) The duties that must be performed in each.

(c) The role of fire department members in each.

BIBLIOGRAPHY

[1] *Fire Protection Handbook,* 14th Ed., NFPA, Boston, 1976, p. 9–29.

[2] ———, 13th Ed., NFPA, Boston, 1969, p. 3–7.

[3] "What's Your Apartment Problem?," *Fire Command!,* Vol. 42, No. 11, Nov. 1975, p. 16.

[4] BOCA *Basic Building Code/1975,* 6th Ed., Building Officials and Code Administrators International, Chicago, 1975.

[5] NFPA 1, *Fire Prevention Code,* NFPA, Boston, 1975.

[6] *NFPA Inspection Manual,* 4th Ed., NFPA, Boston, 1976.

Chapter Eight

Loss Prevention Activities —

Prefire Planning and

Related Functions

PREFIRE PLANS

The purpose of prefire plans is to enable attack preparations and fire fighting operations to be carried out at the scene of a fire as efficiently and effectively as possible. At the fireground operation, attack preparations can begin more quickly if details about the fire site are known prior to the arrival of the fire fighters and if positions of apparatus and possible hose layouts have been predetermined. When effective prefire plans have been made, much less time needs to be spent on making decisions concerning the fire site during and after the size-up process.*

Prefire Planning Process

Prefire planning should involve all fire suppression personnel on a continuous basis. It is a course of action against a probable fire and is based on the collective experiences of those involved in the planning process, and on known or existing conditions, on the relation of cause and effect, and on reasonable expectancy. The four steps that are part of the prefire planning process are: (1) information gathering, (2) information analysis, (3) information dissemination, and (4) class review and drill.

---

*The mental process known as "size-up" is one of the most important tactical operations that takes place prior to any physical activity at the scene of a fire. Size-up is a continuous mental evaluation of the situation and all related factors that may determine the success or failure of the fireground operation. This mental evaluation should begin as soon as companies are alerted and should be continuous throughout the incident. Size-up should not be limited to the fireground commander; it should be practiced by each fire fighter and officer involved with the incident.

Information Gathering: Collecting pertinent information at the selected site that might affect fire fighting operations, such as building construction features, occupancy, exposures, utility disconnects, fire hydrant locations, water main sizes, and anything else that would affect fire fighting operations if a fire should occur.

Information Analysis: The information gathered must be analyzed in terms of what is pertinent and vital to fire suppression operations. Then, an operable prefire plan must be formulated and put into a usable format that can be used on the fireground.

Information Dissemination: All companies that might respond to each pre-fire planned location should receive copies of the plan so that they become familiar with both the plan and the pertinent factors relating to it.

Class Review and Drill: Each company that might be involved at the pre-planned location should review the plan on a regular schedule. Periodic drills with all companies involved should be scheduled on the property if possible.

Prefire plans are necessary for all target hazards and special risks, but need not be developed for occupancies such as single-family dwellings or other smaller occupancies since a standard operating procedure should be sufficient. Prefire planning is a necessary adjunct to tactical operations and, if used, should aid in operational efficiency, reducing fire losses, and helping to provide an optimum level of fire protection.

Description of a Prefire Plan

Prefire plans usually consist of two parts: (1) a data sheet, and (2) a building layout. (See Figs. 8.1 through 8.4.) In combination, these two parts should present information on any or all of the following:

1. Details about the location of the building and the best response routes at various times of the day and for different weather conditions. Such information would eliminate delays on steep hills, or delays caused by heavy traffic or flooding.

2. A building layout showing access routes, dimensions, construction materials, location of stairs, windows, exits, sprinklers and their valves, standpipes, hydrants, and all other fire protection equipment and utilities, as well as any other pertinent information about building construction. Supplementary water supplies from other mains might also be indicated for companies other than those making the first response.

3. Details about the type of occupancy, special volatile materials, and hours that the building would be occupied.

4. Information about the type of occupancy and construction of any adjacent buildings.

5. The best positions to station apparatus in relation to water supply, space, incline, and traffic conditions. Figure 8.1 details a sample of the Portland (Oregon) Fire Bureau's company assignments, positions, and prefire plan for an apartment complex. (This information could be entered for the various possible types of fires if department resources permit such detail.)

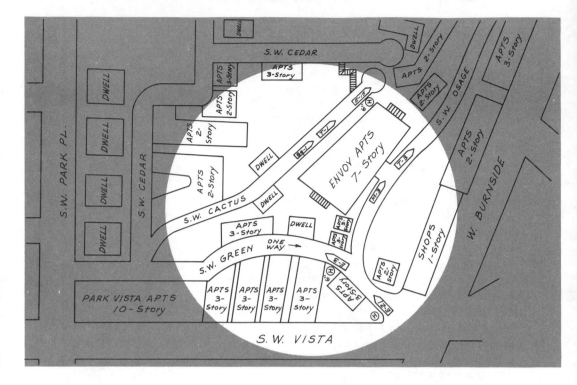

ASSIGNMENTS

| E-3 | E-15 | E-21 | T-3 | T-1 | Sq.-1 |
| C-2 | | 102 | | | |

COMPANY POSITIONS

1. Engine 3 connect to hydrant on Green @ junction of Green and Osage, Manifold 3 lay lines from Engine to main entrance.

2. Truck 3 take a position on Osage.

3. Engine 15 spot on hydrant on Cactus Drive.

4. Truck 1 spot behind Engine 15 on Cactus Drive.

5. Engine 21 spot on hydrant at Burnside & Osage. Work off Manifold 3.

6. Squad 1 spot on Cactus Drive behind Truck 1.

NOTES ON ENVOY PLAN:

The building is well constructed of reinforced concrete with slab floors. The only standpipe is a wet-pipe interior one supplied by city pressure. There is no sprinkler system. There are adequate hydrants. The mains are well gridded.

Because of the narrow streets (Cactus and Cedar are dead end) it will not be practicable to change positions once the rigs are committed.

Company officers should give thought to best deployment for other fires in this area.

Fig. 8.1. Description and drawing of the prefire plan for an apartment complex showing company assignments and positions. Note the access routes and water supplies used by each apparatus. (Portland Fire Bureau, Portland, Oregon)

T.I.P.S. PHASE 1 INFORMATION FORM

BF-35 (1/72)

1. ADDRESS   (Include all if more than one)

	UNIT	BATT.	DIV.	DATE

558 Main St.
ALSO REAR 94–96 Lake St.

2. T. I. P. S. HAZARD (S)   Briefly note major item(s) or hazard(s) that made building a T.I.P.S. Bldg. Info to be repeated below in more detail.

LARGE AREA ON ALL FLOORS
HEAVILY STOCKED (CARDBOARD, COTTON ETC.)
BUILDING RUNS FROM 94–96 Lake St. to 558 Main St.

3. BUILDING CONSTRUCTION INFORMATION

CLASS	HEIGHT	WIDTH	DEPTH	SHAPE IF IRREGULAR
	2	25 & 50	200	L

4. EXPOSURES   List rear exposure. Include others only if not visible from street.

END OF PHASE 1   Further information concerning structural data and chiefs operational tips available upon request.

T.I.P.S. PHASE 2 STRUCTURAL DATA INFORMATION

5. LIFE HAZARD (Civilian)

6. STAIRWAYS & EGRESSES   (To upper floors, horizontal, etc., locate each)

TYPE	LOCATION, FRONT/REAR	EXPOSURE SIDE	FLOOR START/STOP	)R START/STOP
ENCLOSED STAIRS	FRONT	ADJ #2	CELLAR/1ST	.AR/2ND FL
ENCLOSED STAIRS	REAR	ADJ #2 & 3	CELLAR/1ST	2ND FL
OPEN INTERIOR STAIR	CENTER	ADJ #4	CELLAR/MEZZANINE	.AR/STREET
FIRE ESCAPE	REAR		/2ND FL	
ENCLOSED STAIRS	FRONT	ADJ #1 & 2	STREET/2ND FL	
ENCLOSED STAIRS	REAR	ADJ #2 & 3	STREET/2ND FL	

IRON STAIRWAY, LADDER TO SCUTTLE IN ROOF

8. OCCUPANCY   (Include only if unusual or not visible from street)

9. FIRE PROTECTION

THERMOSTATIC ALARM – CELLAR

10. OTHER   (Include any special condition or hazard)

LARGE OPEN AREA ON ALL FLOORS, HEAVILY STOCKED WITH FAST BURNING & SMOKE PRO-DUCING STOCK (CARDBOARD, COTTONS ETC.) MEZZANINE ON LAKE ST. ADDS ANOTHER 2500 SQ. FT. OF FLOORING & STORAGE TO 1ST FLOOR.

11. BELOW GRADE INFORMATION   (If this area pertains to T.I.P.S. Hazard #2 above include access, ventilation, life, etc.)

ACCESS TO CELLAR ONLY FROM INTERIOR OF BUILDING FRONT AND REAR AND AT EXP #4 CENTER OF BLDG. THE STAIR AT EXP #4 IS OPEN. STAIRS AT REAR AND FRONT OF BLDG. ARE ENCLOSED STAIR.
CHUTE – REAR OF BLDG. 3' X 4' TO CELLAR.
LARGE CELLAR AREA.

END OF STRUCTURAL PHASE 2: CHIEFS OPERATIONAL INFORMATION AVAILABLE UPON REQUEST

Fig. 8.2. Example of the data sheet part of a prefire plan. (New York City Fire Department, New York, New York)

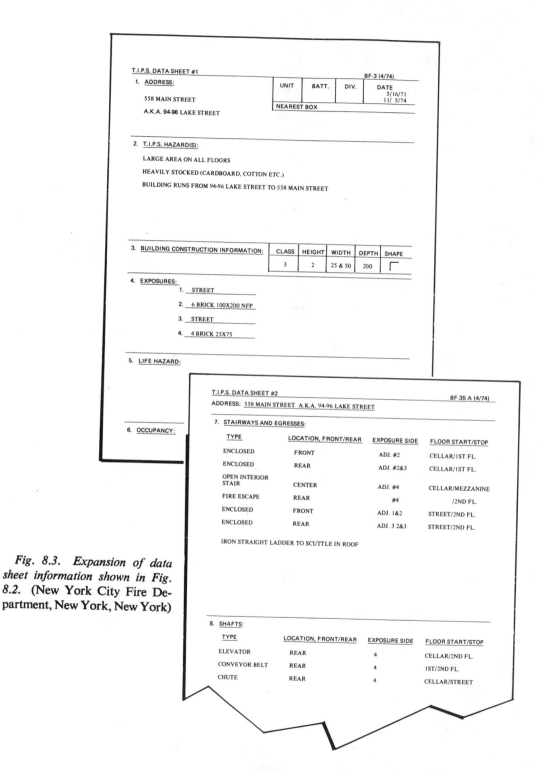

T.I.P.S. DATA SHEET #1

1. ADDRESS:

BF-3 (4/74)

UNIT	BATT.	DIV.	DATE
			5/16/71
			11/ 5/74

NEAREST BOX

558 MAIN STREET

A.K.A. 94-96 LAKE STREET

2. T.I.P.S. HAZARD(S):

LARGE AREA ON ALL FLOORS

HEAVILY STOCKED (CARDBOARD, COTTON ETC.)

BUILDING RUNS FROM 94-96 LAKE STREET TO 558 MAIN STREET

3. BUILDING CONSTRUCTION INFORMATION:

CLASS	HEIGHT	WIDTH	DEPTH	SHAPE
3	2	25 & 50	200	Γ

4. EXPOSURES:

1. STREET

2. 6 BRICK 100X200 NFP

3. STREET

4. 4 BRICK 25X75

5. LIFE HAZARD:

6. OCCUPANCY:

T.I.P.S. DATA SHEET #2

BF-35 A (4/74)

ADDRESS: 558 MAIN STREET A.K.A. 94-96 LAKE STREET

7. STAIRWAYS AND EGRESSES:

TYPE	LOCATION, FRONT/REAR	EXPOSURE SIDE	FLOOR START/STOP
ENCLOSED	FRONT	ADJ. #2	CELLAR/1ST FL.
ENCLOSED	REAR	ADJ. #2&3	CELLAR/1ST FL.
OPEN INTERIOR STAIR	CENTER	ADJ. #4	CELLAR/MEZZANINE
FIRE ESCAPE	REAR	#4	/2ND FL.
ENCLOSED	FRONT	ADJ. 1&2	STREET/2ND FL.
ENCLOSED	REAR	ADJ. 3 2&3	STREET/2ND FL.

IRON STRAIGHT LADDER TO SCUTTLE IN ROOF

8. SHAFTS:

TYPE	LOCATION, FRONT/REAR	EXPOSURE SIDE	FLOOR START/STOP
ELEVATOR	REAR	4	CELLAR/2ND FL.
CONVEYOR BELT	REAR	4	1ST/2ND FL.
CHUTE	REAR	4	CELLAR/STREET

Fig. 8.3. Expansion of data sheet information shown in Fig. 8.2. (New York City Fire Department, New York, New York)

204

T.I.P.S. DATA SHEET #3   BF-35 B (4/74)

ADDRESS: 558 MAIN STREET A.K.A. 94–96 LAKE STREET

9. **BELOW GRADE INFORMATION:**

ACCESS TO CELLAR ONLY FROM INTERIOR OF BUILDING FRONT AND REAR AT

EXPOSURE 4 CENTER OF BUILDING.

THE STAIR AT EXPOSURE 4 IS OPEN.

STAIRS AT REAR AND FRONT OF BUILDING ARE ENCLOSED

CHUTE REAR OF BUILDING 3' X 4' TO CELLAR

LARGE CELLAR AREA

10. **FIRE PROTECTION:**

THERMOSTATIC ALARM IN CELLAR

Fig. 8.3. (Continued). Expansion of data sheet information shown in Fig. 8.2. (New York City Fire Department, New York, New York)

11. **OTHER:**

LARGE OPEN AREA ON ALL FLOORS, HEAVILY STOCKED WITH FAST BURNING AND SMOKE

PRODUCING STOCK. (CARDBOARD, COTTONS ETC.). MEZZANINE ON LAKE STREET ADDS

ANOTHER 2500 SQUARE FEET OF FLOORING AND STORAGE TO 1ST. FLOOR.

T.I.P.S. DATA SHEET #4   OPERATIONAL   BF-35 C (4/74)

ADDRESS: 558 MAIN ST. A.K.A. 94-96 LAKE ST.

FIRE FIGHTING TIPS

VERTICAL EXTENSION: VIA OPEN STAIRS   A. CELLAR TO 1ST FLOOR
                                              B. 1ST FLOOR TO MEZZANINE
                             VIA CONVEYOR CHUTE 1ST FLOOR TO 2ND FLOOR

HORIZONTAL EXTENSION: VERY LARGE OPEN AREAS ON ALL FLOORS.
                             HEAVILY STOCKED WITH FAST BURNING AND SMOKE
                             PRODUCING STOCK (CARDBOARD, COTTONS ETC.).
                             200 FOOT DEPTH AND 25' FRONT ON MAIN ST.; 50' FRONT
                             ON LAKE ST.
                             MEZZANINE ON LAKE STREET SIDE ADDS ANOTHER
                             2500 SQUARE FEET OF FLOORING AND STORAGE TO
                             1ST FLOOR.

CELLAR FIRE: STRETCH ADDITIONAL LINES AT REAR (LAKE ST.)
                             1. TO COVER CONVEYOR OPENING
                             2. TO ADVANCE TO OPEN STAIR ON S/S 1ST. FLOOR
                                TO PREVENT FIRE FROM COMING OUT OPEN STAIR
                                AND ALSO TO PROTECT MEZZANINE OVERHEAD

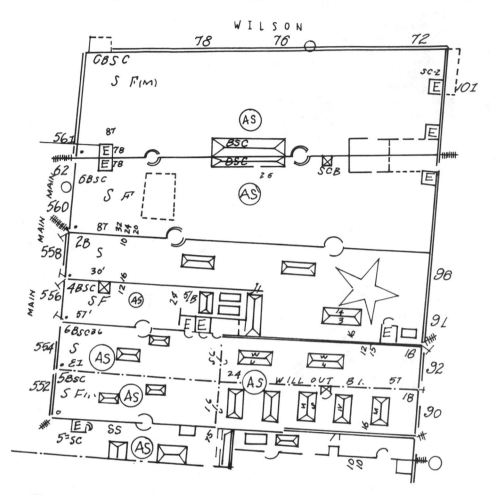

Fig. 8.4. Typical building layout sketch similar to those prepared and presented as part of a prefire plan. This sketch includes the data sheet material from Figs. 8.2 and 8.3. (New York City Fire Department, New York, New York)

In order to be most useful, a prefire plan should contain only that information that does not change readily. Often, not all information that might be valuable is recorded. Secondary information or items that might quickly outdate the plan should be noted in pencil on the plan itself. The inclusion of too much information, however, can complicate a prefire plan, rendering it less effective for the user.

The New York City Fire Department is known for the thoroughness of its prefire plans. Figures 8.2 and 8.4 show the two parts of a prefire plan developed by that department: Figure 8.2 illustrates the data sheet part of the plans, and Figure 8.4 is a sketch of the building layout prepared to accompany the data sheet. Figure 8.3 illustrates how the New York City Fire Department further expands its prefire data sheet material to make it even more comprehensive and useful.

The symbols that are usually used on prefire plans are an important shorthand method for providing information as quickly and simply as possible. Because they are used to save time and space, symbols should be able to be read more easily and more rapidly than words. The use of symbols can be defeated if they are complicated and there are too many to memorize. Different fire departments and organizations use different symbols, and in cases in which the use of a symbol will not sufficiently describe the situation, it is also necessary to label that point on the plan — often by use of an abbreviation. Figure 8.5 is an example of the types of symbols used on prefire plan layouts, and Table 8.1 gives a list of standard abbreviations that can be used. Although brief, the list provides all of the abbreviations that are commonly needed. "Abbreviations for Use on Drawings and in Text," prepared by the American National Standards Institute, provides a list of additional, less common abbreviations.[1] Figure 8.6 shows a prefire plan building layout without symbols, and Figure 8.7 shows the same building layout with symbols substituted for words to demonstrate the extent to which the use of symbols can help simplify a prefire layout.

The symbols and plans presented in this text will enable any inspector or fire fighter to develop an acceptable plan in accordance with widespread convention. However, it should be realized that there are many organizations using slightly different sets of symbols and layouts. When taking information from a plan developed from another source, it is necessary to refer to the legend of symbols used by that organization to accurately interpret the information.

A thorough understanding of the features depicted on a complete plan is necessary. The features of any property can be placed in one of four categories: Construction (C); Occupancy (O); Protection (P); and Exposure (E) — (COPE). These major classifications of important features are comprised of many components. Figure 8.8 shows some of the standard plan symbols that can be used to represent the general location and type of COPE features of a facility.

Drafting Prefire Plans

Generally, a fire department cannot efficiently cover the entire district as frequently as it would like and in the limited time available. Therefore, certain areas or occupancies of high value, or with a great potential for loss of life or property, are given priority. Those sites where the risk is greatest are highest on the list, and are surveyed more frequently. The following paragraphs outline a suggested procedure for conducting a survey.

The Survey: The entire company actively participates in the survey process, which is very similar to an inspection. The department usually supplies checklists that provide the fire fighter with guidelines to follow, making the information-collecting process more efficient. These checklists can be filled in as each

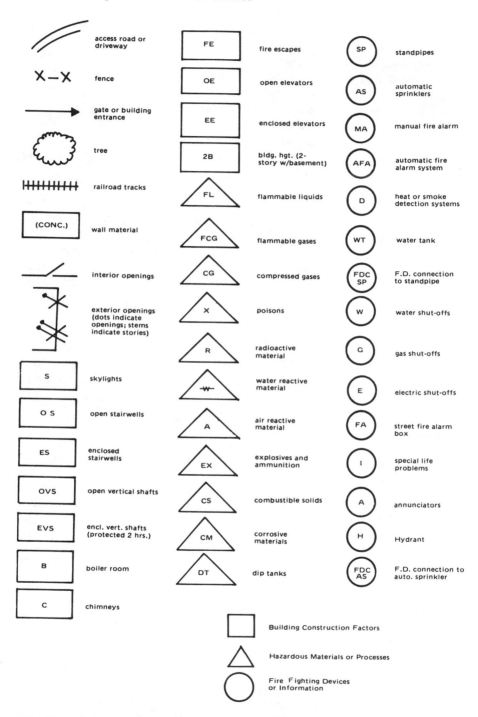

Fig. 8.5.   Examples of types of symbols used on prefire plan layouts. Note: symbols are categorized to facilitate rapid recognition.

Table 8.1
Legend of Common Abbreviations*

Above	ABV	Metal	MT
Acetylene	ACET	Mezzanine	MEZZ
Aluminum	AL	Mill Use	MU
Asbestos	ASB		
Asphalt Protected Metal	APM	Normally Closed	NC
Attic	A	Normally Open	NO
Automatic Fire Alarm	AFA	North	N
Automatic Sprinklers	AS	Number	No
Avenue	AVE		
		Open Sprinklers	OS
Basement	B	Outside Screw & Yoke Valve	OS & Y
Beam	BM		
Board on Joist	BDOJ	Partition	PTN
Brick	BR	(Label Composition)	(ie, WD PTN)
		Plaster	PLAS
Cast Iron	CI	Plaster Board	PLAS BD
Cement	CEM	Platform	PLATF
Cinder Block	CB	Pound (Unit of Force)	LB
Concrete	CONC	Pressure	PRESS
Corrugated Iron	COR IR	Unit of Pressure-Pounds	
		Per Square Inch	PSI
Domestic	DOM	Protected Steel	PROT ST
Double Hydrant	DH	Private	PRIVATE
Dry Pipe Valve	DPV	Public	PUB
East	E	Railroad	RR
Elevator	ELEV	Reinforced Concrete	RC
Engine	ENG	Reinforcing Steel	RST
		Reservoir	RES
Feet	FT	Revolutions per Minute	RPM
Fibre Board	FBR BD	Roof	RF
Fire Escape	FE	Room	RM
Fire Department Pumper			
Connection	FDC	Slate Shingle Roof	SSR
Fire Detection Units		Space	SP
Products of Combustion	POC	South	S
Rate of Heat Rise	RHR	Stainless Steel	SST
Fixed Temperature	FTEP	Steel	ST
Floor	FL	Steel Deck	ST DK
Frame	FR	Stone	STONE
Fuel Oil (Label with		Story	STO
Grade Number)	FO#——	Street	STREET
		Stucco	STUC
Gallon	GAL	Suspended Acoustical	
Gallons Per Day	GPD	Plaster Ceiling	SAPC
Gallons Per Minute	GPM	Suspended Acoustical	
Galvanized Iron	GALVI	Tile Ceiling	SATC
Galvanized Steel	GALVS	Suspended Plaster Ceiling	SPC
Gas, Natural	GAS	Suspended Sprayed	
Gasoline	GASOLINE	Acoustical Ceiling	SSAC
Generator	GEN		
Glass	GL	Tank (Label Capacity	
Glass Block	GLB	in Gallons)	TK
Gypsum	GYM	Tenant	TEN
Gypsum Board	GYM BD	Tile Block	TB
		Timber	TMBR
High Voltage	HV	Tin Clad	TIN CL
Hollow Tile	HT	Triple Hydrant	TH
Hose Connection	HC	Truss	TR
Hydrant	HYD		
		Under	UND
Inch, Inches	IN		
Iron	IR	Vault	VLT
Iron Clad	IR CL	Veneer	VEN
Iron Pipe	IP	Volts (Indicate Number of)	450v
		Wall Board	WL BD
Joist, Joisted	J	Wall Hydrant	WLH
		Water Pipe	WP
Liquid	LIQ	West	W
Liquid Oxygen	LOX	Wire Glass	WGL
		Wire Net	WN
Manufacture	MRF	Wood	WD
Manufacturing	MFG	Wood Frame	WD FR
Maximum Capacity	MAX CAP		
Mean Sea Leves	MSL	Yard	YD

*Some words that have a common abbreviation, e.g. "ST" for "street," are spelled out fully to avoid confusion with similar abbreviations used herein for other terms.

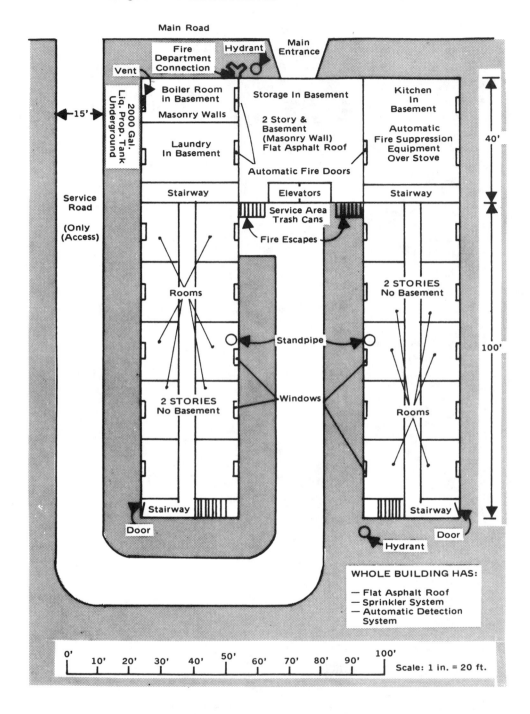

Fig. 8.6.   Example of prefire plan building layout.

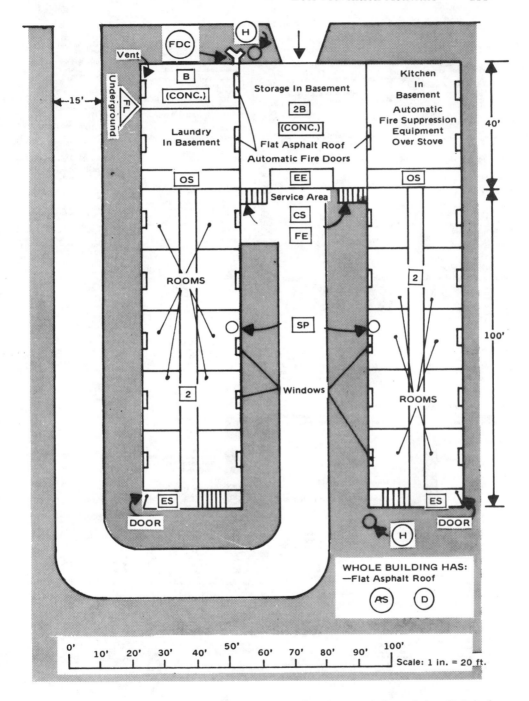

Fig. 8.7.   The same building layout shown in Fig. 8.6, but with symbols substituted for words to demonstrate the extent to which the use of symbols can simplify a prefire plan building layout.

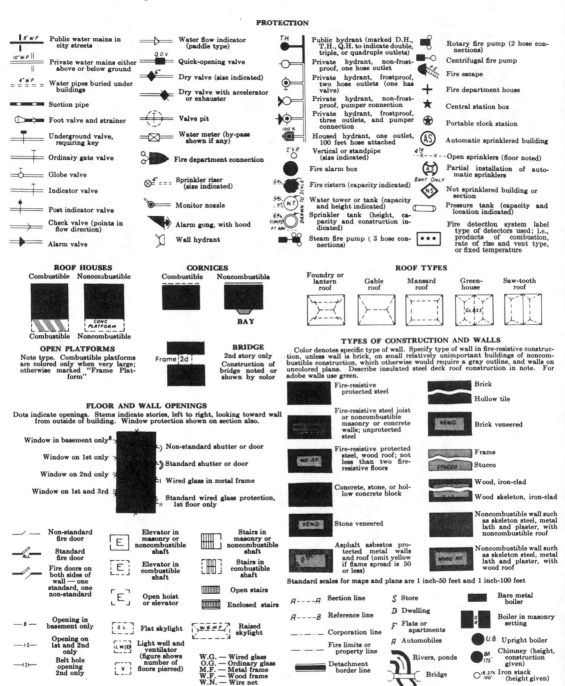

Fig. 8.8. Some of the standard plan symbols used to represent the general location and type of COPE features of a facility. (Includes copyrighted material of Insurance Services Office with its permission. Copyright 1975, Insurance Services Office)

category of information is obtained. Fire fighters can gather data in teams or separately; at times, the company officer might need to collect or verify certain pieces of information without being accompanied by others. When the building has been thoroughly surveyed (the time it will take for this will vary according to the building's size) and the entire company is satisfied that the survey information is correct, a final map of the building and a data sheet showing the specific hazard in the building should be prepared. The best response route and initial attack positions may also be indicated.

The Drafting Process: A fire department formulating a program of prefire planning might use a procedure similar to the following:

1. Determine order of priority for buildings to be surveyed.
2. Plan a schedule for surveys.
3. Notify owners or managers of properties about the prefire plan program, and request permission to make a survey. As with inspections, this request is legally unnecessary. Rather, it is made to help maintain good community relations.
4. Decide which units will carry out the survey.
5. After the survey data is gathered, incorporate it into the prefire plan.
6. Modify prefire plans whenever there are changes in occupancies or buildings, and incorporate all changes into the plan as soon as possible. Also, changing traffic patterns, improvements in apparatus and equipment, and new concepts in fire fighting operations require updating of plans.

Use and Application of Prefire Plans

Prefire plans are often carried on apparatus so that on the way to a fire, company officers and fire fighters can refresh their memories about the details of a building. In some departments, a dispatcher might be assigned the responsibility for relaying prefire plan information to personnel on the apparatus. In either case, availability of this material prior to arrival at the fire scene enables company officers to make rapid decisions about operations once the company arrives.

Further benefit can be derived from prefire plans by using them as a basis for simulation drills. Strategy and tactics for fighting possible fires can be discussed at these drills. The use of prefire plans for training purposes helps to enhance the attractiveness of simulation drills, increases fire fighter interest in departmental procedures, and, most importantly, helps increase company awareness of details of hazards in the district. Further information on the use of prefire plans for training purposes is contained in Chapter Twelve, "Training as a Management Function." It should be kept in mind that the drills in which prefire plans are used may become dull after a while if the only objective is awareness about an emergency that may never occur.

The Future of Prefire Planning

The development of prefire plan strategies for the most likely locations of fires is a large task, particularly for fire departments that have many industrial or commercial buildings. It involves, in addition to the detailed lay-out, several different strategy plans corresponding to possible fire sites for each hazard.

Even if time were available to a fire department so that it could consider formulating such prefire plan strategies in the various commercial and in-dustrial complexes, such plans would contain a vast amount of information beyond the capability of most (and possibly all) fire departments to control. At this moment, the state of the art is not advanced to the point where most departments can process so much information effectively. It would take the most sophisticated computers to accept, organize, and rapidly retrieve such information. Not even the largest fire departments have mobile access to such computer capabilities. If they did, it would also be necessary to have a com-munications system that could transmit such information quickly and clearly to companies en route to the fire. This would require television equipment, since only pictures have the ability to carry this type of information in a form that would permit rapid use. Progress toward such complete prefire plans, including strategy, is being made by limited, highly specialized fire depart-ments that service only a single industrial complex.

Relationship Between Prefire Planning and Inspections

Prefire planning and inspections overlap in several areas, including the fol-lowing:

1. Like inspections, prefire plan surveys often uncover code violations. Reports of violations might be sent to the Fire Prevention Bureau, or to the departmental officer responsible for enforcement of codes.

2. Prefire plan surveys, like inspections, familiarize fire fighters with the buildings in their districts. Prefire plan surveys and inspections reinforce each other in this respect.

3. Prefire plans offer opportunities for good public relations. Although direct contact with people is limited to the initial visit and follow-ups, news-paper articles about prefire plans can help make the general public more aware of the competence of the department. People recognize the advantages of advance planning, especially for emergencies, and are usually impressed by prefire plans.

4. Before an inspection, a company officer could review the prefire plan. Then, if an inspection indicated that certain features of the plan had changed (if an opening had been filled in, for instance, or the location of hazardous material storage had been changed), such information would be incorporated into the prefire plan.

Role of the Company Officer in Prefire Planning

The company officer has the responsibility for managing the process that leads to the development and maintenance of up-to-date prefire plans. The officer can also make use of the plans to increase interest in fire prevention and to create desire for greater knowledge about details of the hazards in the district.

The initial survey of a building is generally accepted as an interesting experience, probably because it is usually more inspiring to do something for the first time. However, unless the officer continues to emphasize the importance of prefire planning and its relevance to the improvement of fire fighting operations, later visits for updating may be treated with less enthusiasm. This would be especially true if the same personnel have frequently inspected a particular building for violations.

The linking elements concept (see Chapter Four, "Modern Management Concepts") can be a useful guide for company officers who are attempting to create a greater interest in prefire planning. To create such interest calls for:

1. Setting goals for development and updating of prefire plans, keeping in mind the eight problem areas that often arise in MBO programs: (1) extent, (2) quality, (3) involvement, (4) frequency, (5) accountability, (6) participation, (7) performance appraisal/evaluation, (8) operational/development. (See Fig. 5.7, Chapter Five, "Managing by Objectives.")

2. Assuring that planning and scheduling for development of prefire plans is thorough and realistic.

3. Making work assignments in such a way that they place equal demands on all fire fighters, considering their respective skills and talents.

4. Providing the necessary training support to eliminate any knowledge/ skill deficiencies that might create apprehension or lead a fire fighter to feel inadequate. For example, the company officer should ensure that all fire fighters understand how to use a prefire plan by coaching them in:

• Drawing maps that show building dimensions.
• Using symbols.
• Deciding which specific pieces of information about a building are important enough to record.

5. Making frequent use of prefire plans in training for interesting simulation or joint planning sessions.

6. Using prefire planning for providing recognition to individuals.

7. Assigning individual fire fighters those tasks that provide greatest satisfaction to them, and rotating the tasks that are widely desired or that present opportunities for developing increased competence.

PUBLIC EDUCATION

One of the most important tasks in the public fire service's loss prevention effort is public education and training. Because lack of public concern for the loss prevention effort can defeat even the best planned public education and training programs, public education should be constantly updated in order to maintain public interest and support.

Purpose of Public Education

As previously explained in Chapter Seven, "Fire Prevention Activities — Codes, Operational Tasks, and Inspections," one of the major purposes of public education programs is to help the fire department achieve increased public support for fire prevention. Thus, if the general public is to be involved in helping to solve the fire problem, it must be kept informed. Also, really effective fire prevention must be based on public cooperation. An increased public awareness of the dangers of smoking in bed, of leaving gasoline cans uncovered, and of leaving boiling water unattended can prevent many fires. For example, "Sparky's Junior Fire Department Programs," a series of educational programs offered by the NFPA, have undoubtedly prevented many fires. A good fire prevention program can bring sympathy for large fire department budgets and create an environment in which inspectors are seen as public servants who perform a most useful service, rather than as intruders. This, in turn, makes fire prevention assignments much more rewarding for fire fighters.

Public Education Through Inspections

Inspections generally make the community more aware of the importance of loss prevention by pointing out the existence of fire hazards in the home, plant, or office. When carried out in a competent and professional manner, inspections can make the public more receptive to further information about firesafety. For example, a good public image and a well thought out plan for publicity and public education programs can do much to encourage homeowners to call up the fire prevention bureau and ask to have their homes inspected.

Howard Boyd, Fire Marshal of Metropolitan Nashville and Davidson County, Tennessee, points out that fire prevention bureau education programs need to zero in on one- and two-family dwellings — the area in which fifty percent of the deaths due to fire occur.[2]

> Unfortunately, I'm afraid that most fire departments are spending very little time on one- and two-family dwellings. This is because 'a man's home is his castle,' and once he gets there he thinks he is safe. Actually, he's in the most dangerous place in America, the home. We need a long program of public education — I see no other way by which we can reach the homeowner in his 'castle.'

Inspections tend to prompt the homeowner's concern for loss prevention matters. Often, the fact that an inspection is forthcoming can stimulate a homeowner into discarding debris, and tidying up any paint cans, papers, and accumulated odds and ends.

Public Education Through Publicity

Publicity through the media and printed brochures, flyers, and handouts are needed to generate interest in private dwelling inspections. A good publicity program can help the public understand the diverse functions of a fire prevention bureau and thus help support the other educational objectives of the department. Such a program can also emphasize the importance of public participation in loss prevention.

To be most effective, a publicity program should adhere to the following principles:

1. Information should be disseminated in a steady and continuous flow over a period of time. (Isolated messages are not as likely to be remembered.)

2. Publicity should be geared to events and seasons. This can be accomplished by emphasizing the current seasonal hazards, Fire Prevention Week, delivery of new apparatus, plans to build a new station, etc. (See Fig. 8.9.)

3. Sometimes news items can be used to pave the way for more specific educational information. For instance, an article describing how the fire department helped bring a specific house fire under control, with minimal damage and no loss of life, could mention that the occupants had recently installed a smoke detector. A follow-up article could then discuss smoke detection equipment.

Using the Media: Gaining the attention of the public through the media is more easily accomplished if the department's personnel are organized to deal with the media. Many departments have officers on their staffs who serve as public information officers; in the absence of such officers, publicity is usually handled by the fire prevention bureau.

1. The chief or designated officer may set up a meeting with the editor of the local paper and/or manager of the local radio station to plan an entire publicity program, and then assign a member of the department to work di-

Fig. 8.9. Example of a poster emphasizing public participation in fire prevention. Shown here is an example geared to a particular event; a Fire Prevention Week poster from NFPA.

rectly with the paper or station in the development of the program. This type of planning can help bring higher priority at times when the media might not normally consider items on fire prevention to be of foremost importance.

2. Television or radio interviews and prepared articles for the newspapers (especially during "Fire Prevention Week") can draw attention to particular hazards and the importance of codes. Some departments look for volunteers to write general interest articles dealing with specific problems. Examples of such articles include how to deal with grease fires in the kitchen, how to plan escape routes, and what to do in case of a fire.

3. The opportunity to publicize the importance of fire prevention comes with every large fire — especially when loss of life is involved. At such times, the press and public are more receptive to ways in which the risk of fire can be reduced. People are then more likely to take steps to protect themselves.

NFPA Posters, Flyers: The NFPA and other organizations having fire protection interests publish many posters, flyers, and other handout materials that can be left with local businesses and in public places. When private dwellings are inspected, flyers with information about specific hazards can be left with the homeowners. School systems often distribute fire prevention flyers and posters to students to take home to their parents.

Public Education Through Programs

The type of community programs that are concerned with the need for greater emphasis on loss prevention are an integral part of the overall public education program. These programs often include activities such as the fire department's "open house" and school visits. During "open house," the public is usually invited to visit fire stations to see demonstrations of training sessions and to inspect the apparatus. School visits, often with the apparatus, usually attempt to explain fire fighting to students. All such activities bring the greatest benefits if they receive wide publicity. (See Fig. 8.10.)

The following excerpt from a recent *Fire Command!* article titled "Department Slashes Fire Losses . . . Can You?" highlighted the dramatic results that can be obtained with a comprehensive fire prevention program.[3]

> As fire losses mount annually around the country, one city has been able to effect a startling reversal of this trend. Although U.S. fire losses increased by 55 percent between 1969 and 1973, fire losses in Winston-Salem, North Carolina, declined by 49 percent during that same period.
>
> The Winston-Salem Fire Department attributes this outstanding record to a five-point fire prevention program that includes scientific fire management and computer analysis; increased emphasis on fire prevention programs such as code enforcement and public education; emphasis on a more firesafe environment; creation of an arson squad to apprehend and prosecute arsonists; and a comprehensive prefire survey program.

The article also presented a summary of the extensive public education effort that played a major part in the total program.[3]

Fig. 8.10.   Captain of the Toronto Fire Department (Toronto, Canada) *receives an award from children who have learned firesafety from him.   (Toronto Sun*, Toronto, Province of Ontario, Canada)

In addition to fire inspections, the fire department places a great deal of emphasis on public education. Approximately 700 radio programs on fire-safety are broadcast yearly. Department members spend 6000 to 8000 hours each year in the school system teaching firesafety to children. Both of these programs are supplemented with a variety of other educational activities designed to disseminate information to the entire community.

Slide Programs: Slide programs usually include slides and talks of a general nature for schools or community groups, or slide sets specifically designed to educate the public on a certain topic (such as fire detection equipment). The multimedia aspect of such programs helps community members assimilate messages quickly and easily.

Special Committees: In some communities, special committees composed of fire department personnel and local business and civic leaders are set up to promote fire prevention programs. These committees offer avenues for the department to discuss community problems relating to fire loss.

Some municipalities organize safety committees composed of representatives from governmental departments concerned with public safety, including representatives from community groups such as the PTA and Jaycees, to discuss various safety problems. Members of these groups who have influential contacts throughout the community can usually help make arrangements for public presentations on firesafety.

Role of the Company Officer in Public Education

Most public education work is handled by a fire prevention bureau where one exists, or by a specific officer who has been assigned the responsibility for public education or community relations. Sometimes, the services of other members of the department who are interested in public speaking or writing are enlisted. Although it might require extra time and effort, this type of work can be stimulating and interesting because it brings rewarding personal contacts or visible evidence of useful activity. However, even in small departments where such talents may be limited, interested and alert officers can usually find citizen volunteers who might be willing to contribute their services for such purposes.

FIRE IGNITION SEQUENCE INVESTIGATION

Investigations into fires that are not considered to be of suspicious origin are conducted by department officers or fire prevention inspectors. They provide the basis for learning about the causes of fires, the reasons for their spread, and the performance of whatever fire prevention equipment had been installed in the building.

Both areas of responsibility — fire detection and fire investigation — are highly technical and specialized. Close coordination of detection and investigation efforts, along with a recognition of the necessity for overlapping in these two general areas, is essential. Often, additional information obtained from interrogations or other aspects of the criminal investigation will corroborate and strengthen the fire ignition sequence factors, and in some cases change the fire ignition sequences altogether.

Purpose of Investigation

The results of fire ignition sequence investigations provide data useful in developing new prevention procedures. Investigations also serve as a means of determining whether fires are due to arson. In addition, if the officer establishes that the fire was due to a code violation, the department can consult its files to determine whether the violation had been discovered during inspections and whether steps were taken to ensure compliance. Finally, investigations provide a necessary service to insurance companies in enabling them to process their claims expediently. (See Fig. 8.11.)

Arson Investigations

The authority for investigating fires of a suspicious nature rests primarily with the state fire marshal's office or, in the absence of this position, with the state police. However, in practice many states delegate this power to local fire department officials who cooperate fully with the police.

Some large departments have arson squads whose special task is the investigation of suspicious fires. Within these squads there are officers, trained by the police department, who may have the power of arrest and the responsibility for preparing cases for prosecution. Others are composed of officers from both fire and police departments. Depending on local ordinances, fire prevention officers may also have such police powers.

Fig. 8.11.   Fire investigators examining debris in the 1971 Lil' Haven Nursing Home fire. (Desert News, Salt Lake City, Utah)

The special training needed for fire investigation may not be available in smaller fire departments. In such instances, when arson is suspected, the work is often turned over to the local police department or to the police department of the closest large community.

The investigation of a suspicious fire usually begins with a search for evidence of the way the fire may have started. The fire scene is searched for clues, and statements are obtained from witnesses and others who can contribute ideas. Sometimes the officer in charge of the investigation may call on the fire fighters for their assistance. Care should be taken to ensure that all possible evidence is collected and that pictures are made of all significant places. As part of the investigation procedure, departmental records are searched for relevant information and the insurance companies are contacted to obtain any light their files may throw on the problem.

Since all state laws establish arson as a felony, after the fire service determines the ignition sequence of a fire to be arson, then that sequence must be further investigated. At the arson investigation phase the police authorities normally have primary responsibility, much the same as for other felonies occurring within their jurisdiction. In many areas of the United States, particularly at the state level or in larger cities, state and municipal laws give fire authorities the power to perform the police function of arson investigation.

Should a suspect be apprehended and charged, it is again the primary responsibility of the fire service to prove the corpus delecti of arson; *i.e.*, that the fire was willfully and maliciously caused.

When developing an arson case, three elements must be established:

1. That there was an actual charring or destruction by fire.

2. That the ignition sequence of the fire was the result of willful and malicious design or intent.

3. That the suspect or an agent of the suspect had the opportunity to cause the fire.

An established motive is of great value in an arson case, although motive is not, from a legal standpoint, considered as an essential element of arson; many incendiary fires might be classified as being without motive. It should also be considered that in the presentation of an arson case, each of the three preceding elements must be established to the satisfaction of the court in the order presented before the next element may be determined. (See Fig. 8.12.)

Fire Loss Reporting

A fire protection duty of equal importance to comprehensive investigation is the accurate reporting of such investigations. This duty has seldom been

Fig. 8.12. A rug clearly shows evidence of an arson fire. After the rug was dried and swept clean, flammable liquid stains established the malicious ignition of the fire. (Portland Fire Bureau, Portland, Oregon)

recognized as an essential part of fire protection, the result being that fire departments and fire protection interests have, in the past, often depended upon unreliable projections and reports in order to effect corrective efforts involving building and fire prevention codes and standards, to point up special fire protection problems, to judge the magnitude of the problem, or to determine whether or not there is a problem.

NFPA 901, *Standard for Uniform Coding for Fire Protection*, establishes uniform language, methods, and procedures for fire loss reporting and coding.[4] This system is designed so that all information can be coded for electronic or manual data processing.

The use of electronic data processing is essential if meaningful and readily retrievable fire loss data is to be collected. The almost unlimited capability of data processing allows for the input of great volumes of individual reports covering all sections of a large jurisdiction, as well as details of reported information relating to the factors and combinations of factors influencing the ignition sequence or communication of fire. By electronic means, the nation's approximately 1,200,000 fire service personnel can now more effectively find, evaluate, and compile fire ignition sequence information. By pinpointing problems, suggesting answers, and eliminating the misdirection of effort and expenditures of the fire protection dollar, analysis of this particular type of information will lead to worthwhile fire prevention programs that have a major effect on fire suppression procedures, structural and fire protection codes, manufacturers and equipment dealers, and on all other areas involved with fire protection.

Role of Company Officer in Investigations

It is the responsibility of the company officer to try to determine the origin of any fire immediately upon arrival at the scene, and to continue the investigation, if necessary, after the fire has been brought under control. If an inspector from the fire prevention bureau is available, that inspector should assist with, or in some departments take charge of, the investigation.

Arson may be suspected by such conditions as: absence of evidence that the fire was due to accident; a smell of gasoline or kerosine; simultaneous start of the fire in several different parts of the building; etc. In such instances the officer should immediately call the arson squad, the fire prevention bureau, or the chief so that a more detailed investigation can be made. As long as there are fire fighters at the scene, the fire department retains control of the property and can prevent members of the public, including the owner, from entering and possibly disturbing any evidence. Thus, fire fighters and other officials conducting investigations can search the premises and collect necessary evidence without obtaining legal sanction.

To help with investigations, company officers must schedule training in fire investigation so that fire fighters can help with finding clues to the causes of fires. Such training would also ensure that pieces of evidence are not disturbed in the clean-up process after a fire.

WATER SUPPLIES AND SYSTEMS
AS MANAGEMENT CONCERNS

An adequate and reliable water supply is necessary for preventing the spread of fires and for extinguishing them. The fact that the 1974 edition of the Insurance Services Office (ISO) *Grading Schedule for Municipal Fire Protection* allocated a possible 1,950 points (or thirty-nine percent) of a total 5,000 points to water supply indicates the relative importance of a good system.[5] (For further description of the *Grading Schedule for Municipal Fire Protection* rating system, see Chapter Ten, "Management of Physical Resources," section titled "Effect of Grading Schedules on Physical Resources.")

A thorough knowledge of water supplies and systems is necessary for members of fire service management. The following paragraphs present a brief history of water supplies for fire defense, and a synopsis of the importance of water supplies and systems to the fire service. For more detailed information on water supplies for fire protection than contained herein, the NFPA *Fire Protection Handbook* should be consulted.[6]

History of Water Supplies for Fire Defenses

While consideration was given to the provision of adequate domestic water supplies as early in history as the time of the Roman Empire, water supplies for fire fighting were neglected until the late eighteenth century. At that time, engineers began to develop details for building waterworks in cities. Much of their emphasis was on systems that could provide water for fire fighting purposes as well as for other uses. Many of these engineers based their calculations on the number of fire streams needed to protect a given population. All this led to research into the cost in a given city for a waterworks that could provide water for fire fighting purposes as well as for other uses (drinking, sanitation, etc.). Several renowned engineers affiliated with individual waterworks examined the problem, and their findings were discussed in technical papers presented at engineering society meetings. Papers by J. Herbert Shedd (1889),[7] J. T. Fanning (1892),[8] and Emil Kuichling (1897)[9] should be consulted for details of the discussions from which standards now followed in American and Canadian waterworks practice developed.

Much of the basic data now employed in hydraulic work in fire protection was developed in a series of extensive investigations conducted in 1888 and 1889 by one of the first fire protection engineers, John R. Freeman.[10] In 1892 Freeman published a paper that noted a relationship pertinent to fire fighting beyond that of proportion between population and fire flow.[11] He reported that sometimes ten or more streams might be needed for a "compact group of large valuable buildings, irrespective of a small population." Fire fighting operations, he noted, required a concentration of water, while domestic needs were a matter of distribution. He drew attention to the need for large main pipes, and to hydrant distribution according to the nature of the buildings to be protected.

Elements of Water Supply

The modern water supply system, whether publicly or privately owned, should be adequate and reliable. Water systems designed today for municipal use have dual functions: they supply potable* water for domestic consumption, and they supply water for fire protection. Domestic water consumption includes water used for human consumption, sanitation purposes, industrial processes, gardening purposes such as irrigating and lawn sprinkling, and air conditioning and similar water-consuming processes. Industrial sites often provide separate systems for supplying process water and water for fire protection. Any dual-purpose system should be able to supply enough water for fire protection and at the same time meet the maximum anticipated consumption for other purposes. A good working relationship between the fire department management and the water company management will ensure that the available supply of water is used most efficiently.

Adequacy: To be considered adequate by the ISO, a water supply must be capable of delivering the required fire flow for a specified number of hours at peak consumption periods. Required fire flow varies according to the type of development in a given district. For example, low-density residential areas need a smaller flow than large industrial parks with buildings that are equipped with sprinkler systems.

A deficiency in available supplies can be caused by an inadequate source of supply, a water utility incapable of delivering the required amount, or a poorly designed distribution system.

1. Water is usually pumped from wells, rivers, or lakes, and cleansed by filtering and chlorination processes. Then it is either stored in elevated reservoirs or pumped directly into the distribution channels. These sources of water may become inadequate during prolonged spells of hot, dry weather or where development of an area has exceeded the limits of available supplies.

2. A water company must have sufficient filtering and pumping capacity, and a distribution system adequate for delivering the required amount of water.

3. A well-designed system would ensure that no large section of the community be dependent upon a single main. Secondary mains would be looped into larger mains, and would be properly spaced. Hydrants would be located according to type of district to be protected, and would be low in friction loss and adequate in size.

Reliability: An adequate water supply must also be reliable. To be as reliable as possible, it should provide some means for compensating for interruptions during an emergency.

1. Breaks in supply can be caused by droughts, silting up of wells, or even chemical pollution. In order to plan for such contingencies, water companies develop storage facilities — either gravity-fed reservoirs, or reservoirs from which the water has to be pumped.

---

*A liquid that is suitable for drinking.

2. Since many pumps are operated by electricity, water companies must provide for alternative power sources should one transformer, or line, be put out of service. Where pumps are operated by steam or internal combustion engines, similar precautions must be taken.

3. The likelihood of damage to the pumping stations by fire or other catastrophe must be considered in the design or evaluation of the system. Standby pumping facilities are usually available to supply pressure in such emergencies. They can be even more useful, though, to supply extra pressure when needed to fight a large fire, or when water consumption by the public is so high that normal pressure is reduced.

4. The reliability of supply mains is also an important aspect of the water supply. The ISO will, for instance, analyze the map of a system to determine whether a break of serious proportions could be compensated for by the remaining mains. This also means that the water company must be able to close the valves to the damaged sections quickly enough to prevent great losses of water.

5. Types of materials used and the method of installation is important because pipes must withstand the fluctuations of weather conditions (especially freezing temperatures). Special construction may be needed at railroad crossings and bridges. Water company records can provide information about the frequency of interruptions due to leaks and breaks at any given location, whenever the adequacy of a system is reviewed.

Standpipes and Sprinkler Systems: Standpipes and automatic sprinkler systems are sometimes referred to as the first line of defense against the spread of fire. Standpipe and hose systems provide a means for the manual application of water to fires in buildings. Although standpipes are required in buildings of large area and in buildings more than four stories high so that fire departments can place hose lines in service with a minimum of delay, they do not take the place of automatic sprinkler systems. Fire losses have been considerably reduced by sprinkler systems, a fact considered by insurance companies in establishing rates.[12] Sometimes the savings in annual premiums is sufficient to pay for the installation of a sprinkler system within a few years.

In his book titled *Automatic Sprinkler & Standpipe Systems*, John L. Bryan comments on the efficiency of automatic sprinkler systems as follows:[13]

> In those fires in which automatic sprinkler systems were unsuccessful, the principal reasons were: (1) closed water control valves, (2) obstructions to sprinkler distribution, and (3) only partial protection of occupancies by sprinkler systems. Primarily, the major cause of unsatisfactory performance of automatic sprinkler systems has been the result of human action: such action involves the closing of water supply control valves before the fire occurs, or before the fire is completely extinguished. Fire department, security, and industrial personnel have all been involved in the premature closing of water control valves.

The overall effectiveness of a sprinkler system usually depends on the adequacy and reliability of the public water supply system. This may be the case even if a water tower on top of, or adjacent to, the building is available. Such supplies, however, are often limited in quantity, and alone may not be adequate for a significant fire. When a sprinkler system exists, the probability is, of course, very small that any fire can spread.

Areas of Overlapping Responsibility Between Water Company and Fire Department: There are several areas in the maintenance of an adequate and reliable water supply in which the water company and fire department cooperate, and in which responsibilities somewhat overlap.

1. When extensive new construction in any community is considered, both the water company and the fire department are involved in determining if a water supply system could provide the required fire flow for the type of development planned.

2. The fire department often has maps of the complete water system. Hydrant checks of the entire district are usually carried out on a rotating basis so that every hydrant is checked at least once a year, and more frequently in high-value areas to determine whether the hydrant is in operating condition and whether it can deliver the required fire flow. The water company is usually responsible for promptly correcting any problems that may exist.

3. When changes of occupancy occur before permits are issued, inspectors should consider the adequacy of water supplies relative to the hazards of the new occupancy.

4. Where the relationship with the water utility is good, all problems affecting the water supply should be immediately communicated to the fire department. Conversely, when there is a major fire, the water utility should be so informed so that it can increase pressure, if necessary, or begin the operation of emergency valves.

Auxiliary Water Supplies — A Fire Department Responsibility: It is the sole responsibility of the fire department to arrange for the availability of auxiliary water supplies. Where these are located on private property, the cooperation of the property owner is needed. Where the water supplies are under the jurisdiction of a public authority, agreements for the use of the water supplies must be established before the need arises.

Some rural and suburban departments maintain large-capacity tank trucks and tanker shuttles for the transportation of water where no hydrants exist. Other departments have apparatus specially designed to draw water by suction from natural bodies of water. A department must, of course, arrange for access to water supply for every possible fire in the district; sometimes this means considerable planning and negotiations with those who control the supplies.

Department Organization to Ensure Adequate Water Supplies: Of major concern to fire department management is departmental organization to ensure adequate water supplies. For example, a large fire department might appoint a special committee to work with the water company to ensure adequate water supplies for fire protection. This committee could include a water liaison officer from the fire department, a water supply company representative, and representatives from governmental agencies affected by the decisions.

Smaller departments usually don't have the need to organize committees for such functions, and generally delegate these responsibilities to specific personnel within the department.

Regardless of the way the handling of the water supply is planned, fire companies must know how to obtain the supply they need at every point in the district. In most well-run departments, at least one person in each first due company knows the water supply system well. In Philadelphia, for instance, great emphasis has been placed on such information.[14] A fire department directive was issued ordering company officers to conduct a physical check of hydrants and the size of mains within their district by using maps supplied by the water department to chart the location and size of mains within each box alarm response. The maps are called "Water Supply Maps."

Some idea of the effort involved in compiling the Philadelphia Water Supply Maps may be gained from the fact that in urban Philadelphia there are more than 26,000 hydrants in the domestic water system and another 1,044 more in the high pressure system for fire fighting. Engine companies received maps of the water main grids in their district. These were used to draw triplicate maps of water supplies within two blocks of each fire box.

The originals of the Water Supply Maps are filed in the numerical order of the street fire alarm boxes noted in the operational manual carried on the apparatus. The second copy is carried in the first due battalion chief's car, and the triplicate copy is in the operational binder of the second due engine company.

It was felt that every officer should know the general range of pressures in the mains and the size of the mains available for fire fighting. Company officers studied the distribution of hydrants and mains in their areas so that pumpers could be properly located without unnecessarily long hose lays. It was stressed that prefire planning for all large buildings or plants should emphasize water supply.

Role of the Company Officer: Water Systems and Supplies

It is the responsibility of the company officer to become familiar with the water supply system maps and the location, flow capabilities, and operation of hydrants in the district. The company officer should also be responsible for supervising the carrying-out of scheduled inspections of hydrants in the district, and for ensuring that the proper importance is attached to the need for inspections of all water supply system components in the department's responsible area.

The fire department connection is mandatory on all standpipe systems, and is recommended on sprinkler systems. It provides the only means of supplying water to the dry standpipe system. The fire department connection should always be inspected by fire companies when in-service inspections are conducted. A regular inspection and testing program relative to fire department connections for both standpipe and sprinkler systems, and the complete testing of both, is a necessity for every fire department. It is the company officer's responsibility for seeing that tests, inspections, and evaluations for all standpipes

Fig. 8.13. Fire department officer checking the condition of the discharge valve from a standpipe system. (Stephen C. Leahy, College Park Volunteer Fire Department, College Park, Maryland)

and sprinkler systems in the department's responsible area are carried out in accordance with accepted procedures. (See Fig. 8.13.)

Automatic sprinkler systems, one of the greatest aids to fire departments, can only function effectively if there is sufficient water pressure. As stated previously, the major cause of unsatisfactory performance of automatic sprinkler systems is, primarily, the result of human action; such action involves the closing of water supply control valves before the fire occurs, or before the fire is completely extinguished. Therefore, upon arrival at a sprinklered building, one of the officer in command's first responsibilities should be to station someone at the operating sprinkler system water supply control valve to prevent the water from being turned off until the fire is extinguished. Another responsibility upon arrival is to supplement the sprinkler system's water supply with hose lines from adequate public water mains or natural sources to the fire department connection on the sprinkler system. These essential and simultaneous procedures are dependent on information obtained during fire department prefire planning. In his book titled *Fire Attack: Command Decisions and Company Operations*, Warren Kimball states:[15]

> In any event, the primary responsibility of the fire department on responding to fires in sprinklered buildings is to see that the sprinklers have ample water supply and pressure, and that small hose teams are provided for mop-up. The fire department will also provide ventilation, overhaul, and salvage service.

Details on the testing, maintenance, and periodic inspection of standpipe systems are contained in NFPA 14, *Standard for Standpipe and Hose Systems*.[16] Details on acceptance tests and water supplies for sprinkler systems are contained in NFPA 13, *Standard for the Installation of Sprinkler Systems*,[17] and details on inspections and prefire planning for both automatic sprinkler and standpipe systems are contained in NFPA 13E, *Recommendations for Fire Department Operations in Properties Protected by Sprinkler and Standpipe Systems.*[18]

LOSS PREVENTION RECORDS AND REPORTS

In loss prevention, as in other aspects of fire department operations, accurate record-keeping is essential. Because it is not always possible to remember precise facts at a later time, most of the necessary information gained from inspections and surveys is usually put into written form — even if only as notes for use as the basis for later reports. Most of this information, together with reports of violation notices issued, follow-up visit reports, and other information pertaining to individual properties, is stored in such a way that it is readily retrievable. Most departments employ record retention, retrieval, and disposal systems that allow for the periodic surveillance of records and reports. Increasingly, fire departments are utilizing electronic data processing for keeping fire records, training records, payroll records, and for statistical analysis. Each fire department should have persons knowledgeable in the use of data processing. It may be desirable to have one officer appointed as coordinator of this work, but commonly there would be an administrative committee in the fire department that would include representatives of plans and research (where provided), administration, fire prevention, and fire suppression. This same committee may also be involved in long-range planning.

When a fire occurs, the information about that fire is, of course, also recorded with all other information concerning the particular structure. These records have many uses, including the following:

1. They can provide data for prefire plans, and thereby reduce the effort and time required for the survey.

2. They are needed to give information about the history of a property and the compliance of the property owners with fire code regulations, and thus help with planning of inspections. If the record is a good one, fewer inspections may be necessary; if the record is inadequate, it may be necessary for the inspectors to become more insistent concerning the immediate removal of any of the violations.

3. They are needed by the ISO, the Board of Underwriters, and by insurance companies for determining rates and ratings.

4. They can serve as the basis for statistical analysis to show what changes in practices and regulations may be desirable to strengthen fire prevention activities, or to reduce the probability of fires through structural changes. The following excerpt from a *Fire Command!* article titled "Department Slashes Fire Losses . . . Can You?" gives an interesting case study on the use of such statistical analysis:[3]

. . . Scientific fire-loss management refers to a systematic and orderly method of identifying fire problems, establishing objectives, developing program strategies, and evaluating results. For example, statistical analysis of Winston-Salem's fire problem showed that residential fire rates were much higher in the first and fourth quarters of the year, and that the increase was due to defective heating systems. Once this problem was accurately defined, it became relatively simple to develop and implement appropriate programs to minimize the number of fires resulting from defective heaters, thereby reducing the overall residential fire rate. . . .

. . . The department developed many of its fire prevention programs as a result of the problem areas identified through computer analysis. It has specific programs for institutions, industry, commercial occupancies, and high-rise buildings. . . .

A listing of typical fire department management records and reports, including those records and reports applicable to fire prevention inspection and education, is presented in Table 8.2, "Typical Management Records and Reports." Suggested forms for certain of the records and reports enumerated are illustrated in the International City Management Associates' publication titled *Municipal Fire Administration.*[19]

LEGAL ASPECTS

The importance placed on fire prevention activities in this country is indicated by the wide range of powers given most fire marshals in rights of entry for fire inspection and investigation, fire marshal's hearings, rights of subpoena of any records or persons who may have information concerning fire ignition sequence, etc. Such powers have been upheld by most courts of law, and should be honored when being used by members of the fire service when performing their duties.

Ordinances and Inspections

Ordinances define the procedures to be carried out for each hazard in the various occupancy category, and recommend the number of inspections that should be made to ensure compliance. The ordinances and regulations also specify the penalties for violation of any code.

Balancing Individual Rights with Those of the Public for Protection from Fire Hazards: Ordinances and regulations also confer the authority for inspection of premises on fire department officials, subject to certain safeguards. These safeguards protect the rights of the individual against unreasonable search and seizure as guaranteed by the U.S. Constitution.

When a conflict arises between the rights of the individual and the department's police powers, the issue is subject to rulings by the courts.

Two example cases — Camara v. Municipal Court of the City and County of San Francisco, and See v. Seattle — involved the right of individuals to refuse

Table 8.2 Typical Management Records and Reports*

GENERAL MANAGEMENT
  Report on Each Alarm by District Chief (consolidates data on operations and investigations)
  Fire Record Journal (chronological list of alarms and fires)
  Consolidated Daily Report (where used)
  Consolidated Monthly Report
  Annual Report
FINANCIAL MANAGEMENT
  Inventory Records (stock records kept by each company or bureau of the department to which land, buildings, furniture, apparatus or equipment is assigned)
  Purchase Records (requisitions, invitations to bid, quotations, purchase orders, reports on goods received)
  Budgetary Control Records
  Payroll Records
PERSONNEL MANAGEMENT
  Company Record of Personnel Attendance
  Department Daily Summary of Personnel Attendance
  Master Personnel Record on Each Member
PUBLIC RELATIONS
  Daybook Record of Programs and Activities
WATER SUPPLY
  Company Records of Hydrants and Cisterns
  Company Records of Sprinklers, Standpipes and other Private Fire Protection
  Daybook Record of Activities of Fire Department Water Officer or Bureau (including reports of water supply interruptions)
  Record of Fire Flow Tests
  Plans of Public Water Systems
  Static Water Source Plans & Files
FIRE PREVENTION INSPECTION AND EDUCATION
  Company Daily Summary of Inspections Made
  Company Record of Individual Properties
  Bureau Daily Summary of Inspections Made
  Bureau Daybook Record of Inspection and Educational Activities
  Bureau Record of Individual Properties
FIRE FIGHTING AND EMERGENCY SERVICE MANAGEMENT
  Company Daybook or Journal (chronological record kept at company watch desk as source of entries in company records)

Company Run Report
  Report on Each Alarm by District Chief (includes consolidation of data on operations of all companies and service units responding to each alarm)
FIRE INVESTIGATION
  Report on Each Alarm by District Chief (includes data for classification of alarm and results of chief's investigation)
  Investigation Bureau Report on Each Alarm Investigated
  Loss Summaries for Consolidated Management Report
  Record of Insurance Losses
  Record of Estimated Uninsured Losses
  Name File of Properties and Persons Involved in Alarms
TRAINING
  Company Record of Training Sessions at Station
  Daybook of Training School Activities
  Records of Training Courses (attendance and grading of participants)
COMMUNICATIONS
  Daily Summary of Alarms Received
  Radio Log
  Daybook Record of Work on Communications System (including disposal of trouble signals)
  Reports of Tests Specified for Communication Equipment
  Record Card on Each Public Fire Alarm Box
  Record or File on other Communications Equipment
  Plans of Wiring
  Record of Installation, Maintenance, Repair, Replacement or Removal
BUILDINGS AND APPARATUS MANAGEMENT
  Periodic Reports Required from Companies and Bureaus on Tests of Assigned Apparatus and Equipment (covers motor fire apparatus, hose and other items of equipment)
  Records Kept by Companies and Bureaus of Maintenance Work Performed on Assigned Apparatus and Equipment
  Shop Reports of Tests of Apparatus and Equipment
  Shop Records of Maintenance and Repairs of Apparatus and Equipment (including cost data)
  Record of Maintenance of Each Parcel of Land
  Record of Maintenance of Each Building

*"Administration and Management," *Fire Protection Handbook*, 14th Ed., NFPA, Boston, 1976, p. 9–21.

admission to the fire department to inspect commercial occupancies, as provided for in fire code safety regulations.*

In both cases, the courts maintained that a person may not be prosecuted for resisting inspection unless a search warrant has been issued by a legally appointed judicial officer.

In the case of Camara, the U.S. Supreme Court ruled in favor of the appellant where the right of entry without a warrant involved a housing code inspector. In the See case (which involved a warehouse), the fire department wanted to inspect under authority of a City of Seattle ordinance granting the fire chief the right "to enter all buildings and premises except the interior of dwellings as may often be necessary." The owner refused to permit an inspection on the grounds that the ordinance was invalid. He said the fire chief had no search warrant, nor any probable cause to believe that a violation of any law existed on his premises. In upholding the constitutionality of the ordinance, the Washington Supreme Court (later overruled by the United States Supreme Court) said:[20]

> The purpose of the fire code inspection is to correct conditions hazardous to life and property. The problem of keeping cities and their inhabitants free from explosions and fires is a serious task facing all fire departments. It is obvious that routine inspections are necessary to ensure the safeguarding of life and property.
>
> The need to conduct routine inspections of commercial premises, in regard to which probable cause for the issuance of a warrant could not ordinarily be established, outweighs the interest in privacy with respect to such premises. The purpose of the inspection contemplated by the code is not unreasonable.

The U.S. Supreme Court reversed the conviction of the warehouse owner on the ground that the Seattle ordinance, authorizing a warrantless inspection of his warehouse, was an unconstitutional violation of his rights under the Fourth and Fourteenth Amendments.

The Court cited its recent decision in Camara v. San Francisco and declared that, "The businessman, like the occupant of a residence, has the constitutional right to go about his business free from unreasonable entries upon his private commercial property."[20]

The Court felt that its recent decisions restricting administrative agencies in their attempts to subpoena corporate books and records supported their view that any agency's particular demand for access should be measured in terms of probable cause to issue a warrant, against a flexible standard of reasonableness that takes into account the public need for effective enforcement of the particular regulation involved. "But the decision to enter and inspect

---

*United States Supreme Court decisions: Camara v. Municipal Court of the City and County of San Francisco, 387 U.S. 523, 87 S. Ct. 1727 (1967); See v. City of Seattle, 387 U.S. 541, 87 S. Ct. 1737 (1967).

will not be the product of unreviewed discretion of the enforcement officer in the field." The Court concluded as follows:[20]

> We therefore conclude that administrative entry, without consent, upon the portions of commercial premises which are not open to the public may only be compelled through prosecution or physical force within the framework of a warrant procedure. We do not in any way imply that business premises may not reasonably be inspected in many more situations than private homes, nor do we question such accepted regulatory techniques as licensing programs which require inspections prior to operating a business or marketing a product. Any constitutional challenge to such programs can only be resolved, as many have been in the past, on a case-by-case basis under the general Fourth Amendment standard of reasonableness. We hold only that the basic component of a reasonable search under the Fourth Amendment — that it not be enforced without a suitable warrant procedure — is applicable in this context, as in others, to business as well as to residential premises. Therefore, appellant may not be prosecuted for exercising his constitutional right to insist that the fire inspector obtain a warrant authorizing entry upon appellant's locked warehouse.

However, while in theory the courts may make the ultimate decision about what constitutes an invasion of privacy for inspection, in practice a search warrant is not often needed because property owners are aware that the fire department can usually obtain one. When a department does face a problem with an owner and seeks a warrant, it must show that "probable cause" exists, based on the length of time since the last inspection, the nature of the building (*i.e*, occupancy), and the condition of the entire area — but not necessarily upon specific knowledge of a violation.

Fire Codes Retroactive Where Life Safety Is Involved: The courts have attempted to maintain a balance between an individual's rights to privacy and the need to protect against potential fire hazards. However, they have consistently recognized the need to protect life through upholding the right of the fire department to enforce regulations retroactively where life safety is involved.

For this reason, a local government may sometimes add to the firesafety code regulations items such as the installation of sprinkler systems in nursing homes and high-rise apartment buildings. Owners would then have to install sprinkler systems in all buildings in both occupancy categories, whether the structure is already in existence, is in the process of being built, or is planned for the future.

Role of the Company Officer in Legal Matters

The company officer must know what the legal responsibilities are as specified in the fire codes and interpreted by the courts. In the performance of duty, the company officer must keep in mind the following:

1. One- and two-family units may normally be inspected only upon a request by the owner. An officer should be aware, however, whether the regulations require or permit an inspection. Upon a complaint by a citizen about

another person's violation of the safety ordinances, the department has the responsibility to investigate and inspect the premises.

2. Officers and inspectors must be aware that they have to inform an owner or person in charge of noncompliance with fire codes before a hazard can be considered a violation.

3. A reasonable period of time must be allowed for correction of code violations. Although unreasonableness in itself is not illegal, an officer must be aware that it would probably invalidate a department's police power to enforce compliance. Judges would tend to dismiss cases brought by the department for failure to comply with ordinances unless a reasonable amount of time for correction has been allowed. Furthermore, harsh interpretation of codes and ordinances could eventually lead to poor public relations.

4. An inspector is legally responsible for recording all violations, and nothing may be intentionally disregarded.

5. An officer or inspector may not recommend a specific company or individual as contractor for correction of deficiencies; only procedures to be carried out may be suggested.

ACTIVITIES

1. Describe the purpose of prefire planning. Then explain the four steps used in the prefire planning process.
2. Your department's existing prefire plan must be expanded to include a recently constructed chemicals storage facility. This building is located at the top of a steep hill in the outskirts of your community. What other information would be needed for the preparation of a prefire plan for this building?
3. (a) Explain why symbols and abbreviations are used in prefire plans. Do you think these symbols and abbreviations should be universal? Why or why not?
   (b) What effect would the following description of a building have in your prefire plan: CEM LOX plant, no FE?
4. (a) Why should prefire plans be continuously updated?
   (b) What methods are used to help fire fighters remember prefire plans before or during a fire in a given occupancy?
5. (a) In what specific ways can prefire plans and inspections be considered as being similar?
   (b) What is the role of the company officer in ensuring that all fire fighters are familiar with prefire planning?
6. With a group of your classmates, discuss the methods a fire department can use for public education in fire prevention. Then, based on your discussion, answer the following questions.
   (a) Does your community's fire department use any of the methods you have listed? If so, describe them.

    (b) What methods of public education are not used by your community's fire department?

    (c) With your group, choose one method that is not being used. Then, discuss and describe how this method could be used in your community.

7. Outline the purposes of a fire ignition sequence investigation.

8. (a) Who is usually responsible for arson investigations within a large fire department?

    (b) How is a suspicious fire investigated, and how is an arson case developed?

9. With a group of your classmates, discuss and list the requirements that determine adequacy and reliability of water supplies and systems for a fire department.

    (a) What water supplies and systems are available to your community's fire department?

    (b) What is the fire department's role in ensuring adequate water supplies and systems for fire fighting?

10. Based on the legal matters involved in inspections discussed in this chapter, determine which of the following statements are false. Then explain why.

    (a) An inspector with a search warrant may be refused entry into a commercial occupancy.

    (b) A local government can force a high-rise building owner to install a sprinkler system.

    (c) If an inspector feels that a building may contain a violation, a search warrant may be obtained without stating the nature or probability of the violation.

    (d) If a citizen complains about a neighbor's firesafety violations, the responsibility to investigate rests with the police department.

    (e) Inspectors must inform a building owner of a violation before a hazard can be considered a violation.

    (f) Violations noted on a property inspected by a fire department officer must be corrected at least five hours after the premises have been inspected.

BIBLIOGRAPHY

[1] "Abbreviations for Use on Drawings and in Text," ANSI Y1.1–1972, American National Standards Institute, New York, 1972.

[2] "Interview," *Fire Command!*, Vol. 42, No. 9, Sept. 1975, p. 27.

[3] "Department Slashes Fire Losses . . . Can You?" *Fire Command!*, Vol. 43, No. 3, Mar. 1976, pp. 20–22.

[4] NFPA 901, *Standard for Uniform Coding for Fire Protection*, NFPA, Boston, 1976.

[5] *Grading Schedule for Municipal Fire Protection*, Insurance Services Office, New York, 1974.

[6] *Fire Protection Handbook*, 14th Ed., NFPA, Boston, 1976, pp. 9-67–9-74, 11-1–11-76.

[7] Shedd, J. Herbert, discussion on a paper by Sherman, William B., "Ratio of Pumping Capacity to Maximum Consumption," *Journal of New England Water Works Association*, Vol. 3, 1889, p. 113.

[8] Fanning, J. T., "Distribution Mains and the Fire Service," *Proceedings of the American Water Works Association*, Vol. 12, 1892, p. 61.

[9] Kuichling, E., "The Financial Management of Water Works," *Transactions of the American Society of Civil Engineers*, Vol. 38, 1897, p. 16.

[10] Freeman, J. R., *Transactions of the American Society of Civil Engineers*, Vols. 12 and 14.

[11] ———, "The Arrangement of Hydrants and Water Pipes for the Protection of a City Against Fire," *Journal of New England Water Works Association*, Vol. 7, 1892, p. 49.

[12] Bryan, John L., "Economic Variables of Automatic Sprinkler Systems," *Automatic Sprinkler & Standpipe Systems*, 1st Ed., NFPA, Boston, 1976, pp. 64–76.

[13] ———, "Fire Department Procedures for Automatic Sprinkler and Standpipe Systems," *Automatic Sprinkler & Standpipe Systems*, 1st Ed., NFPA, Boston, 1976, p. 30.

[14] "How Philadelphia Uses a Water Supply Officer," *Fire Command!*, Vol. 40, No. 5, May 1973, pp. 26–31.

[15] Kimball, Warren Y., *Fire Attack: Command Decisions and Company Operations*, NFPA, Boston, 1966, p. 134.

[16] NFPA 14, *Standard for the Installation of Standpipe and Hose Systems*, NFPA, Boston, 1976.

[17] NFPA 13, *Standard for the Installation of Sprinkler Systems*, NFPA, Boston, 1976.

[18] NFPA 13E, *Recommendations for Fire Department Operations in Properties Protected by Sprinkler and Standpipe Systems*, NFPA, Boston, 1973.

[19] *Municipal Fire Administration*, International City Management Associates, Washington, DC (formerly Chicago, IL), 1967, pp. 284–343.

[20] See v. City of Seattle, 387 U.S. 541, 87 S. Ct. 1737 (1967).

Chapter Nine

Fireground Command
Management Functions

FIREGROUND TACTICAL MANAGEMENT

All of the activities used by a fire department to fulfill its mission come to-gether at the fireground. It is here that the results of all of the effort that has gone into the planning and preparation for emergency procedures come into play in helping to form the basis for the strategy and tactics developed at the fire scene. Thus, fire fighting operations provide a means by which the depart-ment can demonstrate its effectiveness, and by which its personnel, the local officials, and the taxpayers can evaluate performance and the ability to cope with an emergency. The activities that contribute to high-level performance fall into two major categories: (1) preparation, and (2) fire attack.

Preparation

Adequate preparation is necessary for the effective fighting of fires, for en-suring adequate water supplies for the extinguishment of fires, and for helping to reduce the extent of fire spread in order to minimize loss due to fire. In addition to all of the fire prevention activities, each of the following concerns are important aspects of adequate preparation:

1. The efficient distribution of apparatus and personnel in order to make the best use of available equipment, while at the same time providing sufficient coverage for contingencies in each situation.

2. The ability of available personnel and apparatus to apply the necessary fire flow to extinguish any potential fire. This ability results from drills, training, prefire planning, and through the availability of adequate supplies of extin-guishing agents (mainly water).

3. Provision for applying the greatest possible tactical power with the first alarm units (if these companies do not succeed in confining the fire, the re-sponse of additional personnel and equipment may not be rapid enough to prevent serious damage or loss of life).

The level of achievement of these concerns is dependent on the extent of prefire planning involved (which helps to give a first alarm company a head start in attack preparations), and the extent of prior training and drills (which helps to ensure that each unit makes efficient use of time and effort during actual fire fighting operations).

Fire Attack

At the fire scene, the following five factors contribute to the effectiveness with which a fire is attacked and controlled:

1. **Strategy:** The 14th edition of the NFPA *Fire Protection Handbook* defines strategy as follows:[1]

> Strategy is the method employed by the fireground commander to co-ordinate the tactical units (engine and ladder companies) and the management of additional resources, if required, to successfully control the incident or emergency.

It is, therefore, the basic and overall plan upon which the attack on the fire is built. In developing a strategy, the command officer applies everything known about the situation (the needs of the situation, the resources at the scene, and those that will, in time, become available to the total comprehensive plan) to the best possible attack.

Strategy can also apply to departmental operations, where it can be defined as the overall procedures that coordinate personnel, equipment and materials, and the training, fire prevention, and prefire functions.

2. **Tactics:** The NFPA *Fire Protection Handbook* defines tactics as follows:[2]

> The methods or operations employed by the tactical units (companies, task forces, etc.) to achieve objectives such as rescue, confinement, extinguishment, ventilation, salvage, overhaul, and other tasks, as assigned by the fireground commander.

Tactics, then, are the specific and detailed assignments needed to carry out strategic plans. The preparation that goes into drills and the intensive training of individual fire fighters is here translated into more rapid and aggressive attacks on the fire, and a more complete and thorough execution of the fireground commander's orders.

3. **Overhaul and Salvage:** Overhaul and salvage operations are needed to prevent the fire from rekindling, and to hold damage to a minimum. To the officer in charge, they represent a sharply changed situation and require a different type of leadership and different kinds of strategic and tactical decisions than the attack on the fire itself.

4. **Organization:** To be most effective, all stages of fire fighting operations depend upon good organization. Good organization shows up at the fireground by: (1) avoiding wasted motion, (2) eliminating overlapping activities, (3) reducing time spent on unnecessary functions, and (4) putting available resources into operation more quickly.

Good organization allows for effective implementation of strategies and tactics. Good organization, as outlined in the linking elements section of Chapter Four, "Modern Management Concepts," is based on coordination procedures, rules for individuals, clear and rapid communication of goals, and the "esprit de corps" that brings about the best results.

5. **Communications**: Communications is that aspect of fireground activities that provides the commander with the information necessary to evaluate how well strategies and tactics are achieving their desired and expected results, and to make the necessary modifications where the situation is developing in an unanticipated way. Communications also provides information to the subordinate officers and fire fighters about the decisions they have to implement.

A commander can only be as effective as the information received, combined with the personal ability to communicate decisions (based on the information received) to the people who will implement them.

Modern communications equipment enables a fireground commander to quickly obtain the information necessary to formulate an attack strategy, to request help, and to coordinate resources for an effective attack upon the fire.

In combination, these five factors control the effectiveness of the fire attack. The five factors are discussed in greater detail in the following paragraphs.

FIREGROUND STRATEGY

Strategy is the foundation for all the actions that are necessary to achieve the objectives. As Chief Engineer Raymond Hill of the Los Angeles Fire Department points out in an article in *Fire Command!*:[3]

> In fire combat, the ultimate objective is the extinguishment of the fire. Each mission and task must contribute to the ultimate objective. The ultimate objective may not be immediately obtainable and intermediate objectives must be selected. Each intermediate objective must be such that its attainment will quickly and economically contribute to the ultimate objective. The selection of intermediate objectives must be based upon a consideration of the fire itself, the operational environment and the resources available at the fireground.

Hill states that planning is not static, but is a progressive and continuing process; that strategy may need to be modified as changes in the fire situation or the arrival of additional resources dictates; that planning must take all foreseeable contingencies into account; and that careful planning is useful in small fires as well as in the larger ones. The article also points out that:

> The great majority of fires are small and their control and extinguishment becomes routine in nature. In fact, their handling becomes so routine that they are fought without making plans. This is a dangerous trap to fall into because when the large or critical fire comes along there is a tendency to fight this one too without a plan. So — develop the habit of *planning* for every fire, no matter how routine it may seem.

In order to make the best strategy decisions, the officer in charge must, in effect, follow the basic decision-making process. This means defining the problem, obtaining the data, identifying the alternative courses of action, selecting the alternative that is best for the moment, and conducting continuous evaluation and correction on the basis of new data to ensure that the best approach is being used. At the fire scene, the definition of the problem and the data come from the following three distinct and separate analyses:

1. **Analysis of the fire situation** (What's there?). This includes facts and probabilities pertaining to: (1) threats to life, (2) the involved structures, (3) the fire itself, (4) the exposures, (5) the weather and time, and (6) fire fighting resources that are part of the fire location. (This provides part of the definition of the problem and supplies some of the data.)

2. **Needs assessment** (What does the situation need?). What is needed for the existing situation and the various probabilities that deserve consideration: (1) rescue, (2) exposure protection, and (3) confinement and extinguishment. (This supplies more input for definition of the problem, and additional data.)

3. **Available resources** (What have I got?). These must be viewed in terms of currently available and expected resources: (1) apparatus, (2) personnel, (3) equipment, (4) water and other extinguishing agents, and (5) hose. (This provides further information for thoroughly defining the problem, and for the final segment of the necessary data.)

Once these three analyses have been completed, the strategy for attacking the emergency can be built. Though this is a highly complex process, thorough preparation, practice, and experience allow the competent officer to compare the available resources with the needs of the situation, to quickly review several alternative courses of action, and to select the one course of action that seems to be the best. However, before any discussion of the choice of alternatives can be meaningful, the three analyses outlined in the preceding paragraphs require more detailed exploration.

Analysis of the Fire Situation

Obtaining the Information: Some information needed for analysis of the fire situation would be known in advance, or obtained on the way to the fire. This would include:

1. An officer would be familiar with the fire science likely to be pertinent to the situation.

2. Data about the specific features (the terrain and the building) can be obtained from any existing maps, prefire survey data, or prefire plans, and would either be available on the apparatus or would be relayed by the dispatcher from the communications center.

3. On the way to the fire the officer in charge should make mental notes of factors that might influence decisions on the fireground such as weather and traffic conditions and, during the summer, to what degree open hydrants might reduce water pressures, or to what degree dry weather may have added to the problems.

The remainder of the information related to the fire situation would be acquired at the fireground itself during the initial size-up process. It falls into two categories: (1) the facts of the situation, and (2) the probabilities.

Threat to Life: While all fires, if not confined, are a potential threat to life, some obviously represent a more immediate danger than others. Responding units may be partially aware of the seriousness of the situation from prior data, and from on-site reports being relayed to them from the communication center; still, the first arriving officer must obtain the complete picture from: (1) size-up of the situation, and (2) all other sources, including any individuals who appear to have knowledge of the situation — especially knowledge about any people who may be trapped inside a structure.

In addition to the direct danger to people in a burning structure or vehicle, a fire may indirectly threaten the lives of other people in neighboring buildings. If the fire is spreading rapidly, occupants in adjoining structures may not be aware of the emergency. This applies to those who might be most vulnerable — the handicapped and young children. Also, people not accustomed to hearing sirens may not be conscious of the danger. Direct danger may be imminent to bystanders who gather to watch a fire; they may be endangered by explosions, debris, or falling parts of structures. The potential risk of injury to the fire fighters must also be considered.

The Involved Structure or Fireground: During the size-up process, the officer makes a rapid assessment of the problems presented by the involved structure, vehicle, or materials. While doing so, there are several important factors the officer must consider:

1. Construction features and materials that might contribute to fire spread or intensity.
2. Height.
3. Layout (separation and compartments, access routes, ventilation options).
4. Protective devices (sprinklers, fire curtains, fire doors, etc.).
5. Routes by which a fire may travel and spread, even in sprinklered premises (raised floors, suspended ceilings, cable ducts, air ducts, open stairwells, or elevator shafts).
6. Contents and the special problems that they may present (highly flammable materials, volatile liquids, potential of poisonous gases and smoke, etc.).
7. Location (terrain features that may influence decisions).
8. Special problems of outdoor fires (dry brush or timber, unknown contents in trash, storage areas, trucks, etc.).
9. Water sources.

Fire: The fire itself must be considered in relation to:

1. Location within a structure or vehicle.
2. Extent of involvement.
3. Type of combustible.
4. Heat volume.

Exposures: Exposures that need immediate attention to prevent the spread of fire include all the problems presented by adjacent exposures. These fall into the same categories as the involved structures themselves.

Weather and Time of Day: These considerations include:

1. Wind direction and intensity.

2. Temperature.

3. Precipitation (rain or snow, and the extent to which lack of rain may have dried out the materials in the area).

4. Time of day, which may determine traffic, number of people to be evacuated, or other related problems.

Fire Fighting Resources That Are Part of the Fire Location: Prefire plans or data about the location provide the responding officer with information about resources (fire flow from hydrants, external and internal fire protection equipment, and other automatic fire extinguishing systems and extinguishing agents where available).

Probabilities: The second category of information about the fire situation concerns the "probabilities" that define the likelihood that various events will occur that will affect the course of the fire and the kind of resources and strategies needed to bring it under control.

Probabilities change during the course of fireground operations. They are influenced by weather, time, features of the involved structure, and by the actions of the fire fighting team.

A set of complex decisions faces the officer in charge of the size-up. The officer in charge must be able to look at the facts and select from the large amount of surrounding data those that are the most relevant to the particular situation. Then, based on these, the officer must forecast various possibilities about the future course of the fire. For example, in assigning probabilities to a fire on the top floor of a seven-story building, an experienced officer would assess the likelihood of fire spreading to the sixth floor and estimate the dangers associated with that possibility. The officer would consider the chances of damage to the fifth floor and give some thought to the probability of the fire going through the roof and involving adjacent structures. At the same time, the officer may consider the chance of involvement of the fourth floor or lower-level floors as being so small that they would not affect strategy at all.

In preparing to make strategic decisions (that is, the allocation of resources), an officer would assess probabilities in many areas including:

1. Danger to life from smoke, heat, poisonous gases, falling objects, explosions, and structural failure.

2. Danger to property from internal and external spread of the fire from heat, smoke, and water.

3. Changes in weather that may affect the fire situation, such as changes in wind direction, heavy rain, or freezing temperature.

In addition to the probabilities that are part of the environment of the scene, the officer must evaluate probabilities of the effect of various fire fighting steps on the course of the fire. For example, the possibility that resources might be reduced through fatigue or injury should be considered.

Analysis of Facts and Probabilities: From the facts and probabilities, a total picture of the fire situation emerges. This total picture is one of the foundations upon which decisions are based. It provides part of the definition of the problem, and a large segment of the data. Another foundation for decision making comes from analysis of what is needed to cope with the situations, and the probabilities such analysis presents.

Needs Assessment

The resources needed to deal with the problems posed by the emergency must be considered in light of the situation as it is at the moment, and as it is likely to develop. Hence, the officer must again think in terms of probabilities — what the probable needs of the various events that are likely to occur will be.

Rescue: Life-saving operations might require specific apparatus, equipment, or skilled personnel.
1. Ladders for evacuation (aerial, elevated, and extension ladders).
2. Equipment to gain access to trapped people.
3. First-aid equipment and materials.
4. Ambulance or rescue truck.
5. Skilled personnel in adequate number.

Exposures, Confinement, and Extinguishment: Attack on the fire requires:
1. Appropriate amounts of extinguishing agents.
2. Apparatus for applying these agents in adequate quantities to the fire.
3. Skilled personnel in adequate number.
4. Ventilation equipment.
5. Various special types of equipment such as lights, cutting tools, etc.
6. Protective gear for fire fighters.
7. Communications equipment.
8. Support services for maintenance, medical aid, utilities, information, traffic, and spectator control.

An analysis of these actual and probable future requirements provides additional information about the problem and more data on which the strategy decisions and the allocation of resources must be based. These needs may change. Therefore, the officer in charge must take into account the need for reserves or personnel to relieve those in action, or the possibilities that the emergency may diminish sufficiently to allow some of the personnel and/or units to return to headquarters.

Resources Available at the Fireground

A third stage in the process of analysis is to assess what is presently available at the fireground.

Apparatus: The pumpers, ladder and rescue trucks, and the specialized vehicles presently at the fireground.

Personnel: The number of skilled personnel available would depend on department manning practices and on apparatus present.

Equipment: The type and amount available would depend on what was carried on apparatus as standard equipment, and what was brought along in addition for rescue, ventilation, suppression, salvage, and overhaul personal equipment such as breathing devices.

Water: Supplies of water should be known to the officer in charge. Supplies of other extinguishing agents would have been brought to the fireground.

Hose: Size and amount of hose carried by apparatus, and type and number of nozzles carried. Supplementary equipment such as suction basins, etc.

Decisions about Resources

At this point in the size-up process, the officer is ready to make decisions about alternative courses of action to meet the emergency. The problem has been defined and the necessary data has been obtained. The final two steps in the decision-making process must now be taken. These involve defining and evaluating the alternatives to determine the best one for the particular situation.

In developing a strategy, a whole series of decisions has to be made. The first one involves comparison of needs with available resources to determine what number and types of reinforcements are required. If additional help is not needed, then the officer in charge can proceed to the other decisions that are necessary to develop a strategy for the emergency, using the resources available on the fireground.

Guidelines for Decisions about Reinforcements: It is often difficult to decide if, when, and how much help is needed. In his book *Fire Attack 1*, Warren Y. Kimball offers the following guidelines:[4]

> Fire experience has shown that in a relatively high percentage of cases where only one or two additional companies have been called, second or third alarm has been required subsequently. In general, recommended practice is to promptly sound a second alarm in all cases where the first alarm response is not adequate. Calling companies piecemeal frequently has permitted further extension of a fire.
>
> There are seven main purposes for which multiple alarms are commonly ordered by officers in charge of fires:
> 1. To obtain extra personnel and equipment to aid in rescue operations.
> 2. To obtain additional personnel and equipment to run and man additional 2½-inch hand lines (this may involve covering additional positions).
> 3. To obtain additional personnel and equipment needed to place heavy streams in service.
> 4. To set up and help staff a command post or field headquarters at major fires.
> 5. To obtain additional help principally for truck duty such as forcible entry, ventilation, and salvage.
> 6. To provide relief personnel in situations where the fire fighting is unusually exhausting.
> 7. To cover exposures downwind from the fire where the main body of fire presents a possible flying brand hazard.
>
> One or more of these situations may be involved in any decision to sound a multiple alarm, and the officer in charge must anticipate the need for extra help and not allow the situation to get ahead of the resources at hand.

Standard operational procedures for the local department and mutual aid companies determine which and how many companies respond to each alarm. Knowledge of local practices would, therefore, allow an officer to decide how many alarms should be called and whether specific items not automatically available through a standard response would be required. Thus, two decisions must be made: (1) how many alarms are needed, and (2) what special equipment and/or extinguishing agents may be needed. When these decisions are made, costs must, of course, be considered. Both decisions are most difficult in borderline cases when it appears as though the resources on the scene might be able to control the situation.

Even though it is costly to bring additional resources to the scene, it is usually wiser to have too many rather than too few pieces of apparatus. This is true because the decision to bring reinforcements is *reversible*. Additional units may be turned back or released if subsequent developments show they will not be required. However, a decision not to call for reinforcements is essentially irreversible because additional fire damage will have been done if they are not at the fire scene at the time they are needed. Whether or not additional resources or reinforcements have been called, the officer in charge has to decide what to do with the available resources.

Very often, one of the resources may be in limited supply. When this occurs, the officer in charge has to rearrange the resources in order to make best possible use of the limited one. For example, in some situations, it may be possible to conserve personnel by compensating for them by means of using a heavier flow of extra water from deluge nozzles. On the other hand, if water or extinguishing agents are the limiting factor, the decisions are much more difficult. Various options may be considered such as calling for tank trucks and running a relay from them to the fire. It may also be necessary to adopt a more defensive strategy such as taking a stand at a defensible wall, or segments of the fireground, instead of attacking the fire directly and thus depleting reserve supplies of extinguishing agents. When water supply is known to be limited, decisions about how to best use available supplies can be made in advance and integrated into prefire plans, thus avoiding the possibility of delays at the fire scene.

Evaluating these alternatives is, of course, difficult. Good practice in decision making can make this process easier and faster, and can give an officer confidence that the best decisions possible are being made.

Selecting the Best Strategy: Strategy must be decided first, before any tactical decisions are made, because strategy concerns the allocation of resources. The officer who begins to make tactical decisions before the resources have been allocated may find that inadequate resources are available for the last tactical decisions, and may then be forced to make time-consuming changes in the field.

To use an extreme example, an inexperienced officer might make the following hasty, incorrect assignments:

1. Send three fire fighters to attack a fire on the first floor with a 1½-inch hose.

2. Assign one fire fighter to ventilate on the top floor.

3. Allocate five fire fighters to attack the fire on the second floor with 2½-inch hose.

The officer may then find that there were no available personnel to protect the exposure in the rear, and may have to withdraw and change the 2½-inch hose to 1½-inch and make other corresponding rearrangements. Mistakes of this type can be avoided if new officers are trained from the beginning to understand the clear distinction between strategy and tactics, and are instilled with an awareness that strategy decisions (the allocation of resources) must be made first.

Decisions on the allocation of resources initially would focus on the following, in order of importance: rescue, exposure protection to reduce life hazard, exposure protection (confinement) to reduce damage to property, and fire attack (extinguishment).

The officer in charge must consider each of these fireground operations and decide what proportions of the resources should be allocated to each.

Different Kinds of Strategy: Basically, there are two major strategy groups: (1) offensive, and (2) defensive.

A primarily offensive strategy may be called for if a fire emergency is routine and first alarm companies are sufficient for an immediate extinguishment of the fire. However, if resources are inadequate, a more defensive approach is necessary. When possible, direct and immediate offense is highly desirable because damage will be least when exposures can be protected at the same time that a vigorous attack on the fire is launched.

Figure 9.1 shows that when more resources are committed to confinement, fewer are available for attack. On the left-hand side of Figure 9.1, the officer arrives on the scene and sees that no exposures need to be protected, and therefore all available resources can be used for direct attack on the fire. At the other extreme, on the right-hand side of the diagram, the structures are so involved and the situation is such that all available resources on the first alarm may be inadequate for confinement, leaving none for direct attack. In that situation an immediate call for several additional alarms is indicated. Figure 9.2 shows what happens when additional resources — one, two, or three alarms — have been called.

There are many possible variations of defensive strategies. Following is an outline of some of the alternatives a command officer would consider. They are arranged in decreasing degrees of defensiveness (or increasing levels of offensiveness):

- At one extreme there is the decision to allow the fire to burn itself out. In some cases it is not a question of whether resources are sufficient for an attack, but whether an attack is worthwhile. If the involved structure or vehicle is no longer salvageable, and if attempts to put the fire out would be potentially dangerous or would mean significant costs, then it might be better to let the fire burn itself out. A small detachment of fire fighters would stand by to make sure there is no extension.

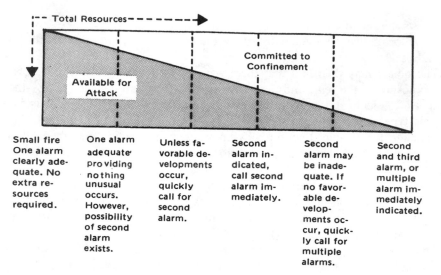

Fig. 9.1. *Options available to an officer on size-up.*

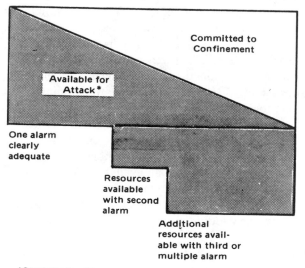

*Shaded area shows resources available for fire attack

Fig. 9.2. *Options available to an officer on size-up, with respect to reinforcements.*

- Next is the strategy that calls for a stand to be taken at a fire wall, allowing everything on the other side to burn. This may be the option chosen when forces on the scene are clearly inadequate for direct attack (see far left of Fig. 9.1), and adequate sources cannot be obtained in time.

- If or when more resources are available, a strategy "to hold" as described above may be modified. The perimeter may be held, while encroachments on the fire are gradually made. These might include cooling a specific area to prevent an explosion or the partial collapse of a structural element, or to prevent an extension in a predictable direction, or even to allow rescue operations to take place at the expense of protecting other extensions. This strategy option might be chosen when the situation with regard to resources is somewhere left of center in Figure 9.1.

• A still lower level of defensiveness (or higher level of offensiveness) would be a strategy in which not only exposures were protected, but also the fire itself attacked to a limited extent in the most crucial areas or gradually from all sides. This kind of strategy would be possible if the availability of resources is close to the middle of Figure 9.1.

The officer in charge would select the strategy combination outlined at the bottom of Figure 9.1 that promises to achieve the objectives of least risk to people and lowest damage to property. Selection would not only focus on the attack alternatives that would hold a fire damage to a minimum, but also on those that would cause the least damage from the fire fighting operations themselves. It is possible to imagine, for instance, that a very poorly trained company might apply such an excessive amount of water to a weak structure that the weight of the water added to the existing load might collapse the building. Less extreme are the actual cases where excessive water causes damage to contents (furnishings, carpets, etc.), thus creating more damage than would be caused by smoke and fire if a less aggressive attack plan were followed.

All these potential and actual costs influence the level of offensiveness. In certain circumstances it may even be more desirable to allow the fire to burn a little longer if less water can be used. This would influence not only strategy, but would also affect tactics such as type and volume of streams. Frequently it may merely demand greater awareness on the part of fire fighters of the potential damage that can be prevented by nondirect actions such as the turning off of sprinkler valves as soon as the fire is sufficiently under control.

Overall Strategic Plan

In most departments it is clearly spelled out that rescue is the first priority for assigning resources, no matter what the personnel limitations might be.

Rescue: In formulating rescue strategies, the officer in charge needs to consider the degree of danger to which occupants and fire fighters will be exposed, the resources available (such as rescue apparatus, first-aid materials, and personnel with emergency medical training), and how to assign them. In so doing, the following questions should be considered:

• What risk would there be to the safety of the fire fighters involved in a rescue mission? What threat of injury and possible loss of life?

• Are resources sufficient for all rescue operations? If not, what rescue efforts can be undertaken? Inadequate personnel may make it impossible to proceed with all desirable rescue operations at the same time and have all of them succeed.

• Which rescue operations should receive priority? The officer in charge would consider which people are in most imminent danger, either from the fire itself or from other hazards. The rescue of those most threatened would receive highest priority, of course, except where danger to rescuers is excessive and personnel is needed for other rescue operations.

• Might the best approach be an indirect one? Sometimes the officer has to weigh the effects of delay against the possibility of greater effectiveness which, however, cannot be predicted with certainty. If a building can be ventilated, for instance, it may be possible to evacuate occupants more rapidly because escape routes would no longer pose danger to them or to fire fighters from smoke and poisonous gases. However, if initial ventilation procedures are ineffective, or if too much time is lost, then the occupants may suffer serious injury in the meantime.

Balancing all these considerations is not only technically difficult, but also involves profound moral issues. Every officer hopes never to be put into a situation where this kind of choice has to be made. When faced with such a situation, training and planning really pay incalculable dividends to the rescuers as well as the rescued.

Based on these considerations the strategic decisions can be made; specifically, what resources to allocate to which of the rescue operations. Only after all the strategic decisions have been made can the tactical ones be considered. This would then involve assigning positions to specific pieces of apparatus and specific fire fighters.

In addition to the direct rescue attempts, the officer in charge must consider protecting those exposures where potential risk to life is serious enough to warrant immediate attention.

Exposure Protection, Confinement, and Extinguishment Strategy Formulation: Strategies are not static; they are never cast in concrete. Instead, to be most effective, strategy must be constantly changed to adapt to new developments. For instance, ventilation of a structure may cause a fire to change its course, requiring revisions to strategy or at least a quick review to determine whether the strategy is still appropriate. If it is not, other options have to be reevaluated and the plan altered accordingly. Ventilation procedures may have been considered when probabilities were first evaluated, and these probabilities may have to be revised to fit the changed situations.

Although the entire decision-making process as discussed in this chapter might seem to be a lengthy and complex sequence, in reality it may take only seconds to consider all the data, to evaluate all the alternatives, and to make the strategy decisions. The same questions may be considered several times. At first an officer would have evaluated the probabilities with respect to ventilating vertically, horizontally, early in the attack, and later in the attack, and established what might happen in each possible situation.

If the decision was made to delay ventilation procedures, the same decision-making process may have to be repeated at a subsequent stage in fire fighting operations. A strategy that had been decided upon, and implemented, can bring results different from those to which the highest probabilities were assigned originally, for various reasons. This, in turn, may require a reevaluation of the approaches; such a reevaluation may again have repercussions on operational tactical decisions. Thus, the process repeats itself, continuing until the fire is under control.

However, the allocation of resources for one purpose — that is, to achieve one objective — cannot be made in isolation from the other objectives that have to be considered in an emergency situation. Every operation, and each segment of the operation, requires resources. The allocation of these must therefore be coordinated in order for each to receive an adequate amount. It is the officer's understanding of this process, combined with the ability to perceive the relationship between a particular decision and the whole plan, that contributes to the overall success of fireground operations.

As the strategy evolves and portions of the total resources are committed to the various activities, the officer in charge must estimate whether resources for exposure protection, confinement, and extinguishment are sufficient for a direct attack against the fire, or whether they must be devoted in part or completely to protecting against fire extension until additional resources arrive.

If additional alarms have been sounded, as reinforcements arrive on the scene they would be integrated into the overall plan. This might call for a redirection of strategy from a defensive to a more offensive one, or to a more comprehensive attack on the fire than has hitherto been possible.

Strategies for exposure protection, confinement, and extinguishment revolve around the best methods of applying the required fire flow to the fire. In this case, the line between strategy and tactics is not a clear one. While consideration of elevated streams as opposed to hand streams, for instance, may be a strategic decision because it involves a fundamental choice about the way in which the fire attack should be approached, the ladder work required would be a tactical consideration. To extinguish fires in buildings where nothing is stored, a heavy flow of water can be used. However, where contents may be easily damaged or the structure itself weakened, a more judicious use of water should be considered so that losses are reduced to a minimum. This is very important during periods of freezing weather, when ice formations may cause considerable damage.

Here again, the allocation of resources must precede the tactical implementation of strategy — how much is needed to cover certain positions and activities. Only when these decisions have been made can thought be given to specific tasks for particular fire fighters and the location of pieces of apparatus.

FIREGROUND TACTICS

Tactics involve the implementation of elements of strategy; they are the methods that are used to carry out the activities upon which strategy depends. Tactics tells the "who," "what," and "how" about the achievement of an objective.   Tactics prescribe the exact apparatus, its location, and the specific way that hoses will be run.   They dictate the specific assignments of personnel to the various tasks.

While the formulation of strategy is usually the responsibility of the fireground commander, unless the fire emergency is so small and routine that it can be handled by a single company, the tactical decisions — implementation of the specific strategies — generally fall to the officers in charge of individual units.

Implementation of Commands

The more thorough the drills and the better the training, the more rapidly the various tactics can be implemented and the less instructions will be needed for fire fighters to understand what is required of them.   In this way fire fighters can move immediately to carry out any tasks as soon as the instructions are given.   As far as possible, orders should be in the form of general guidelines as to what course of action should be taken so that the specific decisions involved can be made by the fire fighters themselves.   The following example shows the difference in the degree of detail needed by a well-trained or veteran fire fighter in order to be able to implement a command, and a poorly trained or new fire fighter.   The instructions for a well-trained fire fighter are listed first.

An officer tells a fire fighter to find a way to get into a building that is on fire; the closest door has four window panes.

1. For most experienced, most thoroughly trained fire fighter.	Get into the building.
2. For more experienced, more thoroughly trained fire fighter.	Get into the building through that door.
3. For experienced, trained fire fighter.	Get into the building through that door; those could be plastic windows — be sure you have the tool to cut with.
4. For least experienced, least trained fire fighter.	Get into the building; take a cutting torch so you can cut the window if it is not glass. Cut the lower left-hand window so you can reach in and open the door from the inside. If that doesn't work, cut both panes so that you can climb in.

When a fire fighter can implement a command without requiring detailed instructions, not only is time saved, but also the officer in charge is free to concentrate on other problems by knowing that the fire fighter will not return for more step-by-step directions if by chance one stage in the plan of action was not adequately communicated.   The advantages of good training are reflected in the more rapid development of strategies, in swifter decisions about tactics to be used, and in improved communications of those tactics, as well as by the

fire fighters themselves who benefit psychologically from the mutual understanding and close working relationship that comes from being a member of
an efficient, well-functioning, competent team.

SALVAGE AND OVERHAUL

Salvage and overhaul operations, while part of the overall strategy, constitute a different stage in fireground activities. The excitement of the emergency has diminished somewhat by the time search and rescue operations have
been completed and the streams are in operation. If some fire fighters are
free, they can be directed to start preventative salvage operations.

Importance of Overhaul Operations

Overhaul ensures that a fire is completely extinguished. Overhaul operations
also enable a department to investigate the cause of a fire. Hot spots are checked
to make certain the fire is not spreading behind walls and between ceiling
spaces, and that anything that is smoldering is doused in water. Even though
there may be no visible burning, fire fighters may still encounter hazards such as
toxic fumes and flammable or otherwise hazardous materials that have been
exposed to water and heat. Sometimes hydraulic overhaul is the best method
to overhaul abandoned buildings so that time can be saved at the expense of
a little extra water.

Although overhaul and salvage are basically different from fireground activities in that they demand their own strategies, tactics, and differing considerations, the decision-making process that an officer must follow is essentially
similar to that followed for fireground activities. Both require that the officer
in charge consider how best to use the human resources at the fireground,
how to minimize damage, and how to return the structure to its owner in as
good a condition as possible.

Salvage Operations

The term salvage operations includes all operations required to protect
a property from unnecessary damage caused by excessive water or other extinguishing materials. Salvage operations include covering objects with salvage
cloths and removing water from the property so that it doesn't seep through
floors and cause damage to the contents of lower floors. In this way a building
can be restored to a reasonable condition before the fire fighters leave.

Strategic Factors in Salvage and Overhaul Operations

Strategic factors for salvage and overhaul operations are often somewhat
similar. Following are some of the strategic factors to be considered for both:

1. To what extent can and should the human resources at the scene be
used to carry out overhaul and salvage operations, especially if they may
be fatigued?

2. To what degree can damage be prevented by quick action?

3. At what point should units be freed so they are available for other emergencies and duties? When should supplies be replenished, hoses examined and stored away, and apparatus and equipment checked?

4. To what extent should personnel be required or encouraged to work overtime? Fireground operations cost money; although this may be of minor consideration in comparison to the cost of fire damage, as soon as the fire is under control the question of the budgeting of time arises.

5. How long can or should volunteer fire fighters reasonably be kept at the scene?

6. Is the building in the best possible condition for return to the owner — cleaned up and closed up so that vandals cannot easily enter? Overhaul and salvage operations provide evidence to both the people who own the property, and those who see it, that the department carries out its responsibilities in an efficient, effective, and considerate manner, with the best interests of the public in mind.

Tactical considerations for salvage and overhaul operations may also be similar, and include the following:

1. Which companies should be assigned to overhaul, which to salvage, and when?

2. Where is action needed, in what sequence, and who should be assigned to it?

3. Who should be assigned to check out equipment and supplies?

Although the strategic and tactical thinking process involved in salvage and overhaul operations is similar to other phases of fireground operations, it is applied to an entirely different environment. While the leaders and subordinates are the same, a different leadership style is required because the actual situation is different.

Leadership Styles During Salvage and Overhaul

During preventive salvage (and even more so during overhaul and clean-up operations), the time pressures on the fire fighting team are nowhere near as great as they were before the fire was under control. Overhaul and salvage, therefore, call for a different goal-setting/decision-making style. Substantially more consultation is warranted. Competent fire fighters and lower-level officers can be given considerably more freedom in deciding what should be done, how it should be done, and in what order.

In overhaul and even more in salvage operations, officers and other managers often overlook the significant potential for developing subordinates and for providing them with substantially greater job satisfaction than would occur if those same officers switched immediately to a more participative style the moment the situation allows. It should be remembered that, with a well-disciplined and organized team, even the commands during fire fighting are, in effect, participative decisions; they are, however, primarily one-way communications. In order to conserve as much time as possible, the lower-level officer or fire fighter would not express any reservation or problems except ones of a serious nature. Once the emergency is over, however, these "lesser" problems become more important in relation to other aspects of the task, and failure to provide an easy outlet for discussion can stifle the desire of lower-level officers and fire fighters to perform their duties as enthusiastically as possible and in the way they deem best.

ORGANIZATION FOR FIREGROUND OPERATIONS

Good organization facilitates the effective implementation of all fire department activities, particularly those related to fireground operations. Good organization results primarily from two of the linking elements that were discussed briefly in Chapter Four, and which are dealt with more specifically here. These two linking elements are: (1) coordination, and (2) rules.

Coordination Procedures for Good Organization

The major avenue for achieving coordination of resources in any organization is through a chain of command. In its simplest form, it is the pyramidal line organization.

Chain of Command: The pyramidal line organization allows for a command, or instruction, to flow from the "top" of the organization down through the organization to the people at the "bottom," where implementation will take place. Most productive organizations that use a large number of people in the direct performance of work, especially military and pseudomilitary agencies like fire departments, function in this way.

Figure 9.3 shows a typical pyramidal structure starting with the chief at the top. In this case, the chief has two direct subordinates. In turn, the chief's

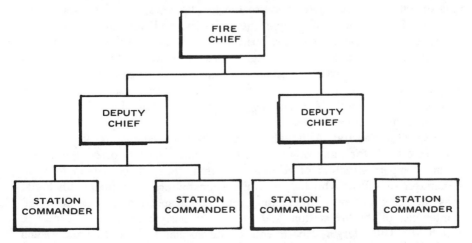

Fig. 9.3. Typical pyramidal line organization in its simplest form, which allows for every person to have one single superior to whom to report.

subordinates have their subordinate officers, and so on down the line.   This kind of simple organization allows for every person to have one single superior to whom to report.   All communications, directions, and instructions flow through that hierarchy, and all assignments are delegated in this way.

In the pyramidal line organization, communications between the different levels is handled as in the following example:

If, in Figure 9.3, station commander Three would like to coordinate something with station commander One, the only way that this can be done is for the commander to talk to deputy chief Two, who would then confer with the chief.   In turn, the chief would discuss the matter with deputy chief One, who would relay the information to station commander One.

In this type of organization, direct communications and direct resolutions of problems cannot occur on the same level, thus ensuring that the higher levels are properly informed and that all instructions flow only through one path.

Honoring the Chain of Command: It is important for a higher-level officer to honor the direct line command structure in order to eliminate the problems and confusion that can occur when a high-level officer bypasses a lower-level officer, and gives orders directly to that officer's subordinates.   Such actions undermine the authority of the lower-level officer and make it difficult for the subordinates to decide whose instructions to follow.   Their dilemma is even greater when instructions conflict, or when minor discrepancies exist.

In fireground situations, violations of the chain of command can cause conflicts and misunderstandings that can result in serious loss of time.   Fire fighters who are given instructions by a high-level officer can conceivably misunderstand those instructions.   If a lower-level officer tries to clarify those instructions, the fire fighters may resist believing they are proceeding according to orders from a higher authority.

Sometimes it is indeed necessary for a higher-level officer to give instructions directly to a fire fighter because the fire fighter's immediate supervisor may be fully occupied with important activities, and any interruption may not be in the best interests of the operation.   It may, therefore, be not only expedient, but also most effective to give direct instructions to that individual fire fighter.   In such a case, the command officer must, of course, immediately inform the fire fighter's direct superior in order to re-establish the integrity of the chain of command.   As much as possible, competent fire service officers avoid such direct interference.

Functional Authority: Although a pure chain of command provides the basic framework for most organizations, in reality there is often a need for a more complex structure of relationships than those described up to now. A manager or officer who has general responsibilities over many functional areas including not only fire fighting, but also inspection, prefire planning, maintenance of the fire station, and so on, obviously cannot be an expert in each field.   Thus, larger departments create special bureaus to handle such functions as fire prevention, and staff them with experts who are given the responsibility to see to it that the entire organization follows the best practices in their respective fields. These positions are considered "staff," as distinct from the direct "line" relationships in the pyramid itself.

Staff specialists must work through the line structure by obtaining orders for their suggested policies or procedures directly or indirectly from the chief. In itself, this does not interfere with the direct line of command. However, for example, a staff officer in headquarters may have the responsibility to ensure that all units conduct their respective inspections in accordance with the department's procedures. That person must have some direct contact with the operational units in order to resolve any questions that may arise. The chief obviously cannot become involved in every small problem related to the staff officer's functions.

The responsibilities of the specialist are, therefore, clearly communicated to the line organization, and line officers usually accept their suggestions directly. When conflicts occur, line officers can obtain clarification by taking the matter to their respective superior for resolution. The more important differences may have to be taken to the chief for resolution.

Figure 9.4 illustrates the relationship between a staff officer, the head of the fire prevention bureau, and line officers. The deputy chief for fire prevention may work directly with and through the station commanders, or may also monitor the fire prevention activities of captains. Since staff officers work primarily in an advisory capacity to line officers, they usually give recommendations rather than direct orders that can, of course, be rejected. A fire prevention officer, for example, may suggest that drills be held on how to conduct company inspections. The captain may feel that all drill time should be used to upgrade fire fighting operations. In order to get the drill changes implemented, the fire prevention officer would then have to work through the hierarchy, either at the deputy chief's level or directly through the chief.

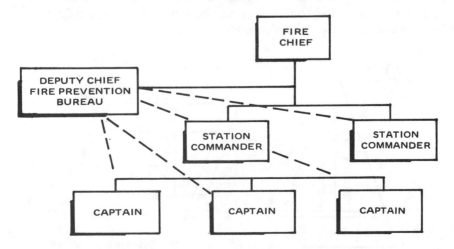

Fig. 9.4. The relationship between a staff officer, the head of the fire prevention bureau, and line officers.

Span of Control: Although the chain of command can expand vertically in a pyramid shape through many levels of subordinates, in the fire service a short chain of command is often most effective since it simplifies communications and allows all levels (including the fire fighter level) to feel close to the top of the organization.

However, when an organization has few levels, it automatically means that more people have to report to one supervisor. The number of people who report to one person are called the *span of control*. The span of control varies with different organizations; but, whenever supervisors or officers have to provide close and specific support, a span of six is generally considered to be the upper limit.

In very large departments it is conceivable that a higher-level officer could have a span of control that is greater than the optimum. This presents a problem. High-level officers must provide services to the people reporting to them. They must set mutually acceptable goals with their subordinates, train and supervise them in the implementation of assignments, evaluate the way in which these are carried out, provide feedback (both positive and negative about performance), and make available the necessary resources. In addition to this, high-level officers must provide the required technical information, skills, and materials, and must also help create an environment in which psychological needs are satisfied.

Thus, an organization can be thought of not only as a pyramid, but also as an inverted pyramid. (See Fig. 9.5.) If any of the higher-level officers do not perform their duties properly and do not see themselves as supporting the organization, the organizational unit may be in danger of collapse.

On the fireground, the command structure would be organized with a small span of control to provide for unity of command at all times, regardless of the complexity of the situation. Although this may lead to much longer chains in large operations, good coordination can be achieved through tight organization and clear definition of assignments.

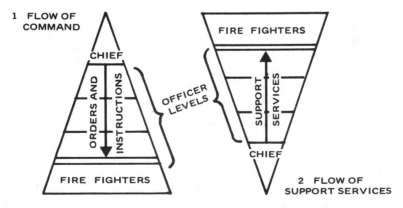

Fig. 9.5.   An organization shown as a pyramid and as an inverted pyramid.

Figures 9.6 through 9.9 show how this type of command structure is accomplished in one large department, the Los Angeles Fire Department.[3] The same principle might be applied by smaller departments by means of mutual aid organizations.

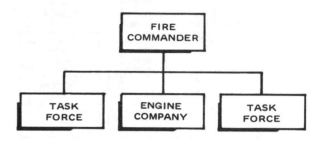

Fig. 9.6.   For small fires, the first attack team consisting of not more than five fire companies, under command of a battalion chief, is sufficient.   Each task force consists of one engine company and a truck company.

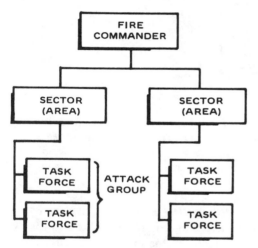

Fig. 9.7.   For greater alarm fires, fire suppression task forces organized into attack groups are assigned to fireground sectors. These sectors may be areas (such as a side or floor of a building fire), or they may be functional (such as rescue or salvage operations).   A battalion chief could be in command of each sector, and a deputy assistant chief would be the fire commander.

Fig. 9.8.   When there are three or more sectors at a fire, an extra battalion chief is assigned to the command post to be in charge of support services such as communications, maintenance, supplies, and medical assistance. The extra battalion chief may also act as command staff to the fire commander.

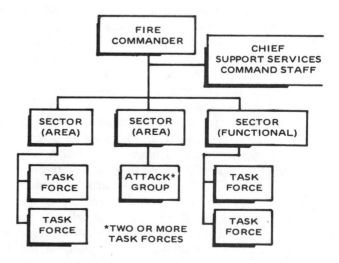

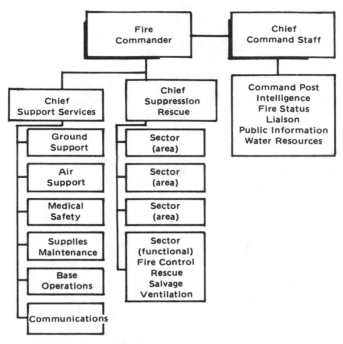

Fig. 9.9. Major emergency: Fire command has been split into three functions — support services, suppression and rescue, and command services. The chief of the command staff is responsible for liaison, supplying the commander with information on the status of the fire and water resources, issuing news releases, and all other activities related to the command post.

Delegation and Control: Figures 9.6 through 9.9 show that the span of control at the top is small, despite the increasing complexity of operations. Not more than three subordinates report directly to the fire commander. The fire commander in Figure 9.9, although far more remote from the actual fireground operations, nevertheless remains in control of the entire operation.

This same principle applies to all areas of fire department activities. The command principles embodied in fireground operations are paralleled in the framework of the fire service as a whole. The fire commander delegates authority for certain specific functions according to the nature and scope of the emergency while, at the same time, maintaining overall control. In much the same way, the head administrator or fire chief, when setting up the specific organizational structure, will delegate general authority to subordinates to act within prescribed limits. The limits may apply to a functional assignment such as training, or to a line responsibility such as battalion command; in either case, the span of control can remain small and coordination with other organizational elements can best be achieved through clear communication of responsibilities. Careful delegation is a necessity if the organization operates with many levels and with an extensive staff complement.

Effective Delegation: It is generally assumed that when the achievement of an assignment is delegated to a subordinate, that person (or "delegatee") has the responsibility to make decisions concerning the tasks that have been delegated within the general guidelines that have been spelled out by the "delegator," or by department policy.

Because it is difficult for some managers to allow their subordinates the freedom to use their own judgment and initiative, subordinates are prevented from acting on their own. Other managers may delegate to such an extreme that they lose contact with the assignments delegated, and thus fail to help those they supervise to achieve their goals. Effective delegation, then, lies somewhere between these two extremes, as illustrated in Figure 9.10.

Fig. 9.10. Effective delegation lies in shaded area, between the extremes shown in the areas on the far left and right.

Decisions are most effective when they are made at the lowest possible level at which all the essential information and expertise are available. This level naturally differs, depending on the type of decisions.

While each fire fighter must obviously decide on matters such as how to hold a nozzle and where to step within a room, decisions about how far to advance a line, or whether to take a line into a room, are made by the officer in charge. How good such a decision is depends, of course, on the adequacy of the information and on the judgment of the person making those decisions.

Effective delegation, then, depends on an organization's ability to achieve a high degree of decision-making competence and judgment at all levels; this can be achieved with thorough, carefully planned and executed training.

Besides the decision-making capabilities of delegatees, four major factors determine the degree to which delegation will be effective: (1) selection of appropriate projects to delegate, and an understanding of the limits of "effective" delegation; (2) selection of the "best" delegatees; (3) thorough mutual understanding of the responsibilities being delegated, and (4) good working relationship between delegator and delegatee.

Selection of Appropriate Projects: In order to maintain good balance between retaining full control and giving up all responsibility, the delegator must select those projects that require enough decision making on the part of the delegatee so that they will not appear to be mere task assignments (see Fig. 9.10). If projects do not allow this broad delegation, they should be handled on the basis of, "Can you help me with this project?" This approach signals to the person assuming the task that the project is not being delegated, and that the superior retains control.

It is not sufficient, however, merely to delegate responsibility for the appropriate projects. The delegatee must also be given considerable decision-making authority so that the delegated projects can, in fact, be completed without constant contact with the superior for approvals on a step-by-step basis.

Selection of the "Best" Delegatee: Selecting the most appropriate individual to carry out a delegated assignment requires correct assessment of subordinate capabilities and characteristics. For people involved in fireground operations, these may include:

- The necessary physical, mental, and emotional capabilities such as the ability to withstand stress, quick reflexes, stamina, etc.
- The technical knowledge that the assignment might require.
- Sufficient confidence to assume responsibility and carry out assignments.
- The confidence and respect of persons the delegatee may work with.

Understanding of Responsibilities Delegated: Both delegator and delegatee must have a clear understanding of the responsibilities being delegated and of those that have been retained by the delegator, in addition to a common view of the goals that are to be achieved. This may involve some joint planning and the establishment of certain priorities. Mutually understood and accepted performance standards must also be set so that both supervisor and subordinate have a means for measuring the degree of success achieved. This involves a realistic workload and time schedule, as well as recognition of the obstacles that may stand in the way of complete achievement of the selected goal. Most of these requirements have to be met during routine work and training, planning, and drill sessions so that, at the fireground, a mutual rapport exists that allows both parties to know what the other expects, without detailed discussion.

Working Relationship Between Delegator and Delegatee: A successful working relationship between delegator and delegatee requires that both parties work together in an atmosphere of trust and mutual understanding. The development of such a climate is enhanced by good two-way communications and the early participation in the decision-making process by the delegatee. Furthermore, the delegator must encourage independence, provide help and the necessary training when required, show interest but not surveillance, and give recognition for satisfactory performance. Also, effective delegators recognize that subordinates will make mistakes; in such cases the effective delegator is willing to accept the responsibility for mistakes, often realizing that if the job had not been delegated, some of the mistakes would not have been made. The effective delegator is one who:

- Understands the learning process and will offer opportunities for initiative and self-development.
- Is secure.
- Can accept that different methods can lead to a favorable outcome.
- Will allow subordinates to share in the benefits brought about by successful operations.

Conditions When Delegation Works Best: Delegation occurs most naturally when the delegator and delegatee are not physically close at all times, when the pressures of workloads are heavy, and when the organization encourages problem solving and self-development. Delegation, therefore, is an appropriate function on the fireground where time must be conserved and personnel must be able to take the responsibility and initiative for working by themselves.

Role of the Delegator: The role of the delegator is to monitor how the delegatee is carrying out the assigned task. This implies that:

1. In assigning a task, the delegator would invite some kind of commitment that the goal could and would be achieved.

This principle of accepting a goal also applies to the more direct commands associated with emergencies and the need to save time. While the command "Rescue those children" may evoke a rapid response, it is still automatically a mutually set goal (although imposed) since the delegatee has the responsibility to accept the assignment. If rescue appears impossible with the available resources, the delegatee must point that out while proceeding to attempt it. But, if the delegatee does not respond at all, the commander is then not aware that a problem exists, and therefore assumes the command is being carried out.

2. As the task is being implemented, the delegator would maintain contact so that additional support, such as more or different equipment, can be provided. Sometimes it might be possible to correctly anticipate what kind of support might be needed. At other times it may be necessary to reassess the whole strategy so that the required support can be provided; this would be especially applicable if the commander has had to set strategy in a highly fluid situation where changes are occurring rapidly.

3. The delegator has to assess how the job has been carried out so that delegation can be made more effective the next time. The questions that have to be asked include:

- If the assignment was not fully achieved, to what extent were the tactics appropriate and what were the reasons for lack of success?
- Was it within the capabilities of the delegatee and, if not, why not?
- Was the task intrinsically too difficult, were the instructions too vague, was the delegator supportive enough? etc.

Role of the Delegatee: A delegatee has several responsibilities to the delegator:

1. A delegatee must decide whether or not an assignment can be accepted with the authority and resources provided. Once this question has been resolved, the delegatee must lay out a plan for accomplishing that particular task.

2. If problems arise, the delegatee must modify the plan within the limits of delegated authority, or report back that the assignment cannot be handled with the presently available resources.

3. The delegatee has the responsibility to help the superior officer plan resources.

Principles of Effective Delegation: Following is a summary of effective delegation principles, of obstacles to delegation, of obstacles to acceptance of responsibilities, and of the circumstances in which delegation works best:

- Principles
     Careful selection of jobs or assignments to delegate.
     A clear view of the limits of 'effective' delegation (task assignments on one hand, abrogation on the other).
     Detailed planning and establishment of priorities.
     Knowledge of delegatees' capabilities and characteristics.
     Selection of proper delegatee.
     Establishment of goals and objectives for delegated tasks.
     An understanding and agreement on standards of performance.
     Agreement on areas of no delegation.
     Provision for support as needed (volunteered and when requested).
     Assessment of results and correction of errors.
     Encouragement of independence.
     Rewards or recognition where justified.
     Acceptance of methods other than those preferred by the delegator.
     Establishment of trust and mutual understanding.
- Obstacles to Delegating
     Inability of delegatee to handle the job (actual inability).
     Lack of confidence in delegatee (perceived inability) in judgment, attitudes, respect of others, etc.
     Fear of competition from delegatees.
     Loss of credit or recognition by delegator.
     Exposure of weaknesses of delegator.
     Lack of time for instructions and training.
     Liking of delegator for doing the particular job alone.
     Belief by delegator in own ability to delegate adequately.
     Perfectionism.
     Political realities.
- Obstacles to Acceptance of Responsibility
     It is often easier to ask the boss than to work it through.
     Fear of criticism, especially when it is often not fully warranted.
     Lack of necessary information.
     Lack of adequate resources.
     Lack of self-confidence.
     Lack of adequate incentives or existence of negative incentives (the "eager-beaver" syndrome, for instance).
     A feeling that the boss always gets own way, regardless.
- Delegation Usually Works Best
     When delegatees are physically distant.
     When delegator is absent frequently.
     When workloads are heavy.
     When there are many tight deadlines.
     When the organization is young and vigorous with emphasis on problem solving.
     When standards of performance are attainable and fair.

When the delegator feels personally secure.

When a favorable environment exists that emphasizes development, growth, innovation, creativity, and human dignity.

When a great deal of mutual trust exists at all levels of the organization.

Rules for Good Organization

As stated earlier, good organization results primarily from two of the linking elements, namely: (1) coordination, and (2) rules. Coordination procedures were discussed earlier in this chapter in the section subtitled "Coordination Procedures for Good Organization." The second element necessary for good organization, a sound set of rules, is discussed in the following paragraphs.

Duties and Responsibilities: One category of rules pertains to duties, responsibilities, and the standards of general conduct expected of all members and ranks. These rules are embodied in the job descriptions that list the particular responsibilities associated with each position in the department. On the fireground, as elsewhere, when jobs and assignments are clearly defined and everyone knows exactly what they are responsible for, there is less confusion.

The benefits that thus accrue in terms of increased efficiency and greater job satisfaction are outlined as follows:

- *Greater accountability.* Officers and fire fighters assuming a designated line position or assignment know what they are responsible for, thus enabling a department to hold them accountable for the manner in which those functions are carried out.
- *Supply of specific skills or technical knowledge.* While ideally all members of a unit have some knowledge of all elements of fire fighting, such knowledge is sometimes limited. By ensuring that the organization always has at least enough people so that the information or technical help that is needed can be provided, the department ensures that it will be available.
- *More highly motivated and efficient team.* On the fireground, good teamwork requires that all members know what is expected of them in terms of their contribution to the team effort. Department regulations specify positions as well as duties associated with each position.
- *Performance is more easily evaluated and tasks are more appropriately assigned.* This works to the advantage of both manager and subordinate. The manager has a basis for assigning work and evaluating how it is carried out. The subordinate has the security of knowing that work performance cannot vaguely be labeled inadequate. Shortcomings must be specified and clearly related to the job description.

On the fireground, more detailed rules than are contained in job descriptions and listings of responsibilities are needed to ensure a rapid and safe response to the emergency from the moment the alarm sounds, to the final overhaul procedures and return to duty. These rules fall into the following three broad categories: (1) response to alarms, (2) command structure, and (3) safety.

Response to Alarms: Departments have rules, or "running cards," for standard response to each alarm. This applies to alarms within the district and for mutual aid responses.

The response varies according to the department's staffing practices and resources. The level of officer responding also varies according to the nature of the emergency and the size of the department. The greater the potential for loss of life and property, the higher the level of officer responding. This might mean that in a big city department where there are several layers of high-level officers, the chief may respond only to emergencies of major proportions; in a very small department, the chief might respond to all but the most routine fires.

Command Structure: Rules governing fireground operations show clearly who is in charge at fires, based on the chain-of-command structure. The highest-level, first-in officer (often the company officer) is fireground commander until relieved by a superior, and the highest-level local officer assumes command at fires where mutual aid companies are working.

Safety: Rules are also necessary to ensure the safety of personnel. This is especially important where positioning of equipment or apparatus may endanger the safety of people. Set procedures for safe operation may govern many aspects of fire fighting, including the following:

- When and how breathing apparatus are to be worn, and who has the responsibility to ensure they are worn when specified.
- The use of protective clothing.
- The placement of ladders.
- How and when units are to be relieved for rest.
- Use of hoses.
- Use of communications procedures and equipment — symbols, commands, relay and priority of messages, etc.

Enforcement: The existence of rules and regulations alone does not determine how effective they are in helping to achieve goals. Rules must be communicated to all department personnel, and the purpose behind them explained so they are understood. Furthermore, they are not useful if they are not enforced.

Rules may be broken for many reasons. Sometimes infractions are the result of poor training or misunderstandings, and can be corrected easily with suitable explanation. Others may necessitate stronger penalties, especially if first warnings have gone unheeded. The procedures for handling noncompliance are described in Chapter Eleven, "Personnel Management."

Penalties are needed to protect the well-being of the organization and its ability to carry out its mission. Any malfunction of its parts affects the operation of the whole. Officers or fire fighters who do not follow orders because they do not reflect their own assessment of the situation may imperil the outcome of the operation and the safety of others.

When rules are broken during an emergency, the officer in charge should note the infraction but postpone discussion of it in order to devote all time, thought, and effort to extinguishing the fire. Each officer has the responsibility for the enforcement of fireground rules. Disciplinary actions are usually handled by the appropriate officer in the chain of command, according to the seriousness of the infraction. However, when rules are broken by mutual aid company members, it is not possible for an officer of one department to discipline personnel from another. All reports of misconduct by a member of another district or department are usually reported to the highest officer on the scene from the district; written notice is then sent to the appropriate officer.

However, since rule infractions tend to reflect unfavorably on the other district's competence, officers often try to protect (publicly at least) the specific fire fighter or subordinate officer. The result is that discipline is difficult to improve for multi-alarm responses unless the various jurisdictions meet regularly to anticipate any problems, to set up review procedures, and to agree on disciplinary actions that may be taken to enforce rules. After this, joint drills can be arranged to help clarify procedures and rules for all concerned.

Review of Rules: Rules and procedures should be reviewed from time to time to ensure that those which are no longer appropriate are modified and, if necessary, dropped. Rules and procedures are usually modified when new conditions and situations arise, such as new hazardous materials, new apparatus, and as new union agreements become effective. Other rules sometimes persist, though they are no longer valid. Such rules will often diminish respect for all rules; *i.e.*, a person who can see that one rule is unreasonable may assume that some of the others are too. This weakens control and department morale.

It is often difficult for organizations to anticipate change and meet new needs. Unfortunately, because an organization itself will sometimes fail to admit that there is a need for change, changes will be resisted as much as possible. Sometimes, all that is needed is a reorganization and shifting of duties. At other times, an extensive review of all rules may be necessary. To avoid the problems that major rule changes can bring, officers who are aware of outdated rules should work to obtain revisions of existing rules by regularly pointing out some of the discipline problems that can result if changes are not made gradually. The "rule book" should be a living document, not cast in concrete.

FIREGROUND COMMUNICATIONS

While good communications are a fundamental requirement for effective leadership in any organization, they are of paramount importance on the fireground where, in order to hold misinterpretation to a minimum, directions must be precise. In the giving of directions at any level, preciseness is important; for example, to and from fireground commander, headquarters, fire fighting units, staff units, company officers, and fire fighters. Since time is of the essence on the fireground, conciseness and lack of ambiguity in communicating are essential. Unfortunately, however, there are many barriers to good communications that can make clarity difficult to achieve. These barriers can obstruct the transmission of one person's thoughts to another person.

Success in verbal communication depends on the ability of the "sender" to find words that appropriately express the thought that is to be transmitted to the "receiver." How well this is done depends on the sender's vocabulary, the ability to choose the correct words, and the time available for explaining the thought. The sender must also think about how the thought should be presented to the receiver in order for it to be received in the best possible way. To do this includes an awareness on the part of the sender of the language that the receiver is best able to understand.

Often, the words that come from a sender's mouth are not as explicit as they are meant to be. Sometimes, such words can mean something slightly different from what the sender intends. At other times, such words can be substantially different because the sender may have been distracted either by some external element, or by other thoughts that interfered with the one that was being phrased into language.

When the words leave the sender's mouth, there is a brief moment in time before they reach the receiver. During that time, all kinds of things can happen. One thing that can happen is that the voice level could be so low that it is not capable of traveling the full distance to the receiver. Or, there could be loud, interfering noises. Most important, though, is that in most instances the words are accompanied by a facial expression or possibly a gesture. These nonverbal symbols that accompany words become part of the message; they can change the meaning of the message by reinforcing or weakening it. For example, a different meaning is carried by words that are spoken with a smile than by ones accompanied by a frown.

When the words finally reach the receiver, another complex series of processes take place before the total communications step is completed. The message reaches the receiver as a complete package of words, gestures, and other symbols — including the relationship between the sender and the receiver, and the situation that surrounds them at the moment. At the same time, there are other impulses that vie for the attention of the receiver. These include all the possible distractions — visual or audible — in the environment, including other people who may be speaking at the same time. Therefore, because of the distractions that have interfered, what the receiver hears and sees of the message may be only a part of what has left the mouth of the sender. But even if the entire message is received together with the symbols that accompany it, the words have a different meaning for the receiver than they have for the sender. Thus, as the total message is gradually assembled in the receiver's mind, it can take on a totally different picture from that which the speaker had intended. The listener or receiver has to translate words into thoughts; again, this involves the vocabulary, the meaning the words have taken on for the receiver, and all the same complications that the sender has faced. In addition, many words trigger various thoughts in the receiver's mind. These thoughts become combined with the message, and the message may grow substantially.

Misinterpreted and misunderstood communications on the fireground can be avoided when:

- There is a good understanding of the communications process by both the officers giving the orders and the fire fighters receiving them.
- Joint drills have been conducted, with attention to standardized orders or instructions to ensure that the same meaning exists for both the senders and receivers.
- The sender-receiver feedback on the way the message is understood by the receiver.

The Meaning of Words

The degree of understanding achieved from a verbal or nonverbal order depends upon the symbols — the words, sounds, codes, or mental pictures — used to relay the order, and the way they are used. Words can have widely different meanings in different situations and for different people. Understanding the meanings of words depends heavily on such things as previous experience with particular words, knowledge about the way other persons use them, the environment (such as expectations about the other person's attitude), and the context in which they are used. For example, the word "truck" — depending on who hears the word, when, and in what circumstances — can produce images that range from a toy truck to an ice cream truck, from a tow truck to a delivery truck, or from an emergency repair truck to a pumper. And, in slang usage, "not to have any truck with so-and-so" refers to nothing concrete, but rather to a lack of relationship to some other person.

Some words are more precise or general than others, and some can have several meanings. Also, to further complicate the transmission of an order or a message, there are some words that sound alike. Thus, in most situations, words like the word "two" have very precise meanings, unless misunderstood to have the same meanings as other words that sound like them ("too" or "to"). Words are the symbols for thoughts that are often highly complex. Therefore, single words are rarely adequate for most purposes. They are usually more effective when strung together to form sentences, and thus add more meaning and specificity to an order or message.

Ladder of Abstractions

Sentences that are used for transmitting orders or messages are more effective when their meanings are made as specific as possible. Such specificity can help prevent misinterpretations and misunderstandings. An order or message that uses specific terms is better able to convey as exactly as possible the meaning the sender intended than ones that don't use specific terms. The ladder of abstractions concept used by semanticists and linguists illustrates how the meaning of an order or message can be made more clear by showing in ladder form the increasing degree of specificity, or levels of generality, of statements. (See Fig. 9.11.)

The statement at the top of the ladder is more abstract or broader in meaning than the statement at the bottom. An officer who understands this principle can adjust orders and directions to the particular requirements of the situation. Messages must be geared to the receiver.

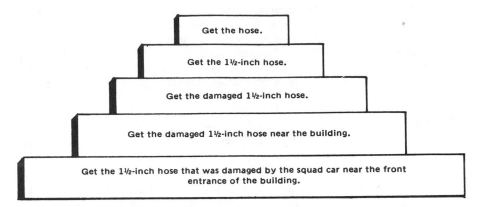

Fig. 9.11. Ladder of abstractions showing the increasing degree of specificity of a statement. Such specificity can help prevent misunderstandings.

With experienced people, where there is a high level of mutual understanding, instructions can often be given in fairly broad terms — high up on the ladder of abstractions. The less experienced the other person, or the less closeness in the relationship, the more detailed instructions or messages have to be so they will be clearly received. For example, while a comparatively new recruit may feel insecure unless all the necessary details about how to enter a building are spelled out, a seasoned, well-organized fire fighter may not need — and might even resent — step-by-step instructions. (See also earlier section titled "Implementation of Commands.")

Specialized symbols are an excellent means for helping to eliminate excessive verbiage from messages. Organizations that rely upon the rapid implementation of directions to achieve a goal often develop sets of symbols — numbers, codes, terminology, etc. — so that the information communicated is clear, precise, and quickly translated into action. In the fire service, numbers may be assigned to apparatus, companies, stations, or even sections of a fire so that there will be no doubt as to which piece of equipment, apparatus, etc., is being referred to. Some departments also give numbers to officers to facilitate radio communication. Numbers or letter codes are also used to convey various standard messages such as those concerning false alarms, the status of companies, the fire situation, and requests for additional personnel.

Specific terminology or jargon, which is often unintelligible to all but those who use it, develops in most organizations, industries, and fields of endeavor. Such terminology enables people to communicate with each other in terms that have a narrow and specific application. The words "BLEVE" and "fire loading," for example, mean little or nothing to people outside the fire service.* Some departments use the terms "working fire" or "all hands" to denote a serious fire that may require multiple alarm response.

---

*BLEVE — Boiling liquid-expanding vapor explosion; fire loading — the weight of combustibles per square foot of floor area.

Giving Assignments and Instructions

In giving assignments and instructions on or off the fireground, or in reporting back, it is important to organize the information to be communicated so that it will be relayed in a logical sequence that is clearly understandable. This can usually be accomplished by:

1. Organizing the information.

    *   What are the main points (topic, activity assigned, etc.)?
    *   What are the relevant details for each main point?
    *   In what order should the main points be presented?

2. Presenting the information to a subordinate (directing) or to a superior officer (reporting back).

3. Obtaining feedback — making sure the information was understood.

Use of this process does not necessarily take more time than it does to transmit messages in a less carefully organized way because once such use becomes a habit, the thought processes involved are almost instantaneous. The benefits of such habits can be substantial.

LINKING ELEMENTS AND
THE COMPANY OFFICER'S ROLE ON THE FIREGROUND

There are several important areas relevant to the linking elements that directly affect the role of the company officer on the fireground. These areas include goals and leadership style, enforcement of rules, post-emergency critique, and sample goals for fireground command.

Goals and Leadership Style

The company officer must be able to use a wide range of leadership styles. Different styles are required at the beginning and through the climax of the emergency than are required during overhaul and salvage. For example, rarely is it advisable on the fireground to hold a conference immediately after size-up to discuss the next steps that should be taken. Instead, the fire officer must be decisive and quick about laying out attack strategy and implementing it immediately. However, this does not mean that participative decision making and goal setting is totally inappropriate; a great deal of participative goal setting takes place with a smoothly coordinated team, although at first this might not be apparent.

Sometimes, something that might appear to be a command often, in reality, is not. If a charge officer and the individual line officers have the kind of understanding characteristic of a well-trained team, there will be deeper meanings to the commands. For example, the instructions or orders from the fireground charge officer to a line officer may sound brief, but may be highly complex in meaning. Both officers are aware, if the working relationship between them is a thoroughly professional and competent one, that they have entered into a contract. The subordinate officer has accepted the goal given by the charge officer's instructions or orders, and can now be held accountable for working toward it. The officer in charge has the right to expect that the subordinate officer will respond as soon as the instructions are given. If the subordinate officer feels that the goal is unrealistically high or is beyond the capability of the team to achieve, then it is that officer's responsibility to so state. By accepting the instructions or orders, the subordinate officer has assumed the responsibility to:

1. Lay out the tactical steps to achieve the goal.
2. Change these steps if it appears as though they will not achieve the goal.
3. Immediately notify the officer in charge that the resources are inadequate as soon as it becomes apparent that the goal might be in jeopardy. For instance, considerable advance notice should be given of the fact that the team will soon be reaching the point of exhaustion, or of any other matter related to the safety of the fire fighters.

Thus, even though most of the goals are decided upon by the officer in charge, more participative decision making is practiced on the fireground by an effective team than might at first be apparent. The effectiveness that results from a sound working relationship between the officer in charge at the fireground and subordinate officers should also result from an effective working relationship between company officers and fire fighters. While the ultimate responsibility for the coordination of all effort rests with the officer in charge at the fireground, responsibility must also be delegated to line officers and fire fighters in order to ensure the close coordination of the efforts of all of the members of the company.

Enforcement of Rules

The enforcement of rules on the fireground is an important responsibility of an officer. On the fireground there is little time to explain rules, and a thorough understanding of the reasoning behind them must have taken place beforehand. When an officer gives instructions to withdraw or accept relief, for example, a fire fighter who attempts to resist must be aware that such resistance is a major breach of the command authority, even though such devotion to duty may seem to be exemplary.

Obviously, to achieve compliance with an order, the officer in charge cannot use force on the fireground. Firmness helps to ensure that instructions are made with serious intent and, through prior training, it should have been made known that disciplinary consequences will result from instructions not being followed.

Post-emergency Critiques

Most fire fighting teams conduct critiques after each run (except the most routine ones) to review strategy and tactics and to draw conclusions on which to base suggestions for improvements. Such conclusions can have limited application if they concentrate, as they often do, on fire fighting strategy and tactics and do not take into consideration other elements that contribute to more effective operation. For example, indication that the goal-setting process is not understood by all can become the foundation for team training and practice sessions. Such training and practice could help impart an understanding of the principles of the delegation of goals — an important part of effective team work, as distinguished from a work group that continually depends on instructions from its leader.

In critiques of what occurred during a run, many opportunities exist to elicit from the fire fighting team methods for improving effectiveness. To help accomplish this, an officer can:

1. Allow members of the team to express their views.
2. Thoroughly explore these views to give credit for any ideas that would be beneficial in the future.
3. Plan, jointly with the team, training and drills that would be beneficial.
4. Agree on objectives that should be set.

There are other facets to the critique that can also be valuable, yet frequently receive little attention. They concern conclusions that can be drawn about steps that would enhance coordination or rule adherence. Then, of course, there is the need to analyze whether, and to what extent, the emergency has helped to cement and increase esprit de corps, or to what extent it may have done damage to the cohesiveness of the team.

The extent to which the goal-setting process has worked is another important subject that should be reviewed in the critique of every emergency. Finally, such review sessions can include a discussion of how the emergency may have added to the satisfaction that team members receive from their work and of ways to improve work-related satisfaction in a more general way.

Every emergency provides many opportunities for the company officer to analyze, either alone or jointly with the team, what impact the emergency has had on the effectiveness of the team. From this analysis, changes can be made that will help the team to more effectively perform its mission in the future.

Encouragement of Team Effort

Considerable social and personal satisfaction can be derived by all members of a team if the team is able to coordinate its activities and thus quickly and effectively respond to the differing needs of a variety of situations. The importance of the image of the company officer as an integral part of such a team effort cannot be overestimated. Only when a team has a high degree of confidence in the competency of its officers can team members gain the full benefit of such team work.

It is necessary for all members of the team to feel that the assignments they have received are fair in relation to those given to other team members. Since judging fairness in a factual way is extremely difficult, it is the feelings of the team members that are important. Assignments, which are more inspiring when they are challenging, must be achievable or they can be discouraging. Assignments also cannot be viewed as containing more of the "dirty jobs" than others receive. Yet these opinions are rarely based on careful comparisons of job assignments. Two different officers can conceivably give identical assignments to members of a team, and the assignments can be received with totally different reactions.

In encouraging team effort, it is essential to instill confidence in team members. To help instill confidence, team members should be allowed to make constructive suggestions and contribute ideas on matters such as where coordination may not have been as good as it might have been among the members of the team or with other companies. Also, they can contribute ideas on how communications might be strengthened, or made more precise and rapid, and they can suggest changes in rules, including those dealing with communications or with other aspects of the fireground activities that could help prevent any future difficulties. And, of major importance, team members can contribute extensively to analyzing the training and drill needs that a particular emergency exposed, or that appear desirable as a result of problems they noted during the emergency. Such open, joint exploration of training opportunities can, in itself, go a long way in helping to encourage team effort and in making training sessions more satisfying. But, what is even more important, it will help to concentrate more clearly on those needs that are perceived by the team — not just on those that the officer may consider important.

Sample Goals for Fireground Command

Following are some sample goals for fireground command, presented here for use as guidelines by company officers when developing fireground goals:

Strategic Goals
- Develop improved techniques so that total response time to start of actual fireground operations is reduced by ten percent.
- Establish coordination procedures that will increase effectiveness of mutual aid companies through better communications during response. and through clearer delineation of responsibilities.
- Develop standards for overhaul procedures.
- Develop standard times for all major hose evolutions.

Operational Goals
- Reduce tie-up time by ten percent by a specified date.
- Establish revised regulations for use of airpacks and ensure adherence.
- Reduce excess water in private home fires to cut water damage by twenty percent.
- Expand coverage of post-fire critiques to include setting goals to meet training needs uncovered at fire fighter and officer levels.
- Include paper and pencil fireground simulations in training sessions.

ACTIVITIES

1. There are two activities that contribute to high-level performance on the fireground. In outline form, describe the factors involved in each

of these activities, including in your descriptions the reasons why they contribute to the effectiveness of fire fighting operations.

2. Write your own definitions of the terms "strategy" and "tactics," emphasizing the major differences between the two.

3. In order to make the best strategy decisions, the officer in charge must, in effect, follow the basic decision-making process. This means defining the problem, obtaining the data, identifying the alternative courses of action, selecting the best alternatives for the moment, and continuous evaluation and convection on the basis of new data to ensure that the best approach is being used. At the fire scene the definition of the problem and the data come from three distinct and separate analyses. Describe these analyses in detail.

4. What factors need to be considered by the officer in charge at the fireground when formulating rescue strategies?

5. (a) With your classmates, discuss the differences between salvage operations and overhaul operations.
   (b) Write your own definition for each term.

6. The pyramidal line organization is the simplest form of a chain of command. Explain why you do or do not think the pyramidal line structure is the most efficient form of organization for a fire department. Defend your reasoning by presenting examples.

7. (a) When giving assignments, instructions, and orders on or off the fireground, why is it important to organize the information to be communicated?
   (b) Explain how the concept of the ladder of abstractions can help sharpen messages, and especially instructions.

8. What is the difference between verbal and nonverbal communications, and why is each one of major importance when giving instructions?

9. Based on what you have learned from this chapter, explain what you feel is the most effective way to delegate tasks. Explain why. (Refer to Fig. 9.10 for use in helping to form your answer.)

10. Two of the elements that are necessary for good organization are: (1) coordination, and (2) rules.
    (a) What is the major avenue for achieving coordination of resources in any organization? How does this work?
    (b) Describe some of the benefits that can accrue, on the fireground as well as elsewhere in the fire service, from a sound set of rules.

BIBLIOGRAPHY

[1] *Fire Protection Handbook*, 14th Ed., NFPA, Boston, 1976, p. 9–27.

[2] ———, p. 9–27.

[3] Hill, Raymond M., "Fire Combat," *Fire Command!*, Vol. 41, No. 8, Aug. 1974, pp. 38–42.

[4] Kimball, Warren Y., *Fire Attack 1: Command Decisions and Company Operations*, NFPA, Boston, 1966, p. 88.

Chapter Ten

Management of
Physical Resources

PHYSICAL RESOURCES OF FIRE DEPARTMENTS

A fire department's primary and most valuable resource is its personnel. Yet no matter how well-trained and well-staffed a fire department is, its personnel cannot perform effectively without the necessary physical resources.

There are basically three types of physical resources available to a fire department: (1) the facilities (the real estate and buildings), (2) the apparatus, and (3) the equipment and supplies. These resources, in addition to personnel, enable a fire department to function and fulfill its assigned objectives. A department's overall effectiveness and the degree to which it can meet its obligation to control fires, extinguish fires, and help prevent fires from occurring, is greatly influenced by the management and coordination of these resources.

Problems in Management of Physical Resources

The constantly changing nature of the job of fire fighting and the updating and modernization of facilities, apparatus, and equipment present many unique management problems to fire department administrators. In order to better comprehend the complexity and extent of some of these problems, it is necessary to understand how frequently and drastically fire fighting building and apparatus needs change as technological advances bring into more common use new construction materials and hazardous substances. For example, the use of plastics and their many derivatives for construction purposes, and the use and transportation of flammable liquids and gases for industrial purposes create new requirements for fire fighters. The advent and popularity of high-rise living has brought about the need for more complex apparatus — such as elevating platforms and aerial towers — for fighting fires in high-rise buildings. The severity of economic loss and loss of lives associated with arson-related fires have provoked the need for new communication and detection equipment, and for more effective inspection and investigative procedures.

Each of these considerations has added to the complexity and scope of the management problems of concern to fire department administrators, and has impact on facilities, apparatus, and equipment needs. Continual changes are therefore necessary in the physical resources required to do the job. These changes might involve purchases such as aerial ladders needed to cope with the rising number of tall buildings in a community, or they might involve management decisions concerning location and construction date of a new station, or modification of an existing one. Expenses involved in the purchase of an aerial ladder may require postponement of a station or, in other cases, may compel remodeling of a station to make room for it. In all stations, it is management's responsibility to establish priorities, keeping in mind that no matter what the changes, the job of fire fighting should never take second place.

The decisions that have to be made in order to establish and meet a department's physical resource needs are often guided by the many applicable existing standards and laws, and those that still have to be passed by state and national legislation. To meet these, the National Fire Protection Association (NFPA) sets standards for nearly every facet of the job of fire fighting. Although these standards are too numerous to list in their entirety in this text, some of the ones that relate to fire service management will be discussed in later sections of this chapter.

Effect of Grading Schedules on Physical Resources

In addition to the help provided by the standards set by the NFPA, the American Insurance Association (AIA) aids fire department management by compiling a grading schedule to rate the effectiveness and efficiency of a fire department. The AIA's predecessor, the National Board of Fire Underwriters (NBFU), originally conducted surveys to establish ratings for individual fire departments. Frequent revisions of schedules and an increase in population since their inception over a century ago have necessitated that regional and state field offices of the Insurance Services Offices (ISO) take over the process of surveying fire department efficiency. A staff of trained engineers from ISO conducts surveys of municipal fire defenses once every ten years and assigns a classification based on 5,000 points that includes ratings in six major categories:[1]

1. Water supply, which analyzes the adequacy and reliability of local water supply.

2. Fire department, which surveys the elements of the fire department organization and grades them.

3. Fire alarm, which is rated on accessibility, speed of transmission, and reliability.

4. Fire prevention, which studies the degree to which codes are enacted and enforced, and the degree of cooperation with other interested departments.

5. Building department, which analyzes the regulations related to building construction and their enforcement.

6. Structural conditions, which involves an analysis of factors in the most important high-value district that would contribute to fire losses.

Table 10.1 Relative Class as Determined by Points of Deficiency*

Points of Deficiency	Relative Class of Municipality
0– 500	First
501–1,000	Second
1,001–1,500	Third
1,501–2,000	Fourth
2,001–2,500	Fifth
2,501–3,000	Sixth
3,001–3,500	Seventh
3,501–4,000	Eighth
4,001–4,500	Ninth[1]
More than 4,500	Tenth[2]

[1]A ninth class municipality is one: (a) receiving 4,001 to 4,500 points of deficiency, or (b) receiving less than 4,001 points but having no recognized water supply.

[2]A tenth class municipality is one (a) receiving more than 4,500 points of deficiency, or (b) without a recognized water supply and having a fire department grading over 1/55 points, or (c) with a water supply and no fire department, or (d) with no fire protection.

Table 10.1 illustrates the breakdown in grading points for fire departments. A municipality is rated in one of the ten categories shown in Table 10.1, with a first-class rating denoting the least amount of deficiency points and a tenth-class rating denoting the highest amount of deficiency points.

When a fire department is evaluated by ISO engineers, the department's buildings, apparatus, equipment, and competence are compared with established standards. Table 10.2 shows a checklist for evaluating fire department response capability based upon the resources required for various occupancies.

Grading schedules are important to fire department management and to the communities they serve because good evaluations reflect the professionalism of the departments and usually mean lower fire insurance rates for the communities. Because of this, the purchase and maintenance of efficient and effective apparatus, buildings, and equipment are of major importance to a fire department's administration. For example, if a fire department has received a sixth-class rating, both the department management and the community will want to improve the department. This will most likely mean enhancing the physical resources available to the department.

The AIA Grading Schedule has brought about extensive improvements in water supply, fire department equipment and efficiency, fire alarm systems, control of special hazards, and structural conditions, with the result that losses due to fire damage have also been reduced.

---

*From *Fire Protection Handbook*, 14th Ed., NFPA, Boston, 1976.

Table 10.2 Evaluation of Fire Department Response Capability*

High Hazard Occupancies (Schools, hospitals, nursing homes, explosive plants, refineries, high-rise buildings, and other high life hazard or large fire potential occupancies)

At least 4 pumpers, 2 ladder trucks, 2 chief officers, and other specialized apparatus as may be needed to cope with the combustible involved; not less than 24 fire fighters and 2 chief officers.

Medium Hazard Occupancies (Apartments, offices, mercantile, and industrial occupancies not normally requiring extensive rescue or fire fighting forces)

At least 3 pumpers, 1 ladder truck, 1 chief officer, and other specialized apparatus as may be needed or available; not less than 16 fire fighters and 1 chief officer.

Low Hazard Occupancies (One-, two-, or three-family dwellings and scattered small businesses and industrial occupancies)

At least 2 pumpers, 1 ladder truck, 1 chief officer, and other specialized apparatus as may be needed or available; not less than 12 fire fighters and 1 chief officer.

Rural Operations (Scattered dwellings, small businesses and farm buildings)

At least 1 pumper with a large water tank (500 or more gal), one mobile water supply apparatus (1,000 gal or larger), and such other specialized apparatus as may be necessary to perform effective initial fire fighting operations; at least 6 fire fighters and 1 chief officer.

Additional Alarms

At least the equivalent of that required for Rural Operations for second alarms; equipment as may be needed according to the type of emergency and capabilities of the fire department. This may involve the immediate use of mutual aid companies until local forces can be supplemented with additional off-duty personnel.

The insurance costs associated with AIA ratings can sometimes have a significant influence on community development. There have been cases where industries seeking locations for new plants have avoided a community where the insurance rates were excessively high. The municipality involved thus lost the tax revenue that could have helped pay for the expenditures on fire defense improvements that should have been made.

The remainder of this chapter deals with managerial methods that apply to the three types of physical resources available to fire departments, and includes information on the use of budgets as tools of management. As stated earlier, the three types of physical resources available to fire departments are:

1. Buildings and location.
2. Apparatus.
3. Equipment.

*From *Fire Protection Handbook*, 14th Ed., NFPA, Boston, 1976.

MANAGEMENT OF FACILITIES

A fire department's facilities are comprised of all of the real estate and buildings utilized by the department. Such facilities can include buildings or areas for housing of personnel, storage of equipment, administrative offices, communications functions, training facilities, maintenance equipment, and supplies. In smaller organizations these functions are usually contained in one building; larger organizations, however, may use several facilities in different locations.

The Fire Station

The fire station is the single, most vital unification force within a fire department. It not only provides a housing element for the department's apparatus and equipment, but also may house the department members themselves. The fire station, as the center of the community's fire fighting operations, is a vital symbol of the protection of lives and property.

The importance of a fire station's upkeep and location involves management decisions by either the chief or by a separate officer or bureau whose specific duties are the handling of all matters related to the station. In volunteer departments a committee representing the membership may "manage" the building and, within the scope of its power, may even be able to recommend the rebuilding of a new station.

When there are no inherent problems with the site and capabilities of an existing fire station, it becomes the responsibility of management to properly maintain the present building so that it will continue to be functional in future years. If the present building is not adequate to meet fire fighter and/or community needs, and if funds have not been budgeted to build a new station in the near future, then department management should try to "make do" with what it has and possibly incorporate new ideas to alleviate some of the problems that necessitate rebuilding. For example, management may realize that the department needs another pumper in order to more effectively handle the community's fires, but may also realize that space requirements would not permit the housing of another pumper within the station. If the station is near a municipal facility that houses trucks and snowplows, management might be able to arrange for storage of the new pumper at that location until a new station can be built. Storage of the pumper at a municipal facility would be a simple, although temporary, solution. In the event that management discovered that the protection capabilities of the present fire station were insufficient because of community expansion, the construction of a new fire station would be considered to be a necessity and major emphasis would be placed on obtaining approval to build it.

Once the decision has been made to build a new station, many decisions have to be made. These concern primarily: (1) location of the station, and (2) design specifications of the station. In arriving at the conclusion that another station is essential, and in convincing the authorities, a department's top managers rely on AIA statistics such as those shown in Table 10.3.

Table 10.3 Relationship Between Number of Apparatus Needed Within a Given Area to Required Fire Flow*

Fire Flow Required	First Due				First Alarm[a] Includes First Due				Maximum Multiple Alarm			
	Eng.		Lad.		Eng.		Lad.		Eng.		Lad.	
gpm	No.	Mi.	No.	Mi.	No.	Mi.	No.	Mi.	No.	Mi.	No.	Mi.
less than 2,000	1	1½+	*1	2++	**2	4	*1	2++	**2	4	*1	2++
2,000	1	1½+	*1	2++	2	2½	*1	2++	2	2½	*1	2++
2,500	1	1½	*1	2	2	2½	*1	2	2	2½	*1	2
3,000	1	1½	*1	2	2	2½	*1	2	3	3	*1	2
3,500	1	1½	*1	2	2	2½	*1	2	3	3	*1	2
4,000	1	1½	1	2	2	2½	1	2	4	3½	1	2
4,500	1	1½	1	2	2	2½	1	2	4	3½	1	2
5,000	1	1	1	1½	2	2	1	1½	5	3½	2	2½
5,500	1	1	1	1½	2	2	1	1½	5	3½	2	2½
6,000	1	1	1	1½	2	2	1	1½	6	4	2	2½
6,500	1	1	1	1½	2	2	1	1½	6	4	2	2½
7,000	1	1	1	1½	2	1½	1	1½	7	4	3	3½
7,500	1	1	1	1½	2	1½	1	1½	8	4½	3	3½
8,000	1	1	1	1½	2	1½	1	1½	9	4½	3	3½
8,500	1	1	1	1½	2	1½	1	1½	9	4½	3	3½
9,000	1	¾	1	1	3	1½	2	2	10	4½	4	4
10,000	1	¾	1	1	3	1½	2	2	12	5	5	4½
11,000	1	¾	1	1	3	1½	2	2	14	5	6	5
12,000	1	¾	1	1	3	1½	2	2	15	5	7	5

[a] Response to building fires should include a chief officer.

*Where there are less than 5 buildings of a height corresponding to 3 or more stories, a ladder company may not be needed to provide ladder service.

**Same as first due where only one engine company is required in the municipality.

+May be increased to 2 miles for residential districts of 1- and 2-family dwellings, and to 4 miles where such dwellings have an average separation of 100 feet or more.

++May be increased to 3 miles for residential districts of 1- and 2-family dwellings, and to 4 miles where such dwellings have an average separation of 100 feet or more.

Location of the Station

The number and location of new fire stations must be continually reevaluated as the buildings and the population of a community change. The number of stations a department will require to accomplish its function is, like everything else, a balance between the costs of the buildings and their maintenance on

*From AIA "Special Interest Bulletin No. 176," the American Insurance Association, New York, NY.

the one hand, and the need for more stations on the other. If a station is located near the most fire hazardous section of a community — such as a heavily populated area of multi-occupancy or wood-frame structures — then station relocation would be inappropriate. Station relocation would be more feasible if the station is located in a rural area that is a considerable distance from the normal population flow and from urban housing and development.

The location of the station in the community goes hand-in-hand with the total response time needed to effectively combat fires. Although a fire station may be centrally located in a community, the majority of the fires that occur might take place at substantial distances from the station. Therefore, an evaluation of the time from receipt of an alarm to the extinguishing of a fire plays an important part in management's determination of the need for relocating a fire station. The total time is the sum of the time it takes to complete each of the following seven fire fighting processes:

Detection: The time it takes to detect a fire, which depends upon the number of people who are in the vicinity of the fire, their rapidity of response, and the time of day. Automatic fire detection systems such as smoke and heat detectors give early warnings of fire and save considerable time before extinguishment. Some detectors are connected directly to a fire station (*e.g.*, central station signaling systems), while others sound only in the building in which there is a danger. In the latter case, detection time is dependent upon human response.

Alarm: The time that elapses between detection of the fire and the transmittal of the alarm to the fire station, which depends upon the availability of alarm boxes or telephones, their reliability, the extent of automation, and the speed of transmission.

Dispatch: The time that is required to record information and to dispatch personnel. If information is recorded automatically and if dispatchers have the use of the most modern communications equipment, the amount of time needed for dispatch is reduced.

Turnout: The speed that personnel — paid, off-duty, and volunteers — can report for duty, board apparatus, and leave the station for the fire, which depends on the location of the personnel at the time of the alarm; *i.e.*, at the station, at work, or in their homes.

Response Time: The travel time from the station to the fire, which depends upon the station's location and the topographical, traffic, and weather conditions at the time. In times of particularly heavy traffic flow, the police department may be needed to aid in traveling to the fire and in preparing for fire attack.

Attack Preparation: The time that is necessary for accomplishing the activities involved in attacking the fire, which includes hose layout and placement of ladders and rescue equipment. The time may vary according to the methods of attack employed.

Extinguishment: This time depends greatly upon the type of fire and the surrounding conditions. Every type of fire calls for a different method of attack and extinguishment, and time must be allowed for making decisions about the particular fire fighting process to be employed.

In addition to total time, the growth changes of a community also bring about new considerations and problems in the location of a fire station. In the past, villages with one main street and a few side streets usually built their fire stations on the main street. But many of these villages expanded into towns and cities that presented difficulties to prompt fire fighting operations. In many cases one fire station wasn't sufficient to handle the expansion of a city's buildings and area. In the case of fire companies that had to respond to fires many miles away but still within their districts, consideration and allocation of funds for a second station or a relocation of the old station became matters of vital importance.

Expansion within a community is another factor that affects the location of a station. Community expansion is reflected in major construction projects such as new roads, bridges, or housing developments. These projects take time for completion and affect the normal routing and traffic flow. Fire departments should be made aware of such projects in order to map out quicker alternate routes in case of fire.

Fire department management should also be aware of the "minor" changes in a community — those changes that can occur so gradually that most people are barely aware of them. For example, vacant lots can be filled in, industrial interests can relocate, a small farm may sell out to a real estate development, and zoning ordinances may be changed to attract more business and people. Such changes affect fire spread and fire fighting abilities, and should be taken into consideration by fire department management when relocation considerations are being made.

Design Specifications of the Station

If a department finds that construction of a new fire station would be beneficial, then a good public relations program should be formulated in advance of announcing the need for a budgetary decision. This involves good communications between the fire department management and the general public so that it is clearly shown that a new fire station is in the best interests of a community.

The reaction of the voting community and the political power for the decision to build a new station depends upon several factors: (1) the professionalism exhibited by the fire department, (2) the ISO rating for the present fire station, (3) the proposed location of the new station, (4) the public's understanding of the need for construction, (5) the manner in which the proposals are presented, and (6) the amount of money involved.

Once the location of the station has been determined, management can focus upon the design needs of the new station. Some of these needs may already be known as they may have determined the viability for building a new station. For example, if the station is solely voluntary, might there be the future possibility that the station will become all-paid? If the area served by the fire department has no high-rise buildings, is there the future possibility that tall buildings might be constructed? If so, could the new station accommodate the specialized apparatus required for fighting fires in such buildings?

Although questions about future changes necessitate discussion with municipal officials, the ultimate decisions that revolve around the department itself, its design, and its general needs are decided by management and its advisors. Therefore, management needs to be aware of all of these factors in order to communicate them to the architect selected to design the new station. To better assist in the planning of facilities, management also needs to know the answers to questions involving traffic flow, terrain features, area characteristics, weather peculiarities, communications needs, fire fighter personal needs, space and storage needs for apparatus, equipment, and supplies, and space requirements for offices, parking facilities, living quarters, and training facilities. (See Figs. 10.1 and 10.2.)

Two other important areas of consideration by management when planning station specifications are the heating and ventilating needs of the station and the set-up of the watch desk area. The design of the station should incorporate a heating system that is able to recover rapidly after apparatus responds to a winter alarm and the doors to the station are not immediately closed. In addition, adequate ventilation of the station should be provided in the apparatus room before the doors are opened to avoid concentrations of carbon monoxide during the usual engine warmup, drilling, or servicing.[2]

The proper set-up of the watch desk area is of major concern to management because it is the area within the station where alarms are received. The watch desk itself should be in the form of a desk-console arrangement with wall space for maps, schedules, and instructions, and with ample space for the necessary radio equipment, alarm control devices, floor controls, and traffic signal controls. The watch desk area should be as soundproof as possible and should allow for clear visibility of the entire apparatus room. A desirable location for the watch desk is near the front entrance to the station — the point where visitors enter and seek information.[3]

MANAGEMENT OF APPARATUS

Whether a fire department decides to construct a new fire station or not, the apparatus within the station is of concern to management in that it is necessary for management to continually analyze and evaluate the effectiveness of the apparatus in terms of its ability to combat the diverse and ever-changing fires of a particular community. In addition to this analysis, management is also aided by the Insurance Services Office grading schedule and survey in the determination of either maintaining present apparatus or purchasing additional and/or newer equipment. From the results of the ISO survey, fire department management and community administrators decide together what major items should be purchased. Specific recommendations

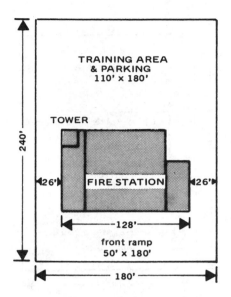

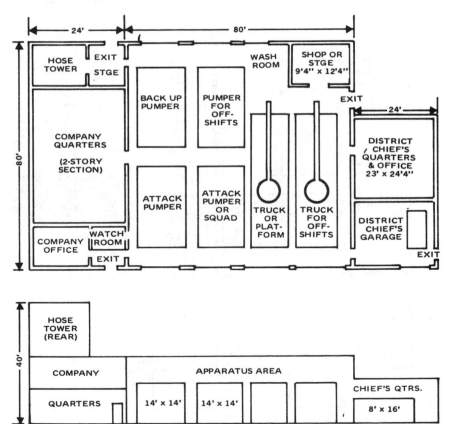

Fig. 10.1. Plot plan (left) for a typical district fire station for urban and suburban services. Minimum recommended plot size is 43,200 square feet. Below is an elevation and plan view of a typical urban fire station. (From Fire Protection Handbook, NFPA)

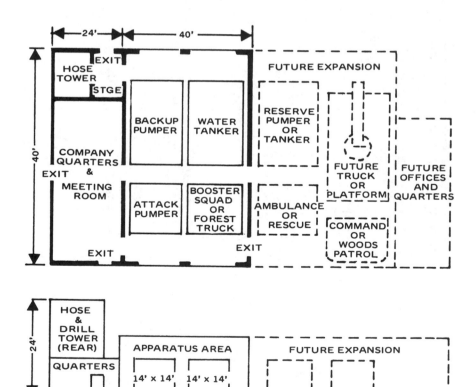

Fig. 10.2. Plot plan (right) for a typical rural station. Minimum recommended plot size is 43,200 square feet. Note the area designated for future expansion. Below is an elevation and plan view of a typical rural fire station. (From Fire Protection Handbook, NFPA)

for apparatus might also come from the battalion or company level of a particular department, or may come from the fire fighters who use the equipment. A well-managed department may wish to rely upon the experience of the fire officers and fire fighters, for they are the ones who have specific knowledge of inadequate features on existing apparatus. Fire fighters may request extra facilities for preconnected hose, additional intakes, or larger compartment spaces for a newer piece of apparatus. First-hand experience may lead to suggestions for the relocation of various appliances and controls, new facilities for storing respiratory equipment, new locations for lights, or for greater availability of lights and generators. These recommendations for improving fire fighting capability and efficiency can be given to a superior officer or directly to the chief. From such recommendations management will be better able to make decisions concerning a station's needs and the appropriateness of types of apparatus.

Purchase and Replacement of Apparatus

In addition to ISO grading schedules, fire department management is also guided in its apparatus decisions by NFPA standards. One standard that applies directly to apparatus decisions is NFPA 1901, *Standard for Automotive Fire Apparatus* (hereinafter referred to as the *NFPA Fire Apparatus Standard*). This standard enumerates various pumper specifications and equipment that should be carried on particular pumpers (to be discussed in detail later in this chapter in the section titled "Management of Equipment and Supplies").

Section 1 of the *NFPA Fire Apparatus Standard* discusses contractor responsibilities for fire department equipment, design of engines, carrying capacity, and the cooling, lubrication, fuel exhaust, and electrical systems of pumpers. The guidelines contained in the *NFPA Fire Apparatus Standard* serve to provide the essential requirements that must be adhered to by the department. In addition to these items, various other component parts of pumpers are summarized:[4]

> **1-3.3.1** The apparatus body design shall be rugged with suitable ventilation and drains where needed and with good visibility to front, sides, and rear. Bodies shall provide readily accessible facilities for carrying hose, appliances and equipment, and riding space for personnel.
>
> **1-3.3.2** Front and rear hooks or rings shall be attached to the frame structure to permit ready towing of the apparatus and/or for towing other apparatus.
>
> NOTE: Where hooks and/or rings are to be so located that their use does not require opening compartment doors, purchaser shall indicate in Special Provisions.
>
> **1-3.3.3** A heavy-duty bumper shall be provided on the front of the chassis and the bumper mounting brackets shall be attached to the frame.
>
> **1-3.3.4** Suitable holders, boxes, compartments, or other attachments shall be provided for all tools, equipment, play-pipes, and other items which the purchaser desires to carry on the apparatus. (*See Chapter 10.*) Equipment holders shall be firmly attached, and so designed that equipment will remain in place under all running conditions and permit quick removal for use.

NOTE (1). Where equipment other than that purchased with the vehicle must be mounted, the purchaser shall indicate in Special Provisions.

NOTE (2). The purchaser shall indicate the space or compartment desired for the installation of radio equipment in Special Provisions.

NOTE (3). Size and location may be critical depending on the nature of the radio equipment. Suitable shielding shall be specified as necessary to permit radio operation without undue interference in Special Provisions.

1-3.3.5 All steps shall be suitably braced and be of heavy gage metal with nonskid safety surface. Minimum width of rear steps shall be 18 inches measuring from the back of the body. Rear steps shall not be required on aerial ladder trucks.

1-3.3.6 Handrails shall be between one inch and one and five-eighths inches in outside diameter heavy metal chrome plated or stainless steel tubing and shall be so arranged as to avoid snagging of the hose or equipment. The minimum clearance between handrails and any surface shall not be less than two inches.

When determining the particular kinds of apparatus needed by a department, management should also consider: (1) the need for effectiveness — to prevent and extinguish fires better than other departments or better than their own present abilities, and (2) the need for efficiency — to perform the mission of prevention and extinguishment at the lowest possible cost. While these needs may seem to indicate that the latest piece of equipment should be purchased and that the oldest piece of apparatus should be sold, management's closer examination of apparatus efficiency and future needs may reveal that this is not necessarily the best policy.

For example, in a small community the average age of apparatus may be as much as eight to ten years. The newest engine may be three years old or even older. When a department considers the ages and capabilities of these pumpers, the department should not consider only the greater acceleration reaped from a new pumper in extinguishing a fire: Also to be considered should be the fact that the older pumper would usually not be the first-in engine, and that it would most likely be used as a backup unit when the newer engines are not able to cover a specific fire. The managerial concern then becomes not how much better the newer engine can fight a fire, but rather how often is the old engine used in a fire attack? If the old engine is used in a fire attack many times, how much damage could probably be prevented if a more modern engine were used? Determining the benefits that a more modern engine will bring is, in itself, a difficult question to answer, but it is not the only one. There are others, such as the following, that also influence the decision. These questions, and less important ones such as fuel efficiency and equipment layout on the engine, have to be considered in making the decision.

1. How much higher is the annual maintenance cost on the old engine?

2. When is it likely that the old engine would be so outdated that it would have to be scrapped, and how much less would its resale value be at that time as compared to today's value?

3. How long before the newest engine will be outdated, making fire attack

less effective than it would be if a newer engine could assume the lead position?

4. Will the new equipment require fewer personnel?

In the world of general industry, equipment replacement decisions are difficult because so many complex questions are involved. However, in industry
such questions are usually answered by considering long- and short-run
profitability. For example, the basis for the purchase of a new piece of equipment usually is whether or not it will "pay for itself" in a specified period of
time. This period of time is usually based on a policy of the organization, established by the financial department, with the approval of the general manager
or president. In industry the following factors are considered in determining
whether a new piece of equipment is worth buying:

- How much more will it produce than the older equipment or, if it is
totally new — for a new product or service — how much will it save over
doing the job by hand, or how much profit will be earned from the product
or service?
- How many years will it be used — and usable; in other words, how
long will there be a demand for the product or service and, if that demand
will be for many years, how long will the equipment or service last, and
what will its depreciation factor be?
- How fast is technology moving? How long will it be before much more
productive equipment will be available so that competitors with newer
equipment will not have a greater advantage?
- What will be the replacement cost (what will new equipment probably
cost) when the older equipment becomes worn out?
- How much will the equipment bring, as second-hand equipment, if it
has to be sold earlier than expected?
- How much will it cost to operate the equipment? How much personnel
time will be needed to operate it, and how much material?
- How much will the utilities (electricity, gas, oil, etc.) cost?
- How much will it cost to maintain the equipment in satisfactory working
condition?
- What is the interest rate? How much would the organization save in
interest charges if it did not buy the equipment? Most companies have
mortgages, bank loans, or outstanding bonds on which they pay interest.
If equipment is not purchased, these loans could be repaid, partially or
fully, and interest would be saved.

In addition to the preceding factors, there usually are some others concerning the auxiliary equipment that will be needed — such as expendable
tools and adaptors, control tapes, etc. These factors are also applicable to
the fire services. But, as difficult as it is to obtain valid answers to many of
these factors in the world of general industry, it sometimes seems that valid
answers are even more difficult to obtain in the fire services. For example, in
view of the possibility that a life may have been lost without the new piece of
apparatus, how should one evaluate the probability that the person would
indeed have suffered serious or fatal injury? Most people would agree that an

aerial ladder has justified its purchase if it can definitely be credited with saving one single life; however, what about third-degree burns over most of an arm? These questions are vastly more difficult than those that general industry faces in most instances because they involve moral and social issues. Thus, traditional business analysis, in the strict sense, does not always apply to fire service apparatus replacement decisions.

Fire District Influences on Selection of Apparatus and Equipment

When ISO engineers evaluate a fire department, they compare its features (buildings, apparatus, equipment, competence) with the established standards. These standards recommend location of stations and distribution of companies (apparatus and personnel) based on response time under normal conditions. (Refer again to "Effect of Grading Schedules on Physical Resources" earlier in this chapter.)

The American Insurance Association table shown earlier in this chapter as Table 10.3 relates the number of apparatus needed within a given area to the required fire flow.[5] Fire flow is the gallons of water per minute (gpm) the water supply is capable of delivering, and required fire flow is determined by size of community, population density, and related factors.

The AIA table is an optimum to reach, or a basic guideline to be modified, according to local conditions. Fire departments do not strictly adhere to the Table 10.3 apparatus guidelines because they need to consider their particular districts in relation to three basic influences. These influences are: (1) the size and type of district, (2) the hazards in the district, and (3) the types of fires in the district.

Size and Type of District: Despite the fact that two fire departments may have the same number of people to protect, their individual needs may vary greatly due to the particular area and type of district served by each. For example, districts that have areas in which the population is widely dispersed might want to pay particular attention to the "roadability," or driving characteristics, of the vehicles they purchase, with particular emphasis upon a fast response time. On the other hand, a district with steep grades, narrow winding roads, or difficult terrain might be especially interested in a vehicle's shifting characteristics. In the latter consideration, a four-wheel drive, extra-large tires, or a tank-like base can have an influence on response time despite difficult driving conditions or where there may be no roads at all.

In districts having narrow, winding streets, an important management consideration in selection of apparatus might be reduction in overall dimensions for an engine in order to make it easier to maneuver around curves. These districts may also consider whether purchasing pumpers without the forward-cab design would give an improved maneuverability that would outweigh the advantage of having fire fighters ready for action immediately upon arrival. If many minutes would be saved by the elimination of these features, then the extra time saved might more than offset the time it would take for fire fighters to don breathing apparatus.

Rural areas would need large water tank trucks, portable suction basins (which allow tank trucks to unload their water next to the pumper and go back to the nearest hydrant or static source for more), portable pumps, and suction hose since most of the water would have to come from a static source or from water carried to the fire scene. Grass fire trucks or ladder trucks in rural areas often have auxiliary ("booster") pumps with capacities of less than 500 gpm. Auxiliary pumps are useful on small, nonstructural fires.

Urban or suburban areas might want to consider the advantages of each type of aerial device so that buildings over three stories in height would be adequately protected. In addition, they would have to take into account factors that require the use of mechanized aerial devices (such as obstacles above roadways, width of streets, and parking spaces available near buildings). The number of people who could be rescued, potential use of such equipment, and frequency of use should be major considerations before any purchase.

In a district where many fire hazards exist, or where the fire department is frequently called in to help in other emergencies, additional rescue vehicles might be needed.

Hazards in District: Some other hazardous conditions that bring about the need for additional companies and fire department personnel are: (1) numerous wood-shingle roofs, (2) large concentrations of closely spaced, wood-frame buildings, (3) large blocks having structures weak in fire resistance and lacking adequate private fire protection, (4) large, individual structures with inadequate private fire protection, (5) narrow streets and traffic congestion, including parked cars that may interfere with fire fighting, and (6) a record of severe climatic conditions such as frequent droughts or heavy snows.

All of these conditions are usually considered in the ISO survey and are taken into account in establishing the grade classifications. However, a department's management may have valid views that differ from the conclusions of the ISO survey; in such instances, the department is likely to be successful in taking its case to the authorities only if it can objectively show why the need is more or less serious than ISO engineers found it to be.

Types of Fires in District: In suburban or semirural areas where there is a high incidence of brush fires or fires in rubbish dumped in vacant lots, management might consider purchasing a grass or brush fire truck instead of a regular pumper, or may consider such a vehicle as an addition to the standard pumper fleet. Equipped with booster pumps, these trucks are better adapted to fighting small fires than are regular pumpers. They are less expensive than regular pumpers because they can be built from regular commercial truck chassis. Grass or brush fire trucks are easier to drive and faster to place in position than are regular pumpers, and they eliminate the possibility of taking a standard pumper from fighting a structural fire.

Although districts with flammable liquid fire hazards are likely to have specially equipped apparatus for delivering foam or other chemical extinguishing agents, most districts may at some time be confronted with explosives or flammable liquid fires. Gasoline station tanks must be filled from commercial gasoline tankers. Such tankers often catch fire when they overturn on a slick surface or at an angular bend in the road. A fire department should be equipped to fight such fires, and its apparatus must carry an adequate number of extinguishers having the capacity to deliver foam.

Major Types of Apparatus

Once the various fire district influences have been determined, management can consider the specific types of apparatus that will be needed and the specification requirements for each particular piece.

Vehicles for Specialized Purposes: Although standard pumpers and ladder trucks carry their own supply of specialized equipment for dealing with specific hazards and situations (such as vehicle rescue and salvage operations), many of the larger fire departments find use for special-equipment vehicles that are outfitted for one specific type of operation or purpose. Such special-equipment vehicles can be trucks that carry extra hose and nozzles to lend a greater degree of flexibility to fire fighting operations, power and lighting trucks with large generating capacities to supplement the portable generators included on standard equipment, or they may be trucks that are specifically designed for specific hazards.

Some community airports and industries having unusually high flammability risks maintain their own fire fighting units. Such situations require

Fig. 10.3. Large waterfront area protected by an elevating platform on the fireboat William Lyon MacKenzie. (Toronto Fire Department, Toronto, Ontario)

adequate pumpers primarily equipped for the purpose of fighting specific types of fires. Whether or not to obtain and use specialized types of vehicles and equipment is a management decision.

A municipality that has a large waterfront area with commercial docks or marinas might decide to purchase one or more fireboats that are specially equipped with turrets that can throw heavy streams. Since fireboats represent an enormous financial investment in relation to their limited use, departments with very small areas of waterfront to protect may consider purchasing a used fireboat or making arrangements with neighbors for joint purchase and use. Figure 10.3 illustrates an elevating platform in use on a fireboat that was specifically designed for a particular fire department.

In certain dry climates having heavily wooded areas, forest and brush fires present a serious hazard. Departments confronted with this problem usually either have their own special equipment, or they make arrangements for leasing forest fire protection devices. Aircraft and helicopters are used extensively in the control of forest fires, particularly by the National Forest Service. Experiments are also being conducted in the use of large-capacity foam trucks on such fires.

In addition to the specific instances that require specialized vehicles, a department may also consider designing its own apparatus from a piece of used equipment. Used equipment, under some conditions, can sometimes be a wiser purchase than a new piece of equipment — particularly when only limited funds are available. For example, a locality may need a specialized piece of apparatus so infrequently that large expenditures on new apparatus cannot be justified. Or, a department may find that it needs an extra backup piece of standard equipment to replace one that can no longer be maintained economically. The purchase of used apparatus or the rebuilding of the chassis of an older piece of apparatus may represent a satisfactory solution to a serious problem. Figures 10.4 and 10.5 show how two departments solved their apparatus needs by utilizing a piece of used equipment (Fig. 10.4) and a rebuilt model (Fig. 10.5).[6]

Specification Decisions: Once it has been established that a major piece of apparatus is needed, be it for specialized purposes or not, fire department management must decide upon the design specifications. Such specifications are usually influenced by the intended use of the apparatus. For example, management may elect to choose an apparatus with special fire pump capabilities, with an elevating platform, or with a special capacity water tank. Many departments use the *NFPA Fire Apparatus Standard* as a general guideline for making decisions concerning design specifications.

MANAGEMENT OF EQUIPMENT AND SUPPLIES

It is a management responsibility to provide as functional a fire station as possible and to provide an efficient range of apparatus. It is also a man-

Fig. 10.4. The Anaheim Fire Department (Anaheim, California), went bargain hunting and came home with a real deal. The city bought a used 1967-model fire engine from a defunct fire protection district near Seattle, Washington, for $28,500. If the city had waited for a new rig, it would have cost about $86,000 and taken eighteen months to arrive. Included in the deal were two spare power plants for the pumper. Fire department officials had to make only minor adjustments to get the rig ready for use. (City of Anaheim, California)

agement responsibility to make decisions concerning the necessary equipment to be used both at the station and on the apparatus. The *NFPA Fire Apparatus Standard* can be used as a guide for setting standards for the basic equipment to be carried on apparatus (such as ladders, nozzles, hoses, and various tools). Sound management decisions concerning such equipment enable a department to operate at its utmost effectiveness. Such decisions apply to the use of all types of equipment, including personal equipment used by fire fighters, communications equipment, auxiliary equipment, and new and used equipment.

Personal Equipment

Most personal equipment is related to the protection of fire fighters in the performance of their work. Respiratory equipment and protective clothing are two major areas of concern to management. Breathing apparatus is needed to protect against the danger of inhaling noxious fumes, and protective headgear, footwear, and clothing help protect the body from the most adverse environmental conditions such as extensive heat and cold, and from exposure to radiation contamination, chemicals, and water. Helmets also help safeguard the head against injury from falling objects, and turnout protective coats are a necessity. NFPA 1971, *Standard on Protective Clothing for Structural Fire Fighting*, sets specific requirements for such protective clothing.[7]

Although some fire departments feel that uniformity of personal equipment is of greater significance than adaptation to personal preferences and needs, the more enlightened departments allow increasingly greater freedom to the

Fig. 10.5.   The Central Fire Protection District in Santa Clara County, California, was faced with the problem of replacing some tired apparatus.   However, the potential $150,000 cost of new apparatus necessitated the consideration of an alternative.   In San Jose, a heavy-duty truck sales agent had contracted to deliver two cabs and chassis to a refuse company.   When the company decided not to accept the trucks, the sales agent contacted the Central Fire Protection District and it was determined that the vehicles met or exceeded state apparatus requirements: the department bought them for $17,000 each.   The district took bids on converting the chassis to fire apparatus, and a major manufacturer won the contract.   The conversion consisted of adding a body and transferring equipment from the old engines.   One engine was converted at a cost of $15,400.   The second cost $19,200 when it was equipped with a 1,000-gpm pump, front mount suction, and several minor additions.   The only other cost was $900 for lights and electronic sirens, which the fire district installed itself.   Both units were acquired at a cost savings of about $81,369 to the taxpayers.

rank and file in matters pertaining to equipment selection. As the following excerpt from *Fire Command!*, July 1974, shows, time studies can point the way to some personal equipment decisions:[8]

> With the availability of preconnected lines, the need for rapid donning of breathing apparatus became apparent. Time studies were again conducted to determine the efficiency in donning breathing apparatus. All breathing apparatus until that time had been carried in cases in compartments on all pumpers. Tests showed that even under ideal conditions, 45 to 60 seconds were required to don the apparatus. Because the department at that time was using ½-hour oxygen self-contained breathing apparatus, it was decided that conversion to compressed air should be made in accordance with current standards. It was also decided that to increase the safety and improve the efficiency of fire fighters exposed to facepiece leakage, pressure-demand type apparatus should be provided, with existing apparatus being converted.
>
> To shorten the donning time, two walk-away brackets were purchased and installed on the 1961 pumper, mounted on the aft wall near the jump seats so the brackets would swing out 90 degrees to be flush with the pump

panels. These allowed donning of the apparatus in approximately 30 seconds. After further testing, it was proved that donning time could be cut to approximately 17 seconds if the apparatus was inverted within the bracket to allow "over-the-head" donning. Consequently, all pumpers were equipped with two breathing apparatus mounted in this fashion. Once again we had shortened our reflex time considerably.

Also of importance in the category of personal equipment for fire fighters is equipment for use in rescue operations. This includes equipment such as life nets and life guns. Although some fire fighters feel that in rescue operations ladders are easier to use than life nets, others feel that life nets are more valuable for rescuing persons in three- or four-story buildings. Life guns, which are used for shooting rope to persons in distress, usually have limited use in water rescues and rescues from cliffs or canyons; however, if the fire fighters feel that either life guns or life nets are useful for their jobs, management should give serious consideration to such needs.

Communications Equipment

Fire department communications consists of three areas: (1) the means for receiving notification of emergencies from the public, (2) the means for alerting and dispatching apparatus and personnel, and (3) the communications necessary for emergency and routine business.[9] As the municipality that the fire department serves expands in buildings and population, management should simultaneously expand the communications center in order to effectively receive fire alarms and to dispatch personnel and apparatus to the areas needed.

In addition to receiving calls for assistance, the alarm center must be capable of handling all radio communications for the department, keeping a continuous record on the status of all companies, handling communications to each station, and maintaining current files and maps of streets. It must also have the personnel resources for the required record keeping. A desk or console should be provided for the center for use by the dispatcher(s). Equipment requirements for the communications center are dictated by the size of the operation and the type of services provided.[10] (See Fig. 10.6.)

The purchase of communications equipment is an important management responsibility. Such purchasing often represents a large outlay of funds, especially if the communications center is to be completely or even partially modernized. There are many different communications needs in a fire department, all of which require equipment that must operate with minimum interference so that emergency and urgent messages will be transmitted and received on a priority basis. Following are some of the needs, or demands, that should be fulfilled by a communications center:

1. The public must be able to reach headquarters in order to send an alarm or to obtain information.

2. Headquarters must be able to reach its fire fighting personnel, either in the stations or in homes.

Fig. 10.6. Communications center equipped with a status board (top center); controls for the status board to the left and right of the board; and radio controls near the base of the board. At lower left are city telegraph system recorders. A status board is a visual indication of the location of the various stations and the equipment housed in each station. Indicating lights at each location show the current disposition of apparatus; e.g., in service by radio, out of service, etc. Shown is the Monroe County, NY, communications center. (From *Fire Protection Handbook*, NFPA)

3. Headquarters must communicate with personnel on the apparatus.

4. The chief officer must reach remote units and even individual fire fighters.

5. There should be a means for communication between pieces of apparatus and between apparatus and individual fire fighters.

6. Officers must be able to reach headquarters to request aid or further instructions on how to control the fire.

7. There must be some kind of regional intercommunications system for mutual aid calls.

8. All these systems must operate with minimum interference so that emergency and urgent messages are easily understood.

There are several different ways to satisfy these communications needs. Some may be more efficient than others, or cheaper, or more suited to existing conditions. Which one to select, therefore, should require management's careful analysis of the specific advantages, drawbacks, and equipment requirements of each. The following background information outlines some of the concerns of importance to management when considering ways to satisfy the communications needs of a department.

Public to Fire Department: Most people still communicate with fire departments by public or private telephones. However, persons discovering a fire can also use public alarm boxes. Such alarm boxes can be wireless or interconnected with wires. Wireless types are transmitters that operate from batteries; some operate with solar energy devices or with small hand-cranked generators. (See Fig. 10.7, which illustrates various types of fire alarm boxes.)

Battery-operated transmitters emit a signal if the battery needs replacing. Alarm boxes that are connected by wire circuits to a communications center usually have several different boxes connected to the same circuit. These separate circuits can be tested; if one is not operating properly, the defective alarm box can be traced by checking out each box in that circuit.

Fig. 10.7. *Various types of fire alarm boxes.* (a) *A coded alarm box showing the actuating lever (arrow) that normally protrudes through the hole shown on the inner door at right. When depressed, the handle releases the springwound mechanism resulting in a coded signal from the code wheel shown at the center of the mechanism.* (G. W. Gamewell Co.) (b) *A telephone-type alarm box.* (c) *A combination telegraph-telephone type. Both doors are open* (d) *to show the relative positions of the coding movement and telephone handset.* (e) *A telegraph-type alarm box.* (f, g, and h are radio-type alarm boxes). (f) *Battery-powered box by G. W. Gamewell Co.* (g) *Battery-operated box by Eagle-Pitcher Industries.* (h) *User-powered box by American District Telegraph Co.* (From *Fire Protection Handbook*, NFPA)

Alarm boxes are usually situated outside public facilities in the more densely populated sections of a municipality and in areas where private or public telephones are not available. This is because many industrial areas are deserted throughout the night, thus making telephones inaccessible. Even in those areas where public telephones are readily available, increasing incidences of vandalism often make them inoperable.

In addition to alarms and requests for emergency assistance that come in by telephone, there are those that are radioed in by the police, by fire department vehicles in the field, by first-aid squads, and by private persons with citizen-band radios.

An ever-increasing number of alarms come from automatic alarm systems installed in homes, factories, and offices. Such systems have direct connections to fire departments or to private fire protection service organizations that immediately relay the alarms to the fire departments.

The initial fire alarm information is not always received by the fire department. Most small departments rely on the police department to accept emergency calls. Often the police operate a comprehensive communications center intended to service all of the emergency needs in the area. In these instances, there should, obviously, be a direct link between police stations and each fire station. The greatest communications need for a fire department exists, of course, during a fire, or possibly during other emergencies. A fire department, depending on size and available resources, may staff a communications center on a continuing basis. Once a fire alarm has been received, a communications center provides many services to the fire department — including the following:

1. Dispatches apparatus; this is usually routine, but in large communities where multiple fires can occur the dispatching of apparatus may require difficult decisions.

2. Provides information to the officer on the lead engine about locations of hydrants, special hazards, sprinkler systems, and any other data that may be available at the communications center or that may have come in from the field.

3. Provides information to the command officer responding to the alarm.

4. Services the needs of responding apparatus for supplies or other help.

In large fire departments the communications center is an elaborate installation with the ability to simultaneously convey many instructions and receive many calls. More and more, these larger centers make use of computers to store information — especially prefire planning data and information concerning availability of equipment or special resources — so that the responding units can be supplied with important data while they are on the way. As prefire planning becomes more widespread and therefore more detailed, more elaborate communications equipment and procedures will be needed. Currently, smaller computers are being marketed. These computers can help serve such needs. The cost of these smaller computers is such that most fire departments should be able to afford them.

Headquarters to Personnel: Once the alarm is given, the fire fighters on duty or on call must be contacted at their station or, if they are not on duty or are volunteers, in their homes. Volunteers who work in the area may be alerted by the siren sounding the alarm to the community. Many fire fighters have home radio alarm systems through which information about the fire is relayed. As previously mentioned, this information can be sent directly from fire headquarters or can come from the police department. These alert systems are tested regularly (usually at least once a day) to determine whether they are functioning properly.

Headquarters to Personnel on Apparatus: Each piece of apparatus is provided with radio equipment. Headquarters needs to be able to communicate with the personnel on the apparatus. Higher level officers may want to know about the status of fire fighting operations, and a dispatcher must know what apparatus and personnel are available in the event that companies need to be dispatched to a fire or pulled from a fire that is under control in order to respond to an alarm elsewhere.

Since noise level is high on moving apparatus or on one that is pumping, the radio equipment must be loud enough so it is clearly audible above the noise. Sometimes multiple speakers and earphones are used.

Chief Officer to Units and Inter-unit Communication: In case of fire, or when in the field, the command officer must be able to communicate both with headquarters and with the units. During a fire it is necessary that the command officer be in touch with the first response engine in order to obtain a preliminary report and to be as informed as possible upon arrival at the fire scene. Once at the fire scene, the command officer needs to be able to talk to officers and fire fighters already engaged with the fire in order to obtain further information about the fire.

Radio Communication Between Apparatus and Individual Fire Fighters: All apparatus carries radio equipment. Radio communication between fire fighters has been made easier by the introduction of light-weight portable radio sets, some of which are small enough to be carried on the belt or in pockets.

Personnel to Headquarters: The command officer needs to communicate with headquarters by radio in order to request further aid or further instruction.

Mutual Aid: Finally, there must be a system to call mutual aid when needed. Similarly, incoming requests for mutual aid must be processed. Here especially, if the system is not capable of clear transmission without excessive interference, serious delays can occur.

Quality of communications significantly affects the total time needed to gain control of a fire. If each individual component of the communications system can be made to operate more efficiently, then the total time it takes from the sounding of the alarm to the extinguishment of the fire will be shorter. Thus, it is sometimes more beneficial for fire department management to consider investing money in upgrading its present communications system than it is to invest in new equipment and extra personnel.

The modernization of a department's entire communications system, or the improvement of any one component of it, can help increase overall efficiency. As stated in a recent *Fire Command!* article:[11]

> Every one of these items is contributing to the unification of fire departments as effective fire combat teams because command orders, acknowledgments, and other information are being exchanged more rapidly. Consequently, the placement and movement of apparatus, the identification and location of personnel, the flow of needed technical data, and the reassuring contact with headquarters and other important sources all combine to make overall fire department operations easier.

To the competent officer who is alert to opportunities for improving operations, the management of all operational aspects concerning communications equipment offers interesting challenges. Nowhere else is technology changing as rapidly as in this field. Communications equipment with improved features is constantly being offered by the manufacturers. To take advantage of the latest developments in the area of communications equipment, fire department management must:

1. Keep abreast of those changes that could bring significant improvements if old equipment were exchanged for new.

2. Be able to evaluate the benefits of new equipment in factual terms when asking for authorization to purchase it.

3. Learn how to make best use of it once it has been acquired by the department.

Sometimes new equipment must be purchased all at one time, thus necessitating the preparation of capital budget requests. At other times new apparatus can be phased in gradually by making small purchases every year. Management concerns related to equipment decisions involve the setting of goals in order to prepare evaluations for training, for self-study on latest equipment (on the way that new equipment can be used), and for analysis as to whether or not procedural changes can help make existing equipment more effective. Fire department management is also involved with the inevitable decisions that have to be made such as whether to request new equipment in the current year, or whether to wait another year when, usually, still more modern versions will be available.

Auxiliary Equipment

Auxiliary equipment is comprised of those tools, attachments, and small pieces of apparatus that are not an integral part of the vehicle body or hose. The *NFPA Fire Apparatus Standard* lists the standard equipment items that should, or in some cases might, be included on each specific piece. The NFPA listings are similar to the ISO lists that are used for grading purposes of apparatus. Older apparatus may not have all of these items, and departments are sometimes downgraded for not having them. In such cases there often is no convenient way of changing old apparatus to fit modern requirements in this respect.

The list of equipment specified in the *NFPA Fire Apparatus Standard* is only a minimum.   For example, a department that has frequent need for certain pieces of equipment should consider additions.   Also, departments that are frequently involved in vehicle rescue work usually carry additional equipment such as medical equipment and tools to extricate people from wrecked automobiles and trucks.   Rural and suburban departments not specially equipped with brush fire trucks but frequently called to grass and brush fires might include such items as hay forks, buckets, metal rakes, back tanks (Indian tanks), fire brooms, and portable pumps on their standard pumpers.   Since hose in standpipe-protected properties will have sometimes rotted because of age (or in public places may have been cut or stolen by vandals), many fire departments carry in their equipment compartments portable kits containing 1½-inch hose that is automatically connected to standpipes when responding to alarms.

Used Equipment

As previously mentioned in connection with fireboats, under certain conditions used equipment can sometimes be a wiser purchase than a new piece of equipment — especially when only limited funds are available.   Often a locality may need a specialized piece of apparatus so infrequently that large expenditures on new apparatus cannot be justified; or, it may need an extra back-up piece of standard equipment to replace one that can no longer be maintained economically; or, a major accident may have made a piece of apparatus inoperative.   The purchase of used apparatus in such cases can sometimes be the solution to a serious problem.

MANAGEMENT OF PHYSICAL RESOURCES AND SERVICES BY BUDGETS

All physical resources and services other than the services provided by some volunteer fire departments are obtained with money.   So that the available monies will be distributed in such a way that a balanced mix of resources is available, fire department management uses budgets to plan and control income and expenditures.

Budgets thus serve many useful purposes, including the following:

- They are guides, or forecasts, that can help make planning easier.
- They are a communications link, joining the department with the public and with officials.
- They show how fast available monies are being spent, thus permitting better planning of activities during the last weeks and days of the budget year.

Because budgets are important management tools, every fire officer should understand the purposes they serve and the basis for formulating them.   In the simplest terms, fiscal responsibility measures management's ability to live within a certain portion of allocated money by providing for all expenses. This allocated money comes in the form of a budget (usually a yearly budget), which is a prediction of how much money will be available and how much money will be spent.

Except in the case of a fire district, the fire department budget is a portion of the municipal budget. On the average, approximately ninety-five percent of the fire department budget is allocated to payroll. The five percent that remains must cover the following:[12]

> . . . such operating expenses as heat and light for the fire stations, fuel for the fire apparatus and other vehicles, maintenance supplies, minor equipment including breathing apparatus and fire fighting tools, office supplies, repairs to buildings and grounds, etc.

Management uses the budget as a forecast for determining who or what is to receive a particular amount of money, and for what purpose. Management also uses budgets: (1) to make planning easier, (2) to provide a communications link for the department, the taxpayers, and the municipal officials, and (3) to show how fast the money available to the department is being spent in order to ensure that activities can proceed normally, even in the last few days of an appropriated budget.

A typical fire department budget is usually divided into two separate budgets. The first is a budget for recurring expenditures. This budget can be called an expenditures budget, an operations budget, or an operational expenditures budget. Sometimes it comes in several segments such as a salary budget, a materials and supply budget, and a fire prevention budget. Within this budget are "lines" for each separate category of expenditures for which the department or financial authorities wish to keep records. For example, within a salary budget there could be a line for every person, or for clerical personnel, etc. Similarly, a materials and supplies budget could have lines for expenditures such as office supplies, oil and gas, uniforms, etc.

The second type of budget, a capital budget, is used for large-scale and costly expenditures that are necessary, but infrequent. Such expenses might include the purchase of a piece of apparatus, the installation of a new communications center, or the construction or renovation of a building or buildings. This type of budget is usually referred to as a capital expenditures budget or, simply, a capital budget.

The Budgeting Process

The preliminary (or proposed) budget submitted to the municipality or region provides the forecast of what the department expects to need, considering the staff it has, the programs it plans, and the changes in prices of the things and services it buys. The preliminary budget is then reviewed by the top administrators, combined with the budgets from other departments, and submitted to the political processes for approval. In the process, changes are usually made and the budget that emerges is generally smaller than the one that was proposed. In a well-managed department, if these changes mean reductions, the cuts are made in those expenditures that are clearly of lowest priority.

This budget process may be somewhat different for volunteer departments that raise funds for themselves, and for departments that obtain grants for special projects from the state, federal government, or private foundations.

The heads of departments are responsible for formulating the preliminary budgets. Some do so alone, based on past expenditures and their own judgment concerning what will be needed. Other department heads follow procedures that involve all of those persons who can contribute useful information. Such combined knowledge can help department heads make the most favorable decisions concerning budget matters.

More widespread involvement in the budget process can help to improve the motivational climate of a department. However, the level of involvement must be carefully chosen. For example, management in larger departments might see priorities differently than lower-level personnel, and it is often likely that the recommendations of fire fighters or first-line officers will have only slight impact on the final budget. It is important, therefore, that officers consider the realities relevant to budget considerations before deciding on the level of participation and before seeking it.

Lower echelons are generally willing to accept that their priorities can be given only relatively little weight in budget considerations, with the exception of salary-related items. Considerable satisfaction can be afforded lower echelons if they are thoroughly briefed about the way the budget is being prepared and on the reasons for specific priorities. Additional satisfaction can be gained by members of lower echelons if they are given the opportunity to register their opinions and to submit ideas.

Regardless of the specific level of participation, the process of providing the information and of obtaining ideas does not have to be the result of a large meeting where all officers (or possibly all members) of the department attend. It can be achieved through many smaller meetings in the various stations, or possibly on different tours, each one conducted by the officer in charge. These officers, in turn, can attend meetings with their chief officers, at which time all worthwhile suggestions can be discussed for possible inclusion in the budget. In large departments where even more levels of officers are involved, more of such meetings will be needed.

Expense Budgets

There are two operational budgeting systems used in preparing and working with recurring expenses. They are: (1) a line item budget system, and (2) a program budget system (or performance-based or functional system).

Line Item Budget System: A line item budget system is the traditional way to write and use a budget. In this type of budget, each particular expense is noted line-by-line. Salaries, maintenance of buildings and grounds, and other expenses such as fire fighting uniforms, hose, and supplies are listed. On each of these lines, entered next to the appropriate item, is the amount that may be

Table 10.4 Line Item Budget System*

1976 Budget: QUANTITY	ITEM	Actually Spent This Month	Total Spent This Year	BUDGETED
1	Calculator			$ 100
1	Adding machine			140
4	Desk and chair			1,107
2	Filing cabinet			255
4	Mobile radio			3,949
4	Radio monitor			900
3	Typewriter			1,836
3	Automobile			11,100
2	Air conditioner			600
1	Rug shampooer			50
1	Camera			50
1	Bookcase			40
	TOTAL:			$20,127

spent per item during the time covered by the budget; often shown are the actual amounts spent in a given month and in the period since the beginning of the year. (See Table 10.4.)

Because this system lists each expense separately rather than incorporating many expenses under one broad category, it is difficult to determine how much of the budget is spent on nonitemizable functions such as fire fighting, nonfire emergencies, training, supporting of community activities, public relations, inspections, or maintenance of alarm systems. There is no need to allocate staff time or supplies or other expenditures to each separate function. An advantage of this type of system is that the total expense for specific items is readily shown. Line item budgets have the advantage of simplicity and low cost.

Program Budget System: In the program budget system, expenditures are allocated for specific activities. For example, a department will estimate the expense (including salaries, materials used, etc.) of performing a specific function for a specified period of time. This estimated amount becomes the basis for determining the actual amount of funds to be used. As the year progresses, a record is kept of actual monies spent. The difference between this type of budget and the line item budget is that it helps to establish not only how much money is to be spent, but also for what activities the money is to be spent. This itemization allows every officer involved with the budget to know what amounts have been allocated and for what activities.

From year to year as well as within the year, by comparing budget allotments to actual expenses, officers can better decide which functions should be reduced and which functions should be increased in order to allow for emergencies or insufficient funds. A program budget requires more record keeping

---

*Courtesy of Prince William County Fire/Rescue Service, Manassas, VA.

Table 10.5 Form for Program Budget System (Oversimplified)

	Amount Budgeted	Actually Spent This Month	Total Spent So Far This Year
January	1,000	1,000	1,000
February	1,000	1,000	2,000
March	500*	500	2,500
April	500*		
May	1,000		
June	1,000		
etc.			
TOTAL FOR YEAR:	10,000		

than the line item budget, but it also permits a department to consciously direct its work so that the activities that deserve higher priorities receive the appropriate attention. For example, if a department has decided that prefire planning should receive high priority for a year and has allocated a certain number of hours to the project, this type of budget will show on a monthly basis whether the preplanning is being deprived of resources or whether it is receiving its planned share. This allows the officer to check whether the prefire plans that the department has decided on will actually be finished by year-end or whether more time will be needed.

Table 10.5, Form for a Program Budget System, shows an oversimplified form of how program budget systems work.

With a program budget system, as with a line item budget, decisions for items are made on the basis of available data, and the need to make them is highlighted by the budget reports as they become available each month. Line item budgets have the advantage of simplicity and low cost, while program type budgets provide management with a better control tool (adjustments can be made when it is desirable or necessary to achieve goals).

Neither the line item system nor the program budget system allow management to account for large expenditures such as the purchase of a new pumper or the construction of a new fire station. These large expenses that are not accounted for on a year-to-year or on a month-to-month basis are recorded within a capital budget.

Capital Budgets

Capital budgets differ from expense (operations) budgets in one major area: only a small part of each item in the capital budget is paid for with current tax revenues. The operation of a capital budget is somewhat similar to the operation involved in purchasing a car with a bank loan. The local government pays for a small part of the capital budget out of money it sets aside from

---

*Flooding during March and April is expected to reduce nonemergency time, and all non-emergency activities are budgeted at lower levels during these two months.

tax receipts. The remaining balance is borrowed either from banks or through the issuing of bonds. Over the years, the borrower repays a fixed amount annually. The government borrowing utilized in a capital budget thus supports installment buying — a "use now, pay later" device which, for example, enables a fire department to buy a new engine before the municipality or county has saved the necessary funds to pay for it.

Because capital budgets usually involve only a few items, they are not considered to be working tools for a manager in the same sense that expense budgets are. However, while they are an authorization for a department to buy needed equipment, they do not require regular entries or watching for good operation of a department.

The Formation of the Budget: Planning

Although group formation of a budget is valuable and may result in many suggestions for improving and making a department more efficient, the process of budgeting involves considerably more than the submission of opinions. Considerable planning and revisions occur before a budget appears in its final version. Budgets of previous years are reviewed intensively in order to judge their accuracy and application to a new year. (See Table 10.6, "Department Expenditure Summary.") Review of previous budgets also provides a means of updating a department by eliminating outdated expenditures and incorporating newly formed needs. Increases in the standard of living and increases in prices of materials and equipment are also taken into consideration. Finally, specific needs, such as a large investment in equipment or facilities, are accounted for. These considerations are estimated in the preliminary budget, which is submitted to the municipality or region that the fire department serves. This budget provides the municipality with a forecast of what the department expects to need for its staff salaries, for the programs it plans, and for the price changes in the services it uses or needs.

Budget Columns: While a budget is being decided on, a proposed budget sheet is used. The proposed budget sheet contains several columns. These show how much money was budgeted in the previous year, how much was actually spent, how much is being requested by the department for the current

Table 10.6 Department Expenditure Summary*

EXPENSE CLASSIFICATION	1974 ACTUAL	1975 ACTUAL	1976 BUDGET
PERSONNEL	$483,765	$747,079	$ 904,443
CURRENT OPERATING	52,728	65,513	75,430
CAPITAL	32,418	21,379	20,127
TOTAL:	$568,911	$833,971	$1,000,000

*Courtesy of Prince William County Fire/Rescue Service, Manassas, VA.

Table 10.7 Style for Proposed Budget Sheet

ANNUAL BUDGET				
Department Fire	Division	Bureau	Function	Account Salary & Wages _____ Other Expenses_____

EXPENDITURE DETAIL

Acct. No.	Classification	Final Budget 1976	Paid or Charged to 1977	Proposed by Department 1978	Increase or Decrease (+) (−)	Final Budget
	Other Expenses					
02	Contractual Services					
04	Main Building & Grounds					

year, and (usually) how much greater this request is than the previous year's request. The differences in total amounts between the two years will reflect cost and operating increases or decreases, and expenditure increases or decreases. The column headings and divisions are fairly standard, but others can be used, such as ones indicating actual expenditures from previous years. (See Table 10.7.)

Budget Approval: Once a budget has been estimated, management is required to submit the budget estimates to a finance officer or a finance committee. These estimates are then given to the town or city administration.

When a departmental budget has been approved by the town or city administration, it must then be approved by the town or city council; in some municipalities, it must be approved by a financial town meeting. With some municipal charters the council can reduce, but cannot add to, the budget. Once approved, the budget takes effect at the beginning of the fiscal year and becomes an instrument of control that shows a department how much it may spend during a particular time period. If not approved in time, it is customary to permit expenditures at the same rate as the previous year.[13] (As previously stated, this budgeting process may be somewhat altered for volunteer departments who raise funds themselves and for departments that obtain grants for special projects from the state, the federal government, or from a private foundation.)

Budget Worksheets: In order to help management work as effectively as possible within an allocated budget, budget worksheets are sometimes used. Budget worksheets usually show a record of expenditures for a current year, and can either be distributed to officers in a particular department or kept solely for the chief's use. While different departments keep budget worksheets in whatever style is best suited to their individual needs, most of them are set up similarly to the sample shown in Table 10.8. Typically, one column is used for the monthly budget and the other column is used for recording the amount actually spent. Other columns may be plotted to show the difference between the two, or to show previous years' budgets and expenditures. (See Table 10.8.)

Long-range Planning: When preparing budgets for the financial management of a department's capital resources, consideration must be given to the long-range use of such resources — one major reason being that to purchase all new apparatus would be impractical. To do so could mean that the expense of such new products would soon outweigh a department's ability to fund many important activities.

In order to formulate long-range budgetary goals it is necessary for management to consider all possible future expenses and renovations relevant to physical resources by predicting as accurately as possible any future problems and needs that might arise. Because the entire department is affected by all budgetary decisions, management should ensure coordination among all levels of the department and should allow for expression of individual needs and recommendations. Through the coordination of all departmental levels, the department will be better able to work as a solidified unit in accomplishing its primary goal — that goal being the protecting of life and property.

As a management tool, budgets have a great advantage beyond the uses discussed so far. In organizations where budgets are used properly, they bring a form of discipline that forces careful planning and thereby starts the management cycle, or the process of setting realistic and meaningful objectives.

Table 10.8 Budget Worksheet

JANUARY

Item	Budget this year	Actual this year	Diff. (+) (−)	Budget last year	Actual last year	Budget to date	Actual to date	Last year budget to date	Last year actual to date
Contractual Services									
Main. Bldg. & Grounds									
Etc.									

FEBRUARY

Item	Budget this year	Actual this year	Diff. (+) (−)	Budget last year	Actual last year	Budget to date	Actual to date	Last year budget to date	Last year actual to date
Contractual Services									
Main. Bldg. & Grounds									
Etc.									

ACTIVITIES

1. As an officer in your municipality's fire department, what factors about each of the following items would you need to consider when deciding whether or not to purchase them for your department?
   (a) An aerial ladder.
   (b) A new car for the chief.
   (c) A new stove for the fire station's kitchen.
   (d) A console desk for your communications center.
   (e) New uniforms for your fire fighters.
   (f) An additional wing to your fire station.
2. Because many of the fires in your district are in tall buildings that have been built within the past few years, it is necessary for your department to consider the purchase of an aerial ladder or an elevating platform. However, the road from the station to the tall buildings in the center of town is too narrow and steep to handle such new apparatus. Describe how you would solve this dilemma, including in your description the considerations you would need to make to help solve it.
3. Discuss some of the negative aspects of utilizing group planning in forming a fire department budget. Then make a list of the positive aspects, defending your choices in a group discussion.
4. Your fire department's new budget has just been approved and the "go-ahead" to build a new station has been given. As a member of management you must submit your design specifications for the station to the municipal officials in order for them to receive bids on the job. Using as a basis fire departments you are familiar with, make a rough sketch illustrating what you feel would be an ideal floor plan for a station. Label the rooms and areas diagrammed in your sketch.
5. (a) What questions should fire department management consider before making a final decision on the purchase of a new piece of apparatus?
   (b) Why is it sometimes better for a fire department to consider the purchase of used apparatus or the rebuilding of a chassis?
6. Review the purposes of an efficient fire department communications system. Then examine the communications system of your community's fire department.
   (a) What kinds of systems are available for the public?
   (b) Do you feel that these systems are adequate or inadequate? Explain your conclusion.
   (c) As a member of management with your community's fire department, how would you go about making any necessary changes?
7. Your community has recently adjusted its zoning laws to encourage more industry. The first new industry to be built is an oil refinery. How would you adjust the physical resources of your local fire department to better cope with the new fire hazard and with other fire haz-

ards that may become part of your district?

8. Discuss the present location of your community's fire station in relation to the fires that have recently occurred.

    (a) Considering that it might be necessary to relocate the station, what are some possible relocation sites?

    (b) List the factors that should be considered when choosing a relocation site for a station.

9. (a) What categories are rated in the ISO grading schedule?

    (b) What would a seventh class rating mean? How might you go about improving a seventh class rating?

10. (a) Explain the benefits of a budget system as: (1) a planning tool, and (2) as a control device.

    (b) Write a brief explanation of a line item budget system, and a program budget system. Prepare a simplified example of each.

BIBLIOGRAPHY

[1] *Grading Schedule for Municipal Fire Protection*, Insurance Services Office, New York.

[2] *Fire Protection Handbook*, 14th Ed., NFPA, Boston, 1976, p. 9–42.

[3] ———, p. 9–43.

[4] NFPA 1901, *Standard for Automotive Fire Apparatus*, NFPA, Boston, 1975, pp. 1901–14, 1901–15.

[5] AIA "Special Interest Bulletin No. 176," American Insurance Association, New York.

[6] "So you need new apparatus . . . or do you?," *Fire Command!*, Vol. 43, No. 6, June 1976, p. 27.

[7] NFPA 1971, *Standard on Protective Clothing for Structural Fire Fighting*, NFPA, Boston, 1975.

[8] "How Canonsburg Designed Its New Pumper," *Fire Command!*, Vol. 41, No. 7, July 1974, p. 23.

[9] *Fire Protection Handbook*, 14th Ed., NFPA, Boston, 1976, p. 9–34.

[10] ———, pp. 9–44, 9–45.

[11] "The Full Scope of Communications," *Fire Command!*, Vol. 41, No. 6, June 1974, p. 21.

[12] *Fire Protection Handbook*, 14th Ed., NFPA, Boston, 1976, p. 9–19.

Chapter Eleven

Fire Service

Personnel Management

WHAT IS PERSONNEL MANAGEMENT?

Private industry uses labor, material, and capital to produce goods or services that it sells, hopefully at a profit. Likewise, federal, state, and municipal governments use labor, material, and capital (obtained from taxes) to provide services to the public. In both situations the key resource is people, and the administration of this resource is a basic responsibility of management if the goals of the organization are to be accomplished.

In effect, personnel administration is concerned with maintaining effective human relations within the organization. As such, personnel administration is an integral part of the job of all persons in supervisory capacities and is as much a part of their job as the work that has to be done.

Organization for Personnel Management

To assist management in the personnel function, many large organizations have a separate department staffed with personnel specialists. However, because most local governmental units cannot afford a separate personnel department for the fire service, the personnel function may either be in a personnel office for all departments or may be one of the responsibilities of a single fire department officer. In many instances, fire departments rely on the Civil Service Commission's personnel procedures for guidance. In other fire departments the personnel function may be the responsibility of the fire chief and the fire director or commissioner.

But whether it is the part-time responsibility of a single individual or the full-time responsibility of a fully staffed unit, the personnel activity of any type of organization has many specific responsibilities grouped into the following three general areas: (1) routine personnel procedures, (2) labor relations activities (whether the department is unionized, or not), and (3) advisory activities to management.

Routine Procedures: Routine procedures include hiring, placement, and termination of employees; monitoring employee services; the administration of salaries, wages, other compensations and fringe benefits, and administration of career development programs, including performance evaluations.

Labor Relations Activities: Labor relations activities of the personnel department include recommendations on policy, a role in employee grievance handling (particularly in nonunion organizations), consultation with line managers on disciplinary actions, and contract negotiations if a union represents some or all of the employees.

Advisory Activities: The personnel department also has the responsibility to serve as advisor to all levels of management on human relations policies, on communications needs, and on scheduling of personnel. It maintains close contact with the needs of people in the organization so that it can recommend policy and procedure changes whenever it becomes necessary or advisable.

Fire Department Personnel Policies

The personnel policies of a fire department are subject to many influences, including union contracts and policies, federal, state, and local regulations, the views of the fire commissioner or director and those of the fire chief, and of the general public (taxpayer). Departmental officers play an important role in the implementation of these policies, whether a separate personnel division exists or not. If the department has such an office, the company officer's task is somewhat less demanding because policies and procedures are likely to be more clearly defined and because more support and advice is available. More of the responsibility for good personnel relations rests with the officer if there is no central personnel office in the department and these functions are performed by an office with responsibility for all employees of the municipality or government unit. In such a case, personnel services to the department are less likely to be specifically relevant to the department's needs.

PERSONNEL MANAGEMENT FUNCTIONS

Even though there are some functions that are solely the responsibility of professionals in the personnel field, discussion of these functions is included in this chapter to provide a comprehensive overview of personnel administration. Included are discussions of the following functions:
1. Equal Employment Opportunity.
2. Hiring, selecting, and placement.
3. Salary administration and the management of fringe benefit programs.
4. Complaints and grievances.
5. Disciplinary procedures.
6. Collective bargaining and labor-management agreements.
7. Personnel functions for volunteers.
8. Record keeping.

Equal Employment Opportunity

Local governmental organizations including the fire service must operate within the guidelines of federal and state statutes. One of the most significant pieces of legislation affecting all personnel functions is the prohibition against discrimination on the grounds of race, color, religion, sex, national origin, or age. It applies not only to hiring and firing practices, but also to all aspects of employment opportunities.

The Civil Rights Act: Originally, the Civil Rights Act of 1964 and its subsequent amendments and executive orders applied only to federal organizations and to those companies doing business with the federal government. Then, many state legislatures, following the lead of the federal government, passed equal opportunity laws that applied the same principles to local businesses and government bodies. In summary, Title VII of the Civil Rights Act of 1964 states that it is unlawful employment practice for an employer:[1]

1. To fail or refuse to hire, or to discharge any individual, or otherwise to discriminate against any individual with respect to that individual's compensation, terms, conditions, or privileges of employment, because of such an individual's race, color, religion, sex, or national origin; or,

2. To limit, segregate, or classify employees (or applicants for employment) in any way that would deprive or tend to deprive any individual of employment opportunities, or otherwise adversely affect that individual's status as an employee because of such individual's race, color, religion, sex, or national origin.

Affirmative Action Programs: The Age Discrimination in Employment Act of 1967 added age to the list of prohibited discriminators, and in 1972 Congress amended Title VII extending coverage to most governmental activities. The legislation encouraged employees to prepare plans to actively seek out minorities and women qualified to hire and/or promote. Those employers doing business with the government, and that violated the laws or did not prepare federally approved affirmative action plans, were warned that they were subject to federal court suits. Such suits could be entered by the Equal Employment Opportunity Commission.

Affirmative action programs require that standards for selection or promotion must be essential to the work. This does not mean that the standards must be lowered in order to provide employment for women and minorities. For example, if the job requires a fire fighter to carry a physical load a certain distance, then a person applying for the job may be asked to demonstrate the capacity to do the job (see Fig. 11.1). But tests that measure abilities not necessary for the work may not be used. Thus, many of the intelligence tests that were in wide use only a few years ago can only be given if the employer can show proof that the test really measures qualities that are essential to the work.

Those employers who are required by law or regulation to prepare affirmative action plans must submit to the respective agency (often the Equal Employment Commission):

Fig. 11.1. In the Palo Alto Fire Department, California, fire fighter apprentices Patty Zimmerman (standing) and Joan Leidenthal participate in a program that will guarantee them a full-time fire fighter's job when a regular position opens on the city fire department. The women include weight training in their apprenticeship, and Joan currently bench presses 145 pounds (66 kg). Her goal is 200 pounds (90.7 kg). (Ken Yimm, Palo Alto Times)

1. A statement of commitment.

2. A specific allocation of time and money to implement an affirmative action program.

3. An analysis of the present organization to determine whether discrimination exists.

4. Specific plans to rectify the imbalance if discrimination exists.

5. Goals at all employment levels and timetables for accomplishing them, with procedures for measuring how well they are being achieved.

Typical goals and specific actions to remedy the problems are:

1. To achieve a work force that represents the population of the community. This would require:

    a. Increasing the number of women and minority employees being considered for all position levels.

    b. Restructuring entry level positions to allow potential minority and women employees to become eligible.

    c. Establishing a procedure for assuring that recruiting materials, vacancy announcements, etc., reach minority groups and women in the community.

    d. Appointing individuals to coordinate the program with minority and women's community organizations.

2. Provide lower grade employees with the opportunity to prepare for higher positions and give economically or educationally disadvantaged persons the opportunity to gain more marketable skills. This might require:

    a. Restructuring positions to allow movement from dead-end jobs.

    b. Establishing percentage goals for enrolling employees in career development programs.

   c. Identifying positions requiring bilingual ability, and encouraging
      those with poor English language proficiency to study English.
   3. Establish procedures to process discrimination complaints, to assure
prompt resolution, and to provide corrective action procedures. This could
be achieved through:
   a. Review of procedures to assure that they do indeed bring improve-
      ment, and revising procedures when they do not.
   b. Assuring that the appeals procedure is fair, and assuring that it is
      revised if necessary.
One dramatic result of these laws and regulations was described in an article
in *Fire Command!* magazine. The article, which discusses the extent to which
women have begun to enter fire departments, explained a survey that resulted
in the following information:[2]

> As results from *Fire Command!*'s December survey of women fire fighters
> continue to come in, one point is clear: there are more women working
> in the Fire Service than previously had been imagined. Not counting the
> women who work in communications or join the Women's Auxiliary, there
> are hundreds of women in the country who participate in fire fighting as vol-
> unteers, and a small but significant number who are joining the ranks of
> the fully paid departments.
> The first forty survey returns indicate that more than 250 women take
> part in fire fighting in those rural, semi-urban, and private fire departments.
> The women make up four percent of the fire fighting forces of those de-
> partments that responded to the survey. The percentage figures varied
> from one department in Mississippi, where three of its four volunteers were
> women, to the Baltimore County Fire Department, Maryland, where only
> five of the 2500 volunteers were women. In addition to the number of female
> volunteers around the country, fifteen women were reported to be work-
> ing full time.
> The women have been given the same training as men, and none has
> asked for special accommodations because of her sex. In places where
> minimum fire fighter standards and training courses are required by the
> state government, the women have fulfilled all the requirements. Mike
> Johnston, a fire fighter and member of the Board of Directors of the Parker
> Fire Protection District, Colorado, said 'a women's division was formed
> in February 1973, but by February of 1975 the division was so well trained
> and integrated that it was disbanded and no distinction is made between
> the sexes. Men and women now are on equal standing.'
> In addition to the serious side of the survey, Chief Jack Belden of the
> Seneca Volunteer Fire Department, Illinois, added what turned out to be
> a light touch. 'I made a statement once,' he wrote, 'saying the only dif-
> ference between the men and the women is that the women may use lipstick.'
> It seems that many fire departments are finding that to be true.

International Association of Black Professional Fire Fighters (IABPF): Another
effect of the Equal Employment Opportunity laws has been the formation of
the International Association of Black Professional Fire Fighters (IABPF).

The IABPF is a life member of the National Association for the Advancement of Colored People (NAACP). This association was organized in 1970 to:[3]

1. Create a liaison between black fire fighters across the nation.

2. Compile information concerning injustices that exist in the working conditions in the fire service, and implement action to correct such injustices.

3. Collect and evaluate data on all deleterious conditions where minorities exist.

4. To see that competent blacks are recruited and employed as fire fighters where they reside.

5. Promote interracial progress throughout the fire service.

6. Aid in motivating other blacks to seek advancement to elevated ranks.

Selecting, Hiring, and Placement

A personnel division must determine a fire department's staffing needs and organize to fill any openings as they occur, keeping in mind the Equal Employment Opportunity requirements. These openings may be the result of planned expansion, retirement, disability, voluntary terminations, or dismissals.

When the department is subject to Civil Service regulations, the Civil Service roster is used to obtain qualified candidates. Otherwise, a department recruits through normal procedures such as advertising, maintaining a list of interested persons, etc. Once applicants are identified, the selection is usually made through most, or all, of the following: (1) reviewing applications, (2) interviewing applicants, (3) testing to determine capabilities and physical fitness, (4) analyzing the interview results, (5) checking of references, (6) repeating interviews where necessary, and (7) selecting the most qualified individual.

In many states the Civil Service Commission maintains a roster for individuals who wish to join a paid fire department. To become eligible, a candidate must usually pass a written examination, possibly a practical one, and a physical checkup. Those who qualify are usually entered on the roster in order of their test results. Several names from the top of the list are submitted to a fire department for specific selection. Either a personnel officer, the company officer, or a small selection team must then choose from these candidates the one who is best qualified to fill the position.

Since human life and safety may be at stake, competency in the fire service is of major importance; therefore, the interviewer must try to establish how an applicant is likely to perform under adverse conditions. The procedures discussed in the "Use of Questions" section of Chapter Four, "Modern Management Concepts," can be helpful in determining personality characteristics, in predicting what an applicant will do when under pressure, and deciding how the applicant will fit into the team — to what extent the applicant will bring to the team the strengths it needs.

Considerations for Effective Selection Interviews:[4] Planning of interviews is of great importance. It provides an opportunity to thoroughly review what needs to be done. Then, during the interview when the interviewer's mind is on many different subjects, none of the important questions will be overlooked. While new questions can be developed during the interview, the basic structure of the interview can be decided beforehand. Planning of each interview can best be done by preparing a checklist to include:*

1. Ideas for starting the interview informally so that the candidate will feel comfortable.

2. A few notes to help explain the requirements, difficulties, and opportunities of the position.

3. Notes to serve as reminders of specific information to be obtained in order to help round out the picture the application presents. These might include: (a) family and work background, (b) special interests, (c) feelings about new experiences, (d) interest in learning and self-development, (e) career aspirations, and (f) attitudes about people, work, responsibility, etc.

In obtaining information, it is useful to help the applicant speak as freely as possible about background and experiences. This can be achieved with open-type questions that elicit more information than simple questions that can be answered merely with a "yes" or a "no." Many interviewers have a tendency to accept factual information about experience as being equal in importance to the more subjective judgments about knowledge and abilities. Experience is much easier to measure than the potential of an applicant; it is, therefore, understandable that experience is given considerable weight. However, the extra effort it takes to explore beyond experience usually proves to be worthwhile, even though such exploration requires searching questions and continuous, careful evaluation during the interview.

During the interview, some personnel representatives develop a list of questions for later use when checking references. If the references prove satisfactory, they often call one, two, or three applicants for a second interview before making the final selection.

Interviewing for volunteer fire departments is not much different from interviewing for paid staff positions. The primary difference, however, is that, in all probability, applicants for paid positions will be screened to determine to what extent they fit a particular position. Applicants for volunteer positions are usually also reviewed to see how their services might be used in activities other than the ones for which they are applying. Often, the interviewing of volunteers is not done specifically at a time when an opening exists, but rather when the volunteer applies. Following are some specific suggestions for interviewing volunteers:

1. The position, its requirements, and the amount of time it will take to do the job should be clearly and honestly described.

2. Training requirements should be explained in detail.

3. The psychological impact of fire service on the volunteer's family should be outlined clearly.

---

*Excerpts have been adapted from *Personnel Administration: Basic Administrative Skills — Reading Material*, copyright © 1976 by The American National Red Cross, Washington, DC, Rev. Ed. 1977, reprinted with permission.

4. Policies and procedures of the department should be discussed.

5. Volunteers should be allowed some time to think about the position and its requirements before acceptance.

6. It should be made clear what support the volunteer can expect from the paid staff, if one exists, and what financial assistance will be provided.

7. Under no circumstances is it desirable to use high-pressure tactics or to continue to persuade a volunteer who shows reluctance.

8. Volunteers should be informed that the early time of affiliation is a trial period.

9. Opportunities for obtaining prestigious positions should be described realistically.

If accepted, new volunteers should be assigned as soon after they offer to serve as possible, and the fire department should confirm such assignments. A letter is an appropriate way to confirm assignments, training dates, uniform requirements, and other job specifications. A file copy of the confirmation letter gives the department a record of the details of specific assignments. If training is required before assignment, letters may be sent after the volunteers have successfully completed the course.

Acceptability of Pre-employment Interview Questions: Questions that have been proven as having a discriminatory effect on the selection process are explicitly prohibited by court rulings under Equal Employment Opportunity legislation, and may not be asked. The following considerations apply not only to interviews, but to any part of the selection procedure, including the tests that are used to separate qualified candidates from those who are not. The basic principle that should be applied is that all selection must be based on criteria that actually are job related — not just in the mind of the interviewer, but in fact. To ascertain whether or not an interview question is discriminatory, consider:

- Does this question tend to have a disproportionate effect in screening out minorities and females?
- Is this information necessary to judge this individual's competence for performance of this particular job; *i.e.*, is it job related?
- Are there alternate, nondiscriminatory ways to secure necessary information?

Major questions that should be eliminated from employment interviews, or carefully reviewed to assure that their use is job related and nondiscriminatory in effect, include:

1. **Maiden Name or Previous Name if Name was Legally Changed:** Inquiries concerning whether the applicant has worked or been educated under another name are allowable only when the data is needed to verify the applicant's qualifications.

2. **Birthplace:** It is discriminatory to inquire about the birthplaces of applicants and their parents.

3. **Race, National Origin, Religion:** Pre-employment inquiries con-

cerning an applicant's race, color, religion, sex, national origin, or age are looked upon with disfavor by the Equal Opportunity Commission and the Wage Hour Administrator. None of the federal civil rights laws specifically outlaws such questions; but, in the absence of any logical explanation for the questions, they will be viewed as evidence of discrimination since the minority, sex, or age status of an applicant has nothing to do with job performance. Inquiries as to religion, sex, national origin, or age are allowed in the case of "bona fide occupational qualifications" requirements for a job.

4. **Education:** Educational requirements that are not job related, and that have a disparate effect on protected groups, are a major area of illegal discrimination. The Supreme Court has explicitly affirmed the Equal Employment Opportunity Commission guidelines prohibiting requirement of a high school education as a condition of employment or promotion where this requirement disqualifies minorities at a substantially higher rate than others, and where there is no evidence that it is a significant predictor of job performance.

5. **Arrest and Conviction Records:** An individual's arrest record has been ruled by the courts to be an unlawful basis for refusal to employ, unless a "business necessity" for such policy can be established. An arrest is not indication of guilt; courts have found that where minorities are subject to disproportionately higher arrest rates than whites, refusal to hire on this basis has a disproportionate effect on minority employment opportunity. Also, a federal court has ruled that conviction of a felony or misdemeanor should not, by itself, constitute an absolute bar to employment, and that the employer should give fair consideration to the relationship between the nature of the act resulting in conviction and the applicant's fitness for the job in question.

6. **Credit Rating:** A negative employment decision based on an applicant's poor credit rating has also been found unlawful where credit policies have disproportionate negative effect on minorities and the employer cannot show "business necessity" for such rejection. Inquiries about charge accounts, or home or car ownership (unless the latter is required for the job) have been found to have an adverse effect on minorities and may be unlawful unless required by "business necessity."

7. **Sex, Marital, and Family Status:** Whether a candidate is male or female, married or single, and the number and age of children are examples of questions frequently used to discriminate against women. Such questions rarely relate to capacity for job performance. Any such question directly or indirectly suggesting or resulting in limitation of job opportunity in any way is unlawful. While an employer may believe that married women with young children are more prone to absenteeism or turnover, actual studies show that in total employment there is little difference in the absentee rates of men and women. Turnover is more related to type of job and pay level than to sex or family status. Investigation of an applicant's previous work record is usually a more valid method of evaluating employee stability. It is a violation of the law for employers to require pre-employment information on child-care arrangements from female applicants only. The Supreme Court has ruled that an employer must not have different

hiring policies for men and women with preschool children.

8. **Physical Requirements:** Questions related to height, weight, and other physical requirements should be asked only where necessary for performance of a particular job. Court and Equal Employment Opportunity Commission decisions have found that height and weight requirements violate the law where they screen out a disproportionate number of Spanish-surnamed persons, Asian-Americans, or women, and the employer cannot show that these standards are reasonably related to job requirements.

9. **Experience Requirements:** Such requirements should be reviewed and re-evaluated to assure necessity for specific jobs. Requirements should be eliminated where jobs can be quickly learned, or reduced if not necessary for job needs.

10. **Age; Date of Birth:** A request on the part of the employer for information such as "Date of Birth" or "State Age" on an employment application form is not in itself a violation of the Age Discrimination in Employment Act of 1967. Employment application forms that request such information by using such phrases will be subjected to close scrutiny to assure that the request is for a permissible purpose and not for purposes prohibited by the Act.

11. **Availability for Saturday or Sunday Work:** Although it may be necessary for an employer to have this information, the law requires that employers make reasonable accommodation for an "employee's or prospective employee's religious observance or practice without undue hardship on the conduct of the employer's business."

12. **Friends or Relatives Working for the Department:** This question may reflect a preference for friends and relatives of present employees, and would be unlawful if it has the effect of reducing employment opportunity for women or minorities. (It would have such effect if makeup of present work force differs significantly from proportion of women or minorities in the relevant population area.) Such a question may also reflect a rule that only one partner in a marriage may work for the employer. There is growing recognition that such rules have a disproportionate, discriminatory effect on employment of women, and that they serve no necessary business purpose.

13. **Appearance:** Employment decisions (hiring, promotion, discharge) based on factors such as length or style of hair, apparel, and other aspects of appearance have been found to violate the law if they disproportionately affect employment on the basis of race, national origin, or sex. Some courts have ruled it illegal to refuse to hire or to discharge males with long hair where similar restrictions are not imposed on females. Hairstyle requirements also may be racially discriminatory.

After selection of an individual, the personnel officer must make the new employee aware of the department's organization, insurance and health benefits, duty hours, vacation, sick leave, holiday policies, educational benefits, retirement and social security plans, and any other rules and regulations necessary for policy adherence. When new fire fighters are assigned to duty stations, they are usually subject to a probationary period of several months so that their capabilities and attitudes can be evaluated before they are given permanent status.

NFPA Guidelines: NFPA 4, *Standard for Organization for Fire Services,* provides recommended guidelines for selection of fire service personnel as well as for minimum qualifications for fire fighters. Applicable sections from the standard are paraphrased as follows:[5]

62. SELECTION, PROMOTION, RETIREMENT
62.1. Selection of Personnel.

62.11. Recruitment. The fire department should establish a recruitment program. It should be coordinated with procedures of municipal or other personnel or civil service agencies having jurisdiction. It should consist of the following steps:

(a) Conducting an active search for the best qualified persons available for membership in the department and encouraging them to apply for appointment.

(b) Rejecting, without examination, candidates who show on their application forms that they clearly fail to meet department standards of education, height and weight and age.

(c) Interviewing each candidate and giving tests measuring aptitudes, physical and personality characteristics.

(d) Subjecting candidates to a thorough physical and medical examination which they should pass in order to be eligible for fire department work.

(e) Investigating the character of candidates by interviewing former employers and others familiar with their records, taking fingerprints and clearing for police records, if any.

(f) Requiring applicants to complete a program of work and training in the department in which the applicant receives a satisfactory rating. The rating should be based on reports from supervisors to whom they have been assigned and from the fire department training officer. A satisfactory rating should include passing an examination to discover the extent to which they have assimilated information on fire department practices and the extent to which they have responded to training.

62.12. Age. A maximum age limit should be specified for acceptance to membership in the fire department which will tend to produce a force of candidates with physical fitness and mental flexibility. A minimum age limit should also be specified to assure members who are mature physically and mentally.

62.13. Education. A high school education should be required as a minimum.

The wide variety of activities in which fire fighters now participate have made it desirable that recruits have more school training than that which can be secured in elementary schools. It would be desirable to interpret the high school education requirement to exclude graduates who have not completed high school courses in physics, chemistry, algebra, plane and solid geometry and trigonometry. This requirement could be readily administered because, if there is any doubt about an individual candidate, the candidate could show that the College Entrance Examination Board's examinations in these subjects were passed. It is not too practical to recognize experience in lieu of education, because personnel for the department should be recruited when they are young, and this means limited experience at best.

62.14. Character. The candidate's application should be required to give an employment history and references. When asked to report for an interview or tests, fingerprints should be taken. The applicant's credit rating should be checked to weed out irresponsibles. Police and motor vehicle records should be obtained.

62.15. Physical Requirements. Basic physical requirements should be stated in applications to eliminate candidates who are physically unacceptable. Tests should be given after the medical examination to determine the applicant's strength, coordination, agility, dexterity and endurance.

62.16. Medical Examination. The fire department should adopt its own medical standards unless those of a personnel agency serving it are adequate. It should require all applicants to pass an examination to reveal physical handicaps, deformities, disease or organic deficiencies which would be cause to reject. It should designate the physician or medical facility which is to be responsible for the examination.

62.17. Aptitudes. Tests for aptitudes and intelligence should be given when facilities for such tests are available to the fire department. In most departments, aptitudes should be determined in a preliminary way at the time the candidate is interviewed, and from reports of supervisors and the training officer during a period of probationary training.

One source of suggestions for aptitude tests is the Public Personnel Association, 1313 East 60th Street, Chicago, Illinois 60637.

62.18. Adaptability. For a period of at least six months before appointment to the department, applicants should be assigned to probationary training classes. During part of this same period they should be assigned to a fire company for a test of how they fit into fire department life and routine. Reports from their supervisors during this period and from the department training officer should be used to evaluate the cooperativeness of the individual and the ability to be a successful member of the department.

Fire fighting is primarily a team function, especially in the case of a very large fire or emergency. Furthermore, the everyday life of a fire fighter is a group life. A fire fighter must therefore have a high degree of ability to get along with others. It is desirable that a fire fighter work under at least three supervisors during probation and receive a satisfactory rating from each.

62.19. Appointment. Applicants should be kept in candidate status until all features of the selection process are completed including the period of probationary training. The chief should dismiss any candidate at any point in the period of probation for unsatisfactory performance.

The chief's authority may be limited to recommended action where a personnel agency outside the fire department has jurisdiction over probationers or where another agency makes the actual appointments. Where a probationary training procedure is not used, it often turns out that personnel who can meet physical and written tests for candidates cannot meet the actual performance requirements of department work. Many probationary fire fighters voluntarily drop out when they find that they cannot handle the work during the probationary period.

62.2. Promotion.

62.21. Promotion Program. The fire department should establish a program for the promotion to the various ranks. It should be coordinated with procedures of municipal or other personnel or civil service agencies having jurisdiction. It should consist of the following steps:

(a) Preparing lists of members for in-service training for promotion to company officers, chief officers and to positions requiring special qualifications.

(b) Arranging assignments so that officer candidates may have a variety of duties (in several companies or districts) and experience in various staff work such as fire prevention, training, maintenance, and communications.

(c) Requiring supervisors to report on the aptitudes and attitudes of candidates for the purpose of evaluating the candidates' qualifications for promotion.

(d) Requiring candidates to complete an in-service training program, based on a job analysis for each position, and the passing of an examination on such training.

(e) Arranging assignments so that interested members may pursue courses for academic credit or college degrees at accredited schools.

(f) Appointing candidates to positions after procedures of the fire department as well as those of personnel jurisdictions have been met.

Salary Administration*

Another major function of a personnel department is the proper administration of salaries and fringe benefits, and the recommendation to higher authority as to appropriate pay scales if not already set by state civil service regulations. Even though fire service officers rarely become directly involved in salary administration matters, some of the general principles of salary administration are presented in the following paragraphs in order to acquaint fire science students with them. From a practical perspective, this knowledge can help to explain salary structure to new fire fighters, and can be useful in discussions of salary-related problems that may arise. The key elements of a good salary administration program include the following:

1. **Job Analysis:** In job or position analysis, information about the position must be determined. This information concerns the purpose of the job, the job to be performed, working relationships, inherent authority, etc.

2. **Preparation of Job Descriptions:** Job descriptions are used to record the facts and information obtained during the job analysis process. Job descriptions provide a written record of job duties and responsibilities. They are usually written in a uniform manner, utilizing a standard format. In addition, the descriptions frequently outline the education, experience, special knowledge, and desirable qualities necessary to perform duties.

3. **Job Evaluation:** In job evaluation, the relative worth of the job with-

*Excerpts have been adapted from *Personnel Administration: Basic Administrative Skills — Reading Material*, copyright © 1976 by The American National Red Cross, Washington, DC, Rev. Ed. 1977, reprinted with permission.

in an organization is determined. There are basically four formal job evaluation methods in use, and many variations of these basic systems. They are described briefly as follows:

(a) *Ranking* — This is the least complex method, and simply is a comparison and ranking of jobs in the order of most difficult to least difficult. Ranking is a nonquantitative method and, because it is subjective in nature, is often difficult to explain and justify.

(b) *Classification* — This method establishes predetermined definitions for each salary classification or grade. Jobs are compared against these predetermined definitions, and are then slotted into the classification that best describes the characteristics and difficulty of the job. This is also a nonquantitative system. This method is used by the federal government and some state and local governments.

(c) *Point System* — This method first defines factors that are present in all jobs. Different degrees of each factor are also identified, and point values assigned to each degree in order of relative importance. Jobs are evaluated and points compiled based on this method. The total point value then determines the relative worth of the job. This is a quantitative system, and it is the method used most widely today.

(d) *Factor Comparison* — This method is similar to the point system, except that factors are selected and assigned values. Jobs are compared to one another, one factor at a time, and are ranked accordingly. This also is a quantitative system, and also widely used.

4. **Job Pricing:** Based on the job evaluation results, jobs are grouped and grades assigned. The next step is to price these grades. This is normally accomplished by conducting an outside salary survey utilizing key or "benchmark" jobs to make comparisons of salaries being paid by other agencies. As a result of this survey, base salary and pay ranges are established consistent with the organization's wage policies (above, below, or comparable to what is being paid on the outside). Salary ranges (minimum to maximum) within each classification differ between different organizations. The most commonly used are based on a scale ranging from 30 to 50 percent of the minimum salary.

5. **Determination of Pay Increases:**

(a) *Individual* — In addition to grades and pay ranges, methods by which an individual moves within a salary or wage grade must exist. The increases can be either automatic, or a merit (pay for performance) basis, or a combination of both. The automatic system provides increases at a fixed rate based primarily on longevity or seniority. Under this system, an individual receives either a predetermined fixed amount if performance is satisfactory, or no increase at all if the performance of duty is less than satisfactory. The merit system, on the other hand, compensates employees on the basis of individual performance and output. In such a system, an employee receives an increase that is directly related to performance of duty. In general, automatic increases are small as compared to the increases to which an individual may be eligible under a merit system. But, together with a merit increase, a capable and competent person will receive more than under the automatic system, while a poor performer receives much less.

(b) *Frequency and Timing of Increases* — Frequency and timing of increases must be part of the system. Generally, increases under a merit system may occur more frequently depending on the individual's performance rating and location in the salary range.

In addition to individual pay increases, most organizations raise all ranges simultaneously from time to time in order to maintain a comparable relationship with salary ranges in the community, and to keep salaries compatible with rises in the cost of living.

6. **Communications:** The salary administration plan must be communicated to supervisors and fire department personnel so that they have the information to carry out and support the program. In addition, for purposes of information and guidance, administrative practices and procedures relating to the program should exist in writing.

7. **Control:** Large departments not only need budgetary controls for salary increases, but also need a system to assure that proper approvals are obtained for individual, promotional, and special salary increases.

8. **Other Considerations:** Interwoven with the preceding elements are a number of principles that have application to sound salary administration.

(a) Equal pay for equal work.

(b) Appropriate pay differentials for work requiring different levels of knowledge, skill, and physical exertion.

(c) Pay scales that have a reasonable relationship to the salaries and wages paid in the job market in which the organizational unit competes, taking into appropriate consideration all the tangible and psychological benefits the position offers.

(d) Each position has a pay range that allows for raises over a number of years. These pay scales should have an appropriate relationship to each other with respect to the principles in preceding item (c).

(e) Capabilities of the individual, which are beyond the requirements of the position the person holds, are not considered when a pay scale for a position is established.

(f) Employees with several years of service receive somewhat higher pay than new employees in identical positions. These differentials, however, become very small between employees with several years of service and those with many years of service.

(g) Salaries reflect in some way an individual's contribution to the mission of the organization.

(h) As much as possible, pay scales are known to employees.

(i) Pay scales are in keeping with the organization's ability to pay.

Some of these principles are in conflict with others; this explains why it is so difficult to develop a salary system that all employees consider fair and acceptable.

Fringe Benefits and Employee Services

The members of most paid fire departments are considered civil service employees. As such, their benefits are usually determined by state or municipal legislation. For example, the pension plan may be under control of a legislative commission, while insurance may be under the jurisdiction of the Fireman's Benevolent Association or the union. When fringes are not subject to outside control, the department must provide administration of these benefits. They involve some or all of the following insurance-type benefits in addition to workmen's compensation, which is always a statutory requirement: (1) life insurance, (2) hospitalization and medical (surgical) expense insurance, (3) accidental death and dismemberment insurance, (4) major medical expense (nonoccupational) insurance, (5) disability insurance (weekly payments in case of illness or accident), and (6) retirement income (pension).

Other important fringe benefits that require administration include: (1) annual leave or vacations, (2) holidays, (3) sick leave, and (4) other leave with pay such as death in the immediate family, time to vote, administrative leave, military training, and short-term educational leave.

There are some personnel functions that are usually considered among fringe benefits, and which can contribute toward satisfying social and esteem needs by encouraging fire fighters and officers to participate in service-oriented activities. Programs that satisfy tangible needs may include: (1) credit unions, (2) educational-incentive programs, and (3) vending machines, whose income is used to purchase sports or recreational materials.

Programs that provide social needs satisfaction include: (1) blood banks, (2) car pools, and (3) bowling and baseball teams.

Esteem needs can be met by special commendations and awards for such activities as: (1) training and educational achievements, (2) special services, (3) transfers and travel, and (4) action above and beyond the call of duty.

Training and Development

Training and development of fire fighters is not only necessary for operational effectiveness, but also to prevent injury and possible death. For these reasons, as well as for self-preservation, fire fighters are motivated to learn about the problems they will encounter and about good solutions. Even though many aspects of training are personnel functions, in most organizations in the fire service the basic job training is the responsibility of the line officer. Analyzing and advising management of training needs in other areas, such as in personnel work, or in supervision, on the other hand, is usually done by the personnel division or officer. In addition, representatives from personnel often assist line officers in improving their on-the-job training techniques. This is an important function because most fire departments do not hire several people at any one time, and therefore must train new fire fighters one at a time. The entire subject of training and development is so important to the fire service that Chapter Twelve, "Training as a Management Function," is entirely devoted to the subject.

Career Development

On December 14, 1972, the National Professional Qualifications Board for the Fire Service directed four technical committees to develop minimum standards for each of the following areas: fire fighter, fire instructor, fire investigator, and fire officer. These standards were planned to accomplish several major objectives, including the following:

- To identify and define levels for an effective organization so that positions can exist that assure that each company has the skills available to accomplish its mission.
- To provide a basis for comprehensive training programs and testing of competence.
- To provide a set of career steps for the individual.

During 1973 and 1974, the Fire Service Professional Development Committee for Fire Fighter Qualifications met in several general sessions during which vast amounts of material related to the fire fighting profession were reviewed and discussed. The committee concluded that the area of fire fighter standards relates to: (1) the fire fighter, (2) the airport fire fighter, (3) the driver/operator (engineer), (4) the emergency medical technician, (5) the alarm operator, and (6) the master mechanic. At this point the committee digressed from levels within six areas only to develop minimum measurable performance standards in each category.

The intent of the committee was to develop performance standards in such a clear and concise manner that they can be used to determine, without doubt, that any person so measured does truly possess the skills to be a fire fighter. The committee further contends that these performance objectives can be used in any fire department in any city, town, or private organization throughout North America. To this end, the committee has recommended basic disciplinary areas of study for the fire fighter, and areas that will lead to advancement into other areas of the fire service.

On November 20, 1974, NFPA 1001, *Fire Fighter Professional Qualifications Standard*, was adopted by the National Fire Protection Association, on recommendation of the Professional Qualification Standards for Fire Fighters Committee. The "Preface" of the NFPA *Fire Fighter Professional Qualifications Standard* explains the standards it sets as follows:[6]

> The standards are designed so that any member of the fire service can achieve the level required by various means; these include participation in state and local training programs, self-study, attendance at colleges offering suitable courses, and by combinations of these means.
>
> The standards are the first step: there must also be a controlled testing procedure by which personnel can be officially certified when they have demonstrated their competency. The Board stresses that such testing procedures are essential to a meaningful program of professionalism and, accordingly, is prepared, in conformance with the directions of the Joint Council of National Fire Service Organizations, to review the validity and quality of testing procedures established by state and local authorities, and to accredit such procedures.
>
> The Board strongly recommends that certification procedures be established on a statewide basis in every state where no such system exists at present, and that every fire department participate in the program.

The establishment of standards and testing procedures will not, in themselves, ensure that all personnel will achieve the required levels of competency. It follows that training programs should be developed to prepare members of the fire service to acquire the skills and knowledge necessary to achieve the terminal performance objectives of the standards.

Throughout the standards, levels of numerical ascending sequence have been used to denote increasing degrees of responsibility: e.g., Fire Fighter I, II, III, the lowest or basic level being I. A similar sequence will be used in each standard; the total number of levels varying in accordance with the number of steps involved in the individual standard.

The NFPA *Fire Fighter Professional Qualifications Standard* states that an individual classified as Fire Fighter I must be capable of demonstrating certain skills and knowledge regarding such subjects as forcible entry, protective breathing apparatus, first aid, ropes, fire hose, nozzles and appliances, and fire streams. In order to qualify for Fire Fighter I, the NFPA standard states that the following level of achievement must be met concerning fire streams:

3-8 Fire Streams.

3-8.1 The fire fighter shall define a fire stream.

3-8.2 The fire fighter, given the necessary resources, shall manipulate the nozzle so as to attack at least two live fires including: a Class A fire and a Class B fire.

3-8.3 The fire fighter shall define water hammer and at least one method for its prevention.

In order to obtain a Fire Fighter II rating, the fire fighter is expected to have achieved a higher level of skills and knowledge. The NFPA standard specifies the following requirements regarding fire streams:

4-8 Fire Streams.

4-8.1 The fire fighter, given fire situations, for each situation shall:
   (a) Identify the phase of burning.
   (b) Select the proper nozzle and hose size.

4-8.2 The fire fighter shall identify characteristics of given types of fire streams.

4-8.3 The fire fighter, given five fireground situations, shall select and identify the proper adaptors or appliances.

4-8.4 The fire fighter shall identify several precautions to be followed while advancing hose lines to a fire.

4-8.5 The fire fighter shall identify three conditions that result in pressure losses in a hose line.

4-8.6 The fire fighter shall identify four special stream nozzles and demonstrate at least two uses or applications for each.

4-8.7 The fire fighter shall identify and explain foam making appliances used, and shall produce a foam stream from all types of foam making appliances used by the authority having jurisdiction.

4-8.8 The fire fighter shall identify three observable results that are obtained when the proper application of a fire stream is accomplished.

4-8.9 The fire fighter, given the necessary resources, shall identify, select, and assemble those items required to develop at least three types of fire streams.

Similarly, to achieve Fire Fighter III, the following skill and knowledge should be demonstrated:

5-4 Fire Streams.

5-4.1 The fire fighter shall construct a diagram to identify three types of fog nozzles, and identify the major parts and trace water flow through them.

5-4.2 The fire fighter, given a selection of nozzles and tips, shall identify their type, design, operation, nozzle pressure, and flow in GPM for proper operation of each.

LABOR RELATIONS

Labor relations can be broadly defined as management's relationship with the nonmanagerial people of the organization. It has often been said that good labor relations is hardly more than good human relations because an organization where every supervisor establishes a wholesome climate for the team is likely to have equally good labor relations.

Labor Relations With Paid Fire Fighters

The concept of labor relations applies to all organizations, whether a union contract is in effect or not. In a unionized organization there is a formal contract between management and an agent (the union) representing the employees. The contract specifies the rights and obligations of all three parties — management, the union, and the employees. In nonunionized organizations an implied contract exists in the form of verbal agreement, customary practices, statutes, and possibly employee handbooks and manuals for supervisors.

The personnel office is an active participant in the labor relations aspect of personnel management because it provides advice and guidance relevant to labor relationships. Supervisors can best use the services of the personnel office by relying on it to help when problems arise. It can perform the following labor relations functions:

1. Provide a personnel policy manual for statement of personnel practices.

2. Determine whether personnel policies are fair and equitably administered throughout the department.

3. Determine whether personnel policies are kept current with existing court rulings and statute changes.

4. Investigate and recommend changes in policy that are unfair, inequitable, or no longer applicable.

5. Arrange for discussions and conclusions on any significant incidents and problems between supervisory personnel and fire fighters or their representatives that might affect the labor relations climate, or the labor-management agreement, if one exists.

To achieve the purposes of both management and labor (*i.e.*, job performance and job satisfaction), both sides must be committed to a course of cooperative action. The key factors in achieving cooperation are determined by the attitudes and approach of all parties involved; management, however, has the primary responsibility for leading towards a wholesome relationship, and every officer has an important role in that endeavor.

Labor Relations in Volunteer Fire Departments

In the volunteer fire department, there is no clear management-employee relationship because every member of the department can be, potentially, a manager next year. There is, therefore, no clear line between manager and fire fighter because management is selected by the members at an election. Many volunteer organizations have two lines of command: (1) the administrative line, and (2) the tactical, or fire fighting, organization.

The administrative organization is usually headed by elected officers and operates like any democratically run organization. Members can bring up any policy or procedural change at a regular meeting. Any changes that are made must be in accordance with the constitution and the bylaws of the fire department or volunteer organization.

At a fire or fire drill, the situation is different. Here there is a clear line of command. The elected chief is in charge, and officers are in command of the respective units. If members are dissatisfied with matters such as the way the chief sets strategy or determines tactics, or about how an individual officer performs, the matter can be brought up at a regular administrative meeting. On the other hand, officers can discipline member fire fighters in a manner similar to that of paid fire fighting companies.

Nonunion Labor Relations

In a nonunion environment, serious dissatisfaction on the part of the employees can lead to performance problems and can bring employees to seek outside representation. Major sources of dissatisfaction include:

Threat to Job or Position Security: This can stem from several reasons, including inattention to complaints or grievances, unsympathetic management, harsh or erratic disciplinary steps, or other high-handed actions on the part of officers. Such actions are viewed as favoritism or unfair treatment.

Wages, Salaries, Benefits, and Promotions: These may not be competitive with comparable community positions or with other communities. The granting of increases and promotion selection procedures may be unknown or unfair.

Employees Do Not Know Where They Stand With Management: This is generally the result of inadequate, improper, or irregular appraisals of work performance, or the failure to communicate to employees the established criteria used in making an evaluation.

Lack of Involvement Concerning Policy and Decision Making: Employees feel they are not involved in decisions affecting their jobs, or do not know what policies are in effect. Employees like to know not only what is happening, but why it is happening.

Poor Working Conditions: If the physical environment is poor, it creates an unfavorable effect on employees.

Discrimination: Discrimination, in any way and on any basis.

Because many employers, both in industry and in government, have failed to create a climate where these dissatisfactions are minimal, employees have sought the protection of unions and the safety that labor-management contracts are intended to provide.

Early in this century, joining a union was a dangerous thing to do because employers were quick to fire the people they believed engaged in union activities. The results of the conflict caused by such firings were, at first, many lawsuits, and later, new laws, so that today an employee has extensive rights to join a union or to participate in union organization activities without the fear of retaliation.

Labor Relations Laws

Prior to 1932, labor relations was the realm of the courts. Judges, through the use of common law, decided the rights of both management and labor. Since the advent of the "New Deal," four pieces of federal legislation established the rules and regulations for the present collective bargaining system. These four laws are: (1) the Norris-LaGuardia Act of 1932, (2) the Wagner-Connery Act of 1935 (often referred to simply as the Wagner Act), (3) the Taft-Hartley Act of 1947, and (4) the Landrum-Griffin Act of 1959. These laws, together with the Railway Labor Act of 1926 and some antitrust legislation, are the basis for all labor negotiations in the United States.

The Norris-LaGuardia Act: The Norris-LaGuardia Act set the stage for all of the following labor relations laws by specifying that an employee cannot be forced into a contract by the employer in order to obtain and keep a job. Before this act, many employers made workers sign a pledge that they would not join a union as long as they were employed by the company. Violating the pledge subjected the worker to job termination. Unions called those who signed the pledge "yellow dogs," and the contracts were so named.

Partly because the "yellow dog" contracts were legal, and partly for other reasons, courts were apt to side with management in a labor dispute and issue an injunction that prohibited striking or, if a strike was in effect, prohibited picketing. These injunctions were enforceable by the police.

The Norris-LaGuardia Act did two things: (1) it said that the "yellow dog" contract is not enforceable in any court in the United States, and (2) it made the conditions for getting an injunction to prevent strikes so difficult that it became almost impossible to get one.

It is important to note that, in 1932, the only way a union could gain recognition was by striking or by threatening to strike. In effect, the employer had to be forced to recognize the union. Even with the passage of the Norris-LaGuardia Act, employers could threaten and discharge workers engaged in union activity. What the act did was to give the unions the right to use their major weapons to gain recognition: striking, picketing, and boycotting without interference from the courts.

When Franklin Roosevelt took office in 1933, the so-called Great Depression was three years old. In an attempt to bolster the faltering economy, Roosevelt took many steps — including instituting the National Industrial Recovery Act (NIRA). Section 7a of the NIRA guaranteed to the unions the right to collective bargaining in order to keep wages up and thus maintain the purchasing power of the workers. This was the shot in the arm the unions needed. Workers flocked to join both the American Federation of Labor (AFL) and the new Congress of Industrial Organizations (CIO).

The Wagner-Connery Act: In 1935, the Supreme Court struck down the NIRA as unconstitutional. Senator Robert Wagner (NY) then introduced his bill, the Wagner-Connery Act, which was quickly passed by Congress. In 1936, an auto industry strike brought the act before the Supreme Court where it was upheld. The Wagner-Connery Act:

- Allowed workers to decide, by a majority vote, who was to represent them at the bargaining table.
- Established the National Labor Relations Board (NLRB).
- Defined unfair labor practices, and gave the NLRB the power to hold hearings, investigate such practices, and to issue decisions and orders concerning them.
- Prohibited management from interfering or coercing employees when they tried to organize.
- Required management to bargain with a union, although management was under no obligation to agree to any of the union's terms.
- Outlawed "yellow dog" contracts entirely (the Norris-LaGuardia Act had only made them unenforceable).

The entire area of unfair labor practices, as covered by the Wagner-Connery Act, restrained management. The act, in effect, was an attempt to equalize the positions of both management and labor. However, the act imposed no penalties for any violations, nor did it provide the NLRB with any real power to enforce its decisions or orders. Not until the matter went to the courts did the act become effective. For example, when the NLRB decided that some employees had been fired in violation of the Wagner-Connery Act, the courts upheld the decision. The result was the employees were reinstated with back pay.

Through the Great Depression and World War II, unions, under the protection of the Wagner-Connery Act and favorable court decisions, continued to grow; with their growth came increasing strength. Shortly after World War II, a series of industry-wide strikes threatened the smooth return of the economy to civilian production. During these strikes it became apparent that the power of unions had grown to such an extent that they were now substantially stronger — thanks to government protection — than their management adversaries. Congress, in an attempt to redress the balance, passed the Taft-Hartley Act of 1947 over the veto of President Truman.

The Taft-Hartley Act: Besides spelling out specific penalties, including fines and imprisonment for violations, the Taft-Hartley Act modified the Wagner Act in the following major areas:

- **Union Representation:** The act gave workers the right to refrain from joining a union; the closed shop was outlawed; the act specified that only one election a year can be held to determine whether a union, and which union, should represent the employees; it gave employers the right to express "any views, argument, or opinion" about union representation provided "such expression contains no threat of reprisal, or force, or promise of benefit."
- **Unfair Labor Practices for Unions:** The act protects employees from coercion by the unions; employees are protected from paying exorbitant dues and initiation fees; nonunion employees are protected against possible reprisals by the union if they refuse to join by preventing unions from forcing employers to fire anti-union people. The act requires unions to "bargain in good faith," as the employers had previously been forced to do by the Wagner-Connery Act.
- **Bargaining Procedures:** The Taft-Hartley Act provides for a sixty-day cooling-off period when a labor agreement ends. Section 8(d) of the act stipulates that written notice must be served if one party to the agreement is terminating the agreement. The written notice must be given to the other party sixty days before the contract ends. Thirty days later the Federal Mediation and Conciliation Service must be notified of the dispute.
- **Regulation of the Union's Internal Affairs:** Union rules regarding membership requirements, dues, and initiation fees, elections, etc., must be made available to the government and to the union membership.
- **Strikes During a National Emergency:** In the event an imminent strike affects an entire industry or a major part of an industry and imperils the health and safety of the nation, the president has been granted certain powers to help settle the dispute.

The Landrum-Griffin Act: In 1955, the AFL and CIO merged. Two years after the merger, Senator John McClellan (AR) conducted committee hearings that revealed evidence of crime and corruption in some of the older locals. At the height of the resulting furor, the Landrum-Griffin Act was passed by Congress. The Landrum-Griffin Act of 1959:

- Established a Bill of Rights for members of labor organizations so that unions would be run in a more democratic manner.
- Required that labor unions file an annual report with the government listing the assets of the union and the names and assets of every officer and employee of the union. In addition, every employer is required to report on any financial relationship it has with a union or union representative.
- Established minimum requirement guidelines for the election, responsi-

bilities, and duties of all union officers and officials.

• Amended portions of the Taft-Hartley Act concerning secondary boycotts, union security, the rights of some workers to strike, and imposed additional restrictions on the rights of unions to picket for recognition.

Unions in the Public Sector

Federal legislation had allowed the unions to grow in the private sector, and labor relations between management and unions to mature. However, fewer than one million government employees were members of unions in 1956. But by 1970, membership in public employee unions had grown to four and one-half million persons.

Until 1970, under existing legislation, government employees were forbidden to strike. The unions' most effective weapon, therefore, was denied to them. The first rumblings of discontent and rebellion to this "disenfranchisement" began in the late 1960s. Several major cities, notably New York City and Baltimore, suffered strikes by sanitation workers, teachers, police, and fire fighters. The federal government was not immune. At one point, air traffic controllers called in sick in such large numbers that commercial flight operations were severely hampered.

In 1970 post office employees went on strike and thereby set the tone for all government employees. Although the strike was illegal and the postmaster general was, by law, forbidden to negotiate with the strikers, he nevertheless did. The result was that the strikers were reinstated without penalty, received raises, and Congress recognized the union as representative of the employees for the purpose of collective bargaining.

What had precipitated the growing militancy of the government employee was the civil rights explosion of the 1960s. In January, 1962, President Kennedy issued Executive Order No. 10988 which, for the first time, allowed federal employees the right to bargain collectively under restricted rules. The order stipulated the rights of management, grievance procedures, and the rules for union recognition. In 1969, President Nixon further expanded the rights of the government employee unions when he issued Executive Order No. 11491. This order established a Federal Labor Relations Council that is similar to the NLRB for the private sector unions.

At the state and municipal level, little union activity had occurred prior to the favorable climate of the 1960s. If they belonged to any organization at all, state and local employees were members of associations that did not try to represent their members in collective bargaining but, rather, tried to work through the governing bodies and existing civil service regulations.

International Association of Fire Fighters (IAFF): As the other government employee unions began growing, so did the International Association of Fire Fighters (IAFF). Today the IAFF represents over eighty percent of the full-time paid fire fighters in the country.

Unlike most unions, the IAFF enrolls and represents supervisory personnel in the fire service. Although not all of the unionized departments have everyone in the union, some departments are completely unionized, including the chief. In many of the communities where the IAFF represents the fire fighter at the collective bargaining session, some members also hold membership in benevolent associations. Some benevolent associations provide health and insurance benefits, while others are more concerned with professional activities (such as continuing education) and with social activities.

Like unions in the private sector, the IAFF also has taken a more militant attitude. In 1968 it removed a fifty-year-old rule prohibiting strikes. Subsequently, fire departments in several communities have gone on strike when they could not reach agreement with the municipality.

Collective Bargaining Procedures in the Public Sector

The collective bargaining procedures at the local level in the public sector are different from the methods used by private industry. In the private sector, management and labor leaders generally "hammer out" an agreement and, once ratified by the employees, the agreement becomes the contract. However, state and local employees generally go through a two-stage process. The labor leaders and a government-appointed representative or committee negotiate the terms of the new contract. Once agreement has been reached at this level and the employees have ratified the agreement, the contract must go before the governing body for final approval.

Because in many cases legislative approval is customary, the contract is often subject to further modifications and negotiation.

The Collective Bargaining Agreement

As a result of the previously discussed labor relations laws, management and labor must bargain collectively and in good faith on the subjects of wages, hours, and working conditions. The result is an agreement containing a series of clauses, each relating to a particular area. The agreement outlines the conditions to which both parties agreed, and the duration of the agreement. One-year agreements are most common, although recently the trend has been toward three-year agreements with, at times, two-year agreements becoming compromises.

Typical types of clauses found in all labor-management agreements can be grouped into five segments: (1) the routine clauses, (2) union security, (3) management rights, (4) grievance procedure, and (5) conditions of employment (the largest group). Routine clauses contain the preamble and purpose, term(s) of the agreement, reopening condition(s), and amendment(s). Included in union security clauses are the bargaining unit definition and union recognition. The management rights clause reserves to management the right to make decisions in any area not specifically covered by the agreement, and stipulates in detail those areas that are solely the rights of management. Grievance procedure clauses spell out the steps in the grievance procedure and arbitration procedures, and conditions of employment clauses present details concerning matters such as wages, hours, strikes and lockouts, holidays, vacations, leaves, reporting, shift differentials, discharges, benefits, safety, apprenticeship training, etc. Further details of union security clauses, management rights clauses, and grievance procedure clauses are contained in the following paragraphs.

Union Security Clauses: A union must develop and maintain a secure organization so that it can speak with assurance for its members. A union must have strength in order to be able to bargain effectively with management. To help develop and maintain a secure organization, unions insist on a clause that defines the bargaining unit and recognizes the union as the agent (third party) representing the employees in that union.

The bargaining unit is an important concept during organizing drives. The union prefers to define the bargaining unit in such a way that a majority is assured during an election vote. Management, on the other hand, usually prefers a different, wider, bargaining unit. In the event of a dispute, the final decision on the bargaining unit is made by the National Labor Relations Board when it certifies the election. A bargaining unit may be selected by function, by craft, by location, or by some other logical entity. For example, in some locals of the IAFF, officers are members of the bargaining unit; in other locals, officers are excluded.

A municipality may have agreements with separate unions representing police, fire, and municipal employees, or one union that represents all municipal employees. When several unions represent employees of the department, the possibility of jurisdictional disputes (disputes over who represents whom) can occur. In such an event, the personnel officer has the responsibility of cautioning all supervisory personnel to remain neutral and to refrain from taking sides in the union dispute. This is most important because any comments or actions by a supervisor showing or implying favoritism toward one union can be considered by the regulatory agency as an unfair labor practice. In addition to the bargaining unit definition contained in the agreement, union security clauses may also contain one or several of the following provisions:

- *The Preferential Shop* — Management agrees to give the first chance for employment to union members. (Not usually applicable to the fire service.)
- *Maintenance of Membership* — New employees do not have to join the union to gain employment; however, any employees who *voluntarily* join the union must maintain their membership for the duration of the contract.
- *Union Shop* — New employees must join the union to retain their jobs after the probationary period.
- *Agency Shop* — Employees do not have to join a union, but they must pay dues to the union.
- *The Checkoff* — Employers must deduct dues from the wages of employees and remit them to the union.

Management Rights Clauses: Initially, unions came into being because employees believed, often with good justification, that management misused its power in order to gain economic advantages at the expense of others. Employees formed or joined unions for mutual protection. After the formation of the unions, capricious and arbitrary decisions by management brought more and more detail into the contracts to protect against unjustified detrimental actions. Management frequently objected that some areas, such as work assignment or overtime, were not subject to bargaining. Arbitration awards and court decisions, however, have gradually established that any subjects not specifically reserved for management must be negotiated. To protect its rights against encroachment, management has always endeavored to maintain and strengthen management rights clauses in contracts.

Management rights clauses reserve to management the right to make decisions in any area not specifically covered by the agreement. In addition, such clauses stipulate in detail those areas that are strictly the rights of management. They usually include the right to:

- Direct the work force.
- Hire, promote, transfer, and assign without interference.
- Suspend, demote, discharge for cause, or take other disciplinary action.
- Take action necessary to maintain the department's efficiency.
- Make reasonable rules and regulations.

When management is weak, arbitrary, or inept, the union often has cause to demand that one or the other of these rights be removed from the management rights clause and be made the subject of separate contract clauses that specifically delineate what managers can and cannot do. To avoid such additional restrictions on their freedom to manage, management people must be careful not to abuse any of these rights, and management spokespersons at the bargaining table must be skillful in protecting their rights clause.

Grievance Procedure: In negotiating an agreement, both management and labor realize that it is impossible to anticipate every conceivable problem. Both parties also realize that some problems will occur that are not directly covered by the agreement. Therefore, every contract provides for a grievance procedure that is intended to serve as a mechanism for bringing about peaceful settlements and resolution of such problems. Grievance procedures are so important to contracts that any agreement with a federal agency that does not contain such a clause is in violation of Executive Order 11491.

While actual grievance procedures may vary somewhat from contract to contract, most of them are comparable to the following example (all of the steps have time limits):

- The aggrieved fire fighter discusses the problem with an immediate supervisor.
- If the problem is not settled at that point, the fire fighter discusses the problem with a union representative who then submits the grievance in writing either to the same officer or to the officer at the next higher level.
- If the grievance is not settled, the union can appeal to the chief, the fire commissioner, or the governing body.
- If the grievance is not answered or resolved to the satisfaction of the

employee or the union, it can be submitted to an arbitrator or a panel of arbitrators. Arbitrators usually are agreed on by both parties or, depending on the stipulations of the contract, may be appointed by an impartial group such as the American Arbitration Association or the Federal Mediation and Conciliation Service. Once an arbitrator has handed down the decision, it is final. Either party can, of course, challenge the decision in court; however, judges rarely overturn the rulings of arbitrators, and do so only when the arbitrator has clearly gone beyond the authority granted by the contract.

Sometimes the grievance procedure is deliberately used by either management or union to obtain a ruling on an issue where the wording in the contract is not clear. For example, if there is a difference of opinion and no agreement can be reached, either party may act on its interpretation. The union or employee would file a grievance, or management would take some disciplinary action to bring the issue to an arbitrator for a decision.

This is very rare, however, because unions and management generally try to avoid referring disputes to an outsider. Both unions and management consider it a failure of their abili.y to maintain a good working relationship with each other, and both are concerned that the outsider (unfamiliar with all the subtle relationships that exist) may inadvertently resolve the issue in a way that is unsatisfactory to both sides.

An officer can take several steps to assure that grievances due to misunderstandings do not arise, and that those grievances that reach arbitration will be resolved in favor of management. These steps require that the officer:

- Assures that all the facts are available to both sides. It is always possible that either side misunderstood the situation or did not know all the facts.
- Maintains accurate and complete records of every occurrence related to the problem.
- Maintains as cordial a relationship with the aggrieved employee as possible.

Administration of Grievances in Departments Without a Union

In any organization, there are times when an individual or group of individuals has occasion to be dissatisfied. What sometimes starts as a minor complaint can lead to a more serious grievance if the supervisor does not give it fair consideration. If the department is unionized, the contract spells out the procedure a fire fighter can follow to obtain satisfaction. If there is no union, there must be an established procedure that specifies the way in which fire fighters can air their complaints. This is necessary, because the way grievances are handled is important to the atmosphere of the department. Effective handling of a complaint at the earliest possible moment prevents dissatisfaction from building up. This does not mean that officers should accede to all requests from fire fighters or lower-level officers. It is important, however, to give everyone a serious and fair hearing. If a request must be denied, thorough explanations are necessary to assure that the petitioner at least clearly understands why a favorable resolution of the request is not possible.

Employees are often dissatisfied when they believe that a particular situation is unfair, even if such an opinion is based on incomplete knowledge of the facts. Often, therefore, a thorough airing is all that is needed to remove the complaint.

Sometimes the problem is primarily an emotional one where the employee does not really expect any action on the part of the officer. In such cases, a friendly, empathetic listener is usually all that is necessary. As the fire fighter discusses the problem, it may turn out that the problem is not as important as it first seemed to be, that nothing can be done about the problem, or that something has already been done to avoid a similar problem in the future.

Sometimes the problem an employee presents cannot be resolved through discussion and explanation. In such instances, considerable dissatisfaction can build up and spread if the fire fighter cannot go to higher authority to file an appeal against the first officer's decision. Therefore, a grievance procedure that is clearly communicated to all fire fighters and officers represents an important and necessary safety valve. The procedure must be a fair one that does not subject the fire fighters to possible reprisals for using it.

In departments in which the officers are alert about identifying practices and policies that could lead to complaints, few complaints are likely to become serious. This points to the need for managers on all levels to maintain good communications with their subordinates so that all actions that affect people will at least be explained if they cannot otherwise be decided upon through some form of participative process. Complaints can stem from many sources, including trivial ones, as shown in the following brief listing:

- Inadequate or unsafe parking facilities.
- Favoritism in the assignment of jobs.
- A suggestion that is given little consideration.
- Any privilege that is not granted.
- Physical conditions in the station.
- Uniforms.
- Facilities for personal belongings.
- Any rule that is disliked.
- Any disciplinary action, etc.

Administration of Disciplinary Action

By its very nature, the fire service is a paramilitary organization. Thus, strict adherence to rules and regulations by its members is necessary — particularly when engaged in fighting fires. As in similar organizations, because there are times when an individual or group of individuals fails to adhere to reasonable rules, some form of disciplinary action becomes necessary. Since disciplinary action is a serious matter and a significant source of dissatisfaction not only for the individual involved, but also for others who sympathize with that person, it is of utmost importance that such actions be taken only on rules that have been thoroughly communicated and understood by all. Furthermore, every officer is responsible for identifying and helping to change rules that are no longer appropriate. However, while seemingly inappropriate rules are in effect, officers must enforce them fairly and impartially.

In many fire departments the rules are established by the chief, or by volunteer committees. The penalties for infractions are often established the same way. In some states and municipalities, the penalties for infractions are stipulated by legislative action. Typical penalties for various offenses are shown in Table 11.1.

Whether or not the disciplinary procedure is mandated by higher authority, employees can appeal any action through the grievance procedure and, if treated unfairly, appeal to the courts. Thus, the procedure must be thorough, and must effectively protect an employee against unfair and arbitrary disciplinary action so that any action sustained through the procedure will be upheld in the courts.

Where grievances are subject to the Civil Service Procedure, an appeal from a disciplinary action is usually heard by a three-member board that has been established by law or is appointed by the head of the fire department. One member of the board is often elected by the employees or approved by the employee making the appeal. Even in the case of volunteer fire departments, a board may be convened to hear and settle the dispute.

Whatever the appeals procedure, it may result in an officer's action being overturned. Since this possibility always exists, it is important for officers to

Table 11.1 Typical Penalties for Various Offenses

Infraction Penalty	First	Second	Third
Consumption of alcoholic beverages or using nonprescription drugs while on duty.	Warning* and suspension of 1–5 days	Suspension (4–10 days)	Dismissal
Reporting for duty while under the influence of alcohol or drugs	Warning and suspension (1–5 days)	Suspension (4–10 days)	Dismissal
Violation of a safety regulation.	Warning	Warning and suspension (1–5 days)	Dismissal
Fighting while on duty.	Warning and suspension (1–30 days)	Dismissal	
Stealing from fellow workers.	Warning to dismissal	Dismissal	
Stealing from the department.	Warning to dismissal	Dismissal	

*The word warning usually refers to a written warning. For less serious rule infractions, the procedure might call for one or two verbal warnings before a written warning is issued.

be careful in resorting to formal disciplinary action. Nevertheless, to preserve the validity of rules and policies, disciplinary action must be taken from time to time. On such occasions, the following precautions should be observed by the officer involved:

- The fire fighter or other person involved should be clearly informed that a rule violation is involved and that disciplinary action may result. At this point, it is generally wise for an officer not to be specific about the consequences in order to avoid commitment to a specific course of action.
- If the employee persists in the rule violation, or if the violation is in the past, it is usually best for the officer to move deliberately and slowly by first consulting either with a personnel officer or with a superior officer before imposing any penalty greater than a verbal warning.
- To avoid possible future embarrassment, an officer should always point immediately to the appeals procedure and suggest that the offender utilize such procedure if it is felt that the disciplinary action is not warranted.

Negotiations

Management and union representatives meet to negotiate the terms of a new agreement either immediately after a union has been recognized as the collective bargaining agent, or when a contract approaches the expiration date. This process is usually initiated by the union with the submittal of a list of requested changes to the previous agreement. Since the union is a political body operating under a constitution, bylaws, and democratic procedures, these requests are either the result of meetings by the union members or by a large group of union officials who have been elected for this purpose.

During contract negotiations, management representatives listen to these proposed changes and then, after discussion, submit counterproposals. The counterproposals may just be responses to the items brought up by the union, or they may contain contract changes that management would like to make. Union representatives answer these counterproposals, and either side (or both sides) will gradually make concessions that narrow the issues that separate them. From these discussions and compromises the new contract gradually emerges. Often there is considerable tension as the contract renewal date approaches, or as negotiations continue beyond the renewal date. Threats of strike or other job actions such as refusal to perform nonessential duties are not uncommon. In the event that talks break down, management, union, or both may call upon the services of a third party (a mediator) to break the deadlock. The mediator has no specific powers, but acts strictly as an impartial go-between in reconciling differences.

The attitude of both parties is extremely important during negotiations. In order to achieve an amicable agreement, each side must exercise restraint. On the management side, this places heavy and often difficult responsibilities on company officers, especially if they are, themselves, members of the union. As managers, they must see to it that the work of the unit continues to be performed without interruption. Simultaneously, as human beings, as union members, and as members of the team, they are under great pressure to help their subordinates achieve the negotiating goals to which they aspire. Considerable competence and good judgment are needed during these negotiating periods to retain the "esprit de corps" that required so much effort to build.

The major function of the department's personnel officer (if one exists) during negotiations is to prepare for the negotiations and to serve as a source of information and technical expertise for the other members of management's negotiating team. Some of the data personnel officers should have available during negotiations includes:

- Information about settlements by other fire departments or local governments, and by industrial facilities in the area.
- A list of contract changes that would help to improve the effectiveness of operations. These should have been obtained from the officers in the department during the life of the contract.
- Basic statistical information about numbers of fire fighters, hours worked, costs of benefits, benefits used, etc., that would help to estimate the probable cost of the union's requests.

Union/Management Relations

The relationship between union leaders and managers contains some curious contradictions. This is understandable because, on the surface, each represents a threat to the other. The general public and rank and file see their role that way.

During the heat of negotiations, union leaders usually visualize management representatives as their antagonists — as the force that prevents them from obtaining the legitimate improvements in working conditions, salary, and benefits that they believe are deserving of, or due, their members. At the same time, managers often see the union leaders as irresponsible opportunists who would do thoughtless damage merely for the sake of getting their way. In many ways, this picture can be said to be correct. Managers and union leaders can plot strategy in such a way that any confrontation will result in their respective sides "winning" in the negotiations. Also, both of them can often claim victory by comparing a particular feature of the settlement with initial demands, or offers, or with other settlements.

At any one moment, with respect to any one issue, the union leaders and the organization's managers are clearly antagonists. They sit at opposite sides of the table. That, however, is not the whole story. While it seems as though, in every issue, the interests of one side are opposed to those of the other, on closer examination it becomes apparent that many of these differences are not as fundamental, or serious, as it first seems. Whenever management and union discuss a grievance, wages, fringe benefits, or working conditions, their positions are opposed. On each issue a serious loss for one side may endanger the security of the individual manager or union leader. If their respective sides see them as frequently losing, or as coming up with unfavorable compromises, sooner or later they will not be able to retain their respective positions. This is the situation as far as the tactical considerations are concerned.

However, strategic, long-term thinking shows a different picture in which the three major issues are: (1) wages and fringe benefits, (2) working conditions (including satisfaction of psychological needs), and (3) the job security of the union leaders and of the organization's managers, respectively.

Wage and Fringe Benefits

The union leaders' objectives in negotiating for wages and fringe benefits are to obtain the best possible package as defined by their membership. It must be remembered that the requests the union places on the table early in the negotiations have been arrived at by a political procedure, at one or many union meetings, where these requests have been established through a democratic process. During these discussions, all the people who are involved are clearly aware that, by asking for more, it is likely they will receive more than if they started by asking for less. Certainly, during negotiations there is more room to give and still obtain as much as the minimum that they are willing to accept. The restraints on the union to request more than most members believe can be obtained are, therefore, not very strong. Obviously, the union will not come in with requests that are foolish; nevertheless, it generally requests substantially more than the union leaders or the members expect.

Management's immediate interests are to hold cost increases to a minimum. In a profit-making enterprise, amounts that are not paid out as additional wages are available as profit to the owners. In a governmental organization, there are so many demands on the funds available to the governmental unit that managers are under pressure to avoid giving greater increases or benefits than necessary. All are aware that, to some extent, their performance is evaluated on the basis of their ability to achieve "favorable settlements."

However, this is only the immediate picture. In the long run, no organization can remain healthy and effective if it fails to adhere to reasonable salary administration principles. One of the most important principles of salary administration concerns the requirement that an organization pay wages and fringe benefits that are equal, or possibly even superior, to those for similar positions in the community. Every manager is aware that, if the organization can pay higher wages and provide a richer benefit package, the opportunities for obtaining and holding people with exceptional competence and high abilities are much greater than if wages are low, or lower than the average. For this reason, competent managers do not oppose a union's legitimate and reasonable demands when such demands are based on good salary and fringe-package administration principles; nor will competent managers try to obtain the very lowest settlements they are able to force on the union when they are in a position to do so. They will, instead, start to bargain at a figure that is lower than what they believe the membership should receive; at the same time, however, they will work diligently to obtain agreement either from stockholders or from higher-level government officials for amounts that will establish a fair salary and fringe benefit picture.

Working Conditions

The term "working conditions" includes more than just the physical facilities and amenities: it also concerns the extent to which supervisory personnel can help provide satisfaction of psychological needs. Also, to some extent, what is true of salary and fringe benefits is often true of working conditions. Organizations having substandard working conditions have greater difficulty retaining qualified and competent people.

Managers know that good working conditions, including reasonable work rules, provide a more desirable work climate and lead to higher productivity. Similarly, union leaders prefer to work with organizations where little conflict exists and where employees have few complaints. Such organizations demand little attention, thus permitting union leaders the freedom to pursue activities they consider more important than settling grievances or working on complaints. Because it is in the best interests of the unions that their members have good working conditions and adhere to reasonable rules, competent union leaders willingly help management establish such environments.

Job Security of Union Leaders and of Managers

Since unions are political bodies, union leaders advance in their careers or remain in office only if they are competent leaders, or if they do exactly what the membership wants them to do provided the membership is not too badly split in its opinions. On the other hand, managers advance, in part, on the basis of their competence in working with union officials. If union leaders and managers have difficulty establishing a good relationship, and if grievances mount, their career goals may become more difficult to achieve.

Consequently, there is mutual interest in the competence of the people on the opposite side. Capable managers never try to use the powers available to them in efforts to undermine the strength of capable union opponents. Enlightened managers are aware that, ultimately, competent union leadership is in everybody's best interest because only capable union leaders are able to control those members who make unreasonable demands or who attempt to undermine a fair settlement that they consider inadequate. Similarly, competent union leaders are aware that when they do have the power, it is not wise to use it in such a way that it will endanger the security or career advancement opportunities of competent managers. This is true even though competent managers are difficult to take advantage of, and that less competent management might allow a union to obtain more favorable settlement in the short run. Over a long term, lack of management competence combined with the repercussion of excessive settlements can lead to a period of considerable unhappiness when either fewer increases or no increases at all can be obtained, or, even worse, if the organization loses the strength to survive.

The Role of the Steward

Management's actions are restricted by the union agreement and, as previously discussed, the Labor Relations Act of 1935. However, the agreement and the Taft-Hartley Act of 1947 similarly restrict the activities of the union. Supervisors can still run their organizations by insisting on adherence to safety rules, attendance regulations, maintenance standards for equipment, apparatus, and facilities, and regulations that apply to fire fighting. The major affect of the union agreement for the first line officer is that day-to-day operations now involve another individual — the union's shop steward.

Establishment of good relations is the joint responsibility of both the line officer and the shop steward. New contract clauses, in particular, are subject to varied interpretation. When a question arises, competent officers consult with their respective superiors who often seek the advice of the personnel officer to obtain clarification on what a clause really means. Only after having obtained such clarification of the management position should an officer take a firm stand with a steward.

The American Federation of Government Employees (AFGE), one of the largest unions representing government workers, describes the shop steward as "Mr. Union to the members . . . and to the supervisor." It is the steward that most workers interface with on union matters. In most organizations having unionized employees, the supervisor will deal only with the steward in day-to-day activities in which the union is legitimately involved. As the AFGE description points out:

> These two must work together in good faith on departmental problems. They must promote and maintain morale and friendly relations. They must be willing to cooperate.

The steward occupies the same position, relative to the union, that the supervisor enjoys with the organization. However, the steward is elected by the employees, is never paid, and the job is totally voluntary. Therefore, in dealings with the steward, the supervisor must keep in mind that the steward, whose job is awarded by constituents, may conceivably lose the position at the next election should constituents become displeased. The supervisor must also remember that, although the steward may be well-informed on union matters, stewards rarely have any formal training in leadership.

One of the responsibilities of the line officer is to maintain a good working relationship with the steward. Of equal importance is the line officer's responsibility concerning the protection of the management rights clause of the contract. Thus, the supervisor must be aware of all policy directives and procedures. Any changes or deviations from the existing rules and regulations must be accomplished through prescribed channels. For example, in the fire service, although duty hours are as assigned by management, it is likely that a fire fighter may desire to take a day off other than the allotted time. Although the fire fighter may be able to find someone with whom to exchange times, the exchange should not take place until the supervisor has approved the action and is satisfied that such action will not represent a precedent that might cause other fire fighters to demand similar privileges, if such privileges cannot also be granted to them.

RECORD KEEPING

An important function of the personnel officer is the maintenance of complete and accurate records. Records are necessary for volunteer departments as well as for paid and for partially paid departments. Such records provide:

- The department and employees, including fire fighters, with a detailed history of an individual's association with the department.
- Management with data for determining personnel availability and qualifications for planning purposes.
- Management with information necessary for future contract negotiations.
- Records for tax and insurance purposes.

Volunteer Personnel Records

A volunteer fire department has responsibility for maintaining records relating to the overall relationship of the volunteer to the organization. This responsibility includes keeping:

1. A master file containing complete data relating to the selection of the individual such as application, interview report, committee investigation report, and physical examination form.

2. A record of training received.

3. Insurance information.

4. An overall record of the volunteer's participation in various areas of activity, including leadership positions; information regarding interest in and availability for other assignments.

5. Information on performance evaluations and on recognition, such as service awards, expressions of appreciation, and honor awards.

6. A record of the reason for discontinuance of service.

Paid Employee Personnel Records

If records are not kept by a personnel office in the local government, the fire department must maintain a complete file on each employee. Besides containing the data necessary to provide reports to government agencies, such a file enables management to objectively select individuals for promotion. The file should include:

1. The completed application form together with the interviewer's notes, reference checks, and results of all tests taken.

2. Payroll records including salary or grade status; federal, state, and municipal income tax deduction authorizations as well as those for bond, credit union, insurance, union, and pension deductions; annual leave and sick leave dates; and insurance claims filed.

3. A work record that includes complete information pertaining to on-the-job training programs, courses or schools attended; performance evaluations; commendations and special awards; grievances, complaints, and disciplinary actions; and positions held (including dates).

In addition to records on individuals, a personnel office in a unionized department should maintain a record of significant factors that may affect future negotiations with the union. These would include records of:

- Complaints about unilateral policy changes by management.
- Complaints about changes in job assignments.
- Complaints about promotions or transfers.
- Problems encountered in job assignments.
- Numbers and types of disciplinary actions by types of infraction.
- Contract settlements by other departments, etc.

ACTIVITIES

1. Describe the organization of the personnel function in your community's fire department.
2. There are basically four formal job evaluation methods currently used by most supervisors of salary administration programs when determining the worth of particular jobs within an organization. In outline form, describe the method you think is the most objective. Discuss your choice with a group of your classmates. Use your outline in defense of your choice.
3. In 1972 the National Professional Qualifications Board for the Fire Service directed four technical committees to develop minimum standards for certain job categories in the fire service.
   (a) What were these categories?
   (b) What major objectives were these standards planned to accomplish? How?
4. Prior to 1932, judges — through the use of common law — decided the rights of both management and labor in labor relations disputes. Following 1932, four federal laws established the rules and regulations for the present collective bargaining system. Explain how each of these laws contributed to establishing these rules and regulations.
5. How do collective bargaining procedures at the local level in the public sector differ from the methods used by private industry?
6. Collective bargaining agreements contain a series of clauses, each relating to a particular area.
   (a) What are some of the typical types of clauses found in all labor-management agreements?
   (b) Write brief descriptions of the purposes of at least two of these clauses.
7. While grievance procedures vary somewhat from contract to contract, most of them follow steps comparable to the example presented in this chapter. Review the example, and then prepare what you feel could be a more satisfactory procedure for settling management/labor problems by either: (1) rewriting the procedure in the example, or (2) adding other steps to the example.

8. What are some of the ways to achieve a work force that is completely representative of the population of a community?
9. What advances has your community's fire department made in fulfilling affirmative action program requirements?
10. (a) Explain the usual procedure for selecting individuals for paid fire departments in those states subject to Civil Service regulations.
    (b) Explain the usual procedure for selecting individuals for paid fire departments in those states not subject to Civil Service regulations.

BIBLIOGRAPHY

[1] Title VII, Civil Rights Act of 1964 (Congress amended in 1972), U. S. Government.

[2] "Women are Fire Fighters, Too!," *Fire Command!*, Vol. 43, No. 2, Feb. 1976, p. 17.

[3] *Fire Protection Handbook*, 14th Ed., NFPA, Boston, 1976, p. A-6.

[4] *Personnel Administration: Basic Administrative Skills — Reading Material*, The American National Red Cross, Washington, DC, Rev. Ed. 1977.

[5] NFPA 4, *Organization for Fire Services*, NFPA, Boston, 1971, pp. 38, 39, 40.

[6] NFPA 1001, *Standard for Fire Fighter Professional Qualifications*, NFPA, Boston, 1974. pp.v–vi.

Chapter Twelve

Training as a Management Function

IMPORTANCE OF TRAINING PROGRAMS

No one factor has more ultimate effect on a fire department's operations than its training program. One reason for this is that rather than basing the selection of fire fighters on experience alone, factors such as physical condition, mechanical ability, personality, educational background, and ability to learn are also considered. Many people enter the fire service each year, most with no previous experience as fire fighters. Training, therefore, is essential for effective performance, and it is only with a comprehensive training program that a fire department is able to establish and maintain a competent and well-trained force.

The importance of training in a fire department's operations and the responsibility of the fire service instructor in such training is emphasized in the following excerpt from the "Introduction" to *Fire Service Instructor's Guidebook*, by Anthony R. Granito, Deputy Superintendent of the National Academy for Fire Prevention and Control:[1]

> The fire service's main objective is protecting life and property, so all people employed in it must be fully qualified to successfully and efficiently perform the wide range of skills necessary to accomplish this goal. This competency is, in large measure, the responsibility of the fire service instructor.
> Great pressure, from both public and private sectors, requires that the level of efficiency and the level of performance of all fire service personnel be constantly and consistently upgraded. The instructor is accountable for the level of up-to-date efficiency, education, and skills.
> The instructor is one of the important cohesive forces in any fire department. Whether a group functions like a well-oiled machine or like the scattered pieces of a puzzle is due in large part to the training, guidance, and encouragement of the instructor.
> The instructor's role is demanding and challenging. The instructor must not only consider training personnel who show various levels of proficiency,

350

but also must train personnel of all ranks within the department. In addition to ensuring that the recruit understands the duties and responsibilities of the position, the instructor must train the recruit for specific job skills. Experienced fire fighters and officers also must be kept familiar with all of the latest prevention and suppression techniques. They must be aware of updated standards, new laws, and new procedures. They must be able to recognize their current performance levels and skills, and correct any deficiencies or weaknesses. The instructor must prepare them for promotions, make them proficient in all fire-related skills, and generate a spirit of pride and commitment to the fire service.

This chapter briefly outlines some of the principles of learning and training design relevant to the fire service. A fundamental principle — that people learn best when highly motivated — is the foundation for the discussion of principles and techniques. The instructor is described as the manager of a learning process that is based on the following procedures:

- Analysis of learner's needs.
- Setting of learning goals.
- Identifying and overcoming obstacles to learning.
- Providing an environment where learning can take place.

This means that the instructor must place equal emphasis on *process* of learning and on *content*, and thus strive for a motivational climate in which learners seek greater knowledge and improved skills. Following a discussion of the principles of learning and various techniques, the chapter presents how these can be applied to on-the-job training and to classroom instruction.

PRINCIPLES OF LEARNING AND TRAINING DESIGN

Because most people spend a significant portion of their lives in classroom situations where learning involves the presentation of information, the traditional conception of an instructor is that of a person who dispenses information. In this type of "learning" situation, the instructor lectures to the class and the students strive to absorb meaning from the words to which they are exposed. There is some give-and-take when class size and instructor temperament permit questions during the lecture; however, usually only very few learners avail themselves of that opportunity.

The Learning Process
Currently, the traditional conception of the instructor is changing to one in which the instructor pays as much attention to the *process* of learning as to the topic *content* with which learners should become familiar. Process refers to the particular steps necessary to ensure that learners gain the greatest benefits from the learning experiences to which they are exposed. The instructor who strives to be a manager of the learning process seeks to shift

the responsibility for the achievement of learning to the learner. Such an instructor does not concentrate on the topic and how it can best be presented in logical fashion, but instead, as a basis for a teaching approach, asks the following questions:

- What do my students know now, before I work with them next?
- What is it that is most important for them to learn next?
- How can I best help them to learn it?

These questions are especially important in the fire service where learners are adults who have usually been exposed to the topic of the session the instructor is planning.

The diagrams shown in Figures 12.1, 12.2, and 12.3 illustrate the importance of this approach to instruction. Figure 12.1 illustrates how a lecture can be self-defeating — at least for those learners who do not seek complete understanding themselves. At first it would seem that a clear, logical presentation would help students to learn the topic by leading them step-by-step from the fundamentals to a thorough picture of the topic. Although this is correct to a limited extent, the educator who strives to increase quality must also evaluate trade-offs between the clear and logical presentation of the material and optimum student comprehension. While it might seem contradictory when stated this way (that logical subject explanation and learner understanding should be in conflict), this is often the case. The well-organized learning experience often provides learners with little awareness of the limits of their new knowledge: because learners follow the presentation, they assume they fully understand the message. Few questions come to their minds and, even though they have mastered some difficult thoughts, they leave the training environment with only a shallow comprehension of the subject — a comprehension that is inadequate for application to complex, real-life situations.

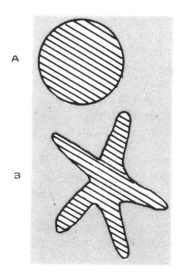

Fig. 12.1. (A) Depiction of a learning experience in which learners, having little contact with the unknown that surrounds the small island of knowledge gained and where they have developed a seemingly adequate picture of the subject, are not likely to probe beyond the circle of knowledge for more information. (B) Depiction of a learning experience in which only sufficient explanation is offered in order to give learners a basis for exploration. In this latter experience, the rugged, uneven format affords learners the opportunity to probe for further understanding in terms most meaningful to each individual.

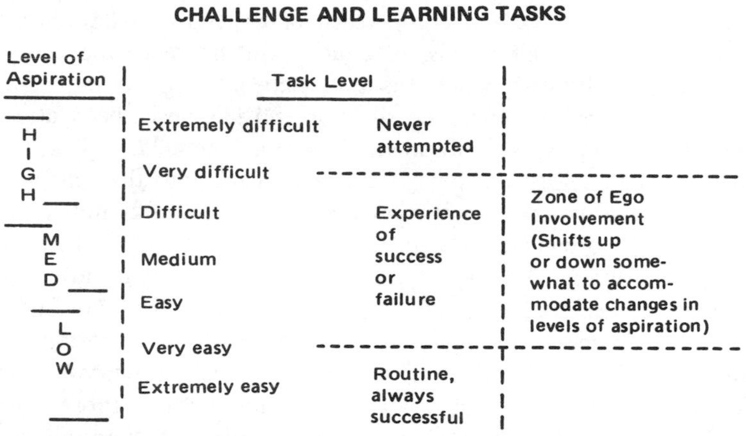

CHALLENGE AND LEARNING TASKS

Level of Aspiration	Task Level	
H I G H	Extremely difficult	Never attempted
	Very difficult	
M E D	Difficult	Experience of success or failure
	Medium	
	Easy	
L O W	Very easy	
	Extremely easy	Routine, always successful

Zone of Ego Involvement (Shifts up or down somewhat to accommodate changes in levels of aspiration)

Fig. 12.2. Comparison of the level of aspiration with the task level. (Based on work by Wallace Wohlking, New York State School of Industrial and Labor Relations, Cornell University, NY)

The circle in Figure 12.1 graphically depicts this kind of learning experience — a learning experience in which learners have little contact with the unknown that surrounds the small island of knowledge gained, where they have developed what seems to them an adequate picture of the subject, and where they are therefore not likely to probe for more information. At some later time, when they attempt to apply what they have learned to the solution of a problem, they discover their lack of understanding. By this time the educator is no longer readily available to supply guidance, and the learner must either devote more effort to learning the necessary material or forego a clear picture of the subject.

The star-shaped part of Figure 12.1 depicts the presentation of information in a rugged, uneven format that is far less satisfying to instructors schooled in the more orthodox methods. In presenting material this way, only sufficient explanation is offered to give learners a basis for exploration. In this type of learning situation, learners probe for understanding in terms most meaningful to each individual. If such a learning experience is carefully designed, it involves some form of problem solving and provides for answers to questions that arise in the process — as they are needed, and asked for, by the learner.

Figure 12.2 illustrates the need for an instructor to be concerned with the level of difficulty the topic or learning goal presents to the learner. The diagram compares the level of aspirations (how strongly the learner wants to achieve) with the task level (how difficult the learning experience is for that particular learner), in order to define the zone of ego involvement at which the learner can devote maximum attention to the task of learning. As shown in Figure 12.2, the three factors involved are: (1) level of aspiration, (2) complexity of the task level, and (3) ego involvement. These factors suggest that high motivation is possible only if the task level is set so that it is perceived to be within the experience and competence of the individual (even if some failures are expected). Aspirations, of course, will influence the way a task is seen and the attitudes with which it is approached.

If a task is perceived as much too difficult and has never been attempted, it is outside the zone of ego involvement shown in Figure 12.2. For example, for most Americans a Russian literacy test would fall into this category. At the other extreme, any task that is immediately recognized as much too easy also fails to bring ego involvement and, therefore, presents little challenge and will quickly be considered a waste of time. Most satisfying are those experiences that are achieved by a narrow margin: failure is a constant threat, and challenge is highest. Here, of course, the payoff in satisfaction of accomplishment is high and motivation to tackle the task is greatest. According to Wallace Wohlking's reports on research with children, those who have a history of success will usually set realistic goals, while those who fail regularly tend to set unrealistic goals — either too high or too low.[2] Those who set goals that are too high seem to do so because they are usually rewarded for trying, while those who set goals that are too low do so as a defense against possible failure. Thus, the conclusions for training design are fairly obvious:

- For all complex tasks, the designer of a training experience must set subgoals.
- Subgoals must be attainable so that successful experiences are developed.
- A specific effort must be made to teach toleration of failure.

The four diagrams in Figure 12.3 emphasize the importance of motivation and show the limits of teaching presentations from still another perspective. If, as shown in Part A of Figure 12.3, the large rectangle (rectangle No. 1) can be considered to completely contain the currently available knowledge about a specific subject, then it can reasonably be assumed that an instructor will know, at best, only a portion, as indicated by rectangle No. 2.

The instructor, faced with limited class time, prepares an outline that presents that portion of knowledge the instructor considers to be most important. Often, the instructor encounters various interruptions and delays, and thus talks about less than had been planned on the outline. The prepared material and what is actually discussed are represented by the two smaller rectangles (No. 3 and No. 4) shown in Part B of Figure 12.3.

The communications process being what it is, different people assign different meanings to words and phrases. This is because there are lapses of student attention, screens of personal biases, misunderstandings, misinterpretations, and false impressions of concept clarity. All in all, what reaches the student is far less than what that student was exposed to. What is remembered a few weeks, months, or even years later is still another matter. The three small rectangles (No. 5, No. 6, and No. 7) in Part C of Figure 12.3 can be considered to represent: what the student actually hears (No. 5), what penetrates the student's consciousness (No. 6), and what the student remembers at some later date (No. 7).

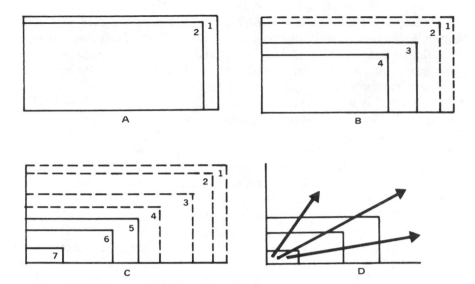

Fig. 12.3. Pictorial representation indicating the importance of motivation and the limits of teaching presentations.

The intention of this somewhat exaggerated analogy is not to portray the futility of conscientious effort; rather, the analogy is included to help illustrate the point that *how* a subject is presented is often far more important than *how much* of the subject is presented. The curiosity of learners can be aroused by presenting only that portion of the material they can readily absorb. If presented in an interesting, stimulating format, learners will usually reach out for more information. (See Part D of Fig. 12.3.) Thus, more will be absorbed, more will be retained, and the ability to apply the newly acquired knowledge will be substantially enhanced. However, to do this is more easily said than done. To change the traditional emphasis, instructors must make use of all the teaching techniques that are geared to stimulating inquiry on the part of learners and thus motivate learners to accept the responsibility for their own learning.

To achieve an environment in which learners can find maximum motivation requires the consideration of all of the elements of the linking elements concept discussed in the earlier chapters of this text — including, in particular, linking elements concerned with goal setting. This, in turn, must start with an understanding of the current situation — what learners know, and what their knowledge or skill deficiencies are.

Learning Needs Analysis

Before an instructor can determine the sequence in which topics should be presented and the specific subtopics to be taught, a learning needs analysis must be made. Such an analysis is necessary in order to help determine the type of information to be presented.

Analyzing Individual Learning Needs: It can often be assumed that new trainees know very little, if anything, about the subject. Classroom sessions or on-the-job training can be planned by looking solely at the topics the learner must master, and at the characteristics of the learner so that learning materials can be presented in the most stimulating way.

The situation is more complicated when planning on-going or continuing development. Not only must the instructor be concerned with logical sequence of topic segments and with presenting them enticingly, but the plan must concentrate on those subtopics (knowledge or skills) where additional learning is desirable. Thus, in the formal sense, a learning needs analysis attempts to obtain answers to the following two basic questions. Based on the answers to these questions, a specific learning program can be prepared and scheduled.

1. What do learners need to know or be able to do?
2. What do learners now know or are now able to do?

The tool with which a learning needs analysis can best be conducted is a knowledge/skill profile that lists all the things the learner should know or be able to do. Table 12.1 is a sample of a knowledge/skill profile for a fire fighter. There are many ways such a profile can be constructed, including the following three:

1. A knowledge/skill profile can be based on a detailed job description if one exists, even though it usually cannot match the job description exactly. For example, a line on the job description for an officer might read:
   • *Supervise the activities of the company's fire fighters during overhaul operations.*
   Similar knowledge and skills are needed for that part of the job, as for a similar line on a job description that reads:
   • *Supervise the activities of the company's fire fighters during salvage operations.*
   These two lines cover many things an officer must know, or be able to do — from communication to the technical aspects of the respective operation, and to all the knowledge and skills involved in supervision. On the other hand, consider a job description line that reads:
   • *Must be thoroughly familiar with hydraulic principles related to fire streams.*
   This latter line could also be a line on a knowledge/skill profile, since it concerns a single topic the officer must know.

2. A knowledge/skill profile can also be constructed from a thorough list of goals that apply to a particular position. The need to convert from goals to knowledge and skills applies to this method of preparing a profile as much as it does to the one in which the profile is based on a job description (preceding No. 1).

3. The profile can be developed by the officer, or cooperatively between an officer and a subordinate. In the latter case, both the officer and the subordinate prepare a profile and then, in discussions, compare their views and create a common one. Such a jointly developed profile is often most likely to provide a basis for learning goals that are challenging and that the subordinate would really attempt to achieve.

Table 12.1   Sample Knowledge/Skill Profile for Fire Fighters

KNOWLEDGE	SKILLS
Organization of fire department	Hose evolutions
Scope of fire department operation	Ladder evolutions
Standard operation procedures	Breathing apparatus use
Fire department rules and regulations	Forcible entry
Safety policies	Ventilation operations
Fire behavior — chemistry of fire, types of fire, etc.	Hydrant operation and connection
Respiration	Resuscitation
Fire streams and use of nozzles and couplings	Salvage operations
	Rope use
Use and types of equipment, such as breathing apparatus	Basic apparatus maintenance operations
Life-threatening injuries	Cleaning, maintaining, and inspecting equipment such as breathing apparatus, ropes, salvage equipment, ladders
Ventilation methods	
Salvage process	
Inspection procedures and standards	Care of hoses and nozzles
Reporting	
Safety	

Analysis of Team Learning Needs: An analysis of learning needs cannot concentrate exclusively on the knowledge and skills that individuals must acquire. There are team needs that go beyond the individual needs of the members of the team. Even when every person on the team has all of the knowledge for performing specific tasks, should the team not have learned how to coordinate them, many problems can occur. These problems can be prevented only through the type of joint team practice that gradually develops the necessary coordination. Team skill needs must, of course, first be identified. For example, each fire fighter in a specific company may have clear knowledge of the standard attack evolution:

- Officer and fire fighter #1 advance one preconnected 1½-inch line to fire for immediate fire attack.
- Operator charges 1½-inch line from engine tank.
- Fire fighter #2 pulls supply hose from body and connects to hydrant, and then prepares to advance 2½-inch line.
- Fire fighter #3 assists fire fighter #2.
- Operator switches from tank to hydrant supply as soon as connected.
- Operator connects 2½-inch hose to pump discharge gate and charges it.

While these evolutions will be followed, without joint drills to develop team skills, fire fighters #2 and #3 will not perform their tasks as fast as they would had they practiced together. It is conceivable that a snag could develop in the timely switching from tank to hydrant, thus making the team's skill deficiencies a major problem.

Setting Learning Goals

The end result of new learning is often a change in behavior. This is especially true in the fire service where it is important that everyone continue to improve the way the job is done. Goals, when properly set, represent a contract to oneself or to others to achieve such change. For this reason, when educators discuss the goals learners have agreed to achieve, they often speak of a "learning contract."

As discussed under goals programs in previous chapters, joint goal setting defines both what is expected of the subordinate and what support the manager is expected to provide. Similarly, a learning contract defines the goals and the responsibilities of learner and instructor and thereby places these responsibilities clearly where they belong.

After the knowledge and skills needs of a person or team have been identified during a needs analysis, goals can be set and developmental experiences can be planned to stimulate the greatest desire for achieving the goals. For planning a learning program, the concept described in the following paragraphs can serve as a useful guide.

The Goal Achievement Spiral: A complete learning experience consists of the three phases shown in Figure 12.4, described as follows:

1. *Acquisition* — During this phase of the learning experience, new knowledge is obtained through the written word, from live presentations, in group discussion, etc.

2. *Demonstration* — The new material is made more meaningful, or more explicit, through the use of demonstrations, where the practical application of new data, principles, or concepts, is shown. This can take the form of dramatic presentations, films, slides, audio or video tapes, actual demonstration with models, etc.

3. *Personal Application* — Here the learner comes face-to-face with his or her own ability to apply the material to various situations. If the learning experiences during the personal application phase are properly designed, they will be quite similar to those the learner normally faces in his or her own environment.

Instructors who work with simulations and other participative learning experiences consider the third stage to be the most important one. Following is what occurs during the personal application phase:

1. This step offers an opportunity for the learner and the instructor to check how well the picture that has built up in the learner's mind meets

Fig. 12.4. The three phases of a complete learning experience.

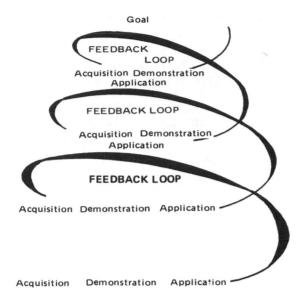

Goal

FEEDBACK
LOOP
Acquisition Demonstration
Application

FEEDBACK LOOP

Acquisition Demonstration
Application

FEEDBACK LOOP

Acquisition Demonstration Application

Acquisition   Demonstration   Application

Fig. 12.5. Basis of the continuing process for achieving learning objectives.

the needs of reality. In so doing, the following two feedback loops immediately come into being:

   • *A loop for the instructor with which to observe the progress of the group in meaningful terms.*

   • *A loop for the learner with which to diagnose areas where particular knowledge deficiencies exist.*

   2. As a result, the two feedback loops become the basis for a continuing process that can be used to achieve any learning objective that is not blocked by attitudinal or emotional obstacles.

The process of achieving such an objective involves a spiral-type repetition of the three phases (acquisition, demonstration, and application) and the feedback loops; less and less new knowledge has to be acquired in each turn. (See Fig. 12.5.) This becomes especially apparent to instructors when they experiment with various types of simulated experiences. Serious-minded learners inevitably ask more precise and penetrating questions during and after the personal application than they are able to ask beforehand.

It should be kept in mind that for new knowledge to be meaningful, it must be explored in the learner's own terms. Although this might seem obvious, the point cannot be overemphasized because to every person words and images have individualized, personal meanings. Therefore, application of new knowledge in the classroom or training session must be to situations that are similar to those the learner normally experiences in the work environment. Also, learning must proceed at the learner's own pace, must be adapted to personal ability, and should be related to previous experience. Therefore, learning programs should make use of techniques that are flexible enough to permit adaptation to the needs of the individual in order to help instructors and learners achieve learning goals as easily as possible.

Identifying and Overcoming Obstacles to Learning

The spiral shown in Figure 12.5 can be used to help learners overcome knowledge/skill deficiencies only if learning is not subject to some blockage. Some types of learning blockages are peculiar to the individual learner. Such blockages are based primarily on the attitudes, emotions, and physical limitations of the learner. For example, learners are sometimes opposed to training. At other times a subject can be so complex that understanding is not easily gained. At still other times, both these obstacles become blockages to the achievement of learning goals.

Although in the fire service there is generally little negative attitude towards learning (fire fighters instinctively realize that learning is essential to effective performance), the learning process can be obstructed by physical or emotional obstacles and by negative attitudes with respect to specific topics or instructions. These obstacles can be referred to as blockages. Figure 12.6 depicts most of the common blockages as well as some of the basic strategies for overcoming them.

Attitudes Toward Subjects to be Learned: An example of a blockage to learning that results from a negative attitude toward a topic would be a fire

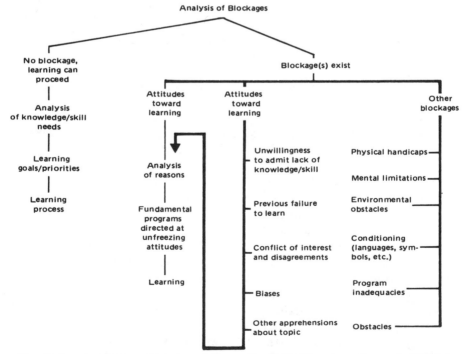

Fig. 12.6. Acquisition of new knowledge and/or skill. (Based on the work of Erwin Rausch, Didactic Systems, Inc.)

fighter who believes that a good fire fighter is a "fire eater." This conception of the good fire fighter is based, for one thing, on the fire fighter's impression that the person who can last the longest in the dense smoke of a fire is, in some way, "superhuman." Such a fire fighter might view instruction in the use of protective breathing apparatus as being negative or unnecessary, and the instruction would be in conflict with the fire fighter's feelings about what a good fire fighter should do. This type of learning blockage can be considered as belonging to the category labeled "Conflict of interest and disagreements" in Figure 12.6.

In attempting to overcome this type of learning blockage, the instructor must first determine the fire fighter's actual reasons for such a belief. If the reasons for the belief are based on the perception or attitude of the learner, the instructor can use several methods to "unfreeze" such a belief, including the following:

1. **Direct Order:** Although this may often not be the most desirable way to achieve the result, it is sometimes the only way to oppose strongly held attitudes. Many behavioral scientists claim that training cannot be effective against strong attitudes unless there is first an organizational requirement that learners must follow. Training can then help people satisfy the requirement more easily, and that, in turn, frequently leads to revised attitudes toward the subject.

2. **Peer Pressures:** When specific learners become clearly aware that their attitudes are different from those of their peers, or if they find that acting on their own views and attitudes will actually hurt team effort, then it is likely that they will question and modify their views. An instructor can therefore make individuals aware when their attitudes are either different from those of their peers, or when their attitudes might hurt team achievement.

3. **Conflict with Views or Actions of Respected and Successful Persons in the Field:** When a learner becomes aware of such a conflict, attitudes are also likely to be questioned. Presenting unrefutable evidence of the attitude of successful professionals in the field (through guest appearances in classes, or through testimonials) can help an instructor cultivate better student attitudes toward the subject.

4. **Apprehension About the Subject:** Such apprehension brings other possible blockages to learning. As shown in Figure 12.6, this type of blockage results from an unwillingness to admit lack of knowledge/skill. For example, people are sometimes reluctant to admit that they have a specific knowledge or skill deficiency and are ashamed to admit that, after having been exposed to the subject, they still do not understand an idea, principle, or procedure — especially if others seem to understand it.

5. **Previous Failure to Learn a Topic:** Similar to the preceding No. 4, such failure to learn can result in the learner feeling that the subject is "too difficult"; thus, learners often fail to devote the effort necessary to master a particular subject. If learners believe that something is simply "common sense," they will sometimes tune out in the erroneous belief that the message does not con-

tain anything of value to them. If, however, the subject is perceived to be too theoretical or irrelevant, learners may not pay adequate attention.

Other Types of Blockages: The extreme right side of Figure 12.6 lists blockages to learning that result from limitations that are not based on attitudes or emotions. The instructor should be aware of any physical handicaps and mental limitations, and sensitive to the fact that some learners may be embarrassed about such handicaps and unaware of mental limitations. For example, a fire fighter may be aware that an old knee injury makes it increasingly difficult to climb a ladder, and may have successfully hidden this minor handicap during the physical examination and during the probationary period. This fire fighter might resist training sessions on ladder evolutions. If an instructor is not aware of the fire fighter's handicap, considerable effort can be wasted in misdirected attempts to achieve learning. A more common example concerns hearing and sight defects. People with these deficiencies are often reluctant to obtain and wear hearing aids and glasses. The obvious blockages to learning that result from these types of defects cannot be resolved unless the instructor is aware of them.

Mental limitations are of a more serious nature, yet once they are recognized, they too can be overcome. Such limitations can include reading problems and minor emotional problems. Like many physical disorders, learners may be reluctant to face mental limitations objectively. Only when the instructor is aware of such problems can the learning program be adjusted to take them into account. Often, only a slower pace and some personal extra help are needed to help the learner achieve the same learning goals as other members of the group.

Environmental obstacles can become blockages to effective learning. They include noises, movement, and other similar distractions that interrupt the thought processes of instructor and learners alike.

Finally, illogical presentation of topics and other instructor-related deficiencies such as talking above the learning level of students, talking condescendingly to students, or ineffective use of chalkboard and other visuals, can detract from a learning experience. These instructor-related deficiencies apply primarily to lectures and demonstrations. Similarly, participative types of learning experiences that provide personal application, while usually so involving that interruptions and distractions have relatively little effect, can be poorly designed so that they are not perceived as relevant or, for other reasons, stimulating to the learning of a specific topic.

SPECIFIC LEARNING PRINCIPLES

In addition to the application of the goal achievement spiral shown in Figure 12.5 and the approaches to learning blockages, there are several major and minor principles that must be considered by the manager of the learning process. An important learning principle previously mentioned in this text is that:

- Learners who are motivated will learn to master a subject faster and more thoroughly than learners who are less motivated.

Motivation is achieved only if the climate is such that learners can find sufficient benefits in the learning experience. The pleasure of gaining new, useful information or desired skills is one of the strongest psychological satisfactions for learners and can be provided through interesting, varied presentations that hold the learner's attention. When the learner is motivated, the learning situation can be compared to being as emotionally rewarding as entertainment if it is truly appropriate to the learner's interests and capabilities. The varied use of techniques that involve learners, together with good selection of media and topic sequence, can help achieve learning sessions that almost totally capture the learner's attention. The satisfaction of psychological needs (which is essential to motivation) can also be provided by evidence of rewards in the form of a sense of greater professionalism, better self-protection, winning in a competition, or achieving something the learner wants to achieve. Additionally, to achieve a learning climate where learners can find appropriate instruction, the other linking elements must be satisfied, with consideration given to the following:

1. As previously discussed, learning goals must be properly set. This means that as much attention must be given to satisfying the concepts embedded in the eight problem areas that usually arise in MBO programs as in managing any other goal-setting situation. (See Chapter 5, "Managing by Objectives," section titled "Making MBO Programs Successful," and Fig. 5.7.)

2. There must be good coordination of learning activities with learning needs, through use of knowledge/skill profiles or otherwise, to avoid the demotivating impact of confusion or lack of clear direction. Topic sequence must also build logically and carefully to ensure that all new concepts are explained before they are applied as explanations for other matters as a basis for drawing conclusions.

3. Clearly communicated and enforced rules, if they are appropriate, contribute to a motivational climate by helping to reduce doubts, confusion, and distractions. Simple rules, such as insistence on the completion of learning assignments on time, or on the rigid starting and stopping time of learning sessions (when emergencies do not interrupt), can have significant influence in providing confidence in the underlying professionalism of a training program.

Another learning principle that instructors should be familiar with is:

- Conditioning (stimulus-response programs) can enhance the learning of simple tasks.

Around the turn of the century, Russian psychologist Ivan Pavlov, while studying automatic reflexes associated with digestion, noted that:[3]

> When meat powder is placed in a dog's mouth, salivation takes place; the food is the unconditioned stimulus and the salivation the unconditioned

reflex. Then some arbitrary stimulus, such as light, is combined with the presentation of the food. Eventually, after repetition and if time relationships are right, the light will evoke salivation independent of the food; the light is the conditioned stimulus and the response to it is the conditioned response.

Conditioning is important in the fire service because some tasks must be performed almost instinctively in the prescribed way to ensure that they are accomplished in the shortest possible time. Such tasks require extensive practice. In *Company Leadership and Operations*, Anthony R. Granito, Deputy Superintendent of the National Academy for Fire Prevention and Control, states that:[4]

> The fire fighter verifies his understanding of the subject through various practice sessions. The intention of the instuctor is to have the trainee remember indefinitely; therefore, a sufficient number of drills or practices are conducted to ensure that the mental processes will become well fixed in his mind. To ensure that the fire fighter remembers until the time he has need for the information, the instructor will have him practice repeatedly what he has learned and understands. Practice of some subjects and drills may involve repetitious work over long periods. Repetition of an operation over a long period of time will give the fire fighter the necessary practice to help him retain what he has learned.

Still another important learning principle concerns the speed with which new concepts are presented to learners.

● Learning pace must be adapted to the learner's ability to absorb, if the learning process is to proceed without interruption.

All learners have different capabilities for learning. Some have quick understanding, others have good memories, and still others have good attention spans. For these reasons a lecture that is fairly fast-paced can lose some learners, and a slow-paced lecture usually holds only the attention of the least capable learners.

● Learning will be absorbed better and retained longer if it is directly work-related and can be applied on the job.

Most subjects covered in fire service training are work-related, although some of them are rarely applied. If the task is one that may be very important during fire fighting, then this principle suggests that regular practice in a simulated environment may be necessary to assure adequate skills when they are needed.

● Things that are learned and understood tend to be better retained than things that are learned by rote.

This learning principle suggests that adequate testing should be done to make sure that the subject is thoroughly understood.

- Practice distributed over several periods is more economical in learning than the same amount of practice concentrated into a single period.

If an important skill has to be practiced extensively in order to achieve full mastery, single practice sessions need not continue until this goal is reached; pauses of several days between relatively short sessions can help to bring about better retention.

- The order of presentation of materials is of major importance.

While this learning principle might seem obvious, many programs attempt to present more complex topics prior to establishing an adequate foundation for them.

- It is easier to recognize something than it is to recall it.

This principle is of great importance in selecting ways to test the knowledge of learners. Testing should emphasize recall, not recognition.

- Learning something new can interfere with remembering something that has been learned earlier.

This learning principle is one that is often overlooked by instructors who, when helping learners acquire new skills or new knowledge, fail to reinforce previously acquired subject matter or skills. Consideration of this principle is especially important when the new subject overlaps a previous one, or is similar to a previous one. For example, learning a new set of code numbers can have strong impact on retention of the previous group.

- Knowledge of results helps learners maintain motivation to continue learning effort.

If learners are unsure as to whether or not they are acquiring knowledge correctly, or are unsure as to whether or not what they are learning is correct, they will be hesitant about devoting their full efforts to learning. Therefore, testing, or participative activities in which learners can receive feedback on the correctness of the knowledge or skills they are acquiring are important segments of satisfactory learning experiences.

While the previous learning principles are not the only ones to be considered when planning an instructional program, they are of major concern. The instructor who successfully incorporates these principles into a teaching plan can be considered to be the manager of a motivational learning experience rather than a mere dispenser of information who relies heavily on lectures.

Techniques

Once learning needs have been identified and goals set, the instructor can plan the instructional strategy. An instructional strategy consists of two major segments: (1) topic sequence (content), and (2) processes to be used for each segment. As discussed earlier in this chapter, these two are closely interlinked. Segments of the subject must be presented in a logical progression of thought with the simple concepts or skills that form the foundations for later concepts and skills being presented first, followed in logical sequence by still more complex concepts and skills (or those based on, or using some of, the fundamental ones). Also, in order to further improve the motivational aspects of a learning situation, each topic segment must include the three stages shown in Figure 12.4: acquisition, demonstration, and personal application. The remainder of this chapter presents a discussion of the techniques that can be used for all three of these stages, followed by an in-depth presentation of their application in the two major teaching environments — classroom instruction and on-the-job training.

INSTRUCTIONAL STRATEGY

When preparing an instructional strategy (program), a planning chart is useful since it can help to ensure that: (1) topic segments are arranged in logical sequence, (2) appropriate techniques will be used for each topic segment, (3) acquisition, demonstration, and personal application will have been considered for each topic segment, and (4) there is sufficient variety in techniques to present a stimulating environment for the learners. Such a chart could look like the sample for a segment of a course in communications shown in Table 12.2.

The more varied instructional techniques an instructor can use effectively, the more interesting and stimulating the learning experience will be for learners. Instructors and officers should, therefore, constantly strive to become acquainted with a wide range of instructional techniques, and should experiment with using these techniques as tools for helping their people learn.

TECHNIQUES FOR ACQUISITION OF NEW KNOWLEDGE AND SKILLS

While everyday environment and past experience account for the major portion of how the average person becomes exposed to unknown subjects, the material in this section of the text is concerned with how the learner becomes exposed to unknown subjects in an educational environment. For most persons, the first educational exposure to unknown subjects usually comes from: (1) lectures, (2) reading from straight text or programmed instructional materials, (3) audiotapes, and (4) films, filmstrips, or videotapes.

Lectures

Lectures are the most widely used instructional technique for transmitting information. Often, lectures are the least expensive and the most readily available instructional technique.   They are flexible, they can be changed on the spot by the instructor who perceives a previously hidden learning need, and they can be used to teach one person or many.   Lectures can be given by one lecturer, or by a variety of lecturers.

Like all instructional techniques, lectures have disadvantages as well as advantages.   In the book *Training in Industry, the Management of Learning*, lectures are explained as follows:[5]

> However, a lecture generally consists of a one-way communication. The instructor presents information to a group of passive learners. Thus, little or no opportunity exists to clarify meanings, to check on whether trainees really understand the lecture materials, or to handle the wide diversity of ability, attitude, and interest that may prevail among the trainees. Also, there is little or no opportunity for practice, reinforcement, or knowledge of results.

Many of the disadvantages of lectures can be reduced through good practices in the handling of questions.   While group discussion is usually more practical with small groups, instructors of any size group who encourage students to ask questions can overcome most of the disadvantages of straight lectures. One disadvantage of lectures frequently encountered by instructors exists when the group contains several highly motivated learners who give the impression of heavy participation.   In such a situation, it might seem to the in-

Table 12.2   Planning Chart for Segment of a Course in Communications

TOPIC SEGMENT	ACQUISITION	DEMON- STRATION	PERSONAL APPLICATION	CORRECTION OF DEFICIENCIES
Receiving and recording fire calls	Lecture (communications officer)	Simulated call in dispatcher room and discussion	Receiving and recording of four simulated calls	During comprehensive drill and supervised work assignment as dispatcher
Establishing location and nature of emergency	Discussion	Demonstration role play by instructor and experienced dispatcher	Role play participation by learners (as dispatcher)	Supervised work assignment as dispatcher
Dispatching equipment and apparatus	Assigned reading	Discussion and equipment demonstrations	Individual use of equipment for specific tasks	Written and verbal tests
(Continued)	(Continued)	(Continued)	(Continued)	(Continued)

structor that the entire group is exploring the subject to gain thorough understanding when, in reality, only a small percentage is doing so while others, often seriously confused by the subject, are reluctant to speak.

The use of media is generally considered an excellent way to enhance the ability of a lecture to transmit knowledge. A Minnesota Mining and Manufacturing Company booklet titled *A Guide to More Effective Meetings* explains the effects of the use of media in instructional situations as follows:[6]

> *People Are Visual-minded:* We are visually-oriented from birth. People grow up surrounded by the visual influences of television, movies, books, school chalkboards and projectors, road signs, advertising signs, all kinds of visual stimulation. People *expect* visuals in meetings. And visuals help the presenter control the meeting and maintain the group's attention.
>
> *Retention Is Increased:* Speeches may motivate, but what about retention? When relying on verbalization alone to communicate, an estimated 90 percent of a message is misinterpreted or forgotten entirely. We retain only 10 percent of what we hear! But consider this: Adding appropriate visual aids to verbalization increases retention to approximately 50 percent.
>
> *Visualization Encourages Organization:* Visualizing forces a presenter to organize his or her thoughts in an orderly fashion that will lead to a conclusion. In so doing, the presenter will learn to simplify and condense the message into a concise, understandable story. This saves both time and expense.
>
> *Misunderstandings Are Less Likely to Occur:* By both seeing and hearing the message simultaneously, meeting participants can understand the presenter's intent easier and quicker. Misinformation can be effectively avoided.

There are many forms of media. Those that are most often used with lectures are primarily visual and include: chalkboards, transparencies, storyboards, display posters and materials, slides, and filmstrips. Because of their versatility, each of these forms is used by effective instructors as much as available materials permit.

Reading

For the acquisition of new knowledge, independent study through reading of text or programmed instruction materials is an alternative to the lecture. Reading affords the learner the opportunity to stop when necessary, to make notes, to clarify meaning by referring back to earlier material, and to consult various sources for more detailed information. With reading, obtaining answers to questions is usually more difficult than during lectures when a question can be explored with an instructor.

Programmed Instruction: Programmed instruction is a special form of guided reading program that is usually used as the basis for an independent learning situation. In programmed instruction, frequent questions are included for the learner to answer before proceeding. The learner is told whether the response is correct by comparison with an appropriate answer in the program. The advantages of programmed learning are that:

1. Knowledge is acquired at the individual's own pace.
2. The learner follows a logical progression of thought.
3. The learner must actively respond to the questions included in the presentation, thus permitting an on-going testing of learner acceptance and retention of the materials.
4. A wide variety of supplementary materials and media (such as audiotapes, filmstrips, flat pictures, etc.) can be presented as extensions to the programmed instruction.
5. Programmed instruction is self-administered and is ready to teach whenever the learner is ready to learn.

Programmed materials, however, are often considered to be tedious. Currently, there are limited programmed courses of instruction available.

Conference Technique

Use of the conference technique for imparting instruction can be especially successful when used with small groups. This technique can be combined with brief lectures to provide a mixture of acquisition, demonstration, and somewhat impersonal application.

Group discussion (upon which the conference technique is based) can provide some immediate reinforcement to newly acquired knowledge. For this reason, group discussion often follows a lecture. Unlike the lecture, discussion is a two-way communication: it affords the learner the opportunity to compare personal reactions to subject matter with the reactions of other learners to subject matter, and with the views of the instructors. In the American Management Association book titled *Conference Leadership*, a conference is described as a:[7]

> . . . pooling of knowledge, experiences, and opinions among a group of people who have something to contribute toward achieving specified objectives, or among people who are capable of analyzing information relevant to these objectives.

A conference, therefore, is a planned learning experience where the instructor's role is not one of lecturer, but rather as a facilitator. The instructor encourages group thinking and, when necessary, provides background information that enables all learners to take part in the discussion. The instructor also summarizes, at the end of each discussion segment, what the participants should have learned from the experience.

Advantages of the conference technique are many. It tends to get learners or trainees to give more thought to the subject matter. It helps to show each conferee how others think about a subject or problem. It adapts the presentation of the subject matter to the needs of the group and, by exposing group opinions, helps to change those attitudes that are detrimental.

One major disadvantage of the conference technique is that it requires a skillful instructor — one who can carefully plan for a variety of unknown eventualities that could occur during the conference program. Another disadvantage is that it has limited usefulness since it lends itself only to those topics where the participants, together, have adequate knowledge of the subject.

TECHNIQUES FOR DEMONSTRATION

Demonstration is the phase in a learning experience where learners are shown how the information, concepts, or materials that were discussed during the preceding acquisition phase can be applied to their respective situations. Demonstrating a piece of equipment and showing how to don breathing apparatus are demonstrations, as is a role-playing situation in which an instructor takes the part of a building owner while a student explains a violation.

Demonstrations can use most of the techniques available to an instructor, including: lectures (by themselves or supported by props, in classroom, or on-site), slides or filmstrips, and audio or videotapes. Demonstrations can also utilize some of the forms of the participative techniques that will be discussed more fully later in this chapter, including: case study exploration, simulated use of equipment (or of a concept), and role-play demonstration.

Although they are usually considered to be some of the most important parts of the learning process, demonstrations are often overlooked. The result of such oversight is a gap in the student's learning experience — a gap that can take considerably more effort to fill at a later date than would have been necessary immediately after the acquisition phase.

TECHNIQUES FOR PERSONAL APPLICATION

The instructional techniques used for a classroom (as distinct from field practice) during the personal application phase are based, in one way or another, on case studies. While there are many kinds of case studies, all of them are basically descriptions of real or imaginary situations that range in length from single paragraphs or brief verbal statements to small, greatly detailed books about the organization that is the subject for the case.

Case Studies or Case Method

The applications of the case method to learning situations vary as widely as their types. Sometimes they serve as foundations for simulations and role playing, but most often they are used more directly in various ways, including the following.

As Simple Descriptions: Learners are expected to review the case, decide what issues it raises, and then draw conclusions about these issues. For instance, a case method session could start by presenting fire fighters with a prefire plan of a particular building, and with instructions to review and comment on it.

With Somewhat More Instruction (Structure): At the end of the case, a few specific questions are asked for learners to answer.

With Very Detailed Questions: At the end of the case, many detailed questions are asked that learners have to answer.

As Staged Cases (Called Incident Process): In this use, learners are provided with only part of the information necessary to thoroughly analyze the case. They must first decide what additional information is needed so that they can work on the case. After they have asked for and received the additional information, they can work on the case. For instance, in a case describing a specific fire situation, items such as distances from the hydrants and wind direction and other weather conditions may have been omitted in the description even though they are important to the case.

With Varying-sized Classes: Cases can be used with single learners, with small groups of learners, and with large classes made up of many learners.

Cases help stimulate creative thinking because learners are asked to ferret out what is essential about the situation and then decide what actions, if any, should be considered. Cases are easy to use because much of the material available to instructors can form the basis for case studies — records of previous fires, prefire plans, history of inspections at any one location, portions of articles from fire magazines, newspaper stories, etc. Also, cases can be used spontaneously when it becomes clear that learners need to explore certain issues, especially after a lecture during which many questions indicate inadequate comprehension, or in situations where it is obvious that the learning process clearly needs a change of pace in order to maintain learner interest.

Simulations

If learners are asked to imagine that they are one of the people described in a case (but not to actually act out the role of that person), they begin to participate in a simulation. Invariably learners are asked to solve specific problems in the case when they are working on it as a simulation.

Simulations are an ideal vehicle for learning in the fire service. They can dramatically enhance interest in training sessions and contribute greatly to awareness of the crucial features of hazards in the district. In addition, they can help to make valuable use of existing prefire plans and, coincidentally, they can also serve as a basis for continual improvement in the prefire plans and in the allied inspections.

A company officer or instructor who decides to build most instruction around exploration of strategies and tactics at local properties can expand them into simulations. These can concentrate on rescue, fire streams, forcible entry, ventilation, or on ladder evolutions as well as on specific fire fighting tactics and strategies based on various different assumptions of fire locations, weather conditions, or time of day. The inevitable outcome of such simulations is greater interest in learning, greater knowledge of local conditions, enhanced interest in inspections, and improvement of prefire plans.

Simulations can be supported with transparencies or can be worked out on paper. Some can be programmed for use with computers, some can be expanded into field work, and still others can become actual fire drills at actual locations (in instances when the owner's or official's permission has been obtained to do so, usually during nonwork hours or days).

Simulations, like case studies, can be elaborate descriptions of a situation with detailed data, pictures, charts, graphs, or floorplans, or they can be simple verbal descriptions used spontaneously just like cases, and for the same purposes. With simulations, learners can all assume that they are the same person or they can take on different roles in the situation. Simulations are usually more appropriate for more student-involving learning experiences than case studies; therefore, they can be more enjoyable for the learner and can better hold the learner's attention.

Role Plays

If the simulation question "What should be done in this situation?" is sharpened to ask "Exactly what words should be used?," then the simulation is likely to become a role play. The words "role play" do not have precisely the same meaning to all instructors. Sometimes, simulations in which learners assume different roles are referred to as role plays. More common, however, is the use of this name for those instructional activities in which learners act out the specific roles that are assigned to them. Role plays are primarily applicable to instructional situations in which the learning objectives involve communications between individuals or groups.

Even though the most common form of role playing is a live demonstration staged with one person per role and all others as observers, this is rarely the most effective form. Much more effective for skill development is the type of role-playing technique that involves all the members of the group simultaneously.

Role-playing sessions can become an enjoyable activity because they can be made stimulating and interesting to the participants (learners). Some of the ways role-playing sessions can be made more interesting are:

Use of Recorders: A simple role play can be recorded on an audio tape or video tape and the taped segment used with a large group to critique it. In this type of situation the members of the group do not feel that they are criticizing actual people, and they are more willing to discuss the errors they have observed. This is particularly true if they are not certain who recorded the interview, or if it was done by individuals who are strangers to the group. Various topics for which such taped role plays can be useful include: consoling a grieving relative of a victim, calming an irate owner, explaining a violation, a performance discussion between officer and fire fighter, and responding to a citizen inquiry.

Taped role plays can, of course, be used to help in self-development. For this use, a participant is asked to perform in a simulated situation such as facing a member of the public, a subordinate, or a supervisor in real life. In this type of role play, the other role is usually assumed by the trainer or the role player's manager. At the conclusion of the role play or after some time, it can be used to critique all of those instances where the participant could gain useful insights into better approaches. Self-realization or self-recognition of mistakes is believed to be more effective than if they are pointed out by an authority figure.

Role Playing in Small Groups: When role playing is done with several observers or under the critical eye of a supervisor, it often contains threatening aspects. On the other hand, in the intimacy of a small group of friends or peers it does not carry the same implications. As a result, it is a much more relaxed activity in which each participant behaves naturally and realistically.

Number of Participants Per Role: Another important feature of successful role plays can be the number of participants who play a given role. In most role plays, only one person assumes a given role. A possibly more effective way to analyze the significance of specific phrasing or approaches is to have two people play each role. They must consult with each other before any words are uttered.

In addition to the major variants of role playing, there are other variations that help make it an effective teaching device. For example, a role play can be interrupted after a few moments and participants told about a change in the situation (such as someone announcing a particular emergency, or a telephone call, etc.). Still other variations can result from a specific hidden point that must be uncovered by the person playing the learner's role. It could be that the fire fighter will accept the goal only when a given "hot button" is touched. Or, hidden feelings must be uncovered.

APPLYING LEARNING PRINCIPLES AND TECHNIQUES TO COACHING

Classroom training and drills can provide most of the knowledge and skills needed by fire fighters or officers for their jobs. However, due to the many variances in ways people perceive their jobs and in the amount of learning they obtain from classes and drills, there is considerable need for individual coaching by superiors. Such coaching is usually in one of the following forms:

1. Suggesting self-study goals to eliminate deficiencies and prepare for advancement, and helping with any difficulties the learner encounters.

2. On-the-job training in the particular knowledges and skills that require individualized attention in order to help eliminate deficiencies, or where only one person needs training.

Self-study

Self-study recommendations (such as guided reading programs) and individualized help (such as advice from superiors) in achieving training goals are excellent methods for the continuing development of professionals. Such methods are always specifically geared to the needs, aspirations, and the knowledge and skill level of the individual.

On-the-job Training

Many topics, especially skills, are so important that they cannot be left to the more leisurely self-study approach; thus, they require the more intense activity of on-the-job training. As a general guide for the training of civilian employees, the U.S. Army uses a chart that comprehensively describes the four steps in the on-the-job training process (see Table 12.3).[8]

The four steps shown in Table 12.3 parallel the stages of the complete learning experience illustrated earlier in this chapter in Figure 12.4, as follows:

- *Acquisition* is covered in Step 1, "Preparing the Learner," and in the first part of "Presenting the Task."
- *Demonstration* is covered in the remainder of "Presenting the Task."
- *Personal Application* is covered in Step 3 where the learner repeatedly performs the task until it is mastered.
- *Followup* assures correction of any remaining deficiencies.

This four-step process also satisfies the following learning principles and techniques discussed earlier in this chapter:

- *Motivation* is enhanced through the careful attention to the learner's personal needs in Step 1 and through the thoroughness with which the learner is helped to master the task.
- *Blockages* are recognized and overcome during Step 3 when the learner begins to try the task.
- *Conditioning* occurs during the repeated trials.
- *Understanding* is assured when the learner explains the task.
- Subtasks are presented in *logical order* since they are practiced in exactly the same way they are demonstrated.
- *Knowledge of results* is immediately available since the learner's performance is checked several times as the total task is learned.
- *On-the-job training* can or does employ several of the techniques previously discussed.
- *Lectures* are used during the explanation of the task.
- *Simulation* is used during the first trials of the task by the learner if either danger, inconvenience, or considerable costs are involved. For example, nozzle operation, forcible entry, ventilation, etc., may all be practiced in simulated fashion before they are fully practiced (even in a practice environment).
- *Role plays* can be useful even before more thoroughly simulated practice when the learner explains, in detail, how tasks involving other people will be performed.

APPLYING LEARNING PRINCIPLES AND TECHNIQUES TO CLASSROOM INSTRUCTION

Unlike on-the-job training (which is highly structured and follows a very specific pattern), classroom instruction is extremely varied in form. However,

Table 12.3
The Four Steps of On-the-job Training

STEP	PURPOSE	HOW ACCOMPLISHED
1. Prepare the learner.	A. To relieve tension. B. To establish training base. C. To arouse interest. D. To give him/her confidence.	A. Put him/her at ease. B. Find out what he/she already knows about task. C. Tell relation of task to mission. D. Tie task to his/her experience. E. Ensure that he/she is in a comfortable position to see you perform the task clearly.
2. Present the task.	A. To make sure he/she understands what to do and why. B. To ensure retention. C. To avoid giving him/her more than he/she can grasp.	A. Tell, show, illustrate, question carefully and patiently, use task analysis. B. Stress key points. C. Instruct clearly, completely, one step at a time. D. Keep your words to a minimum. Stress action words.
3. Try out learner's performance.	A. To be sure he/she has right method. B. To prevent wrong habit forming. C. To be sure he/she knows what he/she is doing and why. D. To test his/her knowledge. E. To avoid putting him/her on the job prematurely.	A. Have him/her perform the task and do not require that he/she explain what he/she is doing the first time through. If he/she makes a major error, assume the blame yourself and repeat as much of Step 2 as is necessary. B. Once he/she has performed the task correctly have him/her do it again and this time have him/her explain the steps and key points as he/she does the task. C. Ask questions to ensure that key points are understood. D. Continue until you know that he/she knows.
4. Followup.	A. To give him/her confidence. B. To be sure he/she takes no chances, and knows he/she is not left alone. C. To be sure he/she stays on the beam. D. To show your confidence in him/her.	A. Put him/her on his/her own; praise as fitting. B. Encourage questions; tell him/her where he/she can get help. C. Check frequently at first. D. Gradually reduce amount of checking.

if the principles of learning and training design discussed in this chapter are to be honored, some pattern should be followed. Therefore, the following general guidelines are suggested:

1. Lectures should be of sharply limited duration. Many educators feel that uninterrupted lectures that last more than twenty minutes are likely to result in seriously reduced attention.

2. The sequence of acquisition, demonstration, personal application, and correction of deficiencies should be carefully followed. One way to almost constantly do so is to proceed in the following order:

    (a) A lecture to explain concepts, supported with visuals if possible, that offers learners as much opportunity to ask questions as the environment permits.

    (b) An appropriate activity that is worked individually by the learners, in small groups, or preferably both ways, one after the other.

    (c) A review of the activity through reports and individual or group discussions of the reports.

    (d) An opportunity for learners to ask questions.

3. As much as possible, the atmosphere should be informal and relaxed so that learners feel free to ask questions and explore points in terms with which they are most familiar. To help create an informal atmosphere, lectures must allow for questions almost continuously, and instructors must answer questions without being condescending or belittling the questioners. At the same time, instructors must be careful not to allow questions to draw the lecture away from the logical sequence of thought necessary for an orderly presentation. Furthermore, the instructor must be honest and open with learners. An instructor who cannot answer a question should admit so, and either offer to obtain an answer or assign one of the learners to research it.

4. There must be opportunities for slower learners (or those whose attention had strayed) to catch up with the class, and for fast learners (or those who are more familiar with the subject) to find challenge in the learning process. Individual and small group activities can provide such opportunities, since the slower learners or those inclined to attention lapses feel freer to ask questions in individual or small group environments. At the same time, those with a better understanding of the topic can verify their command of it by helping to explain it to others. Such explanations serve to further strengthen understanding and help to achieve full mastery, since few things are as well understood as things explained to people who are free to question extensively.

5. There must be effective but polite discipline. This helps learners pay greater attention to the subject matter. Instructors who have difficulty maintaining orderly progress can find help in any of the many readily available books on conference leadership or classroom discipline.

It is obvious that a classroom that satisfies the preceding guidelines is one that also conforms to most of the principles of learning and training design discussed in this chapter. To follow these guidelines requires a willingness to experiment with different ways to manage learning experiences, and thoroughness in keeping the learning process in mind.

It is most important for instructors to become comfortable with allowing the learners to take an active role in the classroom. Much can be gained from allowing the fire fighters to take turns in leading the discussion of the various cases. Assignments for such discussion leadership should be made at a previous session so that fire fighters can appropriately prepare themselves. Such rotation of discussion leadership on team or class activities can be especially valuable if, as has been suggested, prefire plans or records of properties in the district are used as foundations for the activities in the training sessions.

Training in the Fire Service

At present, there is no single national, mandatory formula for training fire fighters to which local fire departments are compelled to conform. The most formal set of basic requirements for fire fighting training programs is issued by the American Insurance Association (AIA) as "Special Interest Bulletin No. 234," titled *Fire Department Training*.[9] In 1971 the Municipal Survey Service of the AIA was transferred to the Insurance Services Office (ISO). The insurance rates set by the ISO are, in part, contingent on the extent to which a fire department's training program is effective.

AIA's "Special Interest Bulletin No. 234," *Fire Department Training*, bases its evaluation of a training program on five major areas: (1) organization of training, (2) fire training facilities, (3) quality of instruction and practice, (4) officer training, and (5) subject of study. The standards applied in grading each of these areas are based on standards suggested by the NFPA, particularly in NFPA 1001, *Standard for Fire Fighter Professional Qualifications*,[10] and the International Fire Service Training Association's training manuals and texts in the *Red Book Series*.[11] "Special Interest Bulletin No. 234" states training time requirements in the following definitive terms:[9]

> Most training at the company level can be undertaken as in-service instruction and practice at or near company quarters. These training sessions should be held daily throughout the year, at a prearranged time, and should be conducted for periods of at least two hours per day. When companies are seriously undermanned, and where inservice conditions permit, it may be advisable to have two or three companies train together. Where department manpower is mainly volunteer, the number and frequency of drills will have to be arranged to fit the available time of the members and the needs of the department, but these should be held at least monthly.

"Special Interest Bulletin No. 234" also lists the following recommended program topics:[9]

Subjects for Study

1. General Fire Department Information
   A. Organization and Administration

B. Duties and Responsibilities
C. Elements of Fire; Extinguishment
   (Continued)

D. Communications
E. Standard Operating Procedures
F. Public Relations
G. Preventive Maintenance
2. Fire Department Apparatus
  A. Pumpers — Pumping — Tests
  B. Ladder Trucks — Elevating Platforms
  C. Other
3. Fire Department Tools & Equipment
  A. Extinguishers
  B. Ladders
  C. Hose — Hose Layouts
  D. Master and Special Stream Appliances
  E. Forcible Entry Tools and Equipment
  F. Breathing Apparatus
  G. Other Special and Minor Equipment
4. Operations and Procedures
  A. Ventilation
  B. Salvage
  C. Hydraulics — Basic and Advanced
  D. Automatic Sprinkler and Standpipe Systems
  E. Relaying
  F. Rescue and First Aid

G. Size-up and Extinguishment
H. Fire Problems
I. Occupancies with High Life Hazard
5. Fire Alarm System
  A. Municipal
  B. Private
6. Water Supply
  A. Municipal — Location of Hydrants — Fire Flow Tests
  B. Other Sources
7. Fire Safety Control
  A. Local and State Fire Prevention Regulations
  B. Hazardous Materials and Processes, including Radioactive Materials
  C. Inspection Procedures
  D. Local and State Building Construction Regulations
  E. Types of Construction
  F. Safety to Life and Protection Against Spread of Fire
8. Prefire Planning
  A. Fire Department Inspections and Reports
  B. Use of Information on Item 4H
  C. Fire Investigation and Arson Detection

Various organizations in the public and private sectors supply fire departments with a wealth of materials that influence local training programs: these organizations include the AIA, ISO, NFPA, and the Department of Commerce. How departments organize to fulfill most of these requirements is as varied as the information that can be found on training programs. This is understandable since the construction of fire department training programs — their priorities, content, and methods — all ultimately are left to individual localities, to their chiefs, and to training instructors. For this reason, it is difficult to talk about a "typical" training program. The most a discussion on the training process can do, therefore, is discuss those aspects of training that seem to be common elements.

One common aspect of training is a formal method of introducing probationary fire fighters to the job. New fire fighters are provided with a course of basic training that attempts to provide the foundation for more thorough on-the-job training. Table 12.4, "Suggested Basic Training Course for Fire Fighters," illustrates what the first page of a basic training course for probationary fire fighters might look like. Some of the material contained in

Table 12.4   Suggested Basic Training Course for Fire Fighters*

Drill 1 — History and Organization of the Fire Service   5 Hours
  Coverage:
    Departmental history, traditions, development, and organization; personnel
    policies; operation of the fire department; duties and responsibilities of all
    personnel in the fire department; trainee duties and responsibilities; con-
    ditions of employment; general rules and procedures; employee activities
    and services; pay; benefit plans; self-improvement opportunities; F.M.B.A.
    information; facilities available to, or through, the department; community
    facilities and obligations; participation in community activities; the job; hours;
    compensation; training; promotion policies; overview of the fire fighter in
    the department; and the department in the community.

Drill 2 — Communications   4 Hours
  Coverage:
    Receiving and recording fire calls; establishing the location and nature of
    the emergency; dispatching equipment and apparatus; relaying information
    to the proper authorities; transmitting and receiving voice messages; overall
    communications mediums; maintaining the daily activity logs and records
    on personnel; equipment movements and status; fires; alarms; communi-
    cation equipment tests; visitors protocol; special events, etc.; interpersonal
    communications; fire department radio and receiving equipment operations
    and terminology; and channels of communications in the fire service.

Drill 3 — Fire Department Records   3 Hours
  Coverage:
    Records system accomplishments; and file maintenance on all fire depart-
    ment equipment, apparatus, and activities.

Drill 4 — Chemistry — Chemistry of Fire   3 Hours
  Coverage:
    Chemical changes; inorganic, organic, analytical, bio-, physical and nu-
    clear chemistry, mixtures and compounds, elements; analysis and synthesis;
    atomic weights; compounds of hydrogen, oxygen, carbon, hydrocarbons,
    carbohydrates; ions and ionization; acids, hydrochloric, nitric, sulphuric,
    acetic, tartaric, other organic acids, alkalies or bases; sodium hydroxide,
    sodium carbonate, sodium hydrocarbonate, potassium hydroxide, salts;
    chemical equations; and chemistry of fire.

---

such a basic training course is usually also used in the refresher sessions of
in-service programs.

Basic training periods vary from one week long to six weeks long. Generally, the content for most basic training courses is based on materials from
the following sources:

- NFPA — *Fire Protection Handbook*.
- NFPA — *Guides to Standards* (Pocket Editions).
- IFSTA — *Red Book Series*.

---

*Courtesy of Bloomfield Fire Department, Bloomfield, N.J.

- ICMA — *Municipal Fire Administration.*
- Transparencies such as those supplied by IFSTA.
- Pictures and films produced by local fire departments.
- Records and fire reports.

A training officer, usually a high-ranking officer approved by the chief, coordinates all classroom activities. The training officer in medium- to large-sized municipal fire departments is responsible for selecting textbooks, writing department manuals, presenting materials in the classroom, and seeing to it that training records are kept on probationary and in-service fire fighters throughout their terms of employment.

The training officer's role is as important in on-the-job training as it is in classroom instruction and record keeping. For example, once a trainee has completed a basic course (sometimes called "bread and butter" course), the training officer will assign that trainee to a company where on-the-job application of all the information learned is made possible. The company officer then assumes the responsibility for arranging trainee schedules so that evolutions of every type are covered as soon as possible.

The in-service training of fire fighters is an on-going process. Fire fighters cannot maintain their skills in all essential fire fighting evolutions. Many of these operations are used only at large or special types of fires. It is, therefore, essential that all members of the department be required to put in enough training work not only to retain their skill in performing standard evolutions, but also to keep abreast of current technical developments in their field. Good fire departments devote part of every day to drill and training work.

Through regular drill procedures at a training school, methods of performing all operations are standardized so that personnel may be transferred to various companies without impairing efficiency. In well-run departments, companies are periodically assigned to drill schools. For example, in Boston as in many other cities, two engines and a ladder company go to drill school each day. Annually, each company has at least three weeks at drill school, usually divided as follows: (1) one week is devoted to "bread and butter training" consisting of review of standard operations, (2) one week is devoted to special courses of advanced training, and (3) the remaining week is devoted to training in special problems and techniques.[12]

All company training activities are usually recorded by the company officer and presented to the training officer for inspection. Figure 12.7 is an example of a record of the training activities of the Bloomfield Fire Department, Bloomfield, New Jersey. The report includes such information as date, company number, attendance count, location of training activity, type of activity performed, company officer's name in charge of training activity, and total time used in training. These reports, usually prepared by the various company officers throughout the department, supply the training officer with the information for a consolidated monthly training activity report that is periodically reviewed by the chief. A final consolidated report is then prepared for the record. Figure 12.8 shows a typical consolidated monthly training report.

BLOOMFIELD, N.J.
FIRE DEPARTMENT TRAINING ACTIVITIES*

STATION #2 ___ Group #1 ___ MONTH Nov. 19 76

DATE	COMPANY NUMBER	GROUP NUMBER	MEN ATTENDING	TRAINING SESSIONS	AT DRILL TOWER	IN QUARTERS	EVOLUTIONS PRACTICED	EVOLUTION NUMBERS	TALKS LECTURES FILMS SUBJECT	DRILLS ALL TYPES	INSTRUCTOR	TIME HOURS	TOTAL MAN HOURS
11/1	E	2	1	4	1		✓				#14	Capt. a Caridad	1	4
11/1	E	2	1	4	1		✓			Insp.	#33	Capt. a Caridad	4	16
11/11	E	2	1	4	1		✓		15	Forcible Entry		Capt. a Caridad	1/2	2
11/1	E	2	1	4	1		✓				#25	Capt. a Caridad	1/2	2
11/2	E	2	1	4	1		✓				#25	Capt. a Caridad	1/2	2
11/2	E	2	1	4	1		✓		15	Forcible Entry		Capt. a Caridad	1/2	2
11/2	E	2	1	4	1		✓			F.D. Insp.	#34	Capt. a Caridad	4	16
11/4	E	2	1	4	1		✓			F.D. Orders	#1	Capt. a Caridad	1	4
11/4	E	2	1	4	1		✓		15	Forcible Entry		Capt. a Caridad	1/2	2
11/4	E	2	1	4	1		✓				#25	Capt. a Caridad	1/2	2
11/5	E	2	1	4	1		✓			Streets	#35	Capt. a Caridad	2	8
11/5	E	2	1	4	1		✓		15	Forcible Entry		Capt. a Caridad	1/2	2
11/5	E	2	1	4	1		✓				25	Capt. a Caridad	1/2	2
TOTALS			52	13		4				9		16	64

*Courtesy of Bloomfield Fire Department, Bloomfield, NJ.

Fig. 12.7.   Example of a typical training activity report.

BLOOMFIELD, N.J.
CONSOLIDATED MONTHLY
TRAINING REPORT*

FIRE DEPARTMENT   MONTH _June_ _ 19_76_

A TRAINING SESSIONS		THIS MONTH	LAST MONTH	THIS MO LAST YEAR	THIS YEAR TO DATE	LAST YEAR TO DATE
ENGINE	1	152	141	145	793	791
ENGINE	2	143	143	122	731	607
ENGINE	3	157	133	124	773	593
ENGINE	4	140	132	85	726	602
ENGINE	5					
ENGINE	6					
TRUCK	1					
TRUCK	2					
TOTAL		592	549	476	3,023	2,593

B ANALYSIS OF TRAINING	THIS MONTH	LAST MONTH	THIS MO LAST YEAR	THIS YEAR TO DATE	LAST YEAR TO DATE
NO. TRAINING SESSIONS	592	549	476	3,023	2,593
ATTENDANCE ALL SESSIONS	3,253	3,010	2,654	17,142	16,017
AVERAGE ATTENDANCE	5.5	5.48	5.6	5.67	5.9
TIME OF TRAINING SESSIONS AVG.	.85	.9	.9	.85	.9
1-MAN HOURS OF TRAINING	2,771	2,670	2,210	14,712	13,671
2-HOURS TRAINING PER MAN AVG.	26.9	24.9	21	142.8	131
EVOLUTIONS PRACTICED	213	254	239	1,349	1,245
DRILL - ALL TYPES	379	295	243	1,675	1,501
TALKS - LECTURES - FILMS					
TOTAL AUDIENCE					
INSTRUCTOR HR'S	524.5	477	399	2,518.5	2,362

C WATER USED FOR TRAINING					
AT DRILL TOWER	66,000	34,000	67,000	100,000	411,520
OTHER					

1. HOURS SCHEDULED THIS YEAR MONTH -   _1441_

2. HOURS PER MAN   _ _14_ _ _

REMARKS: 103 Men Training

SIGNED	D C IN CHARGE:	DRILL MASTER:

*Courtesy of Bloomfield Fire Department, Bloomfield, NJ

Fig. 12.8.   *Example of a typical consolidated training activity report.*

Small departments having budgets that do not allow for full-time training staffs usually train new fire fighters to an adequate level of efficiency and competence by sending them to statewide or regional fire fighter's training programs. These programs, now in operation in most states, include state or regional fire schools, and are conducted annually with sessions held either for a few days or for a full week of intensive training. The state courses include officer and leadership conferences, instructor training classes for fire department instructors, industrial fire brigade training courses, and training conferences for fire prevention officers. A substantial number of states (especially larger states such as New York and California) have traveling training instructors working year-round with those local fire departments that are too small to have full-time training officers.[13]

ACTIVITIES

1. (a) How has the current conception of the role of the instructor changed from the traditional conception of the instructor as merely a person who dispenses information?
   (b) Include in your explanation definitions of the terms "process of learning" and "topic content."
2. Explain the importance of motivation in training design.
3. Describe the three major phases that make up a complete learning experience.
4. What is the difference between simulation and role playing as instructional techniques?
5. List at least five common blockages to learning and some of the basic strategies for overcoming them.
6. There are many major and minor learning principles that must be considered when preparing a training course. Ten major principles are highlighted in this chapter. Choose five of these principles and, in your own words, describe the importance of each as they apply to learning situations.
7. Briefly outline a set of guidelines for applying to classroom instructional situations the learning principles and training design techniques discussed in this chapter.
8. As a learning technique, a conference is a planned learning experience in which the instructor's role is that of facilitator rather than lecturer. Thus, there are both advantages and disadvantages to this technique.
   (a) What are some of the advantages of the conference technique?
   (b) What are some of the disadvantages?
9. (a) Explain the use of a planning chart in the preparation of an instructional strategy for a fire science course.
   (b) Using Table 12.2 as a general guide and based on what you have learned earlier in this textbook, prepare a planning chart for a

segment of a course titled "Prefire Planning." Compare your chart with those prepared by your classmates, and discuss any suggestions for improvements. Revise your chart to include appropriate suggestions.

10. Write a brief, informal essay that explains the importance of training in a fire department's operations. Include in your essay the responsibility of the fire service instructor in such training.

BIBLIOGRAPHY

[1] Granito, Anthony R., *Fire Service Instructor's Guidebook*, NFPA, Boston, 1976, p. 1.

[2] From the works of Wallace Wohlking, New York State School of Industrial and Labor Relations, Cornell University, NY.

[3] Hilgard, Ernest R. and Bower, Gordon H., *Theories of Learning*, Appleton-Century-Crofts, NY, 1966, p. 48.

[4] Granito, Anthony R., *Company Leadership and Operations*, NFPA, Boston, 1975, pp. 74–75.

[5] Bass, Bernard M., *Training in Industry, The Management of Learning*, Brooks-Cole, Belmont, CA, 1966, p. 94.

[6] *A Guide to More Effective Meetings*, Visual Products Div. of Minnesota Mining and Manufacturing Co., St. Paul, MN, 1975.

[7] *Conference Leadership*, American Management Association, NY, 1947, p. 5.

[8] United States Army, "The Four Steps of On-The-Job Training," U. S. Government Printing Office, Washington, DC.

[9] *Fire Department Training*, "Special Interest Bulletin No. 234," American Insurance Association, NY, Rev. Ed., Dec. 1975.

[10] NFPA 1001, *Standard for Fire Fighter Professional Qualifications*, NFPA, Boston, 1974.

[11] *Red Book Series*, International Fire Service Training Association, Oklahoma State University, Stillwater, OK.

[12] *Municipal Fire Administration*, International City Management Associates, Washington, DC (formerly Chicago, IL), 1967, p. 73.

[13] ———, pp. 73, 74.

Subject Index

A

AIA (*see American Insurance Association*)

A Guide to More Effective Meetings, by 3M, 368

"A Piece Rate System," by Frederick Taylor, 26

Acceptance qualities
  in decision making, 60, 138, Fig. 3.4
  in goal setting, 138

Accountability
  definition of, 123
  in goal setting, 123, 125, 134
  of managers, 142
  of subordinates, 133
    in action steps, 134, 135
    in performance appraisals, 140
    in planning, 134, 135
    results of, 135
  questions concerned with, 123

Accounting
  as function of fiscal management, 153
  management responsibilities in, 135, 155

Achievement, of objectives
  level of dependency of
    on drills, 239
    on extent of prefire planning, 239
    on training, 239
  measure of, by goal accomplishment, 140
  performance appraisals based on, 140

Achievement motivation studies, by David McClelland, 52

Action steps
  accountability of subordinates in, 135
  as basis for evaluation, 125, 134
  definition of, 117
  evaluations based on, 125, 134
  of company officer, 165
  to accomplish multi-level goals, 126
  viability of, 135

Activities, management of
  advisory, personnel management, 313
  fireground
    overhaul as a stage in, 253
    salvage as a stage in, 253
  fire prevention, 238
  labor relations, 313

loss prevention, 200
prefire planning, 200

"Address to Superintendent of Manufacturers," by Robert Owen, 43

Adequacy
  as element of water supply, 225
  of sprinkler systems, 226

Administrative management
  in a fire department, 159
  roles of officers in, 160

Advisory activities, in personnel management, 313

Adult ego state, in transactional analysis, 93

Affirmative action programs
  goals in, 315–316
  requirements of, 314
  results of, 316
  role of, in equal employment opportunity, 314

Airport fire fighter, standards for, 328

Alarm
  as a factor in total response time, 282
  definition of, 282
  factors in transmittal of, 282

Alarm operator, standards for, 328

Alarms
  multiple, purposes for, 245
  response to, as organizational rules, 265
  role of officer in, 246

Alignment of rules, chief's role in, 162

Ambulance service, emergency services, 149

American Insurance Association (AIA)
  fire prevention activities of, 173
  Fire Prevention Code by, 174
  grading schedule of, 277
  role in National Building Code, 173
  role of, in fire prevention, 173

Analysis
  of deficiencies, technical, 83
  of facts, 243–244
  of fire situation, 241
  of probabilities, 243

Analysis decisions, described, 8

Analysis, job, in salary administration, 324

Fire Command Text and Workbook

C hief Alan Brunacini's textbook, *Fire Command*, takes you step-by-step to develop know-how and confidence on the fireground. By studying *Fire Command* you'll know just what to do and why. You'll know your part as a member of the team because you'll know the whole system.

Then test yourself on the important command concepts with the *Workbook for Fire Command*. The Workbook offers multiple-choice quizzes, tactical exercises and answer keys. Each chapter corresponds to a unit in the *Fire Command* text allowing you to work at your own pace.

Advance toward fireground excellence—order your set today!

☐ **YES! Send me the the Fire Command Text and Workbook Set** (Item No. 2H-SET-70) $27.25 NFPA Members $24.50. Please include $2.85 handling. California residents add 6% sales tax.

Total amount enclosed $_____

Name_____

Company_____

Address_____

City, State, Zip_____

NFPA Member No. _____

☐ I enclose a check (payable to NFPA)

☐ Please bill me

Signature_____

NFPA® Batterymarch Park Quincy, MA 02269-9101

Fire Protection Handbook

O nly one comprehensive sourcebook answers the full range of today's fire protection and prevention questions — the *Fire Protection Handbook*. With new fire technologies, new materials, and constantly changing fire hazards, the very nature of fire protection grows more complicated every day. The *Fire*

Protection Handbook covers:
- hazardous wastes and materials
- venting
- emergency response
- fire hazards of robotics
- aerosol charging
- mining safety and emergency intervention

It's all here, and more, in one comprehensive volume.

Order your copy today

☐ **YES! Send me the the Fire Protection Handbook** (2H-FPH-1686) $79.50 NFPA Members $71.55. Please include $2.85 handling. California residents add 6% sales tax

Total amount enclosed $_____

Name_____

Company_____

Address_____

City, State, Zip_____

NFPA Member No. _____

☐ I enclose a check (payable to NFPA)

☐ Please bill me

Signature_____

NFPA® Batterymarch Park Quincy, MA 02269-9101

BUSINESS REPLY MAIL

FIRST CLASS   PERMIT NO. 3376   QUINCY, MA

POSTAGE WILL BE PAID BY ADDRESSEE

National Fire Protection Association
Batterymarch Park
Quincy, MA 02269-9904

BUSINESS REPLY MAIL

FIRST CLASS   PERMIT NO. 3376   QUINCY, MA

POSTAGE WILL BE PAID BY ADDRESSEE

National Fire Protection Association
Batterymarch Park
Quincy, MA 02269-9904